The Cambridge Companion to Folk Music

A groundbreaking introduction to folk music and song focusing on questions of community, representation, politics, and popular culture. Written by a distinguished international team of authors, this Companion is an indispensable resource for rethinking the confluence of sound, heritage, and identity in the twenty-first century. A unique addition to the literature, it highlights the fundamentally hybrid and (post)colonial dynamics that have shaped people's cultures around the globe, from the Appalachian mountains to the Indian subcontinent. It provides students with new critical paradigms essential for understanding how and why certain musical traditions have been characterised as 'folk' – and what continues to inspire folkloric imaginaries today. The twenty specially commissioned chapters explore folk music from a variety of perspectives including ethnography, revivalism, migration, race, class, gender, protest, and the public sphere. Among these chapters are four 'Artist Voices' by world-renowned performers Peggy Seeger, Angeline Morrison, Jon Boden, and Yale Strom.

ROSS COLE is Associate Professor of Music at the University of Leeds and author of *The Folk: Music, Modernity, and the Political Imagination* (2021), which won the Society for Ethnomusicology's Bruno Nettl Prize. In 2024, he was awarded a Philip Leverhulme Prize.

Cambridge Companions to Music

Topics

The Cambridge Companion to Ballet
Edited by Marion Kant

The Cambridge Companion to Blues and Gospel Music
Edited by Allan Moore

The Cambridge Companion to Caribbean Music
Edited by Nanette de Jong

The Cambridge Companion to Choral Music
Edited by André de Quadros

The Cambridge Companion to Composition
Edited by Toby Young

The Cambridge Companion to the Concerto
Edited by Simon P. Keefe

The Cambridge Companion to Conducting
Edited by José Antonio Bowen

The Cambridge Companion to Eighteenth-Century Opera
Edited by Anthony R. DelDonna and Pierpaolo Polzonetti

The Cambridge Companion to Electronic Music, second edition
Edited by Nick Collins and Julio D'Escriván

The Cambridge Companion to the 'Eroica' Symphony
Edited by Nancy November

The Cambridge Companion to Film Music
Edited by Mervyn Cooke and Fiona Ford

The Cambridge Companion to Folk Music
Edited by Ross Cole

The Cambridge Companion to French Art Song
Edited by Stephen Rumph

The Cambridge Companion to French Music
Edited by Simon Trezise

The Cambridge Companion to Global Rap
Edited by Richard Bramwell and Alex de Lacey

The Cambridge Companion to Grand Opera
Edited by David Charlton

The Cambridge Companion to Hip-Hop
Edited by Justin A. Williams

The Cambridge Companion to Jazz
Edited by Mervyn Cooke and David Horn

The Cambridge Companion to Jewish Music
Edited by Joshua S. Walden

The Cambridge Companion to K-Pop
Edited by Suk-Young Kim

The Cambridge Companion to Krautrock
Edited by Uwe Schütte

The Cambridge Companion to the Lied
Edited by James Parsons

The Cambridge Companion to *The Magic Flute*
Edited by Jessica Waldoff

The Cambridge Companion to Medieval Music
Edited by Mark Everist

The Cambridge Companion to Metal Music
Edited by Jan-Peter Herbst

The Cambridge Companion to Music and Romanticism
Edited by Benedict Taylor

The Cambridge Companion to Music in Australia
Edited by Amanda Harris and Clint Bracknell

The Cambridge Companion to Music in Digital Culture
Edited by Nicholas Cook, Monique Ingalls and David Trippett

The Cambridge Companion to the Musical, third edition
Edited by William Everett and Paul Laird

The Cambridge Companion to Opera Studies
Edited by Nicholas Till

The Cambridge Companion to Operetta
Edited by Anastasia Belina and Derek B. Scott

The Cambridge Companion to the Orchestra
Edited by Colin Lawson

The Cambridge Companion to Pop and Rock
Edited by Simon Frith, Will Straw and John Street

The Cambridge Companion to Recorded Music
Edited by Eric Clarke, Nicholas Cook, Daniel Leech-Wilkinson and John Rink

The Cambridge Companion to Rhythm
Edited by Russell Hartenberger and Ryan McClelland

The Cambridge Companion to *The Rite of Spring*
Edited by Davinia Caddy

The Cambridge Companion to Schubert's 'Winterreise'
Edited by Marjorie W. Hirsch and Lisa Feurzeig

The Cambridge Companion to Serialism
Edited by Martin Iddon

The Cambridge Companion to Seventeenth-Century Opera
Edited by Jacqueline Waeber

The Cambridge Companion to the Singer-Songwriter
Edited by Katherine Williams and Justin A. Williams

The Cambridge Companion to the String Quartet
Edited by Robin Stowell

The Cambridge Companion to the Symphony
Edited by Julian Horton

The Cambridge Companion to Tango
Edited by Kristin Wendland and Kacey Link

The Cambridge Companion to Twentieth-Century Opera
Edited by Mervyn Cooke

The Cambridge Companion to Video Game Music
Edited by Melanie Fritsch and Tim Summers

The Cambridge Companion to Wagner's *Der Ring des Nibelungen*
Edited by Mark Berry and Nicholas Vazsonyi

The Cambridge Companion to *West Side Story*
Edited by Paul R. Laird and Elizabeth A. Wells

The Cambridge Companion to Women Composers
Edited by Matthew Head and Susan Wollenberg

The Cambridge Companion to Women in Music since 1900
Edited by Laura Hamer

Composers

The Cambridge Companion to Bach
Edited by John Butt

The Cambridge Companion to Bartók
Edited by Amanda Bayley

The Cambridge Companion to Amy Beach
Edited by E. Douglas Bomberger

The Cambridge Companion to the Beatles
Edited by Kenneth Womack

The Cambridge Companion to Beethoven
Edited by Glenn Stanley

The Cambridge Companion to Berg
Edited by Anthony Pople

The Cambridge Companion to Berlioz
Edited by Peter Bloom

The Cambridge Companion to Brahms
Edited by Michael Musgrave

The Cambridge Companion to Benjamin Britten
Edited by Mervyn Cooke

The Cambridge Companion to Bruckner
Edited by John Williamson

The Cambridge Companion to John Cage
Edited by David Nicholls

The Cambridge Companion to Chopin
Edited by Jim Samson

The Cambridge Companion to Debussy
Edited by Simon Trezise

The Cambridge Companion to Elgar
Edited by Daniel M. Grimley and Julian Rushton

The Cambridge Companion to Duke Ellington
Edited by Edward Green

The Cambridge Companion to Gershwin
Edited by Anna Celenza

The Cambridge Companion to Gilbert and Sullivan
Edited by David Eden and Meinhard Saremba

The Cambridge Companion to Handel
Edited by Donald Burrows

The Cambridge Companion to Haydn
Edited by Caryl Clark

The Cambridge Companion to Liszt
Edited by Kenneth Hamilton

The Cambridge Companion to Mahler
Edited by Jeremy Barham

The Cambridge Companion to Mendelssohn
Edited by Peter Mercer-Taylor

The Cambridge Companion to Monteverdi
Edited by John Whenham and Richard Wistreich

The Cambridge Companion to Mozart
Edited by Simon P. Keefe

The Cambridge Companion to Arvo Pärt
Edited by Andrew Shenton

The Cambridge Companion to Ravel
Edited by Deborah Mawer

The Cambridge Companion to the Rolling Stones
Edited by Victor Coelho and John Covach

The Cambridge Companion to Rossini
Edited by Emanuele Senici

The Cambridge Companion to Schoenberg
Edited by Jennifer Shaw and Joseph Auner

The Cambridge Companion to Schubert
Edited by Christopher Gibbs

The Cambridge Companion to Schumann
Edited by Beate Perrey

The Cambridge Companion to Shostakovich
Edited by Pauline Fairclough and David Fanning

The Cambridge Companion to Sibelius
Edited by Daniel M. Grimley

The Cambridge Companion to Richard Strauss
Edited by Charles Youmans

The Cambridge Companion to Stravinsky
Edited by Jonathan Cross

The Cambridge Companion to Michael Tippett
Edited by Kenneth Gloag and Nicholas Jones

The Cambridge Companion to Vaughan Williams
Edited by Alain Frogley and Aiden J. Thomson

The Cambridge Companion to Verdi
Edited by Scott L. Balthazar

The Cambridge Companion to Wagner
Edited by Thomas S. Grey

Instruments

The Cambridge Companion to Brass Instruments
Edited by Trevor Herbert and John Wallace

The Cambridge Companion to the Cello
Edited by Robin Stowell

The Cambridge Companion to the Clarinet
Edited by Colin Lawson

The Cambridge Companion to the Drum Kit
Edited by Matt Brennan, Joseph Michael Pignato and Daniel Akira Stadnicki

The Cambridge Companion to the Electric Guitar
Edited by Jan-Peter Herbst and Steve Waksman

The Cambridge Companion to the Guitar
Edited by Victor Coelho

The Cambridge Companion to the Harpsichord
Edited by Mark Kroll

The Cambridge Companion to the Organ
Edited by Nicholas Thistlethwaite and Geoffrey Webber

The Cambridge Companion to Percussion
Edited by Russell Hartenberger

The Cambridge Companion to the Piano
Edited by David Rowland

The Cambridge Companion to the Saxophone
Edited by Richard Ingham

The Cambridge Companion to Singing
Edited by John Potter

The Cambridge Companion to the Violin
Edited by Robin Stowell

The Cambridge Companion to Folk Music

Edited by
ROSS COLE
University of Leeds

Shaftesbury Road, Cambridge CB2 8EA, United Kingdom

One Liberty Plaza, 20th Floor, New York, NY 10006, USA

477 Williamstown Road, Port Melbourne, VIC 3207, Australia

314–321, 3rd Floor, Plot 3, Splendor Forum, Jasola District Centre, New Delhi – 110025, India

103 Penang Road, #05–06/07, Visioncrest Commercial, Singapore 238467

Cambridge University Press is part of Cambridge University Press & Assessment, a department of the University of Cambridge.

We share the University's mission to contribute to society through the pursuit of education, learning and research at the highest international levels of excellence.

www.cambridge.org
Information on this title: www.cambridge.org/9781009407595

DOI: 10.1017/9781009407601

© Cambridge University Press & Assessment 2026

This publication is in copyright. Subject to statutory exception and to the provisions of relevant collective licensing agreements, no reproduction of any part may take place without the written permission of Cambridge University Press & Assessment.

When citing this work, please include a reference to the DOI 10.1017/9781009407601

First published 2026

A catalogue record for this publication is available from the British Library

A Cataloging-in-Publication data record for this book is available from the Library of Congress

ISBN 978-1-009-40759-5 Hardback
ISBN 978-1-009-40758-8 Paperback

Cambridge University Press & Assessment has no responsibility for the persistence or accuracy of URLs for external or third-party internet websites referred to in this publication and does not guarantee that any content on such websites is, or will remain, accurate or appropriate.

For EU product safety concerns, contact us at Calle de José Abascal, 56, 1°, 28003 Madrid, Spain, or email eugpsr@cambridge.org

Contents

List of Figures   [*page* xi]
List of Contributors   [xiii]
Chronology   [xix]

Introduction   [1]

PART I   PERSPECTIVES

1   The Idea of Folk Music   [15]
    ROSS COLE

2   Observing and Collecting   [35]
    JEFF TODD TITON

3   Folk and the Public Sphere   [55]
    TIMOTHY HAMPTON

4   Towards a Critical Folk Music Studies   [73]
    BRAHMA PRAKASH

5   *Artist Voice*
    Fiddler on the Hoof: Reminiscences of an Ethnographer   [91]
    YALE STROM

PART II   ELEMENTS

6   Complementary Modalities in Celtic Music   [99]
    JOSHUA DICKSON

7   Thinking About the Words to Folks' Songs   [120]
    DIANNE DUGAW

8   Folk Instruments   [140]
    MAEVE CAREY-KOZLARK

9   Folk Dance in a Global Frame   [162]
    THERESA JILL BUCKLAND

10 *Artist Voice*
   An Introduction to Introductions   [184]
   JON BODEN

   PART III IMAGINARIES

11 Folk Music and Nationalism   [191]
   KATHARINE ELLIS

12 Colonialist Hierarchies   [210]
   ERIN JOHNSON-WILLIAMS

13 Reviving the Folk   [231]
   BRITTA SWEERS

14 Music, Migration, and Belonging   [251]
   HELEN PHELAN WITH HALA JABER, JOHN NUTEKPOR, AND EWA ŻAK-DYNDAŁ

15 *Artist Voice*
   Mythopoeic Singing or, The Mythopoeic Singer   [272]
   ANGELINE MORRISON

   PART IV IDENTITIES

16 Reclaiming Black Folk Music   [279]
   KATRINA THOMPSON MOORE

17 Women in the Margins   [299]
   ELIZABETH BENNETT

18 No Neutrals Here: Folk, Class, Labour   [317]
   MARK STEVEN

19 Protest Song and the Popular Voice   [334]
   OSKAR COX JENSEN

20 *Artist Voice*
   Multiple Identities   [354]
   PEGGY SEEGER

   Further Reading   [359]
   Index   [364]

Figures

1.1 Mary Howitt. Frontispiece to *An Autobiography* (London, 1889). Woodburytype. [*page* 18]

1.2 Winslow Homer, 'The Songs of the War', *Harper's Weekly*, Vol. 5 (23 November 1861). Wood engraving. Library of Congress. [22]

2.1 Robert Winslow Gordon, 1923. Photograph courtesy of J. Barre Toelken and the American Folklife Center, Library of Congress. [43]

3.1 Joan Baez at an anti-draft demonstration in Central Park, New York City, 1968. Photograph by Bernard Gotfryd. Library of Congress. [61]

4.1 Gaddar performing in Hanamkonda district of erstwhile Andhra Pradesh in a programme organized by the All India People's Resistance Forum (AIPRF), 28 December 1997. Photograph by G. D. Satyam, processed and archived by B. Narsing Rao. [86]

5.1 Jewish wedding in Roman, Romania with klezmer music from Romani musicians. Photograph by Yale Strom, February 1985. [95]

6.1 A 'primary' pibroch ground as it has been most commonly conceptualized since the 1890s. [106]

6.2 The phrase pattern in Figure 6.1 reconfigured by Lorimer to reveal its structural reciprocity. [107]

6.3 The 'Scottish Measure', one of twenty-four outlined in Robert ap Huw's manuscript of *c*.1613. [108]

6.4 Variations 1–4 of J. S. Skinner's 'Tullochgorm' from *The Scottish Violinist*, 1900. [111]

8.1 Banjo by William Esperance Boucher, Jr., Baltimore, United States, *c*.1845. Metropolitan Museum of Art. [148]

8.2 Appalachian Dulcimer by Charles Napoleon Prichard, United States, late nineteenth century. Metropolitan Museum of Art. [151]

14.1 John Nutekpor in *Kutrikuku / Resilience*, 2020. Photograph by Maurice Gunning. [263]

15.1 William Edward Burghardt Du Bois, 1919. Photograph by Cornelius Marion Battey. Library of Congress. [273]

16.1 '(Traversée) Danse de Nègres'. Engraving from Amédée Gréhan, *La France Maritime*, 3rd Volume (Paris, 1837).   [281]
18.1 Woody Guthrie, 1943. Photograph by Al Aumuller. Library of Congress.   [328]
19.1 Drawings by Walter Crane from *Chants of Labour*, edited by Edward Carpenter (London, 1888).   [344]

Contributors

ELIZABETH BENNETT is the author of *Performing Folk Songs: Affect, Landscape, and Repertoire* (Bloomsbury Academic, 2024). She is an interdisciplinary researcher and educator, with a focus on performance in relation to gender, space, place, landscape, and voice. She was the co-organiser of two ground-breaking conferences: 'Locating Women in "The Folk"' (held at the University of Sussex in 2018) and 'Street Music' (held at the University of East Anglia in 2019). In 2018, she co-authored a public report with George McKay entitled *From Brass Bands to Buskers: Street Music in the UK*, a major output of the AHRC-funded project 'Public Culture and Creative Spaces'.

JON BODEN has been earning his living as a performer of (primarily) traditional folk songs for over twenty years. Through his work as lead singer of Bellowhead, one half of Spiers & Boden, and through his solo songwriting work he has won eleven BBC Radio 2 Folk Awards, sold over 250,000 albums, and performed all over the world. He co-presents *Under the Leaves* with Eliza Carthy, a podcast on the history of folk-song collection. Before becoming a folk singer he studied Medieval history and literature at Durham University and composition for the theatre at the London College of Music. He has been awarded honorary doctorates by Durham and the Open University.

THERESA JILL BUCKLAND is Emeritus Professor of Dance History and Ethnography at the University of Roehampton and Fellow of the British Academy. She is the author of *Society Dancing: Fashionable Bodies in England 1870–1920* (Palgrave Macmillan, 2011) and the editor of *Dance in the Field: Theory, Methods and Issues in Dance Ethnography* (Macmillan, 1999), *Dancing from Past to Present: Nation, Culture, Identities* (University of Wisconsin Press, 2006), and co-editor of *Folklore Revival Movements in Europe post 1950* (Czech Academy of Sciences, 2018). As well as social, popular and folk dance, she writes on cultural memory and the emergence of dance as an academic discipline.

MAEVE CAREY-KOZLARK is a PhD candidate in historical musicology at New York University, where her research examines sonic geographies and material culture under conditions of memory, migration, and cultural imperialism, with a particular focus on Ireland and the Irish diaspora. She has presented her work at a number of conferences including the American Musicological Society, Society for Ethnomusicology, American Conference for Irish Studies, and the American Musical Instrument Society. Previously, she studied at Bennington College.

ROSS COLE is author of *The Folk: Music, Modernity, and the Political Imagination* (University of California Press, 2021), which won the Bruno Nettl Prize from the Society for Ethnomusicology awarded to an outstanding publication on the history of the field. He completed a PhD at King's College Cambridge with Nicholas Cook and was then elected to a junior research fellowship at Homerton College. In 2024, he received a Philip Leverhulme Prize. His recent writing, on a wide range of topics, has appeared in journals including *Modernism/Modernity*, *ASAP/Journal*, *Ethnomusicology*, and the *Journal of the Royal Musical Association*. He is Associate Professor of Music at the University of Leeds.

OSKAR COX JENSEN is a novelist and UKRI Future Leaders Fellow in Music at Newcastle University. He is the author of *Vagabonds: Life on the Streets of Nineteenth-Century London* (Duckworth Books, 2022), *The Ballad-Singer in Georgian and Victorian London* (Cambridge University Press, 2021), and *Napoleon in British Song, 1797–1822* (Palgrave Macmillan, 2015). He is also co-author of *Our Subversive Voice: The History and Politics of English Protest Songs* (McGill-Queen's University Press, 2025) and co-editor of *Music and Politics in Britain, c.1780–1850* – a special issue of *Journal of British Studies* (2021) – and of *Charles Dibdin and Late Georgian Culture* (Oxford University Press, 2018).

JOSHUA DICKSON is Head of Traditional Music at the Royal Conservatoire of Scotland. He studied Scottish Gaelic at the University of Aberdeen and undertook doctoral research in the history of the piping tradition of the southern Outer Hebrides at the School of Scottish Studies, University of Edinburgh. Joshua led the design of the groundbreaking BMus (Hons) Traditional Music programme at the Royal Conservatoire and co-founded the international conference series 'Pedagogies, Practices, and the Future of Folk Music in Higher Education', which has taken place in Glasgow (in partnership with the world-renowned Celtic Connections festival) and Helsinki.

DIANNE DUGAW is a singer/musician, writer, and scholar. Professor Emerita at the University of Oregon, she has published widely on topics in queer and gender studies, folklore, musicology, and literary and cultural studies. Her scholarly books include *Warrior Women and Popular Balladry* (Cambridge University Press, 1989; University of Chicago Press, 1996) and *'Deep Play' – John Gay & the Invention of Modernity* (University of Delaware Press, 2001). Her memoir *California Medieval: Nearly a Nun in 1960s San Francisco* received the 2023 Nicholas Schaffner Award for Music in Literature and was published by Schaffner Press in 2024.

KATHARINE ELLIS is 1684 Professor of Music at the University of Cambridge. A cultural historian of musical France, her books include *Music Criticism in Nineteenth-Century France* (Cambridge University Press, 1995), *Interpreting the Musical Past* (Oxford University Press, 2008), *The Politics of Plainchant* (Ashgate, 2013), *French Musical Life* (Oxford University Press, 2022, winner of the American Musicological Society's Otto Kinkeldey Award), and jointly edited collections on Berlioz and on music and literature. She is an elected member of Academia Europaea, a Fellow of the British Academy, and an International Fellow of the American Philosophical Society.

TIMOTHY HAMPTON is Aldo Scaglione and Marie M. Burns Professor of Comparative Literature and French at the University of California, Berkeley. His research involves the relationship between politics and culture, and focuses on such issues as the ideology of literary genre, the literary construction of nationhood, and the rhetoric of historiography. He regularly teaches courses on the early modern period, on the Baroque, and on lyric. His books include *Bob Dylan, How the Songs Work* (Zone Books, 2019), *Cheerfulness: A Literary and Cultural History* (Zone Books, 2022), and *Fictions of Embassy: Literature and Diplomacy in Early Modern Europe* (Cornell University Press, 2009).

ERIN JOHNSON-WILLIAMS is Associate Professor of Music Education and Social Justice at the University of Southampton. Her research focuses on decolonizing nineteenth-century history, the imperial legacies of music education, trauma studies, gender and maternity, and biopolitics. She is co-editor of *Intersectional Encounters in the Nineteenth-Century Archive* (Bloomsbury Academic, 2022), *Hymns and Constructions of Race* (Routledge, 2024), and the forthcoming *Oxford Handbook of Music Colonialism*. At Southampton, she is Director of the Centre for Music Education and Social Justice and Project Lead for the AHRC Public Engagement with Music Research Hub (2024–2026).

ANGELINE MORRISON is a singer, songwriter, and multi-instrumentalist who makes music infused with elements of soul, sixties beat pop, folklore, myth, and the supernatural. Her original compositions and re-stitchings of traditional songs focus on things that have gone unnoticed. In 2022, she won the prestigious Christian Raphael Prize at Cambridge Folk Festival. Her 2022 album *The Sorrow Songs: Folk Songs of Black British Experience* (Topic Records) was described by *The Guardian* as 'dazzling', and was voted No. 1 Folk Album of the Year. *The Sorrow Songs* uses history and imagination to tell stories of Black British ancestors in the sonic style of folk and traditional music.

KATRINA THOMPSON MOORE is Associate Dean in the College of Arts and Sciences and joint-appointed Professor in the Departments of African American Studies and History at Saint Louis University. She is the author of *Ring Shout, Wheel About: The Racial Politics of Music and Dance in North American Slavery* (University of Illinois Press, 2014), which was selected as a Choice Outstanding Academic Title and recognized as one of the thirteen most important books in Black History by the *Washington Post*. Her writings have appeared in *Journal of American Culture, Popular Culture Studies Journal, Black Women, Gender*, and *Families*, among other publications.

HELEN PHELAN is Professor of Arts Practice and Director of the Irish World Academy of Music and Dance at the University of Limerick. She is a multi-award-winning Irish Research Council recipient for her work on music and migration. Her publications include the monograph *Singing the Rite to Belong: Music, Ritual and the New Irish* (Oxford University Press, 2017). She has co-written the chapter in this volume with three of her recent doctoral students and graduates, Hala Jaber, John Nutekpor, and Ewa Żak-Dyndał, whose research investigates music and themes of belonging, inclusion, and identity negotiation in the context of new migrant communities in Ireland.

BRAHMA PRAKASH teaches theatre and performance studies at Jawaharlal Nehru University, New Delhi. He is the author of critically acclaimed books *Cultural Labour: Conceptualizing the 'Folk Performance' in India* (Oxford University Press, 2019) and *Body on the Barricades: Life, Art and Resistance in Contemporary India* (LeftWord, 2023). He has also published in various scholarly journals, including *Asian Theatre Journal, Performance Research, South Asian History and Culture, Economic and Political Weekly*, and others. His popular columns on art, culture, and politics frequently appear in Scroll, Wire, Outlook, Indian Cultural Forum, and other media platforms.

PEGGY SEEGER is rightly considered one of folk music's icons. A multi-instrumentalist, she is lauded for her feminist, political, and topical songs. Although in her late eighties, her light burns as brightly as ever, with legendary live performances that might include an unaccompanied ballad followed by an anecdote from her remarkable life before a topical song about drugs, war, hormones, politicians, unions, women, love, or ecology. She has made twenty-four solo recordings and participated in over a hundred more with other artists. As Ewan MacColl's partner and muse, she was the inspiration behind the song 'The First Time Ever I Saw Your Face' (the title of her much-praised memoir).

MARK STEVEN is Associate Professor of Literature and Film at the University of Exeter. His writing explores the poetics of social transformation – how different forms respond to the vicissitudes of capitalism, to the practicalities of revolution, and to the possibility of communism. He is the author of *Class War: A Literary History* (Verso, 2023), *Red Modernism: American Poetry and the Spirit of Communism* (Johns Hopkins, 2017), and *Splatter Capital* (Repeater, 2017). He is editor of *Understanding Marx, Understanding Modernism* (Bloomsbury, 2021), and co-editor of *The Cinema of Theo Angelopoulos* (Edinburgh University Press, 2015) and *Styles of Extinction: Cormac McCarthy's The Road* (Bloomsbury, 2012).

YALE STROM is one of the world's leading ethnographer-artists of klezmer and Romani music and history. His findings were instrumental in forming the repertoire of his klezmer band, Hot Pstromi. Strom's sixteen CDs on the Naxos, Transcontinental Music, and ARC UK labels run the full gamut from traditional klezmer to 'new' Jewish jazz. He has directed ten award-winning documentary films, written fifteen books, and produced two award-winning audio dramas. Strom was artist-in-residence in the Jewish Studies Program at San Diego State University between 2006 and 2020. He currently teaches in the Music Department. Prior to this, he taught at New York University.

BRITTA SWEERS is Professor of Cultural Anthropology of Music at the University of Bern, where she was previously Director of the Center for Global Studies. Between 2014 and 2021 she was President of the European Seminar in Ethnomusicology. A central focus of her research is the transformation of traditional musics in a global context, including *Electric Folk: The Changing Face of English Traditional Music* (Oxford University Press, 2005). Britta undertook further fieldwork in the United States, Germany, the Baltic Countries, and Northern Scandinavia. She is co-editor of the *European Journal of Musicology* and the book series Transcultural Music Studies.

JEFF TODD TITON, Professor of Music Emeritus at Brown University, has been active as a folklorist and ethnomusicologist for more than fifty years. He is known for his work in collaborative ethnography, for introducing the concepts of musical and cultural sustainability, for helping to establish the field of applied ethnomusicology, for his appeal for a sound commons for all living creatures, and for his current project theorizing a sound ecology. In 2020 he received the Lifetime Scholarly Achievement Award from the American Folklore Society. His most recent book is *Toward a Sound Ecology: New and Selected Essays* (Indiana University Press, 2020).

Chronology

Folk music seems to defy attempts at chronology. Nevertheless, it is the product of a particular era and set of historical circumstances. This chronology traces the concept from its origins in literary Romanticism through to the tail end of the postwar revival – a 200-year itinerary that has defined the modern world. Essentially Victorian in nature, the terms *folk song* and *folk music* appear in the English language in the wake of railways, steam ships, and the music hall. These terms coincide with the Industrial Revolution and come into wider circulation alongside the Arts and Crafts movement. The Folk-Song Society was founded in London in 1898 at a pivotal moment that witnessed the emergence of the phonograph, electric light, radio transmission, automobiles, the Fabian Society, the Labour Party, and the *Daily Mail*. Although folk music is often associated with two major 'revivals' (the Edwardian and the Cold War), we can see that there was sustained interest in the topic from this point onwards. We might note the ways in which such interest often accompanies periods of rapid social and technological change.

1760s	James Macpherson publishes epic poems purportedly by an ancient bard named Ossian.
1765	Thomas Percy, *Reliques of Ancient English Poetry*.
1773	*Von deutscher Art und Kunst*. Inclosure Act.
1776	United States Declaration of Independence.
1778	Johann Gottfried Herder, *Volkslieder*.
1789	Storming of the Bastille in Paris. Outbreak of the French Revolution.
1798	William Wordsworth and Samuel Taylor Coleridge, *Lyrical Ballads*. Thomas Robert Malthus, *An Essay on the Principle of Population*.
1800	Acts of Union create the United Kingdom of Great Britain and Ireland.
1802	Walter Scott, *Minstrelsy of the Scottish Border*.
1804	Coronation of Napoleon at Notre-Dame de Paris. Haitian independence.

1805	Achim von Arnim and Clemens Brentano, *Des Knaben Wunderhorn*.
1806	Dissolution of the Holy Roman Empire.
1807	Slave Trade Act.
1811	Luddite movement.
1813	Jane Austen, *Pride and Prejudice*.
1815	Congress of Vienna. Battle of Waterloo. End of Napoleonic Wars.
1818	Mary Shelley, *Frankenstein*.
1819	John Keats, 'Ode to a Nightingale'.
1821	John Constable, *The Hay Wain*.
1824	Ludwig van Beethoven, Symphony No. 9.
1828	Thomas D. Rice, 'Jump Jim Crow'.
1829	Felix Mendelssohn's revival of J. S. Bach's *St. Matthew Passion* in Berlin.
1830	Liverpool and Manchester Railway opened. July Revolution in Paris.
1833	Slavery Abolition Act. Great Western Railway founded.
1834	New Poor Law. *Narrative of the Life of David Crockett, Written by Himself*.
1835	Jacob Grimm, *Deutsche Mythologie*.
1836	Ralph Waldo Emerson, 'Nature'.
1837	Accession of Queen Victoria to the British throne. Charles Dickens, *The Pickwick Papers*.
1838	Beginnings of Chartist movement. J. M. W. Turner, *The Fighting Temeraire*.
1839	Introduction of Daguerreotype (early photographic process).
1840	Percy Society founded in London. Uniform Penny Post. Robert Schumann, *Dichterliebe*.
1841	Peter Christen Asbjørnsen and Jørgen Moe, *Norske Folkeeventyr*.
1843	John Broadwood, *Old English Songs*. Virginia Minstrels develop the blackface minstrel show.
1845	Great Famine in Ireland. Isambard Kingdom Brunel, *SS Great Britain*.
1846	'Folk-lore' coined by William Thoms. Saxophone patented. Electric Telegraph Company founded in London. Smithsonian Institution founded in Washington, DC. Mexican–American War.

1847	'Folk's song' used by Mary Howitt. Charlotte Brontë, *Jane Eyre*. Emily Brontë, *Wuthering Heights*.
1848	Wave of revolutions throughout Europe. Karl Marx and Friedrich Engels, *Manifesto of the Communist Party*. California Gold Rush.
1849	John Ruskin, *The Seven Lamps of Architecture*.
1851	Great Exhibition held in London's Crystal Palace. John Everett Millais, *Ophelia*.
1852	'Folk-Music' used by Andrew Hamilton. Canterbury Music Hall opened in London. Museum of Manufactures established (later the V&A). Harriet Beecher Stowe, *Uncle Tom's Cabin*.
1853	Crimean War. Giuseppe Verdi, *La traviata*.
1854	Henry David Thoreau, *Walden*.
1855	William Chappell, *The Ballad Literature and Popular Music of the Olden Time*. Walt Whitman, *Leaves of Grass*.
1857	Charles Baudelaire, *Les Fleurs du mal*. Uprising against the British East India Company.
1858	Government of India Act; beginning of Crown rule (British Raj).
1859	Charles Darwin, *On the Origin of Species by Means of Natural Selection*.
1860	John Williamson Palmer, *Folk Songs*. Edouard Manet, *The Spanish Singer*.
1861	Richard Grant White, *National Hymns*. Beginning of the American Civil War. Unification of Italy.
1863	Emancipation Proclamation issued by Abraham Lincoln. Opening of the London Underground.
1865	Abraham Lincoln assassinated. First Ku Klux Klan founded in Tennessee. Richard Wagner, *Tristan und Isolde*.
1866	Carl Engel, *An Introduction to the Study of National Music*. Bedřich Smetana, *The Bartered Bride*.
1867	*Slave Songs of the United States*.
1868	Harriet Beecher Stowe refers to 'John Brown's Body' as a 'folk-song'.
1871	Fisk Jubilee Singers formed. Charles E. Gover, *The Folk-Songs of Southern India*. William Axon, *Folk Song and Folk-Speech of Lancashire*. Edward B. Tylor, *Primitive Culture*. Paris Commune.
1877	Antonín Dvořák, *Bouquet of Czech Folk Songs*. Invention of the phonograph by Thomas Edison.
1878	Folk-Lore Society founded in London.

1879	Johannes Brahms, *Hungarian Dances*. Thomas Edison demonstrates the incandescent light bulb.
1880	Joel Chandler Harris, *Uncle Remus, His Songs and His Sayings*.
1881	Natural History Museum opens in London.
1882	Francis James Child, *The English and Scottish Popular Ballads* (ten volumes published 1882–98).
1884	Fabian Society founded in London. Pitt Rivers Museum founded in Oxford.
1886	Volta Graphophone Company founded. Benz Patent-Motorwagen. Robert Louis Stevenson, *Strange Case of Dr Jekyll and Mr Hyde*.
1888	American Folk-Lore Society founded in Cambridge, MA. John Ashton, *Modern Street Ballads*.
1890	S. Baring-Gould, H. Fleetwood Sheppard, and F. W. Bussell, *Songs of the West*. William Morris, *News from Nowhere*. Paul Cézanne, *The Card Players*. Claude Monet, *Stacks of Wheat*.
1891	Frank Kidson, *Traditional Tunes*. William Alexander Barratt, *English Folk-Songs*. Oscar Wilde, 'The Soul of Man under Socialism'.
1892	S. Baring-Gould, *Strange Survivals*. Max Nordau, *Entartung*. *Vogue* magazine founded in New York.
1893	Joseph Jacobs, 'The Folk'. Lucy E. Broadwood and J. A. Fuller Maitland, *English County Songs*. Richard Wallaschek, *Primitive Music*. Edvard Munch, *Der Schrei der Natur*.
1894	Francis B. Gummere, *Old English Ballads*. Dreyfus affair in France.
1895	First radio transmission by Guglielmo Marconi.
1896	C. Hubert H. Parry, *The Evolution of the Art of Music*. *Daily Mail* founded.
1897	Peasant Arts Society founded in Haslemere, Surrey. Edvard Grieg, *Symphonic Dances*.
1898	Folk-Song Society founded in London. Gramophone Company Limited founded.
1899	Kate Lee, 'Some Experiences of a Folk-Song Collector'. Jean Sibelius, *Finlandia*. Sigmund Freud, *Die Traumdeutung*. Joseph Conrad, *Heart of Darkness*.
1900	British Labour Party founded in London.
1901	Death of Queen Victoria. Booker T. Washington, *Up From Slavery*.

1903	W. E. Burghardt Du Bois, *The Souls of Black Folk*. Wright brothers achieve first powered flight. Women's Social and Political Union founded.
1905	Lucy Broadwood, 'On the Collecting of English Folk-Song'. Samuel Coleridge-Taylor, *Twenty-Four Negro Melodies*. Industrial Workers of the World ('Wobblies') formed in Chicago.
1906	Béla Bartók, *Hungarian Folksongs, for voice and piano*.
1907	Cecil J. Sharp, *English Folk-Song*. Eugenics Education Society founded in London. Pablo Picasso, *Les Demoiselles d'Avignon*.
1908	Percy Grainger, 'Collecting with the Phonograph'. Ford Model T car introduced.
1910	John A. Lomax, *Cowboy Songs and Other Frontier Ballads*. R. Vaughan Williams, 'English Folk-Song'.
1911	English Folk Dance Society founded by Cecil Sharp. Henry Burstow, *Reminiscences of Horsham*.
1912	Ernest Newman, 'The Folk-Song Fallacy'. *Der Blaue Reiter*. Arnold Schoenberg, *Pierrot lunaire*.
1913	Marcel Proust, *Du côté de chez Swann*. Ballets Russes perform Igor Stravinsky's *Le Sacre du printemps*.
1914	Outbreak of First World War. W. C. Handy, 'Saint Louis Blues'.
1915	Frank Kidson and Mary Neal, *English Folk-Song and Dance*. John Wesley Work, *Folk Song of the American Negro*. D. W. Griffith, *The Birth of a Nation*. Second Ku Klux Klan founded in Georgia. Kazimir Malevich, *Black Square*.
1917	Olive Dame Campbell and Cecil Sharp, *English Folk Songs from the Southern Appalachians*. Russian Revolution. Marcel Duchamp, *Fountain*.
1918	Natalie Curtis Burlin, *Negro Folk-Songs*. Influenza pandemic.
1920	League of Nations established. Communist Party of Great Britain founded. Prohibition Era.
1921	Louise Pound, *Poetic Origins and the Ballad*. Chanel No. 5 launched.
1922	BBC founded. Mussolini appointed Prime Minister of Italy. Creation of Irish Free State. Formation of the USSR. T. S. Eliot, 'The Waste Land'. James Joyce, *Ulysses*.
1923	Jean Toomer, *Cane*. Alfred Williams, *Folk-Songs of the Upper Thames*. R. Vaughan Williams, *English Folk Song Suite*. Ma Rainey, 'Bo-Weavil Blues'. Bessie Smith, 'Downhearted Blues'.

1925	Beginning of electrical sound recording. Virginia Woolf, *Mrs. Dalloway*. F. Scott Fitzgerald, *The Great Gatsby*. Alain Locke, *The New Negro*. Sergei Eisenstein, *Battleship Potemkin*.
1926	Louis Armstrong's Hot Five on Okeh Records. Zoltán Kodály, *Háry János*.
1927	Carl Sandburg, *The American Songbag*. Fritz Lang, *Metropolis*.
1928	Archive of American Folk Song established. Representation of the People (Equal Franchise) Act.
1929	Wall Street Crash; beginning of the Great Depression.
1931	Zora Neale Hurston, 'Hoodoo in America'. 'The Art of India' exhibition, London.
1932	English Folk Dance and Song Society (EFDSS) formed from the merger of the Folk-Song Society and the English Folk Dance Society. Highlander Folk School founded in Tennessee.
1933	Adolf Hitler appointed chancellor of Germany. Beginning of New Deal programs and reforms enacted by US President Franklin D. Roosevelt.
1934	John and Alan Lomax, *American Ballads and Folk Songs*. R. Vaughan Williams, *National Music*.
1935	George Gershwin, *Porgy and Bess*. Fred Astaire and Ginger Rogers star in *Top Hat*.
1936	John and Alan Lomax, *Negro Folk Songs as Sung by Lead Belly*. Workers' Music Association founded by Alan Bush. Charlie Chaplin, *Modern Times*. Spanish Civil War.
1937	Walt Disney Productions, *Snow White and the Seven Dwarfs*. Little Steel strike, US.
1938	A. L. Morton, *A People's History of England*. Benny Goodman performs at Carnegie Hall. First 'From Spirituals to Swing' concert at Carnegie Hall, presented by John Hammond.
1939	Topic Records founded. Outbreak of Second World War. John Steinbeck, *The Grapes of Wrath*.
1940	The Almanac Singers formed. Woody Guthrie, *Dust Bowl Ballads*. Churchill war ministry.
1941	John and Alan Lomax, *Our Singing Country*. W. C. Handy, *Father of the Blues*. Olivier Messiaen, *Quatuor pour la fin du temps*. Orson Welles, *Citizen Kane*. Attack on Pearl Harbor.
1942	Beginning of mass extermination of Jews in gas chambers. Edward Hopper, *Nighthawks*.
1943	Woody Guthrie, *Bound for Glory*. Iain Lang, *Background of the Blues*. Allied invasion of Sicily.

1944   A. L. Lloyd, *The Singing Englishman*. Sister Rosetta Tharpe, 'Strange Things Happening Every Day'. Theodor W. Adorno and Max Horkheimer, *Dialektik der Aufklärung*. D-Day.

1945   People's Songs founded in New York City. Atomic bombs dropped on Hiroshima and Nagasaki. Germany and Japan surrender. Nuremberg trials begin. United Nations established.

1946   B. A. Botkin, *The American People*; A. L. Lloyd publishes a rave review in *Our Time*.

1947   International Folk Music Council founded in London (later, International Council for Traditional Music). Indian Independence Act. Truman Doctrine; beginning of the Cold War. W. H. Auden, *The Age of Anxiety*. Jackson Pollock, *Full Fathom Five*. Christian Dior's 'New Look'.

1948   Folkways Records founded by Moses Asch. The Weavers formed. Pete Seeger, *How to Play the Five-String Banjo*. British Nationality Act. HMT *Empire Windrush* brings West Indian immigrants to London. Introduction of the National Health Service (NHS). Creation of the state of Israel.

1949   George Orwell, *Nineteen Eighty-Four*. Mao Zedong proclaims the People's Republic of China.

1950   First issue of *Sing Out!* Pete Seeger, *Darling Corey*. Alan Lomax sets sail for Europe.

1951   Festival of Britain. J. D. Salinger, *The Catcher in the Rye*. Miles Davis, *The New Sounds*.

1952   Harry Smith, *Anthology of American Folk Music*. A. L. Lloyd, *Come All Ye Bold Miners* and *Coaldust Ballads*. John Cage, *4'33"*. Pierre Boulez, *Structures 1*. Ralph Ellison, *Invisible Man*.

1953   First broadcasts of *As I Roved Out* and *Ballads and Blues* on BBC radio and *Song Hunter* on BBC television. Death of Joseph Stalin. Samuel Beckett, *Waiting for Godot*. Coronation of Queen Elizabeth II. Francis Crick and James Watson discover the structure of DNA.

1954   The IFMC agrees on a definition of folk music founded on Cecil Sharp's ideas. Maud Karpeles gives a series of talks on 'English Folk Music' for BBC radio. Ewan MacColl, *The Shuttle and Cage: Industrial Folk-Ballads*. Television Act. *Brown v. Board of Education*. Elvis Presley, 'That's All Right'.

1955   Peggy Seeger, *Folk Songs of Courting and Complaint*. William Broonzy, *Big Bill Blues*. Skiffle craze in Britain. Beginning of the Vietnam war. Chuck Berry, 'Maybellene'.

1956	*Odetta Sings Ballads and Blues.* Hungarian Revolution. Nikita Khrushchev's 'Secret Speech'. John Lennon forms The Quarrymen. Allen Ginsberg, *Howl and Other Poems.*
1957	'Ballads and Blues club' hosts weekly sessions in the upper room of the Princess Louise pub in Holborn. BBC radio broadcasts a series of programmes presented by Alan Lomax: *Memories of a Ballad-Hunter, A Ballad-Hunter Looks at Britain, A Ballad-Hunter Looks at Ireland.* Izzy Young founds the Folklore Center on MacDougal Street in Greenwich Village. Jack Kerouac, *On the Road.* Richard Hoggart, *The Uses of Literacy.* Campaign for Nuclear Disarmament founded.
1958	The Kingston Trio's self-titled debut album released on Capitol Records. First Berkeley Folk Music Festival. *The Ballad of John Axon*, the first BBC 'radio ballad' by Ewan MacColl, Peggy Seeger, and Charles Parker. March from London to Aldermaston organized by Direct Action Committee Against Nuclear War. Raymond Williams, *Culture and Society. The Black and White Minstrel Show* begins on BBC television. Ornette Coleman, *Something Else!!!!* John Coltrane, *Blue Train.* Alfred Hitchcock, *Vertigo.*
1959	R. Vaughan Williams and A. L. Lloyd, *The Penguin Book of English Folk Songs. Dave Van Ronk Sings Ballads, Blues, and a Spiritual.* Shirley Collins, *Sweet England.* Samuel B. Charters, *The Country Blues.* D. K. Wilgus, *Anglo-American Folksong Scholarship.* First Newport Folk Festival organized by George Wein. Alan Lomax, 'Folk Song Style'.
1960	Joan Baez's self-titled debut album released on Vanguard Records. Paul Oliver, *Blues Fell This Morning.* First issue of *New Left Review* edited by Stuart Hall. The Beatles formed in Liverpool. Harper Lee, *To Kill a Mockingbird.* R v Penguin Books Ltd. Jean-Luc Godard, *À Bout De Souffle.*
1961	Judy Collins, *A Maid of Constant Sorrow.* John F. Kennedy sworn in as US President. Yuri Gagarin becomes the first human to enter space. Berlin Wall is built. Bridget Riley, *Movement in Squares.*
1962	Bob Dylan's self-titled debut album released on Columbia Records. *Peter, Paul and Mary.* First appearance of the American Folk Blues Festival. *Broadside* magazine founded. Rolling Stones formed in London. Cuban Missile Crisis. Andy Warhol, *Marilyn Diptych.*

1963   March on Washington for Jobs and Freedom features performances by Joan Baez, Bob Dylan, Peter, Paul and Mary, and Odetta. E. P. Thompson, *The Making of the English Working Class*. Betty Friedan, *The Feminine Mystique*. John F. Kennedy assassinated.

1964   Simon & Garfunkel, *Wednesday Morning, 3 A.M.* Phil Ochs, *All the News That's Fit to Sing*. Buffy Sainte-Marie, *It's My Way!* Ewan MacColl and Peggy Seeger form The Critics Group. Clashes between Mods and Rockers in British seaside towns. *Top of the Pops* on BBC television. Radio Caroline begins broadcasting from international waters. Labour victory in the General Election. Berkeley Free Speech Movement. Civil Rights Act. The Velvet Underground forms in New York City. Stanley Kubrick, *Dr. Strangelove*. Philip Larkin, *The Whitsun Weddings*. Sergio Leone, *A Fistful of Dollars*. Barbara Hepworth, *Single Form*. George Maciunas, *Fluxus 1*.

1965   Martin Carthy's self-titled debut album released on Fontana Records. Bert Jansch's self-titled debut album released on Transatlantic Records. Jackson C. Frank's self-titled debut album released on Columbia Records. The Watersons, *Frost and Fire*. First Cambridge Folk Festival. Bob Dylan performs with an electric guitar backed by members of the Paul Butterfield Blues Band at Newport Folk Festival. Voting Rights Act. Watts riots. Malcolm X assassinated. Bay Area 'Acid Tests' feature the Grateful Dead. Steve Reich, *It's Gonna Rain*. Sylvia Plath, *Ariel*.

1966   A disgruntled fan shouts 'Judas' at Bob Dylan in Manchester during an electric set backed by the Hawks (later known as The Band). *The Incredible String Band*. The Mothers of Invention, *Freak Out!* Black Panther Party for Self-Defense founded in Oakland.

1967   First Smithsonian Institution Festival of American Folklife. A. L. Lloyd, *Folk Song in England*. Maud Karpeles, *Cecil Sharp*. *Songs of Leonard Cohen*. Love, *Forever Changes*. Bob Dylan records *The Basement Tapes*. Fairport Convention founded. Monterey International Pop Festival. The Jimi Hendrix Experience, *Are You Experienced*. 'Summer of Love' in San Francisco.

Introduction

For her first birthday, my daughter Lila received a book of nursery rhymes. On its cover a moon smiles down upon an array of memorable characters: three blind mice, a cat playing a fiddle, cutlery eloping with crockery, an accident-prone egg. Stars shine and the suggestion is that these short poems will sooth your baby to sleep. A pleasant fiction. Having exhausted the book, I turned to the foreword by the children's author Mary Ann Hoberman and was struck by its echoes of folkloric thinking. She describes these songs and verses as 'treasures of the English language ... handed down through the generations'; reading them aloud, we are 'bestowing a precious heritage' in a world where 'connections to our common past [are] disappearing'.[1] Collectors of folk music would be familiar with this way of understanding tradition: something that needs to be kept alive through creation of small links in a chain stretching back into the storm of history, coupling the present with the past before it's lost forever. Folk song is often thought about in this way as a storehouse of obscure treasures handed down from person to person within a cultural environment becoming ever more saturated by the ersatz delights and detritus of globalized mass consumption. It offers a source of collective memory haunted by the extraordinary and unfathomable, the notorious and quotidian. Its melodies appear to connect us with our ancestors and the common (wo)man, with patterns of labour, ritual, pleasure, and play sunk deep into the landscapes we inhabit. But what makes this music *folk* music?

Defining folk music has proved an extremely difficult thing to do. It took until 1954, for example, for the International Folk Music Council (IFMC) to agree on the following:

Folk music is the product of a musical tradition that has been evolved through the process of oral transmission. The factors that shape the tradition are: (i) continuity which links the present with the past; (ii) variation which springs from the creative impulse of the individual or the group; and (iii) selection by the community, which determines the form or forms in which the music survives.

The term can be applied to music that has been evolved from rudimentary beginnings by a community uninfluenced by popular and art music and it can likewise be applied to music which has originated with an individual composer and has subsequently been absorbed into the unwritten living tradition of a community.

The term does not cover composed popular music that has been taken over ready-made by a community and remains unchanged, for it is the re-fashioning and re-creation of the music by the community that gives it its folk character.[2]

There are several problems with this definition. First, it stresses 'oral' and 'unwritten', whereas we know that promiscuous migrations between print and orality have occurred for centuries. The oral and written are not antitheses. What folk song collectors would later identify 'as the products of an unmediated oral tradition', Adam Fox writes, 'turns out to derive from the print culture of the early modern period' – an era in which 'no one lived beyond the reach of the written and printed word'.[3] Moreover, what are we to make of published collections or guitar tablature of traditional songs: do these then no longer qualify as folk music? And what about recordings? Second, we are told nothing whatsoever about time. The definition is strikingly ahistorical, placing emphasis not on a time-honoured repertory or genre of music, but rather on a continual *process* of alteration by a community, the scale of which is unclear. There's no real indication of how long it takes to generate 'folk' music from different origins and no mention of how old the 'surviving' forms are. Is this evolutionary process still thriving to this day, or has it produced traditions that no longer evolve and are now extinct? Third, it's quixotic at best to believe that any tradition originating in the West is entirely 'uninfluenced by popular and art music' (a claim undercut by the subsequent admission that work by art music composers has been 'absorbed' elsewhere). As Oskar Cox Jensen points out, English ballad hawkers were often remarkably itinerant and their repertoires 'above all else mixed'.[4] Use of the term *popular* here is thus rather dubious, suggesting as it does a misleading binary between music 'of the people' (*folk*) and music 'for the people' (*popular*). The definition, in short, is constructed on a veiled anti-capitalist underpinning – one that has been central to the idea and appeal of the folk.

This definition bears the hallmarks of a specific era, and one song collector in particular. In 1907, Cecil J. Sharp claimed in *English-Folk Song: Some Conclusions* that 'folk-song has not been made by the one but evolved by the many' according to 'the three principles of *continuity*, *variation*, and *selection*'.[5] It is no coincidence that the first paragraph of the IFMC definition is a precise restatement of his theory: Sharp's close associate and literary executor Maud Karpeles not only served on the commission that drafted it, but also offered the provisional definition for a plenary discussion the previous year.⁶ The idea that folk music had 'evolved', however, was nothing more than conjecture – a tenuous metaphor employed in the service of Sharp's politically motivated project to establish that folk and popular musics were 'two distinct species', the former 'a communal and racial product' and hence the true cornerstone of nationalistic education.⁷ Sharp's hypothesis is a sign not only of his Fabian sympathies, but also of a pervasive apprehension about the effects of urbanized mass society and an intellectual climate immersed in evolutionary thinking on account of writers such as Herbert Spencer, Charles Darwin, and the anthropologist E. B. Tylor. The IFMC definition contains traces of this Victorian outlook both in Sharp's choice of language and the reference to 'rudimentary beginnings'. If we turn to Hubert Parry's 1896 book *The Evolution of the Art of Music*, for instance, folk music is situated chronologically as a fulcrum between 'music in the rough, in animals, in savages' and 'incipient harmony' – evidence of a teleological vision in which the apex of global development is European art music.⁸ Such historiographical ideas, like the IFMC definition, carried an undertone of social reproach: as 'the spontaneous utterances of the musical impulse of the people', folk music differed emphatically from the 'vulgarised and weakened portions of the music of the leisured classes'.⁹

What's really going on in these definitions is a habit of opposition in which folk music is situated as a paradigm of authenticity in contrast to something else tainted with commerce, frivolity, or bourgeois individualism. As Richard Middleton notes, 'to define either "folk" or "popular" music is inevitably to offer at least a partial definition of the other'.¹⁰ Folk music, in other words, has always tended to be defined *relationally*. The term conveys a sense not simply of *the people*, but a conception of the people as the humble, labouring, rural population – aging and isolated inhabitants of country hinterlands juxtaposed with the seething, avaricious, and unruly mob of the metropolis. It is this idea of the folk that guides the widespread assumption that their music exists as a counterpoint to the reign of the commodity. To quote Parry's inaugural address to the Folk-Song Society in 1898, folk music apparently 'grew in the hearts of the people before they devoted themselves so assiduously to the making of quick returns'.¹¹ What we find here is not a careful examination of historical or current musical practices among the working class, but (as Simon Frith puts it) 'a nostalgia for how they might have been'.¹² The appeal being made through the term *folk* is to a set of values revolving around community – values that would in turn come to shape the countercultural discourse of rock. In Frith's words, 'the description of folk creation (active, collective, honest) was, in fact, an idealised response to the experience of mass consumption (fragmented, passive, alienating)'.[13] It is no accident that interest in folk music arrives hand-in-hand with industrial modernity in Britain: it offered a reformist antidote to the havoc of social transformation and what Parry depicts with Miltonian zeal as 'unhealthy regions' rife with 'snippets of musical slang'.[14] As I've argued elsewhere, interest in the folk is hence always political – part of an ongoing debate over the identity and scope of 'the people'.[15]

Indeed, it is at this point that we can turn to Theodor Adorno – not usually known for his approval of popular culture – to explain an enduring anti-capitalist fascination with the folk. Reflecting on his and Max Horkheimer's now ubiquitous term 'culture industry' some twenty years after *Dialectic of Enlightenment* was published, Adorno stresses that this coinage had been employed to replace 'mass culture' in their early drafts so as explicitly to refute the idea

> that it is a matter of something like a culture that arises spontaneously from the masses themselves, the contemporary form of popular art. From the latter the culture industry must be distinguished in the extreme. The culture industry fuses the old and familiar into a new quality. In all its branches, products which are tailored for consumption by masses, and which to a great extent determine the nature of that consumption, are manufactured more or less according to plan. The individual branches are similar in structure or at least fit into each other, ordering themselves into a system almost without a gap. This is made possible by contemporary technical capabilities as well as by economic and administrative concentration. The culture industry intentionally integrates its consumers from above.[16]

What we find here is a characteristic form of Marxist nostalgia integral to Adorno's aesthetics: prior to the gloomy, mechanistic reign of mass-market capitalism, there existed an authentic and (comparatively) autonomous popular sphere arising from the people themselves. As Adorno puts it: 'the seriousness of the lower perishes with the civilizational constraints imposed on the rebellious resistance inherent within it as long as the social control was not yet total'.[17] Whereas the culture industry 'transfers the profit motive naked onto cultural forms', pre-industrial forms circulating in a marketplace nevertheless 'sought after profit only indirectly', raising 'a protest against the petrified relations' under which people lived.[18] In folkloric thinking, these old and mythical forms of art are delightfully unruly, disobedient, even defiant – offering the faint susurration of utopian possibility and the model for a culture of opposition. The same theme can be found in a passage Walter Benjamin notes down from Jules Michelet's book *Le Peuple* in which he expresses regret that 'worker-poets' are now 'sacrificing whatever folk originality they might have' by dressing up in suits and gloves, 'thus losing the superiority that strong hands and powerful arms give to the people when they know how to use them'.[19] This leitmotif tends always to accompany mention of the folk, suggesting that their appeal in the modern world has chiefly been as a vehicle of critique – a way of identifying alternative ways of being.

A prime example of this distinctive form of utopian desire grounded in nostalgia can be found in Ananda K. Coomaraswamy's 1909 *Essays in National Idealism*. In it, Coomaraswamy grants art a central role in anti-colonialist opposition to what he portrays as India's 'life and death struggle with an alien bureaucracy'.[20] This struggle, he affirms, 'is much more than a political conflict': it is, rather like Frantz Fanon would argue fifty years later, 'a struggle for spiritual and mental freedom from domination'.[21] How was this freedom to be achieved? Through national awakening and self-realization inspired 'by artists and by poets, not by traders and politicians'.[22] Indeed, he continues, 'I believe that it is not through politics that revolutions are made, and that National Unity needs a deeper foundation than the perception of political wrongs' – an ideology that foreshadowed key elements of European fascism.[23] Coomaraswamy looks back to William Morris for his ideals, noting that the 'vigour and vitality' of such work emerged from a conscious attempt to 'recover the thread of a lost tradition and carry it on'.[24] Towards the end of the book, Coomaraswamy draws on another contemporaneous English socialist: Cecil Sharp. In fact, the kind of spiritual revitalization Coomaraswamy is encouraging shares far more with Sharp's Fabianism than Morris's Marxism: in Indian music, he argues, 'change must be organic, not sudden ... it must be an evolution in accordance with the bent of the national genius'.[25] Quoting Sharp, he stresses the need for folk songs (and those embodying 'love of the land') to be taught orally in elementary schools as a form of nationalistic education in order to create 'good Indian citizens'.[26] With the exception of his belief in the 'fundamental unity' of music across distinctions of folk and art, Coomaraswamy embraces Sharp's ideas unreservedly, berating India for allowing neglect of 'the one thing vital, that is the music living in the hearts of peasants, uneducated and illiterate – but more truly Indian than their "educated" "superiors"'.[27] What's particularly striking here is that we find Sharp's chauvinistic form of English nationalism (in which he bemoans the rise of cosmopolitanism) being used strategically in the service of Indian resistance to English colonialism and cultural imperialism. In both instances, folk music is called upon as a tool to cultivate kinship and resist foreign influence. It is positioned as an art form that springs organically from the humble, ordinary inhabitants of the homeland and is diluted or washed away by the shifting currents of modernity, globalization, and intercultural contact.

We might, then, think of folk music very simply as music that has been framed (and thus received) in a particular way. The terms *folk music* and *folk song* are in truth devices that have been used to collate, animate, and make sense of a diverse range of material. As frames, they belong above all to those who collect and theorize, write and curate. To borrow Michel de Certeau's words, they are examples of an attempt by song collectors and folklorists to 'express what is *other*' that nevertheless 'remains *their* discourse and the mirror of their own labors'.[28] This particular vocabulary emerges around the same time as the seminal work of French painter Édouard Manet, including *The Spanish Singer* and *The Old Musician*. This latter canvas should interest us for a number of reasons. It is among Manet's earliest paintings, inaugurating a body of work widely accepted as a pivotal moment in the history of art. As T. J. Clark writes, the course that painting begins to take around this time 'can be described as a kind of scepticism, or at least unsureness, as to the nature of representation' – a growing awareness that 'things and pictures do not add up'.[29] Debates about the folk are inseparable from this modern world of uncertainty and displacement. Manet's *The Old Musician* shows us an epoch struggling with its own fragmentation: a bucolic scene rendered jarring and unreal, populated by marginal figures personifying urban decay and isolation (from street urchins and the Gypsy violinist to a cloaked and behatted figure on the right, a spectral return from his earlier work *The Absinthe Drinker*). Folk music performs a similar kind of representational act – though one that, instead of revelling in the dark Parisian *demimonde* of Charles Baudelaire, attempts to rescue and restore a lost unity. Such dreams, of course, reveal far more about the plagues and desires of modernity than they do about the pasts they envision. In folkloric hands, history is always a precious talisman for the future.

In exploring folk music, however, our task is not only to confront the troubled contours of its past, but also to analyse its contemporary appeal in an unfinished series of revivals. In so doing, we might better understand what Kay Kaufman Shelemay describes as 'music's generative role in social processes' – the multitude of ways in which music functions to create, galvanize, and sustain communities of people.[30] Folk music has given birth to a vast number of social groupings and continues to inspire new communities in the age of surveillance capitalism.³¹ A prime example would be the 'ShantyTok' trend. Late in 2020, a young Scottish postman by the name of Nathan Evans posted a video of himself singing an old whaling ballad known as 'The Wellerman' on TikTok. The song soon went viral as millions of people listened and offered their own embellishments. News stories proliferated, including a *Guardian* article claiming that such songs were 'at least 600 years old'.³² A little research reveals that the song could be no older than the Weller brothers to whom it refers – English merchant traders who founded a commercial whaling station in New Zealand during the 1830s. Rather than being a timeless product of cultural evolution, the song was intimately related to colonial capitalism and had, in fact, been published in a 1973 compendium entitled *New Zealand Folksongs: Song of a Young Country*.³³ What mattered, however, were not details of the song's history, but the *sense* of history and temporal distance it carried – one indebted to the imagination and the specifics of our modern world. The 2021 revival was closely bound up with social conditions experienced during the Covid-19 lockdowns as people across the globe were forced to confront death, confinement, monotony, dwindling supplies, and a lack of communal activity. The song and the medium afforded not only active participation, but also access to a fading realm of seaborne adventure and rugged outdoor labour, and in consequence a social experience of solidarity and shared, communal endeavour. Shelemay encourages us to consider how such groupings might be unified through 'descent' (collective identity), 'dissent' (opposition), and 'affinity' (shared preference). We can find folk musical communities existing across this spectrum – from the Fisk Jubilee Singers and klezmer ensembles (*descent*) through the Highlander Folk School and Civil Rights movement (*opposition*) to Newport Folk Festival and labels such as Topic Records (*affinity*). Folk music, in other words, is inseparable from the social collectivities it has brought to life.

As the essays in this *Cambridge Companion* demonstrate, folk music has endured in spite of – or rather owing to – such elusiveness and imaginative investment. As Middleton puts it, if such terms are suspect 'they are not necessarily *empty*'.³⁴ In response, this volume brings together repertoires, artists, collectors, and regions in a revisionist attempt to understand folk music from a critical and diverse standpoint. **Part I** opens the book by offering different perspectives on folk music that map the field and provide ways to begin thinking about its history and meaning. In Chapter 1, I show when and how the term 'folk music' entered Anglophone discourse, arguing that it is, above all, an *idea* that has conditioned our reception of culture and the past. In Chapter 2, Jeff Todd Titon provides an authoritative survey of the field's history focusing on tools and methodology, tracing a turn from text-based understandings towards anthropology. In Chapter 3, Timothy Hampton draws attention to how media such as the LP record in conjunction with the countercultural spaces of Greenwich Village afforded a new kind of public sphere. In Chapter 4, Brahma Prakash tackles questions of power, meaning, and critique by paying close attention to the democratic undercurrents of contemporary folk performance in South Asia. In Chapter 5, violinist Yale Strom offers a uniquely personal perspective on klezmer and Romani music, recounting unexpected moments of connection and cultural exchange.

Part II then delves into some of the primary elements that, together, have constituted folk music as a recognizable cultural practice – from instruments and texts to movement and melodic structure. In Chapter 6, Joshua Dickson leads us on a journey through the history and practice of Celtic music by following interlaced threads of function, bestowal, structure, variation, and memory. In Chapter 7, Dianne Dugaw spotlights the lyrics to folk songs, uncovering their formulaic patterning as well as recurrent themes of infancy, lost love, disaster, and social marginality. In Chapter 8, Maeve Carey-Kozlark showcases the nature and uses of folk instruments and the convoluted ways in which they have been employed to serve ideals of authenticity. In Chapter 9, Theresa Jill Buckland takes a synoptic approach to folk dance, paganism, and embodied movement, tracing this nexus from its earliest incarnations as a discipline up to the present. In Chapter 10, Jon Boden of the band Bellowhead confronts a pervasive element of professional folk performance that frames reception and yet often escapes notice: spoken introductions.

Part III widens this focus on specific elements to explore a powerful and entangled series of imaginaries that have animated and continue to sustain folk music in our globalized world. In Chapter 11, Katharine Ellis offers a wonderfully informative take on the troubled relationship between those two great inventions of the European nineteenth century: folk music and the nation. In Chapter 12, Erin Johnson-Williams relates this history to the wider context within which it was nested, exploring visions of difference shaped by colonialism that endure to this day. In Chapter 13, Britta Sweers explains the structure of folk revivals with particular reference to folk rock. Such revivals, she points out, bring imaginaries into play that are at once both nostalgic and utopian. In Chapter 14, Helen Phelan joins three of her former doctoral students to illustrate the extent to which traditional music fosters a sense of belonging among migrant communities in Ireland. In

Chapter 15, Angeline Morrison gives us an exquisite account of what mythopoeic singing means to her and why it is central to reimagining and decolonizing the history of British folk music.

Developing this theme, **Part IV** turns to questions of identity, uncovering how and why folk music has traversed histories of race, gender, class, and political radicalism. In Chapter 16, Katrina Thompson Moore foregrounds marginalized traditions of Black folk music, from their roots in transatlantic slavery and the Middle Passage to W. E. B. Du Bois, blues, and hip hop. In Chapter 17, Elizabeth Bennett looks at another neglected presence in folk music history: women collectors. Her discoveries accentuate the need for a feminist re-reading of the archive. In Chapter 18, Mark Steven drills down into the seams of class conflict, manual labour, and solidarity, showing us how songs such as 'Which Side Are You On?' create political subjects. In Chapter 19, Oskar Cox Jensen situates such questions within a longer trajectory by unearthing the ways in which song has been received as a channel of popular vocality. Finally, in Chapter 20, legendary performer Peggy Seeger draws together – in characteristically virtuosic fashion – the themes of this book as a whole through the trio of song, singer, and community.

Notes

1. Mary Ann Hoberman, 'Sharing Nursery Rhymes with Your Baby', 6. In Penny Dann, *The Orchard Book of Nursery Rhymes for Your Baby*. London: Orchard Books, 2010, 6–7.
2. 'Resolutions'. *Journal of the International Folk Music Council* 7 (1955): 23.
3. Adam Fox, *Oral and Literate Culture in England, 1500–1700*. Oxford: Oxford University Press, 2000, 411, 19. See also Christopher Marsh, *Music and Society in Early Modern England*. Cambridge: Cambridge University Press, 2010.
4. Oskar Cox Jensen, *The Ballad-Singer in Georgian and Victorian London*. Cambridge: Cambridge University Press, 2021, 203.
5. Cecil J. Sharp, *English Folk-Song: Some Conclusions*. London: Simpkin & Co., Novello & Co., 1907, x, 16.
6. See Maud Karpeles, 'Definition of Folk Music'. *Journal of the International Folk Music Council* 7 (1955): 6–7.
7. Sharp, *English Folk-Song*, x. On this point, see Ross Cole, *The Folk: Music, Modernity, and the Political Imagination*. Oakland: University of California Press, 2021.
8. C. Hubert H. Parry, *The Evolution of the Art of Music*. London: K. Paul, Trench, Trübner, 1896, vii, viii.

9. Parry, *The Evolution of the Art of Music*, 80.
10. Richard Middleton, 'Editor's introduction to Volume 1'. *Popular Music* 1 (1981): 3–7, 3.
11. C. Hubert H. Parry, 'Inaugural Address'. *Journal of the Folk-Song Society* 1 (1899): 1–3, 1, 2.
12. Simon Frith, '"The Magic That Can Set You Free": The Ideology of Folk and the Myth of the Rock Community'. *Popular Music* 1 (1981): 159–68, 160. For a corrective, see Peter Bailey, *Popular Culture and Performance in the Victorian City*. Cambridge: Cambridge University Press, 1998.
13. Frith, 'The Magic That Can Set You Free', 160.
14. Parry, 'Inaugural Address', 2, 3.
15. See Ross Cole, 'Notes on Troubling "the Popular"'. *Popular Music* 37 (2018): 392–414 and Cole, *The Folk*.
16. Theodor W. Adorno, 'Culture Industry Reconsidered', trans. Anson G. Rabinbach. *New German Critique* 6 (1975): 12–19, 12. See also Theodor W. Adorno and Max Horkheimer, *Dialectic of Enlightenment*, trans. John Cumming. London: Verso, 1997.
17. Adorno, 'Culture Industry Reconsidered', 12.
18. Adorno, 'Culture Industry Reconsidered', 13.
19. Walter Benjamin, *The Arcades Project*, trans. Howard Eiland and Kevin McLaughlin. Cambridge, MA: Belknap Press of Harvard University Press, 1999, 727. This is a quotation from Jules Michelet, *Le Peuple*. Paris: Comptoir des Imprimeurs-Unis, Hachette, Paulin, 1846. On the legacies of this idea in postwar Britain, see Ross Cole, 'Industrial Balladry, Mass Culture, and the Politics of Realism in Cold War Britain'. *Journal of Musicology* 34 (2017): 354–390.
20. Ananda K. Coomaraswamy, *Essays in National Idealism* (Colombo: Colomo [sic] Apothecaries, 1909), i.
21. Coomaraswamy, *Essays in National Idealism*, i. See for example Frantz Fanon, *The Wretched of the Earth*. New York: Grove Press, 1963. For context, see also Partha Mitter, *Art and Nationalism in Colonial India, 1850-1922: Occidental Orientations*. Cambridge: Cambridge University Press, 1994 and Nalini Ghuman, *Resonances of the Raj: India in the English Musical Imagination, 1897–1947*. New York: Oxford University Press, 2014.
22. Coomaraswamy, *Essays in National Idealism*, ii.
23. Coomaraswamy, *Essays in National Idealism*, ii. See Zeev Sternhell, *Neither Right nor Left: Fascist Ideology in France*, trans. David Maisel. Princeton: Princeton University Press, 1986.
24. Coomaraswamy, *Essays in National Idealism*, 42.
25. Coomaraswamy, *Essays in National Idealism*, 193. See Cole, *The Folk*, 74–103 and 132–58.
26. Coomaraswamy, *Essays in National Idealism*, 193.

27. Coomaraswamy, *Essays in National Idealism*, 195–6. On this theme, see Brahma Prakash, *Cultural Labour: Conceptualizing the 'Folk Performance' in India*. New Delhi: Oxford University Press, 2019.
28. Michel de Certeau, *The Writing of History*, trans. Tom Conley. New York: Columbia University Press, 1988, 36. See also Johannes Fabian, *Time and the Other: How Anthropology Makes Its Object*, new ed. New York: Columbia University Press, 2014.
29. T. J. Clark, *The Painting of Modern Life: Paris in the Art of Manet and His Followers*. Princeton: Princeton University Press, 1984, 10, 12. See also Michael Fried, *Manet's Modernism; or, The Face of Painting in the 1860s*. Chicago: University of Chicago Press, 1996.
30. Kay Kaufman Shelemay, 'Musical Communities: Rethinking the Collective in Music'. *Journal of the American Musicological Society* 64/2 (2011): 349–90, 351.
31. See Shoshana Zuboff, *The Age of Surveillance Capitalism: The Fight for a Human Future at the New Frontier of Power*. London: Profile Books, 2019.
32. 'Not just for drunken sailors: how sea shanties took over TikTok'. *The Guardian*, 13 January 2021. www.theguardian.com/music/2021/jan/13/not-just-for-drunken-sailors-how-sea-shanties-took-over-tiktok.
33. Neil Colquhoun, *New Zealand Folksongs: Song of a Young Country*. Folkestone: Bailey Brothers and Swinfen, 1973.
34. Middleton, 'Editor's introduction', 5.

PART I

Perspectives

1 | The Idea of Folk Music

ROSS COLE

The premise of this chapter is very simple: that folk music is neither a repertoire nor an idiom, but an *idea*. Ideas, of course, have histories, and it is this chapter's contention that folk music and folk song are peculiarly modern notions that emerge in the English language during the middle of the nineteenth century and come to fruition in the twentieth century. It is no coincidence that what I like to call the 'folkloric imagination' is coterminous with Western industrialization, colonialism, nationalism, capitalism, and the advent of mass society.[1] Folk music, in essence, is a reply or retort to the interlaced revolutions and encounters that have defined modernity. In consequence, we should remember that the rubric 'folk music' – as a product of imaginative speculation about the past and other cultures – has transformed our view of the music to which it refers.

As we shall see, the term *folk song* appears as a direct translation of the German *Volkslieder*, though it is associated explicitly neither with the work of Johann Gottfried Herder nor with any particular nation or region. Indeed, it is the *concept* that most enchants British and American writers during this era – writers who are never of the folk they speak about, but rather observers of popular traditions that captivate and beguile. *Folk song* precedes *folk music* into print, indicating that the idea was initially formulated in relation to sung texts and the history of the ballad. In order to trace how and why these two terms arise, this chapter embarks upon a chronological journey from the 1840s to the 1870s, by which time they are widely used and accepted. Ultimately, this story exemplifies what Stuart Hall described as 'a more or less continuous struggle over the culture of working people, the laboring classes and the poor'.[2]

From *Volkslieder* to Folk Song

The term *folk-lore* was introduced in English in 1846 in the *Athenæum* by a pseudonymous antiquarian named William Thoms, who later founded the literary journal *Notes & Queries*. Thoms coined this epithet to better describe what he referred to as Popular Antiquities or Popular Literature:

'it is more a Lore than a Literature, and would be most aptly described by a good Saxon compound, Folk-Lore – *the Lore of the People*'.[3] Foreshadowing later collectors of songs and tunes, his letter called for assistance 'in garnering the few ears which are remaining, scattered over that field from which our forefathers might have gathered a goodly crop'.[4] Here we have an early, exemplary instance of the folkloric imagination: a perception that loss and lack of cultivation in the present should spur a restorative search for the few surviving remnants of an endangered but truly popular culture. Significantly, Thoms does not turn to Johann Gottfried Herder in support of this idea, but rather to the second edition of Jacob Grimm's *Deutsche Mythologie* (1844). Fragmentary records 'of old Time – some recollection of a now neglected custom', he proposes, would 'become of importance when they form links in a great chain', creating a picture of the deep, mythic past as if from isolated and seemingly insignificant jigsaw pieces.[5] Editors of the *Athenæum* were not quite so enthusiastic, fearing they might be inundated by a 'shower of trivial communication'; nevertheless, they promised to offer a few columns here and there for 'some valuable salvage for the future historian of old customs and feelings' under the suggested title.[6] Thoms responded the following year with a series of essays on the 'Folk-Lore of Shakespeare'; an editorial footnote to the first essay expressed 'some satisfaction at the universal adoption of this name [*folk-lore*]', noting that in less than a year 'it has almost attained to the dignity of a "household word"'.[7] Clearly, Thoms had identified a particular way of thinking about the past that struck a chord with the wider public at this precise moment in time.

Intriguingly, the term *folk song* had in fact preceded Thoms' *folk-lore* into print by a few years. In a lengthy 1843 book review concerning 'The Old Hymns and Lays, Sacred and Profane, especially of Germany down to the Time of Luther' in *The Foreign and Colonial Quarterly Review*, the author notes that 'the lais, as folk song, as epic song, and as historic song, the lyric lais, and the German leiche, the church sequence, and the cloister prosæ and cantilenæ, are all most abundantly discussed'.[8] The *lai* referred to here is a medieval poetic form using the Old French word that gives rise to the English term *lay*, describing a simple ballad or sung poem. Such a casual allusion to this form as a kind of 'folk song' suggests that the term was not unfamiliar to well-educated readers owing to its lexical similarity to Herder's much earlier coinage *Volkslieder* from the 1770s. Inspired by the Ossian myth and Thomas Percy's *Reliques of Ancient English Poetry* (1765), Herder had used this expansive term to identify material that shaped and gave voice to a nation's characteristic identity, revealing 'a people in its *naked* simplicity, the happiness with which it *was born*, and all of *nature in its most basic creative potential*' – something best appreciated, he adds, after divesting oneself of 'all the false politeness that has come to generate an inhumane sense of bourgeois life'.[9] Here, just under 200 years before Bob Dylan graced the coffee houses of Greenwich Village, is a blueprint for the idea of folk music as countercultural rebellion – a return to nature that might free listeners from the stifling conformity of middle-class existence. The fact that it is difficult to identify any specific English-language claim to the term *folk song* and that it predates *folk music* by around a decade is strong evidence that Herder's word is the origin, offering a readymade conceptual category that (much like Thoms' handy neologism) began to circulate at an opportune moment. Together, these terms pointed towards a longed-for culture of popular origin and appeal that seemed increasingly elusive, fragile, and remote.

One person in particular was responsible for early circulation of the English term folk song in print: the prolific author and translator Mary Howitt. Along with her husband William, Mary had lived for a short time during the early 1840s in Heidelberg, a focal point of German Romanticism exemplified by Achim von Arnim and Clemens Brentano's collection *Des Knaben Wunderhorn: Alte deutsche Lieder*.[10] With knowledge of German literature and a passion for old songs culminating in her 1847 anthology *Ballads and Other Poems*, Howitt would have been aware of Herder's coinage and the lack of an equivalent term in English. Much like Herder, it was Percy's *Reliques* that had inspired her lifelong fascination with 'old, traditional literature' (a love also stirred by a domestic servant whose capacious memory, as she puts it, was full of 'ballads, old songs, and legends').[11] Howitt had published an English translation of Hans Christian Andersen's autobiography in 1847. In it, she uses the term *folks-song* to describe the old Danish song 'Kong Christian stod ved højen mast', the country's royal anthem.[12] It is revealing that Howitt chooses to place *folks-song* in the plural here, the 's' a tell-tale linguistic spectre of Herder's *Volkslieder*. If further proof were needed that the German term enters the English language around this time, we need look no further than the April 1847 issue of *Howitt's Journal*. Here, Mary labels her translation of a poem entitled 'The Three Little Roses' as 'a German folk's song'.[13] In a brief note she points out that 'the German Volkslieder, or people's songs, bear a great affinity to those of the border and the lowlands of Scotland', given that 'they have the same simplicity and tenderness, the same rudeness and irregularity of construction'.[14] She continues by comparing 'our own folk's songs' with Germany's, noting a corresponding reliance on 'inconsequent reasoning', 'popular superstition', 'rude and irregular rhythm', and regional dialect (which she equates with 'our dales of Westmoreland, bordering on Yorkshire – one of the sweetest and most purely Saxon dialects of England').[15] She ends, however, with what seemed to be a signal difference: 'the ballad poetry of England is a thing of the past, of the feudal ages' whereas 'the Volkslieder of Germany are the people's songs at this moment … spread, and known, and living in the minds of the common people everywhere, as much now as ever'.[16] Here is unequivocal evidence not only of the ease by which *Volkslieder* was rendered as *folk's song*, but also of a nascent definition of folk music: some crude and primitive balladry with a regional flavour bound up with mythology and feudalism existing as a precious and pure form of national heritage. What's more, other countries appeared to be better at preserving or cultivating this art than others. Howitt went on to use the terms *folk-song* – and indeed *folk-dance* and *folk-life* – in her popular translations of books by the Swedish writer and reformer Fredrika Bremer.[17]

Figure 1.1 Mary Howitt. Frontispiece to *An Autobiography* (London, 1889). Woodburytype.

Public interest in things folkloric has tended to accompany periods of rapid transition and social change, the *fin de siècle* and the 1960s being two notable examples. The Victorian 1840s were no different. This was the era of J. M. W. Turner, Giuseppe Verdi, Charles Dickens, the Brontës, John Ruskin, the California Gold Rush, the penny post, imperialism, abolitionism, Transcendentalism, blackface minstrelsy, the Mexican–American War, and the advent of the Daguerreotype. More significantly, the decade witnessed a widespread eruption of political radicalism in the form of the working-class Chartist movement in Britain and the European Revolutions of 1848, not to mention publication of the *Manifesto of the Communist Party* by Karl Marx and Friedrich Engels.[18] Simultaneously, the decade saw a catastrophic failure of potato crops across Europe that led to the Great Famine in Ireland during which roughly one million people died of disease and starvation, and millions more were forced to emigrate.[19] Britain also experienced 'railway mania', a financial bubble related to a massive expansion of the nation's public railway network, along with the introduction of standardized 'railway time'.[20] Indeed, transportation and communications underwent a technological revolution during this period, with the launch of Isambard Kingdom Brunel's vast iron-hulled passenger steamship *Great Britain* in 1843 and the formation of the Electric Telegraph Company three years later.[21] In short, the 1840s were a particularly turbulent and transformative decade. We can begin to see why the idea and appeal of folk music might have begun to arise in response – an unassuming people's culture associated with a dying way of life typified by the character of Bessie in *Jane Eyre*, a nursemaid who sings doleful and mysterious ballads of a bygone era as she goes about her daily tasks.[22] The increasing attention paid to the folk could thus be read as a sign of democratic sympathies, a way of protecting and validating a people's culture in the face of capitalist modernity. We could, however, make a very different argument: that it was no accident this archaic and unthreatening vision of working-class life surfaced during an era of revolutionary awakening – its nostalgic embrace of feudalism the sign of a deep reactionary impulse. As I've argued elsewhere, the folkloric imagination holds this Janus-like tension at its heart.[23]

An Outgrowth from the Life of the People

By the middle of the nineteenth century, terms pertaining to the folk were beginning to appear more frequently in print. In 1852 we find what might be the first appearance of *folk music* in a book by the antiquarian Andrew Hamilton entitled *Sixteen Months in the Danish Isles*. He pauses to describe a 'peasant-woman' with a particular fondness for performing extremely long ballads:

> So we sauntered onwards, and our songstress moved by our side, ever singing in her gentle voice a ditty that, by the time it reached the twentieth or thirtieth verse, began to grow monotonous as to the tone. The melody was sufficiently simple, and, doubtless, as old as the words. It had a slight cast of the wildness almost inseparable from folk-music; but on the whole the ballad airs are not in general so original as other kinds of Danish popular music. It seems as if it had not been designed that the melody should be too attractive, lest it might draw off the attention from the words which would appear always to have been the chief point in a ballad.[24]

Folk-music is introduced here so casually as to be almost self-evident – a term used to designate a simple, old, and natural kind of music used primarily in the service of a text. A verse from one such narrative is included as the epigraph of the book's opening chapter: a long ballad entitled 'The Lady Magdalene: A Legend of an English Hall' by none other than Mary Howitt.[25]

There is a particularly vivid depiction of folk song in the English writer John Berwick Harwood's 1855 novel *The Serf-Sisters: or, The Russia of To-Day*. Again, the term is associated with 'an ancient ballad ... from beyond the memory of man' accompanied by a sad, humble tune:

> It was one of those wailing dirges which all semi-civilized races appear to love beyond all more joyful or more elaborate melodies. Such were the strains which rose and fell amid the Druid's reverenced oaks; which echoed over the cairn of Fingal, and the rune-marked tomb of many a Danish sea-king; which rang through the gloomy woods of New England, before the pilgrim fathers trod those rugged shores; and which were sung around the stone of Irmensul by the idolators of Pomerania; – strains melancholy and monotonous as the sigh of the willow and the murmur of the pine. In a wigwam on the western prairies, or beside one of those grey menhirs that start up like petrified giants from the black Breton heaths, beside the watch-fires of the Arab and Turcoman, or among the outcast gipsies of Hungary, you may still hear those touching though barbarous airs, which appeal to the sable thread that all of us possess, inwoven firmly in the mystic weft of our natures.[26]

There is a striking form of universalism at play here linking the 'untaught pathos of some peasant minstrel of a benighted land' with the nostalgia of a 'lullaby in infancy' and nature itself (stones, woods, weathered shores, moorlands, willow trees, oaks, and pines).[27] The range is extraordinary and varied, comprising Native American history prior to European colonization, ancient Celtic cultures, the Viking Age, Germanic paganism, nomadic tribes of the Middle East, and the Romani people. It is neither a particular repertory of songs nor a musical genre that is being referred to here, but rather an *idea* or fantasy of the wild and pre-modern (rendered as 'semi-civilized' or 'barbarous'). In a trope familiar from early anthropology, exotic cultural difference in the present is being conflated with deep temporal distance – both forms of alterity nevertheless pointing towards some dark and numinous yarn tying together all of humankind as one.[28] Once again, however, there is a Janiform pull between folk music as the signature of shared human nature and such music as the symptom of a racialized and unbridgeable disparity between groups of people. In a word, what's going on in this passage is an eruption of the *imagination*, an image of global cultural history afforded by the new and enchanting concept of folklore.

In 1860, a handsomely bound anthology dedicated to the poet Henry Wadsworth Longfellow entitled *Folk Songs* appeared in the United States, courtesy of John Williamson Palmer. This book presents an idiosyncratic assortment of poems not only by 'Anonymous', but also by Longfellow, Blake, Tennyson, Shakespeare, Burns, Dibdin, Keats, Poe, Motherwell, Byron, Coleridge, Heine, Emerson, Wordsworth, Marlowe, Goethe, the Brownings, Shelley, Pope, and others. Palmer offers the book as a gift containing 'such flowers of lyric tenderness and beauty as have long been precious to my own heart'.[29] A review in the widely read *Harper's Weekly* plainly stated that 'the title is translated from the expressive German *Volkslied*, which means literally a folk-song – a people's song – not a song for the *dilettanti*, for any particular class or sympathy, but a song of the universal heart – a song of passions and emotions which the human heart every where instinctively comprehends'.[30] Although Longfellow himself felt the title was not ideal (despite being 'poetical and rare'), such work echoed the heterogeneity of Herder's earlier folk song collections, which included a variety of literary and vernacular material from both fieldwork and published sources attesting to song's pre-eminence from Shakespeare to German art song, through languages as diverse as medieval Latin, Old Nordic, Spanish, Lithuanian, and Inuit.[31] As Philip Bohlman puts it, Herder saw this project as one 'ontologically unencumbered by the limitations of genre' that conveyed 'the cultural and temporal qualities of universal history'.[32] Palmer's volume demonstrates that (at least in the United States) the concept of folk song was still comparatively fluid, a term serving to indicate a broad range of lyric material that had a wide or lasting popular appeal. There were, of course, limitations, and the fact that its supposedly 'universal' scope downplayed or omitted material of African origin is revealing – especially

Figure 1.2 Winslow Homer, 'The Songs of the War', *Harper's Weekly*, Vol. 5 (23 November 1861). Wood engraving. Library of Congress.

given its date of publication, less than a year before the outbreak of the American Civil War.

Shortly after the war in a chapter on the Union general William Tecumseh Sherman, Harriet Beecher Stowe refers to 'John Brown's Body' as a folk song. On the eve of Sherman's famed March to the Sea, she writes, 'a Massachusetts brigade, its band playing the wonderful "John Brown" folk-song, was the last to leave the city [of Atlanta]'.[33] The music being portrayed was a Union favourite now known as 'Battle Hymn of the Republic', with its refrain of 'Glory, Glory Hallelujah'. The song offered a secular vision of Christ's burial and resurrection that, as Franny Nudelman argues, 'puts religion to work in the service of wartime nationalism', making its titular hero into a martyr that reminded soldiers if they perished it was 'on behalf of a greater cause', one that would rejuvenate the collective body politic.[34] Like many other nationalist songs, it encourages cohesion and unity in the face of adversity, making political struggle into a spiritual call-to-arms – in this case, to end the centuries-long horrors of slavery. The way in which Stowe employs the term *folk song* would come to prevail over and above Palmer's literary anthologizing. Indeed, 'John Brown's Body' is a song that has a convoluted and contested history of authorship encompassing not only revivalist camp meetings (featuring hymns such as 'Say, Brothers, Will You Meet Us'), Civil War military camps, African American spirituals, radical abolitionism, and comic extemporization, but also elite traditions of writing and print (the poet Julia Ward Howe published a well-known version of the lyrics in 1861).[35] Consequently, the song's origins are impossible to pinpoint – and to do so, moreover, would neglect the history and significance of its many variants. Stowe's usage thus implied an alternative definition of folk music: a tradition in which notions of ownership, authorship, and derivation are less important than organic variation, adaptation, and anonymous recirculation among the common people, the 'folk'.

Other sources from this era confirm that the terms folk song and folk music were both derived from the German *Volk-*. In an 1861 book entitled *National Hymns*, the prominent American critic Richard Grant White suggests that true national airs have no composer; rather, 'they are found existing among the people, who are ignorant of their origin. They are, to borrow a German phrase, folk-music.'[36] This would become a commonplace assertion in later folk song collecting, typifying the work of Cecil Sharp. In a similar study, Carl Engel likewise remarks that such music 'exhibits certain peculiarities more or less characteristic, which distinguish it from the music of any other nation or tribe'.[37] In a footnote to this opening gambit he points out that 'the Germans call it *Volksmusik*, a designation which is very appropriate, and which I should have rendered *folk-music*, had this word been admissible'.[38] Why *folk-music* was inadmissible here is unclear and perhaps relates to a publisher's whim, as Engel had used this term in another book two years earlier. In *The Music of the Most Ancient Nations* he had argued that national features are most discernible 'in the popular folks-music, generally originating with and traditionally preserved by the rural population'.[39] A slightly earlier claim in the Folk Lore section of *Notes & Queries* had suggested that it was artisans (skilled manual labourers) who were 'the great purveyors of folk-music'.[40] Whether rural labourers or artisans, a cultural and profoundly political idea of 'the folk' was emerging – a body of people who encapsulated a nation's identity in some unconscious way, being the true source or last remaining storehouse of its distinctive ancestral heritage. What concerned writers such as White was that America as a nation seemed to suffer from a lack of homegrown, indigenous music. When sympathetic voices endorsed 'negro melodies' for this role, White poured out contempt: 'these are no more to us as a people, or even as a nation, because they are heard in this country, than the songs of the birds or the howling of the wolves'.[41] Native American history fared no better: 'the traditions of a savage people which is vanishing away before our race, with which it has not even a single point of affinity'.[42] Such a view demonstrates the extent to which the idea of folk music could be employed in a brutally revisionist way to erase unwelcome others and buttress the project of white supremacy.

By the early 1870s *folk song* had become a recognized and widely used term, finding its way into the title of William Axon's *Folk Song and Folk-Speech of Lancashire* as well as a multitude of other works such as Frédéric Louis Ritter's *History of Music* and an essay in *Putnam's Magazine* by James Vila Blake. These sources share a number of common strands. Axon sings praises to an archetypal balladeer: standing aloof 'he interprets to all who choose to hear the mysterious symbols written in the book of Nature, the tenderness and solemnities of this visible world, the hopes, fears, and passions of the human race'.[43] Such figures, he writes, were usually working-class men, 'sons of the soil, and not mere rhymers, but men who have drunk deeply of the Heliconian spring'.[44] Ritter sees folk song (along with Gregorian chant) as 'the foundation upon which all forms of our musical art rest'.[45] Folk song, he argues, is 'an outgrowth from the life of the people ... unassisted by art, it is true, but yet the product of innate artistic instinct in the people'; its authors are either 'unknown' or artists 'so inwardly connected with the people in their feelings and mode of expression, that their productions seem to spring from the same source'.[46] It displays 'the characteristics of a nation' and hence 'enables us to judge ... of the relationship existing between different races of men'.[47] For Blake, German folk song offered aesthetic respite from 'the whirling, dizzy torrent' of New York City via its 'joy in nature's perfections' and model patriotism based upon military sacrifice for a 'Fatherland'.[48] Folk songs told of temperance, valour, faith, 'the exalted side of lowly things', and 'the secluded freedom of pastoral life'.[49] These writers all define folk music as something near synonymous with Nature – whether as instinct, outgrowth, seed, or rootedness in the land. All agree that it signals an elemental form of creativity akin to the source of a great river. They are comparably equivocal about authorship, preferring to lapse into generalities about bards, ploughmen, and shepherds. Above all, they share a tendency to read folk culture as an idealized reflection of their own values – values that prefigure the rhetoric of blood and soil, a key component in the culture of fascism.[50]

This decade also saw the appearance of a substantial book by the anthropologist and translator Charles E. Gover entitled *The Folk-Songs of*

Southern India, a text demonstrating not only that the concept had achieved a global reach on account of British imperialism, but also that it was not restricted to thinking solely about European or Western musical traditions. Gover's book reveals that the intellectual framework of folk music could very easily be applied to an entirely new environment and yield similar results – in a word, that it was transposable. Gover aspired to seek out and present the anonymous 'songs that pass from lip to lip' containing 'the very essence of popular belief'.[51] The folkloric perspective he adopts was employed to retrieve from obscurity (and from the misrepresentation of missionaries and educated elites) 'the millions who in reality form the mass of the nation' – the Dravidian people.[52] The high-caste Brahmin priesthood too often taken to represent India as a whole, he points out, 'are as different from *the people* in social habit, religious practice, and mode of thought, as the Greek philosophers from the vulgar crowd'.[53] Folk music was thus at one with the labouring population, with streets, markets, and patterns of vernacular behaviour that Michel de Certeau calls 'tactics'.[54] In an exemplary folkloric move, Gover associates cultural purity with both the oldest and the most geographically remote material found amid 'the hill tribes', who 'come into life, are married, and die to the music of some chant, song or requiem'.[55] Although such work might appear to be unusually enlightened, politically radical, and free from ethnic prejudice, we need to look closely at its aims and epistemology. Throughout the book, Gover is preoccupied with the notion that this material is evidence of Aryan identity and kinship. 'There is not one true Dravidian root common to the three great branches, Tamil, Telugu and Canarese', he claims, 'that cannot be clearly shown to be Aryan … the vocabulary of the dialects is almost pure Aryan, and presents the most startling affinities with the grand Teutonic stock'.[56] What we have, once again, is an undeniable illustration of folk music's imaginative authority as a witness to racialized origin and tribal belonging.

Broken and Crumbling before our Eyes

From our brief journey through the earliest uses of *folk song* and *folk music*, we can see that a distinctive network of ideas – or discourse – begins to coalesce around these new terms during the nineteenth century on both sides of the Atlantic. Above all, they signify a people's culture – a rich but unassuming tradition associated with the humble and the commonplace, with the labouring population and those living in close communion with the land. This popular culture was largely consigned to the mythic or feudal past, though it was at times seen to exist in the present in relation to anonymous recirculation (an example being Harriet Beecher Stowe's reference to 'John Brown's Body') or among so-called 'primitive' societies. Crude and marginal, folk music was habitually coupled with Nature, instinctual creativity, and texts (most notably ballads). Given this close affinity between people, place, and song, furthermore, folk music appeared to be not only a vital form of ancestral heritage, but also the bedrock of national or ethnic identity. In consequence, such music played a key role in narrating cultural developments on a global scale, explaining the ostensibly innate differences or commonalities between groups of people. But as we've seen, this avenue of thought led in two irreconcilable directions: towards folk music as an indication of universal human nature and towards folk music as an indication of racial difference, blood-and-soil belonging, and white supremacy. Another fault line runs through this discourse – between folk music as a form of radical support for working-class experience and folk music as a nostalgic reaction against working-class radicalism. These conflicts remain unreconciled to this day, allowing folk music to move seamlessly across the political spectrum from left to right.

What I have been unfolding here, we should remember, is not an accurate reflection of reality. Folk song and folk music are, as ideas, symptoms of an intellectual appetite. They have helped to crystallize a particular understanding of culture and the past, one that feeds a certain historiographical vision or desire. The idea of the folk and their music is predicated on a yearning for the ways of life they represent, a longing that is also a form of sorrow – an acknowledgement of the difficulty of recapturing something lost or on the threshold of extinction. Folk music is thus, inevitably, a kind of lament or swan song. To borrow Susan Sontag's words from an essay on the anthropologist Claude Lévi-Strauss, it is an indication of our sense of 'homelessness' in an era characterized by 'the inhuman acceleration of historical change'.[57] The antidote, she remarks, has often been found in consciously exacerbating such alienation by seeking Self via the Other. The history of folk music in the West supports Sontag's conception of this modern sensibility moving between two related impulses: 'surrender to the exotic, the strange, the other; and the domestication of the exotic, chiefly through science'.[58] The former epitomizes a longstanding infatuation with the primitive, pastoral, and untutored charm of the folk; the latter typifies the work of folk song collectors such as Cecil Sharp (with his Darwinian theories of evolution) and Alan Lomax (with his data-driven 'cantometrics' project). Folk music shares with anthropology this fundamental melancholia about Time: both are forms of necrology, lamenting that 'the past, with its mysteriously harmonious structures, is broken and crumbling before our eyes'.[59]

It was in the twentieth century that the concept of folk music truly came alive despite, or rather due to, its distance from the waning and increasingly mysterious world the folk personified. As Hall reminds us, tradition 'has little to do with the mere persistence of old forms' and 'much more to do with the way elements have been linked together or articulated'.[60] In Britain and the United States, a series of gatekeepers conveyed folkloric materials and consolidated the idea of folk music for a wider public – among them Francis James Child, W. E. B. Du Bois, Lucy Broadwood, Cecil Sharp, Ralph Vaughan Williams, Carl Sandburg, Zora Neale Hurston, John A. Lomax, Alan Lomax, Pete Seeger, Harry Smith, Ewan MacColl, and A. L. Lloyd. Central to this process were a number of monumental collections inaugurating a canon of Anglophone folk music: Child's *The English and Scottish Popular Ballads* (1882–98), Sharp's *Folk Songs from Somerset* (1904–09), Sandburg's *The American Songbag* (1927), the Lomaxes' *American Ballads and Folk Songs* (1934), and Smith's *Anthology of American Folk Music* (1952), a compilation of obscure early recordings that became a talisman of the 1960s revival. These collections linked material together on the terms of curators who selected, classified, and arranged songs. However, the lack of both precision and consensus about what exactly defined folk music (the broad idea, as we've seen, always being more important than the details) led to varying degrees of inclusivity. Whereas Child and Sharp were narrow and exacting, snubbing vulgar broadsides and the music hall respectively, Sandburg and Smith were liberal and capacious. Sandburg's aspiration was to create a markedly American tradition 'as ancient as the medieval European ballads brought to the Appalachian Mountains' and yet 'as modern as skyscrapers, the Volstead [National Prohibition] Act, and the latest oil-well gusher' encompassing 'pioneers, pick and shovel men, teamsters, mountaineers, and people often called ignorant ... along with minstrels, sophisticates, and trained musicians'.[61] Whether stringent or permissive, these collections all succeeded in conveying 'folk' material to a new mass audience – in so doing, (re)articulating the boundaries and constituents of tradition.

Running throughout the history of folk music has been this pull between an anxious, pessimistic view that folk culture is dead or in terminal decline (hence in need of saving) and the optimistic belief that folk traditions are by definition imperishable, always resurfacing in new guises. Much depended on whether emphasis was placed on purity and origin or the manifestly chaotic process of transmission – the fact that, as Sandburg writes, 'thousands of men and women ... made new songs, they changed old songs, they carried songs from place to place, they resurrected and kept alive dying and forgotten songs'.[62] We can trace this position, characteristic of folkloric thinking in the United States, back to the collector Phillips Barry. In a 1911 essay on Irish music, Barry argues that 'folk-song is folk-song, because it *has become* the property of the folk in the widest sense of the word': unlike 'static' art music, folk music is 'dynamic', suggesting that 'folk-song is in reality an idea, of which we can get but the process of actualization, traceable as a history'.[63] It is this conception of 're-fashioning and re-creation ... by the community' that would finally be agreed upon as a definition by the International Folk Music Council in 1954.[64] The idea of a truly authentic working-class tradition distinct from the imperious juggernaut of capitalism nonetheless persisted alongside this more ethnographic consensus. It was this conception that fired the socialist imagination of Lloyd and MacColl, who during the early years of the Cold War achieved a remarkable rearticulation of folk music from pastoral to urban-industrial (one shot through with a distinctive masculine bias).[65] As a good historical materialist, Lloyd reasoned that folk songs 'are evolved by labouring people to suit their ways and conditions of life, and they reflect the aspirations that rise from those ways and conditions'.[66] For Lloyd, such music was therefore not only the result of poverty and economic oppression, but also an expedient tool in a contemporary fight against 'the mumbled withdrawals or frantic despair of the pops'.[67]

As I hope to have shown throughout this chapter, the idea of folk music – however imaginative, idiosyncratic, or erroneous – has bequeathed to us an enduring and highly influential habit of thought. What is worth underscoring is the relative novelty of this habit and the ways in which it has performed an extraordinary yet frequently overlooked form of cultural alchemy, transforming an assortment of merely old, exotic, or commonplace music into *folk* music. The very fact that *folk song* and *folk music* were first employed by highly educated writers in the mid nineteenth century to categorize timeworn material and certain non-Western practices should alert us to an obvious anachronism. As contemporary adoptions, these terms bore no relation to how such music had been understood historically nor how it was practiced by communities in different geographic and social settings. In short, these terms were alien impositions onto contexts that would not have recognized the classifications or assumptions being made. Folk music was therefore a kind of intellectual scaffolding fashioned and applied by antiquarians, authors, and folklorists to make sense of traditions they presumed had something significant in common. In truth, what these traditions had in common was that antiquarians, authors, and folklorists chose to portray them as folklore. To put it bluntly, medieval peasants, ballad sellers, nomadic peoples, Vikings, and Dravidian hill tribes did not use the English terms *folk song* and *folk music* and would have been entirely unaccustomed to thinking about their musical practices in this way.

This should not come as too much of a surprise. Critics have repeatedly pointed out that the concept of folk music is a thoroughly modern invention, one that has falsified (or at the very least falsely coloured) our view of the past.[68] Folk music is one thread within a much broader fabric of invented traditions that characterize the nineteenth and early twentieth centuries. The music and songs were not usually inventions as such – rather, it was the very *concept* of folk music that was invented, a category into which various traditions, material objects, songs, and practices were summarily relocated (sometimes being edited or transfigured in the process). Rather than being strengthened, continuity with the past was broken and consciously reformulated by this 'attempt to structure at least some parts of social life within [the rapidly shifting modern world] as unchanging and invariant', to quote Eric Hobsbawm.[69] This is particularly true of folk revivalism, which would become central to institutions such as the English Folk Dance and Song Society, as well as later events such as Newport Folk Festival. The invented tradition to which folk music made its most prominent contribution, however, was the nation – an ideological artefact of modernity claiming ancient or mythic legitimacy. Nationalism, as Hobsbawm points out, 'became a substitute for social cohesion' principally among the burgeoning middle class, which lacked more established forms of sociopolitical coherence.[70] Folk music delivered an emotive paradigm of unity at this transformative moment. Imaginary traditions of 'the folk' were used to illustrate and authenticate the wider political community of the nation – shoring up what Benedict Anderson describes as its 'philosophical poverty and even incoherence'.[71] In the process, folk music was shaped by and in turn helped to shape long histories of 'race-thinking', whether employed as a reactionary force by racist white collectors such as Sharp or as a tool of national liberation and memory by African American authors such as Du Bois and Jean Toomer.[72]

Today, our critical task is to understand how and why this desire for the folk, conceived during the nineteenth century out of a mixture of colonialist epistemology, nostalgic longing, and nationalist hunger, continues to draw adherents across the globe. What drives a yearning to escape the present into a lost or prelapsarian age; to what extent is such escape a form of critical engagement with the present and a spectral return of Romanticism? Informed by postcolonial consciousness, we should also pay renewed attention to the hybrid adulterations of the popular. Instead of joining in Herder's quixotic hunt for unsullied material that 'encodes the traits with which a people are born', we might turn attention to what he found most inconvenient about such a project: 'the mishmash and imitation of foreign voices, lands, and eras plague German folk song even at the origins'.[73] These fusions are not 'plagues', but rather windows onto the troublesome and intriguing complexities of a people's culture. Popular cultures are always tangled at the root, unruly mishmashes of high and low, oral and written, regional and national, Us and Them; to search for purity would be to ignore and erase these manifold hybridities.

A useful guide here is the song 'My Back Pages' from *Another Side of Bob Dylan* (1964). Turning its back on the 1960s folk revival, the song details a Joycean epiphany: it is all too easy to be seduced by the deceptive clarity of black-and-white thinking (in which politics must be memorized, dogma preached, and watchmen stationed against a legion of threats). How had the young artist inadvertently become trapped by these wildfires of conviction? He had used 'ideas as my maps' – one of these, it's tempting to suggest, being the notion of something 'foundationed deep' and in need of protection, in other words *folk music*. The song is a caution against the dangers of not looking carefully enough at such ideas, of adopting a naive, blinkered, or dictatorial perspective. Properly scrutinized, the idea of folk music reveals a tradition in which the projection of elite ideals and anxieties far outweighs the common, quotidian realities of working-class experience. It has become one in which, as Greil Marcus writes, 'the poor are art because they sing their lives without mediation and without reflection, without the false consciousness of capitalism and the false desires of advertising'.[74] It is a tradition in which these Others – be they poor, Black, marginal, or long-dead – are made to carry the burden of lessening modernity's alienation from an imagined state of innocence and communal being. In this sense, folk music is ultimately a form of social critique driven by a desire to mould an emerging mass society in the image of its outsiders. What would it mean to reconceive the history of folk music as a history from below? This is a radically democratic story still waiting to be told.

Notes

1. See Ross Cole, *The Folk: Music, Modernity, and the Political Imagination*. Oakland: University of California Press, 2021.
2. Stuart Hall, 'Notes on Deconstructing "the Popular"' (1981), in *Essential Essays, Volume 1: Foundations of Cultural Studies*, ed. David Morley, 347–61. Durham, NC: Duke University Press, 2018, 347.
3. Ambrose Merton [William Thoms], 'Folk-Lore', *Athenaeum*, 22 August 1846, 862–63, 862.
4. Merton, 'Folk-Lore', 862–3.
5. Merton, 'Folk-Lore', 863.
6. Merton, 'Folk-Lore', 863.
7. William Thoms, 'The Folk-Lore of Shakespeare', *Athenaeum*, 4 September 1847, 937–38, 937.
8. 'Hymns and Lays of Ancient Germany', *Foreign and Colonial Quarterly Review*, January 1843, 57–100, 94.
9. Johann Gottfried Herder, 'From *Alte Volkslieder / Ancient Folk Songs*' (1774), trans. Philip V. Bohlman, in Philip V. Bohlman, *Song Loves the Masses: Herder on Music and Nationalism*, 26–43. Oakland: University of California Press, 2017, 43. See also Matthew Gelbart, *The Invention of 'Folk Music' and 'Art Music': Emerging Concepts from Ossian to Wagner*. Cambridge: Cambridge University Press, 2007.
10. Susan Drain, 'Howitt [née Botham], Mary (1799–1888)'. *Oxford Dictionary of National Biography* (2004) DOI: https://doi.org/10.1093/ref:odnb/13995.
11. Mary Howitt, *Ballads and Other Poems*. London: Longman, Brown, Green, and Longmans, 1847, v.
12. Hans Christian Andersen, *The True Story of My Life: A Sketch*, trans. Mary Howitt. London: Longman, Brown, Green, and Longmans, 1847, 94.
13. 'The Three Little Roses: A German Folk's Song', trans. Mary Howitt, *Howitt's Journal*, 17 April 1847, 212.
14. 'The Three Little Roses', 212.
15. 'The Three Little Roses', 212.
16. 'The Three Little Roses', 212.
17. Fredrika Bremer, *Hertha*, trans. Mary Howitt. London: Arthur Hall, Virtue & Co., 1856, 285, 300; Fredrika Bremer, *Life in the Old World; or, Two Years in Switzerland and Italy*, Volume II, trans. Mary Howitt. Philadelphia: T. B. Peterson & Brothers, 1860, 164, 354.
18. See Christopher Clark, *Revolutionary Spring: Fighting for a New World, 1848–1849*. London: Allen Lane, 2023.
19. See Ciarán Ó Murchadha, *The Great Famine: Ireland's Agony, 1845–1852*. London: Continuum, 2011.

20. See Boyd Hilton, *A Mad, Bad, and Dangerous People? England, 1783–1846.* Oxford: Clarendon Press, 2006.
21. See Jürgen Osterhammel, *The Transformation of the World: A Global History of the Nineteenth Century*, trans. Patrick Camiller. Princeton: Princeton University Press, 2014.
22. Currer Bell, ed., *Jane Eyre: An Autobiography*, Volume I. London: Smith, Elder, & Co., 1847, 30–31.
23. Cole, *The Folk*.
24. Andrew Hamilton, *Sixteen Months in the Danish Isles*, Volume II. London: Richard Bentley, 1852, 46.
25. Hamilton, *Sixteen Months in the Danish Isles*, 1; see Mary Howitt, *Mary Howitt's Complete Poetical Works*. Boston: Wentworth, Hewes & Co., 1858, 31–41.
26. John Harwood, *The Serf-Sisters: or, The Russia of To-Day*. London: Geo. Routledge & Co., 1855, 43–44.
27. Harwood, *The Serf-Sisters*, 44.
28. See Johannes Fabian, *Time and the Other: How Anthropology Makes Its Object*, new ed. New York: Columbia University Press, 2014.
29. John Williamson Palmer, ed., *Folk Songs*. New York: Charles Scribner, 1860, vii.
30. 'A Gift'. *Harper's Weekly*, 24 November 1860, 739.
31. Andrew Hilen, ed., *The Letters of Henry Wadsworth Longfellow, Volume IV: 1857–1865*. Cambridge, MA: Belknap Press of Harvard University Press, 1972, 175; Philip V. Bohlman, 'Epilogue: Herder's Journey', in Bohlman, *Song Loves the Masses*, 261–84, 277.
32. Bohlman, 'Epilogue', 278.
33. Harriet Beecher Stowe, *Men of Our Times; or, Leading Patriots of the Day*. New York: Hartford Publishing Co., 1868, 441.
34. Franny Nudelman, *John Brown's Body: Slavery, Violence, and the Culture of War*. Chapel Hill: University of North Carolina Press, 2004, 15.
35. See John Stauffer and Benjamin Soskis, *Battle Hymn of the Republic: A Biography of the Song That Marches On*. New York: Oxford University Press, 2013.
36. Richard Grant White, *National Hymns*. New York: Rudd & Carleton, 1861, 29. On this prehistory of the folk concept in relation to the discourse of 'national music', see Gelbart, *The Invention of 'Folk Music' and 'Art Music'*.
37. Carl Engel, *An Introduction to the Study of National Music; Comprising Researches into Popular Songs, Traditions, and Customs*. London: Longmans, Green, Reader, and Dyer, 1866, 1.
38. Engel, *An Introduction to the Study of National Music*, 1.
39. Carl Engel, *The Music of the Most Ancient Nations, Particularly of the Assyrians, Egyptians, and Hebrews*. London: John Murray, 1864, 123.
40. H. D'Aveney, 'Bell Inscriptions and Bell-Founders'. *Notes & Queries*, 4 June 1859, 451–52, 451.

41. White, *National Hymns*, 30–31.
42. White, *National Hymns*, 32.
43. William E. A. Axon, *Folk Song and Folk-Speech of Lancashire*. Manchester: Tubbs and Brook, [1871], 11.
44. Axon, *Folk Song and Folk-Speech of Lancashire*, 12.
45. Frederic Louis Ritter, *History of Music, in the Form of Lectures*. Boston: Oliver Ditson & Co., 1870, 48.
46. Ritter, *History of Music*, 46.
47. Ritter, *History of Music*, 46.
48. J. Vila Blake, 'Folk-Songs'. *Putnam's Magazine*, Volume 6, October 1870, 441–49, 444–45.
49. Blake, 'Folk-Songs', 445.
50. See Zeev Sternhell, *Neither Right nor Left: Fascist Ideology in France*, trans. David Maisel. Princeton: Princeton University Press, 1986 and Zeev Sternhell, with Mario Sznajder and Maia Asheri, *The Birth of Fascist Ideology: From Cultural Rebellion to Political Revolution*, trans. David Maisel. Princeton: Princeton University Press, 1994.
51. Charles E. Gover, *The Folk-Songs of Southern India*. Madras: Higginbotham & Co., 1871, 1.
52. Gover, *The Folk-Songs of Southern India*, 1.
53. Gover, *The Folk-Songs of Southern India*, 2.
54. See Michel de Certeau, *The Practice of Everyday Life*, trans. Steven Rendall. Berkeley: University of California Press, 1984.
55. Gover, *The Folk-Songs of Southern India*, 15.
56. Gover, *The Folk-Songs of Southern India*, vii, 63.
57. Susan Sontag, 'The Anthropologist as Hero' (1963), in *Against Interpretation and Other Essays*, 69–81. London: Penguin Books, 2009, 69.
58. Sontag, 'The Anthropologist as Hero', 70.
59. Sontag, 'The Anthropologist as Hero', 73.
60. Hall, 'Notes on Deconstructing "the Popular"', 357.
61. Carl Sandburg, *The American Songbag*. New York: Harcourt, Brace & World, Inc., 1927, viii.
62. Sandburg, *The American Songbag*, viii.
63. Phillips Barry, 'Irish Folk-Song'. *Journal of American Folklore* 24 (1911), 332–43, 333.
64. 'Resolutions'. *Journal of the International Folk Music Council* 7 (1955): 23; see also Maud Karpeles, 'Definition of Folk Music'. *Journal of the International Folk Music Council* 7 (1955): 6–7.
65. See Ross Cole, 'Industrial Balladry, Mass Culture, and the Politics of Realism in Cold War Britain'. *Journal of Musicology* 34 (2017): 354–90.
66. A. L. Lloyd, *Folk Song in England*. London: Lawrence & Wishart, 1967, 22.
67. Lloyd, *Folk Song in England*, 5.

68. See Joseph Jacobs, 'The Folk'. *Folklore* 4/2 (1893): 233–38; Ernest Newman, 'The Folk-Song Fallacy'. *English Review* 11 (1912): 255–68; Louise Pound, *Poetic Origins and the Ballad*. New York: Macmillan, 1921; Charles Keil, 'Who Needs "the Folk"?'. *Journal of the Folklore Institute* 15/3 (1978): 263–65; Dave Harker, *Fakesong: The Manufacture of British 'Folksong', 1700 to the Present Day*. Milton Keynes: Open University Press, 1985; Robin D. G. Kelley, 'Notes on Deconstructing "The Folk"'. *American Historical Review* 97/5 (1992): 1400–08; Georgina Boyes, *The Imagined Village: Culture, Ideology and the English Folk Revival*. Manchester: Manchester University Press, 1993; Robert Cantwell, *Ethnomimesis: Folklife and the Representation of Culture*. Chapel Hill: University of North Carolina Press, 1993; Regina Bendix, *In Search of Authenticity: The Formation of Folklore Studies*. Madison: University of Wisconsin Press, 1997; Benjamin Filene, *Romancing the Folk: Public Memory and American Roots Music*. Chapel Hill: University of North Carolina Press, 2000; Gelbart, *The Invention of 'Folk Music' and 'Art Music'*; Karl Hagstrom Miller, *Segregating Sound: Inventing Folk and Pop Music in the Age of Jim Crow*. Durham, NC: Duke University Press, 2010; and Cole, *The Folk*.
69. Eric Hobsbawm, 'Introduction: Inventing Traditions', in *The Invention of Tradition*, ed. Eric Hobsbawm and Terence Ranger, 1–14. Cambridge: Cambridge University Press, 1983, 2.
70. Eric Hobsbawm, 'Mass-Producing Traditions: Europe, 1870–1914', in *The Invention of Tradition*, ed. Hobsbawm and Ranger, 263–307, 303.
71. Benedict Anderson, *Imagined Communities: Reflections on the Origins and Spread of Nationalism*, rev. ed. London: Verso, 2006, 5.
72. Paul Gilroy, *Against Race: Imagining Political Culture beyond the Color Line*. Cambridge, MA: Belknap Press of Harvard University Press, 2000, 8. See also Kwame Anthony Appiah, *Lines of Descent: W. E. B. Du Bois and the Emergence of Identity*. Cambridge, MA: Harvard University Press, 2014.
73. Herder, 'From *Alte Volkslieder*', 37, 32.
74. Greil Marcus, *Invisible Republic: Bob Dylan's Basement Tapes*. London: Picador, 1997, 28.

2 | Observing and Collecting

JEFF TODD TITON

It was in the early 1970s when the renowned Harvard folklorist Albert Lord told me, only half-jokingly, that folklore was absent in the United States. We were having one of our monthly lunches in Cambridge, Massachusetts, when the kindly old scholar responded to a Chicago newspaper article I'd brought to him. It featured a Yugoslavian immigrant, resident for many years in the United States, who, it was just discovered, could sing epic poetry and accompany it on the *gusle*, a one-stringed bowed lute. With his mentor Milman Parry, Lord had collected and recorded on aluminium discs many of these epic songs from *guslars* in Bosnia in 1935. Holding forth for hours at a time in coffeehouses, these illiterate singers with their songs of ancient heroes and wars were thought by Parry to be folk musical descendants of Homer. Although Parry died tragically later that year, Lord carried on the collecting work after the War and published *The Singer of Tales*, the most influential scholarly book about oral literature in the last century.[1] But about this Chicago *guslar*, Albert was dismissive: 'He can't be any good.'

'What do you mean?' I asked.

Lord replied that European folklore, when brought to the United States, deteriorated in the absence of its authentic, Old Country contexts. 'Besides,' he said, with a twinkle in his eye, 'there isn't any folklore in the United States, anyway.'

'How can you say that?' I was perplexed and amused. The folklore course I was teaching concentrated on American folklore. Had my subject suddenly disappeared?

'We never had peasants', he said.

Musing on our conversation some fifty years later, I realize again how it confirms that folklorists set the boundaries of our field to suit our inclinations and interests, thereby constituting the objects we set out to discover while excluding others as unsuitable or inauthentic.[2] Our observations are not merely perceptions; we are not like a glass lens struck suddenly by light. Rather, our observations always are already prepared for. Like the European aristocrats who gathered up popular antiquities during the Enlightenment, Euro-American intellectuals began by thinking of folklore as relics from a pre-modern era, showing our own nostalgic anti-modernism. Paradoxically, we then subjected folklore to the information control mechanisms of modernity: identification, observation, investigation, collection, classification, analysis, comparison, interpretation, and evaluation – all in service to science, expertise, universities, and the knowledge production industry. Today, we challenge the inscription of folklore studies into the epistemology of modernity and its institutional power structures, especially in terms of its consequences for minorities and people of colour. In what follows I construct a brief history of folk song observation and collecting chiefly in the United States, the region I know best. I attend to how and why the consensus among American folklorists changed over time concerning who are the folk (if not peasants, then who?), what constitutes folk song, and how folk song is to be studied and understood.

The American democratic ideal requires that the folk be ordinary people, neither peasants nor elites.[3] A definition of folk song is harder to pin down because not all songs the folk sing qualify as folk songs. When regarded as an object, a folk song carries a constellation of characteristics, not all of which need be present and some of which may be compromised. The most important were these: that folk songs and related music such as tunes for dancing must be old; that they are anonymous (that is, the composer has long been unknown); that they are passed down orally in families and delimited social groups (communities, which may be geographical or occupational) and learned by imitation rather than from formal instruction in schools or from books or commercial recordings; and that as a result, folk songs change over time and therefore collectors find them to exist in different variants depending on time and place. For roughly the first two-thirds of the twentieth century, American folklorists did regard folk songs as objects – texts with tunes that could be captured on paper or recordings. Since then, folklorists with academic training conceived of a folk song more as a process, a single performance event in a unique, unrepeatable context. There is an object, a text and tune, generated in the performance; but a song is much more than this residual husk. Today most folklorists acknowledge that whereas folklore must link to tradition, its ontology is contemporary expressive culture, 'artistic communication in small groups.'[4] As a result, folk songs are no longer regarded as quaint remnants that evoke isolated, bucolic, premodern communities. Rather, most folklorists in the United States today reject that idealistic folk imaginary while undertaking fieldwork in contemporary folk groups to study living traditions. And so finally I ask who are the collectors, what institutions have we been affiliated with, what have we been looking for, what is a collection and where is it kept, and how have the methods for observing, collecting, analysing, and interpreting folk songs changed over time?

Summarizing broadly, folk song observers and collectors in the United States fall into two categories: the academic professionals employed in colleges, universities, and museums; and the public folklorists and amateur enthusiasts employed outside the academic world either by the government, NGOs, or in the private sector. For most of the twentieth century, observing and collecting was done by surveying, but in the 1970s academic folklorists increasingly turned away from short-term geographical surveys across several communities towards ethnographic fieldwork in single communities. This fieldwork turn resulted partly from the paradigm shift from folklore as text to folklore as performance, which latter invited a more holistic and ethnographic understanding of sociocultural context. In the 1980s – a period of postcolonial reflexivity that anticipated the present turn to decolonization – academic folklorists became uneasy with the extractive connotations of 'collecting' from 'informants', and looked to find ways to collaborate with their 'field partners' and to share with them the authority of representation. Instead of folklore, scholars wrote about 'expressive culture', and the term 'folk' was even avoided in some quarters because of its associations with colonialism, empire, and white racial superiority. Collections themselves were not spared from critique: was the collecting impulse a peculiarly Western preoccupation? What were the criteria for 'good' collections and was archival preservation only an excuse for mastery? Had the songs really been donated after fully informed consent or were they plundered? Should they not perhaps be 'repatriated' back to their original owners or their descendants?

From Origins to Archives

It is unclear when folklore observation and collecting began, or who was the first folklorist. The word *folklore* was coined in England by William Thoms in the mid nineteenth century after the German *volkskunde*, and came to displace the phrase 'popular antiquities.' But observation and collecting is far older. Herodotus (c.484–425 BC), acclaimed as the first Western historian, is also the first Western folklorist that we know of. He travelled widely, solicited and collected stories circulating in oral tradition, and narrated his *Histories* based largely upon them. In Book One, for example, he recounts the legend, 'as the Corinthians and Lesbians tell it', of the musician Arion of Methymna, a city on the Island of Lesbos. About

600 BC, facing the threat of death from robbers while journeying upon a ship to Corinth, Arion sang a hymn to Apollo then leapt into the sea whereupon he encountered a dolphin that carried him on its back to Taenarum. 'Here,' wrote Herodotus, 'Arion landed, and made his way in his singing costume to Corinth, where he told the whole story. Periander [the ruler] was not too ready to believe it.'[5] But at length the Corinthians gave it credence, and Herodotus underscored their belief by making reference to the statue in the temple at Taenarum of a man on a dolphin.

What constituted folklore and folk song to those early anthropologists and folklorists, who came together for scientific study in 1888 to form the American Folk-Lore Society? The opening article in the first issue of their *Journal*, unsigned and presumably representing the group's consensus, proclaimed that the Society was designed to 'collect the fast-vanishing remains of Folk-Lore in America', which they named as, first, 'relics of Old English Folk-Lore (ballads, tales, etc.)'; second, 'Lore of the Negroes in the Southern States of the Union', third, 'Lore of the Indian Tribes of North America (myths, tales, etc.)', and fourth, 'Lore of French Canada, Mexico, etc.'[6] Who were these American folklorists in the early period (roughly from the 1880s to the 1920s), where were they employed, and what folk songs did they collect? They were professors in universities and their former students, researchers affiliated with ethnology divisions of museums, and serious amateurs with spare time and sufficient wherewithal combined with enthusiasm for the stuff of folklore and a passion for the adventure of collecting. Formal graduate education leading to a degree in folklore as an academic discipline did not begin in earnest in the United States until after World War II, although degrees in anthropology and graduate study in comparative musicology were achievable decades earlier. Cultural anthropologists and comparative musicologists were most interested in observing and collecting folk songs of Indigenous (then-termed 'primitive') peoples such as the American Indian tribes. Most of the early collectors were interested either in the old English relics or the 'lore of the Negroes'.

Among members of the Society there was, then, a powerful anti-modern sentiment similar to that in the United Kingdom described by Ross Cole and exemplified by the collecting, publishing, and educational activities of Cecil Sharp both in England and the United States.[7] Observing, collecting, and preserving were critical because folklore was thought to be disappearing while the United States was accelerating its belated transformation into a modern, industrial nation. But folk song might still be found in relatively isolated places like the Southern Appalachian Mountains and rural New

England, among Native Americans on Indian reservations, and among Black Americans in prisons in the South or on the islands off the coast of Georgia and South Carolina. The most important thing was to gather up the texts and tunes so as to safeguard the folk songs before they disappeared. Later, the academics and intellectuals would analyse, classify, and subject items of folklore to comparative analysis to trace their origins and the history of their diffusion over time and space. This latter procedure, the 'historic-geographic' method, dominated folklore studies in North America until, in the early 1970s, folklorists clustered around the University of Pennsylvania's graduate folklore program induced a paradigm shift from text to performance.[8] At the same time, American folklorists were starting to think of what we were doing, or at least ought to be doing, as fieldwork: documentation and interpretation rather than surveying, collecting, and analysis. In the earlier period dominated by collecting and historic-geographic analysis, however, folklore was valued as an historical curiosity and an object of nostalgia capable of occasioning an aesthetic response. But more importantly, the distribution of folklore and folk song was thought to offer insight into ancient and medieval history and the unrecorded migrations and cultural connections of disparate peoples.

But how, exactly, was folklore to be observed and collected? From the few articles in the early decades of the Society devoted to acquiring folklore one infers that it consisted chiefly of discovering suitable 'informants', soliciting the folklore from them, then noting down the texts and if possible any tunes, and lastly finding out where, how, and from whom they learned it. Collecting was best done in person, but items of folklore could also be solicited in newspaper columns and by printed advertisements. The collector was advised to have a list of examples at the ready to prompt the informant. Fanny Bergen and W. W. Newell published such a list with examples of song lyric prompts such as 'Oh who will shoe your feet ... '.[9] Comparative musicologist Helen H. Roberts published a thoughtful guide, remarking that although folk song collectors resembled natural historians such as botanists, their task was harder because of 'the human factor'.[10] People might misunderstand what the collector was after, refuse to sing, or sing something different from what was being solicited. Roberts instructed would-be collectors in the techniques of recording and notating texts, tunes, and movements (gestures, dance, etc.) and urged them to pay attention to obtaining and translating song texts; to classify and categorize songs while also noting down native categories; to take down information about musical instruments; and to find out about the contexts for the music. All of the specimens were to be gathered 'in the field' and then brought back to 'the laboratory' for analysis and comparison. Although good rapport with informants was necessary for success, the informants themselves were not important except as vessels or carriers of the music. In this way, the collectors found (or failed to find) examples of what they were looking for. Dorothy Scarborough wrote that 'if you aspire to be a folk song collector, you must cast aside the niceties of conduct, must shamelessly eavesdrop, and ask intrusive questions'.[11] Collecting 'without selection based on preconceived categories' seldom occurred until decades later.[12] Folklorists seem to have been so preoccupied with gathering material that they did not much examine their methodology. They knew what folk song was (and was not), and it was chiefly a matter of finding it and setting it down for posterity.

What was collected in the early period? 'Lore of the Negroes of the Southern States of the Union' was already in a collecting phase by the time the American Folk-Lore Society formed. Early collections of Negro folklore and folk song perpetuated a stereotype of the enslaved Negro, the so-called happy-go-lucky 'darky'.[13] The first substantial collection of Negro folk songs included secular songs but emphasized spirituals, both texts and tunes.[14] Capitalizing on popular interest, the Fisk University Jubilee Singers toured and performed these Negro spirituals to great acclaim in the United States and Europe, where they came to stand as folk song exemplars.[15] Around the turn of the twentieth century, sociologist Howard W. Odum collected Negro religious and secular songs in Georgia and Mississippi, and published two important articles based on them.[16] Interestingly, he collected some songs with blues lyrics, but either the singers did not call them blues songs then or Odum failed to find that out.[17] Dorothy Scarborough must have heard the vaudeville blues of Bessie Smith and others on commercial recordings, but she thought any purity they might have had as folk songs was corrupted by the profit motive.[18] Most folklorists agreed with Scarborough about commercial recordings until the 1960s, when they were persuaded that early downhome blues, gospel music, immigrant, and some 'hillbilly' records contained folk songs.[19]

Anthropologists, ethnologists, and comparative musicologists collected the musical 'Lore of the Indian Tribes of North America'.[20] Franz Boas (1858–1942), the most eminent cultural anthropologist in the United States, played an important role in the American Folk-Lore Society's early years. President of the Society in 1904, he was also an editor of its *Journal*. Other collectors included Frances Densmore, who travelled to survey the music of many of the Southwestern and Western tribes systematically. Her sound recordings were deposited in the Smithsonian

Institution's Bureau of American Ethnology archives and the surveys were published in more than a dozen book-length monographs.[21] George A. Herzog offers a good summary and critical appraisal of this early collecting and scholarship on Native music.[22] After World War II, when comparative musicology was absorbed by the new field, ethnomusicology, most of the collections and analyses of tribal musics in the United States were done by ethnomusicologists rather than folklorists or anthropologists.

Lore of French Canada (including much music) was being collected by the Canadian Marius Barbeau, while collecting 'relics of old English folklore' was centred at Harvard University, where Francis James Child had amassed his monumental collection of English and Scottish ballads. Appropriately, Child was the first President of the American Folk-Lore Society (1888–89). In 1896 George Lyman Kittredge succeeded Child at Harvard, wrote a magisterial introduction to his predecessor's ballad collection, and mentored Phillips Barry, the most important American collector of British ballads in the United States during the Society's early period. Barry's collecting efforts in New England resulted in several publications.[23] Barry inspired several others who collected in New England and who liked to think they were in competition with collectors in Appalachia to see who could find more Child Ballads. D. K. Wilgus offers an excellent summary and evaluation of these efforts.[24] The focus on English and Scottish folk song was congruent with the belief, then prevalent among the educated class, that authentic cultural heritage in the United States was Anglo-Saxon owing to the dominance of British settlement in the Colonies and Revolutionary period – an idea that promoted white supremacy at certain folk festivals and other events.[25]

Two others who had studied with Kittredge were interested in collecting a broader variety of American folk song. One, Robert Winslow Gordon, left a professorial appointment in English at Berkeley in 1925 to become a full-time collector, supporting himself by writing columns and articles on the 'old songs', as he called them, in popular magazines. As detailed by Debora G. Kodish in the liner notes to *'Folk-Songs of America': The Robert Winslow Gordon Collection, 1922–1932*, Gordon

carried his heavy cylinder recorder (and later, his disc machine) to the San Francisco waterfront, the Appalachian mountains, and the Georgia coast in order to record the diverse singing traditions of this country. He recorded nearly a thousand cylinders, collected nearly ten thousand more song texts from the readers of his popular articles, and gathered many thousand additional song versions from old camp-meeting and revival songbooks, broadsides, folios, and hillbilly recordings – ephemeral material of which few of his colleagues were aware.[26]

Much of his in-person collecting was done in Black communities. Gordon established the Archive of American Folk Song at the Library of Congress in 1928, and continued his collecting activities until he and the Library parted ways in 1933.

Kittredge's most significant follower was John A. Lomax (1867–1948). With another Harvard professor, Barrett Wendell, Kittredge had encouraged Lomax, then an older Harvard graduate student, to collect cowboy songs from his native Southwest. Lomax did so, and in 1910 published *Cowboy Songs and Other Frontier Ballads* to critical and popular acclaim. John Lomax, later with his son Alan, then Alan alone after his father died, collected folk song over the entire span of the century and became the best-known non-academic folklorists of that era. Theirs was a search for American voices. In 1931 John became affiliated with the Archive of American Folk Song and, with his teenage son Alan, began recording Negro folk songs in Southern prisons, where he thought the songs would be least affected by modern culture. With Alan as co-editor he published *American Ballads and Folk Songs*, notable for not containing a single Child ballad.[27] Rather, the collection was organized both by geographical region and by occupations, chiefly blue collar and male (railroaders, levee camp workers, miners, cowboys and vaqueros [with lyrics in Spanish], shanty boys, etc.), all with a very large helping of Negro songs, secular and sacred. Kittredge wrote a foreword to the volume, vouching for Lomax as a collector and for the songs' authenticity.

Between the World Wars a more inclusive idea of American folk song and cultural history emerged from the collecting efforts of Gordon and the Lomaxes – one that was public rather than academic, and one that promoted an idea of American cultural democracy, connected with the frontier and the open road. Their folk were not all sequestered away in isolated rural areas that 'time forgot'; rather, they were identified as working class Americans – the 'common man', to use the parlance of the time. Moreover, as exemplified in Gordon and the Lomaxes, the folk song collector became, in the popular mind, a romantic hero, a 'song-catcher' who travelled far and wide looking for rare specimens. Roger D. Abrahams proposed that this kind of itinerant, hard-living collector represented an ideal of rough-and-ready manhood identified with the western frontier.[28] The implied contrast was with an effete New England, where the focus remained on ballad collecting and where many of the important collectors were women.[29]

During the New Deal, the Federal Writers Project employed dozens of collectors who gathered hundreds of recordings and transcriptions of texts and, in some cases, tunes from many states in the union. Given direction by

Figure 2.1 Robert Winslow Gordon, 1923. Photograph courtesy of
J. Barre Toelken and the American Folklife Center, Library of Congress.

the Lomaxes, Charles Seeger, and B. A. Botkin, they were more interested in finding native American folk songs than European survivals. Alan Lomax himself made a number of significant field trips, recording hundreds of discs under the Archive's auspices during this period while soliciting folk songs from other singers and collectors. British folklore 'relics' were a part of this mix, but equally if not more important were songs that reflected native American subjects. Immigrant communities and their folk songs were targeted as well.[30] The prevailing thought was that folk songs persisted and thus were best collected from communities that were relatively homogeneous, and where folklore had persisted in oral tradition in homes and families, uncontaminated either by commercial music or the learned, literate traditions of the educated classes. In 1941 John and Alan Lomax published a second and more substantial collection, *Our Singing Country*, based largely upon the material in the Archive of

American Folk Song. The composer Ruth Crawford Seeger painstakingly transcribed the recorded songs and dance tunes into music notation. This important collection was segregated into broad regions: The East, the South, the Negro South, the West, etc. Many Negro folk songs were featured, and the book also contained a small number of Cajun and Creole songs (in French) from Louisiana. They printed the lyric texts with tunes meant for singing. The Lomaxes saw no irony in presenting these old workaday songs from oral tradition to a literate public. In the face of modernization and cultural homogenization they worried that these songs and the histories they represented could disappear. In addition to holding them in archives, the best way to preserve them was to circulate them in a new context, by means of books, recordings, radio programs, and school curricula.

Other academics and amateur collectors were also busy between the 1930s and 1960s. A culture of collecting developed. Dozens of anthologies were published with English and Scottish ballads given pride of place. Whereas the Lomax collections, which continued after the War, emphasized singable texts and tunes with some historical context, precious relics in the ballad collections were carefully arranged, and many were meticulously annotated. Most were centered in a single state or region, such as the *Frank C. Brown Collection of North Carolina Folklore* (1952–1964), which devoted two of its seven volumes to folk song. Record collecting became an obsession among some. Blues record collectors, for example, haunted thrift shops that sold used records and canvassed door-to-door in the South looking for rare blues that, beginning in the 1920s, had been issued on commercial 78s. They swapped records among themselves and bought and sold at auctions all in an attempt to build the finest collections. Dubbed the 'blues mafia', they also became principals in record companies that specialized in reissuing these old 78s on LPs. With that, and in view of their contributions to the 'rediscoveries' and subsequent recording and promotion of singers still living who had originally made those recordings, these collectors shaped public taste in country blues during the blues revival of the 1960s and beyond.[31]

The Anthropological Turn

In the years following World War II a folk music revival occurred in the public arena at the same time that stand-alone graduate degree programs in folklore (and later ethnomusicology) were established in the academic world. However, the folk revival, associated with such singers as Woody Guthrie and Pete Seeger, was problematic for academics owing to its radical Left politics. The Lomax and New Deal focus on the working classes and the leftist association of some prominent folklorists did not play well institutionally during the Red-scare 1950s. Seeger was blacklisted after he refused to testify to the House Committee on Un-American Activities and sentenced to a year in prison. Alan Lomax departed the United States, collected and promoted folk song in the United Kingdom and Europe, and returned when things cooled down late in the decade. At that time the folk song revival expanded, especially on college campuses, with the immense popularity of clean-cut, apolitical folksinging groups such as The Kingston Trio. Guthrie protege Bob Dylan's rise to popularity a few years later nevertheless made it clear that the folk song revival had not lost its associations with protest music and the working classes. At the same time, the ongoing revival inspired a number of musicians to learn ethnic and regional musics such as Cajun, klezmer, polka, and old-time southern Appalachian string band music. Many of these revivalists also became researchers and collectors – first locating, then visiting, learning from, and recording exemplary elder musicians. Meanwhile, the Archive of American Folk Song had turned back into a repository, not a centre for promoting folk song.

During the 1950s and 1960s, certain that folk music's leftist connotations would impede the institutionalization of folklore within American college and university curricula, Indiana University's PhD-granting Folklore Institute led a movement to discredit the revivalists as amateur researchers who did not know (or care) about the differences between folklore and 'fakelore'. Richard Dorson, director of the Folklore Institute, applied this term not only to made-up folklore (such as the legend of Paul Bunyan) but also to performers, journalists, and promoters, as well as to folklorists with tenuous academic credentials such as B. A. Botkin, whose folklore *Treasuries* were best-selling anthologies of regional folklore gathered from various sources. Sensitive to the public's impression of folklore as mere superstition and of folklorists as 'amateurs having a good time puttering around', the professors distanced themselves from the folk revival while taking care to call themselves 'professional folklorists'.[32] They carefully positioned their university work as scientific research, avoiding anything that smacked of folk revivalism or public advocacy. Leading an academic consensus, folklorist D. K. Wilgus blasted careless scholarship in the amateur collections, aiming his sharpest missiles at the Lomaxes.[33] The related field, ethnomusicology, which drew upon cultural anthropology, comparative musicology, dance studies, and folk song studies, was also established then, with graduate degree programs at universities such as UCLA, Wesleyan, Brown, Illinois, Washington, Indiana, and Texas. The US-based Society for Ethnomusicology (SEM, founded in 1955) included members with interests in folk song, which Bruno Nettl defined as 'the music in oral tradition found in those areas which are dominated by high cultures, [and] with which it exchanges material and by which it is profoundly influenced'.[34] However, the SEM resisted an invitation from Maud Karpeles that they instead join with the International Folk Music Council, chiefly because they worried that their status as a scientific organization would be undermined by association with what one of their founders disdained as a 'society of folksingers and dancers'.[35]

During the post–World War II period, folk song researchers relied on a combination of in-person surveying with archival and published sources. Before the War, the Lomaxes had collected folk song chiefly as Gordon had done – by traveling and surveying in likely communities, announcing their presence and their intention to collect and record folk songs, then staying for a while to do that before moving to the next location. In that way they could cover a lot of ground and gather as much material as possible. Upon his return to the United States in the late 1950s and as the folk song revival gathered momentum, Alan Lomax once again surveyed and recorded traditional folk music throughout Appalachia and the South, seeing to it that it was published in the media mainstream on Prestige and Atlantic LPs. In the late 1970s he was at it again, surveying the older forms of Black American folk music in Mississippi, and producing a documentary film based on his travels.[36]

The subject of surveying arose in conversation with Alan Lomax one evening in a Washington, DC tavern. It was October 1985. Barry Dornfeld, Tom Rankin, and I were in the midst of making a folklife documentary film in Virginia, spending a few months living in the community where we were filming and attempting to arrive at a mutual, collaborative understanding of purpose with the people we were filming.[37] But at that moment in the tavern we were on a brief visit to DC to get some equipment repaired. Our visit happened to coincide with the annual ceremony for the Folk Heritage Awards from the Folk Arts Division of the National Endowment for the Arts (NEA), awards which came with financial stipends that were given to exemplary folk artists, musicians, and craftspeople. As we were chatting, Alan suddenly asked Tom why he had quit his job as the Mississippi state folklorist. 'I thought you were our man in Mississippi,' Alan remarked. Tom responded that he was forced to do too much survey work and couldn't spend enough time with any single folk tradition-bearer or group. 'Well,' said Alan, 'I'm a survey man myself.' Indeed, until the 1970s, for most folklorists in the United States, whether in academia or in the public sector, collecting meant surveying. They were after texts and tunes foremost, and the more authentic examples they could find before it all vanished, the better. However, the generation that came of age in the 1960s and 1970s – my generation – was increasingly attracted to anthropological methodologies: longer times spent in single communities rather than broadly surveying over many. In the first book-length guide to fieldwork for folklorists, Kenneth Goldstein wrote that 'we must turn to the cultural anthropologists for anything approaching an adequate methodology for folklore collectors' because folklore's 'methods must be scientifically determined and based'.[38] Folklorists began to adopt terms like fieldwork and documentation instead of surveying and collecting to describe our activities.

Further revolutions took place in folklore and ethnomusicology studies after the mid-1970s, one inside the academic world and the other outside of it. Inside, folklorists started thinking of folklore as performance rather than text. Among many academic folklorists (as with cultural anthropologists) there was also a gradual transformation away from analytical, comparative social science towards the humanities, where meaning and significance was interpretative, ambiguous, and elusive. In the public arena government involvement in folklore was powerfully re-invigorated. Major public sector folklore institutions were established in the 1970s: the American Folklife Center (AFC) at the Library of Congress, which incorporated the Archive of American Folk Song and also undertook collecting surveys; the aforementioned Folk Arts Division of the NEA, primarily a funding agency for organization-based projects intended to preserve and promote traditional, family and community-based arts and artists; and the Smithsonian Center for Folklife and Heritage, which sponsored the annual Festival of (American) Folklife in Washington, DC. This resulted in numerous public sector jobs for folklorists. Aiding the re-invigoration of public folklore was the 1976 American Bicentennial celebration and ethnic 'roots' movements, with a deepening commitment to folklore and folk song's role in portraying America as a culturally pluralistic nation where ethnic traditions flourished. It was, however, some years before public folklorists began theorizing much about methodology; most of their time was spent doing the work: surveying for folk tradition-bearers (including, of course, musicians), identifying them, documenting and promoting the performing folk artists, advocating for their practice, and aiding them in preserving their traditions within their communities.

Folklore's anthropological turn inside the American academic world led to an increased concern with methodology, and those who went into public folklore occupations were exposed to it during their graduate school training.[39] Ethnographic observation and interview techniques – with a focus on in-group language usage as a key into folk cultural worldview – led to a rise in studies of expressive culture in folk groups with a focus on many-layered description (or 'thick description' as anthropologist Clifford Geertz phrased it).[40] Despite the movement towards interpretative rather than analytical writing, fieldwork itself was to be as objective as possible. A field manual for ethnomusicology students advised that 'good observations and sensitivity aid in establishing rapport' and that the good fieldworker, although unavoidably conspicuous at musical events, should aim to be like a 'fly on the wall', refraining from taking sides or interfering. Participation in musical events was permitted, but fieldworkers must remember they were outsiders. Self-observation was also advised, and methods for checking observational accuracy were elaborated upon.[41] In his book *Fieldwork*, academic folklorist Bruce Jackson called attention to observation, noting that it offers 'first-hand reports' and 'gives direct knowledge of matters that, from interviewing, we could only know about through hearsay'.[42] Jackson further claimed that folklorists usually did not attempt the type of long-term, community-based fieldwork that anthropologists did; rather, because they 'do not work in primitive societies' and 'rarely attempt to understand whole communities' they can 'do fieldwork on evenings or weekends; they can also do it full time for a week or a month or a year'.[43] In saying so, Jackson was emphasizing flexibility: folklorists could do ethnographic fieldwork and produce significant community-based studies, but it was also all right to collect folklore episodically in one's spare time.[44]

By the 1980s, most folklore graduate programs were training their students in ethnographic fieldwork so that they could document and interpret expressive cultural performance within folk communities. Instead of focused observation and collection from the moment of arrival, the new fieldworkers preferred to proceed gradually after a period of quietly 'hanging out' and getting to know people. Ethnomusicology graduate programs were likewise emphasizing anthropological methods. 'The purpose of recording field data,' according to the Society for Ethnomusicology, 'is to study and preserve musical traditions ... [Fieldworkers] should assume that whatever is gathered will be of importance to them and to other scholars, or to members of the communities where the recordings were made, at some time in the future'.[45] Yet, while graduate education in folklore and ethnomusicology was expanding, in the troubled American economy of the 1980s the academic job market for folklorists, never robust, contracted along with the market for professors in the humanities generally, and it was not long before folklore graduate programs were under stress as well. By the end of the century many of them either had perished or been absorbed by other disciplines.

Despite folklore's gradual decline in academia, public folklore jobs increased, and the field prospered in the 1990s. In what appeared to be a heavenly convergence, US Presidents appointed folklorists to direct both the NEA (William Ivey), and the National Endowment for the Humanities (NEH; William Ferris). Amateur folklorists and local historians were collecting and submitting more folklore to archives and historical societies. Public folklore's emphasis on ethnicity and cultural pluralism also was having an effect on definitions. A popular undergraduate textbook on the subject defined American folk music as 'music with strong regional ties or a racial/ethnic identity and direct links with its past'.[46] In response to the continuing public interest in folklore, the AFC at the Library of Congress expanded its brief 'layman's introduction to field techniques', a pamphlet outlining what was (and wasn't) folklife, what to collect, and how to collect it.[47] Laymen were, however, carefully distinguished from the 'professional folklorists' who held jobs at public folklore institutions such as the AFC.[48] Surveying, recording, and interviewing were the techniques recommended for amateurs. They were also advised on equipment, consent forms, and how to process their collections prior to donating them to archives such as the AFC. They were given a short equivalent of Jackson's *Fieldwork*, with emphasis on collecting in one's spare time. Meanwhile, in the 1990s the distance between public and academic folklore was closing. Public folklore was becoming respectable among academic folklorists and ethnomusicologists, and in some graduate programs (e.g., at Brown, Indiana, Western Kentucky, and UCLA) students were being prepared for careers in it.[49] Academic folklorists joined in doing, and theorizing, public folklore. Collecting, preserving, and presenting folklore to the general public was not enough. All along, public folklorists had been partisan advocates intending to encourage folk traditions to prosper and continue inside their own families and communities. The new name for public folklore's objective was 'cultural conservation', which in the twenty-first century became 'cultural sustainability'.[50]

Conclusion

It is possible to sum up the academic side of this history by highlighting two themes. The first is the growing importance of personal and cultural context in determining the meaning of a folk song and the procedures by which it should be understood. The second, related to the first, is the growing emphasis on the relationship between a folk song, its meaning, and lived experience. In the first instance, as the historic-geographic method was exhausting itself in the minutiae of typology, folklorists discovered how important it was that the same song could have multiple meanings. Those meanings depended on who sang it, who heard it, and where, when, and why it was sung.[51] Content analysis fails to disclose unique personal meanings and cultural group understandings. In the second instance, the revelation of personal and group meanings of particular folk song texts led folklorists to an interest in how members of the folk group experienced songs and the events surrounding performances. Ethnographic interviews as well as observations of their interpretative comments during performance revealed how these songs were entwined in their lives and how their lives were entwined with one another. Observation and collection shifted: instead of isolating the collected texts and tunes and reducing their study to the comparison of particularities, folklorists studied performance events as wholes. Not only texts and tunes, but also immediate as well as remembered lived experience became part of the quest for meaning, as the locus of meaning itself shifted from history and geography to cultural experience.

Attempts at more collaboratively written ethnographies characterize academic approaches to observation and collecting today.[52] Traditional ecological knowledge became an important object of fieldwork in response to global warming and climate change, while a new interdisciplinary field, ecomusicology, has probed relations between music, sound, expressive culture, nature, and the environment.[53] Reflexive and auto-ethnographic approaches also increased as part of the phenomenological turn that brought in fieldworkers' experiences as well as their relations with field partners and others. For academics, as I've written elsewhere, fieldwork is 'no longer viewed principally as observing and collecting (although it surely involves that) but as experiencing and understanding music'.[54] In the introduction to an oft-assigned volume of essays, Timothy Cooley writes that 'we wish to reframe the critical debate within postmodern social science to consider ... the ethnographic process that position[s] scholars through their fieldwork as social actors within the cultures they study'.[55] Folklorists and ethnomusicologists whose subject positions give them access to insider knowledge provide invaluable information and perspectives unavailable to cultural outsiders.[56] Expanding in number, they are increasingly representing, expressing, interpreting and curating the traditions of their forebears. The latest and most comprehensive attempt to theorize fieldwork, co-authored by an academic folklorist and a public ethnomusicologist, is not only about participation, observation, note-taking, problem-solving, getting familiar with one's gear, and remembering to bring along spare batteries (although all of that is covered).[57] The book instead foregrounds issues such as positionality, ethics, collaboration, and decolonization in such a way as to invite readers to think and decide for themselves. In the end, the authors assert, observing and collecting is about people and relationships, not texts and tunes.

Notes

1. Albert Lord, *The Singer of Tales*. Cambridge, MA: Harvard University Press, 1960.
2. See Jeff Todd Titon, 'Reconstructing the Blues: Reflections on the 1960s Blues Revival'. In *Transforming Tradition: Folk Music Revivals Examined*, ed. Neil V. Rosenberg, 220–240. Urbana: University of Illinois Press, 1993.
3. But see Arthur F. Raper, *Preface to Peasantry*. Chapel Hill: University of North Carolina Press, 1934.
4. Dan Ben-Amos, 'Toward a Definition of Folklore in Context'. *Journal of American Folklore* 84, 331 (1971): 3–15, 13.
5. Herodotus, *The Histories*, trans. Aubrey de Sélincourt. New York: Penguin Books, 1983, 49.
6. Unsigned, 'On the Field and Work of a Journal of American Folk-Lore'. *Journal of American Folklore* I, 1 (1888): 3–7.
7. See Ross Cole, *The Folk: Music, Modernity, and the Political Imagination*. Oakland: University of California Press, 2021.
8. See Richard Bauman, ed., 'Toward New Perspectives in Folklore'. Special issue, *Journal of American Folklore* 84, 331 (1971): v–169.
9. Fanny Bergen and W. W. Newell, 'Topics for Collection of Folk-Lore'. *Journal of American Folklore* IV, 13 (1891): 151–58, 156.
10. Helen Roberts, 'Suggestions to Field Workers in Collecting Folk Music and Data about Instruments'. *The Journal of the Polynesian Society* 40, 3 (1926): 103–128.
11. Dorothy Scarborough, *On the Trail of Negro Folk Songs*. Hatboro, PA: Folklore Associates, 1963 [1925], 3.
12. See Melville Herskovits, 'Some Next Steps in the Study of Negro Folklore', *Journal of American Folklore* 56, 219 (1943): 1–7, 1.
13. Roger D. Abrahams, 'Foreword' to Scarborough, *On the Trail of Negro Folk Songs*, i–ix, vi–vii.
14. William Francis Allen, Charles Pickard Ware, and Lucy McKim Garrison, *Slave Songs of the United States*. New York: A. Simpson & Co., 1867.

15. J. B. T. Marsh, *Story of the Jubilee Singers, with Their Songs*. New York: Houghton-Mifflin, 1881.
16. Howard W. Odum, 'Religious Folk Songs of the Southern Negro'. *American Journal of Religious Psychology and Education* III (1908–09): 263–365 and 'Folk Song and Folk Poetry as Found in the Secular Songs of the Southern Negroes'. *Journal of American Folklore* XXIV, 93 (1911): 255–296; 94 (1911): 351–396.
17. These later were expanded into two books co-authored with his colleague Guy B. Johnson: *The Negro and His Songs* and *Negro Workaday Songs*.
18. Scarborough, *On the Trail of Negro Folk Songs*.
19. See D. K. Wilgus, *Anglo-American Folk Song Scholarship Since 1898*. New Brunswick, NJ: Rutgers University Press, 1959; David Evans, *Tommy Johnson*. London: Studio Vista, 1971; Richard K. Spottswood, *Ethnic Music on Records: A Discography of Ethnic Recordings Produced in the United States, 1893–1942*. 7 vols. Urbana: University of Illinois Press, 1990.
20. Comparative musicology began in Germany in the 1880s; it involved the analytical study of folk and 'primitive' (Indigenous) music all over the world.
21. Frances Densmore, *Chippewa Music*. Washington, DC: Smithsonian Institution Bureau of American Ethnology, *Bulletin* 45, 1910.
22. George A. Herzog, 'Study of Native Music in America', *Proceedings of the Eighth American Scientific Congress*, 2 (1942): 203–209.
23. E.g., Phillips Barry, 'Folk Music in America' *Journal of American Folklore* 22, 83 (1909): 72–81; Phillips Barry, Fannie Hardy Eckstorm, and Mary Winslow Smyth, *British Ballads from Maine*. New Haven: Yale University Press, 1929.
24. Wilgus, *Anglo-American Folk song Scholarship*.
25. See David E. Whisnant, *All That Is Native and Fine*. Chapel Hill: University of North Carolina Press, 2009 [1983].
26. Debora G. Kodish, 'Introduction' to '*Folk-Songs of America*': *The Robert Winslow Gordon Collection, 1922–1932*, ed. Neil V. Rosenberg and Debora G. Kodish, 3–13. Washington, DC: Library of Congress, 1978, 3.
27. John A. Lomax and Alan Lomax, *American Ballads and Folk Songs*. New York: Macmillan, 1934.
28. Roger D. Abrahams, 'Mr. Lomax Meets Professor Kittredge.' *Journal of Folklore Research* 37, 2/3 (2000): 99–118, 108–112.
29. Nevertheless, many women collectors who were contemporaries of Gordon and the Lomaxes, women such as Dorothy Scarborough, Helen H. Roberts, and Frances Densmore, gave the lie to this stereotype, traveling and collecting music in conditions as difficult, if not more so, than those that Gordon and the Lomaxes encountered.
30. Mark A. Davidson, 'Recording the Nation: Folk Music and the Government in Roosevelt's New Deal'. Dissertation, University of California at Santa Cruz, 2015.
31. See Marybeth Hamilton, *In Search of the Blues*. New York: HarperCollins, 2008.

32. Kenneth S. Goldstein, *A Guide for Field Workers*. Hatboro, Pennsylvania: Folklore Associates, 1964, 6.
33. Wilgus, *Anglo-American Folk song Scholarship*, 156–167.
34. Bruno Nettl, *The Study of Ethnomusicology*. New York: The Free Press, 1964, 7.
35. Bruno Nettl, *Nettl's Elephant: On the History of Ethnomusicology*. Urbana: University of Illinois Press, 2010, 143.
36. Alan Lomax, John M. Bishop, and Worth W. Long, *The Land Where the Blues Began*. 1-hour, colour documentary film, 1979. www.folkstreams.net/films/land-where-the-blues-began
37. Barry Dornfeld, Jeff Todd Titon, and Tom Rankin, *Powerhouse for God*. 58-minute, 16 mm, colour documentary film. Watertown, MA: Documentary Educational Resources, 1989, and www.folkstreams.net.
38. Goldstein, *A Guide*, 6.
39. See James P. Spradley and David McCurdy, *The Cultural Experience: Ethnography in Complex Society*. Chicago: Science Research Associates, 1971, and James P. Spradley, *The Ethnographic Interview*. New York: Holt, Rinehart and Winston, 1979.
40. Clifford Geertz, 'Thick Description: Toward an Interpretive Theory of Culture'. In Geertz, *The Interpretation of Cultures*, 310–323. New York: Basic Books, 1973.
41. Marcia Herndon and Norma McLeod, *Field Manual for Ethnomusicology*. Norwood, MA: Norwood Editions, 1983, 72–7.
42. Bruce Jackson, *Fieldwork*. Urbana: University of Illinois Press, 1987, 66.
43. Jackson, *Fieldwork*, 65.
44. Such as Henry H. Glassie, *Passing the Time in Ballymenone: Culture and History of an Ulster Community*. Philadelphia: University of Pennsylvania Press, 1982.
45. Jennifer Post, Mary Russell Bucknum, and Laurel Sercombe, *A Manual for Documentation Fieldwork & Preservation for Ethnomusicologists*. Bloomington, IN: Society for Ethnomusicology, 1994, 7.
46. Kip Lornell, *Introducing American Folk Music*. Madison, WI: Brown & Benchmark, 1993, 10.
47. Peter Bartis, *Folklife and Fieldwork: A Layman's Introduction to Field Techniques*. Revised and expanded edition. Washington, DC: Library of Congress, 1990 [1979].
48. Bartis, *Folklife*, 23.
49. Robert Baron and Nicholas R. Spitzer, *Public Folklore*. Washington, DC: Smithsonian Institute, 1992.
50. See Burt Feintuch, *The Conservation of Culture: Folklorists and the Public Sector*. Lexington: University Press of Kentucky, 1988; Mary Hufford, *Conserving Culture: A New Discourse on Heritage*. Urbana: University of Illinois Press, 1994; Jeff Todd Titon, 'Music and Sustainability: An Ecological Viewpoint'. *The World of Music* 51, 1 (2009): 119–137; and Timothy J. Cooley,

ed. *Cultural Sustainabilities: Music, Media, Language, Advocacy*. Urbana: University of Illinois Press, 2019.
51. Titon, *Powerhouse for God*.
52. Luke Eric Lassiter, *The Chicago Guide to Collaborative Ethnography*. Chicago: University of Chicago Press, 2005.
53. Aaron S. Allen and Kevin Dawe, *Current Directions in Ecomusicology*. New York: Routledge, 2016.
54. Jeff Todd Titon, 'Knowing Fieldwork', in *Shadows in the Field: New Perspectives for Fieldwork in Ethnomusicology*, ed. Timothy J. Cooley and Gregory F. Barz, 87–100. New York: Oxford University Press, 1997, 87.
55. *Cooley and Barz, eds., Shadows in the Field*, 4; see also Titon, 'Knowing Fieldwork', 93–7.
56. See Gerald Davis, *'I've Got the Word Within Me and I Can Sing It, You Know': A Study of the Performed African-American Sermon*. Philadelphia: University of Pennsylvania Press, 1987, and Mellonnee Burnim, 'Culture Bearer and Tradition Bearer: An Ethnomusicologist's Research on Black Gospel Music'. *Ethnomusicology* 29, 3 (1985): 432–447.
57. Lisa Gilman and John Fenn, *Handbook for Folklore and Ethnomusicology*. Bloomington: Indiana University Press, 2019.

3 | Folk and the Public Sphere

TIMOTHY HAMPTON

Folk music is public music. It potentially belongs to everyone and circulates across regions, nation-states, and languages. It has always had an especially dynamic relationship to the common world of the small community. Folk songs help circulate the news. They serve as vehicles for the transmission of attitudes towards current events – political upheavals, changes in property, new customs. And they work as safety valves through which actors who pose threats to stable social systems (outlaws, adulterous women, eccentrics) can be located, represented, and given meaning. More grandly, with the onset of the modern world and the rise of new types of media, folk songs can serve important functions in larger communities. We think, for example, of patriotic songs, or satirical songs about elections or public officials. These are songs that can help bind a country together and, even when countries are divided, give one group an insight into the values and cares of the other.

I will suggest in this chapter that the popular role of folk music changed dramatically in the middle years of the twentieth century. In the late 1950s and early 1960s folk suddenly took on new kinds of social meanings, which brought it into the larger political and cultural world in powerful ways. However, just as quickly, I will suggest, its power faded. It changed its meanings yet again and ensconced itself firmly on the edges of popular culture, where it resides today, as a potent but limited political and artistic force. These rapid transformations were linked to new technological inventions, but also to the ways in which public discourse itself changed, opening up a space into which folk songs could take on new importance as vehicles of ethical and moral value. My focus will be principally on the situation in the United States, though many of the points I make here could be adapted to other contexts in the industrialized West as well.

As a background to this story, we need to recall the concept of the 'Public Sphere', first developed by the German philosopher Jürgen Habermas. Habermas's 1962 doctoral thesis was translated into English in 1989 as *The Structural Transformation of the Public Sphere: An Inquiry into a Category of Bourgeois Society*. Habermas's thesis was that in the eighteenth century in Europe there came into being a new space, outside of both the court societies and the ecclesiastical spheres that had shaped ideas over the preceding centuries. That new space was the space of conversation, of debate and ideas. Through the emergence of this space, in Habermas's formulation, many of the great values and themes of bourgeois modernity were worked out.[1]

Habermas's argument, which has been much debated by historians and philosophers since its publication, is useful for thinking about popular music because it is an argument about space and the media. Bourgeois modernity, he suggests, could not have happened without the rise of new spaces for the production of culture and thought – the coffee house or the public meeting hall where intellectuals and politicians could test ideas, away from the authority of the State or the Church.

Along with these new spaces came new media. The bourgeois 'public sphere' could not have emerged without the influence of the new genre of the newspaper, and, in England, such magazines as *The Tatler* and *The Spectator*. These publications helped found an entire mediascape of print culture that would become ever more extensive in the following two centuries.[2] I will argue that the new technology of the long-playing record both brought folk music to a new listening audience and, by virtue of the combinations of ideas that it expressed, in effect created a discursive space in which political ideas, moral attitudes, and musical expression were intimately intertwined. By the mid-1960s, it was not possible to think about progressive political action without thinking about folk music, nor was it possible to listen to folk without considering its political implications.

In the early twentieth century, the media that Habermas had linked to the rise of the Enlightenment public sphere underwent a transformation, first through silent film, and then through the invention of recorded sound. The early decades of the new century were marked by the explosion of recorded music – symphonic music, popular crooners, jazz. Folk music found its place in the margins of the media world, along with the blues and what came to be called 'race records'. These quasi-ethnographic recordings were later scooped up by eager white urban collectors interested in documenting the life of the rural outback in North America and, to a lesser degree, Western Europe. The first overlapping between what might be called 'folk' music and a broader listening public came in the American South. Its emblems were two artists. Beginning in 1927 the Carter Family issued a series of recorded traditional songs taken largely from Appalachia for a southern and rural audience. In the same year, a Mississippi-born singer named Jimmie Rodgers began recording original songs, billing himself as 'The Singing Brakeman'.

By the end of the decade, he had moved to Texas and rebranded himself as a singing cowboy.

Thus, folk music, when it was recorded, was first linked to regional identity. It stood largely on the edges of official culture, ignored by major magazines and newspapers. Popular in the South and West, it remained, for much of the country, a kind of ethnographic curiosity in a land still dramatically divided along regional lines – a country in which people from the Northeast and people from the South could sometimes scarcely understand each other's accents.[3]

The Greenwich Village Legacy

This situation began to change in the early years of the 1940s. The Great Depression of the 1930s had displaced thousands of people, among them singers. Many working-class performers found themselves traveling the country and, inevitably, coming into contact with all kinds of music, which they collected, changed, and disseminated. This social displacement resulted in the emergence of a left-wing musical establishment in Greenwich Village, a neighbourhood of New York City. There, young singers with progressive political views – often directly linked to the labour union movement or vaguely linked to the American Communist Party – began to promote collective music along with progressive politics. Their assumption was that traditional or folk music constituted the authentic voice of a disenfranchised working class. They aimed to disseminate that music, and in particular any songs that had a political bite to them. From this movement came several notable groups. The first was the Almanac Singers, named for the Almanac House on West Tenth Street. The group was founded by pacifist and isolationist Lee Hays and featured, among others, the Oklahoma-born songwriter Woody Guthrie and the Harvard-educated aristocrat Pete Seeger. For the Almanacs, politics and music were inseparable. Their activities soon narrowed into the more focused approach of a single folk-singing quartet named The Weavers, founded in 1948, which brought Seeger together with Hays, Fred Kellerman, and Ronnie Gilbert. The quartet blended elegant harmony, guitar, banjo, and a dynamic upbeat performance style, hitting it big with 'Tzena, Tzena, Tzena', an adaptation of an Israeli song, backed with 'Irene Goodnight' by the convicted but paroled convict Huddie Ledbetter, known as Lead Belly. Their success was short-lived, however; as the 1950s unfolded under the shadow of the anti-Communist blacklist and McCarthyism, they were driven from the airwaves and the stage. Seeger left the group and began working on his own, playing for peanuts in union halls and churches.[4]

The Weavers' attempt to blend politics and music evoked a paradox that has inflected the entry of folk music into the larger entertainment world: whereas their songs were traditional and simple sounding, their performance style was extremely well polished and much rehearsed. If the 'folk culture' they were bringing to public attention was simple and singable, their version of it was commercially appealing and slick.

The model of The Weavers – traditional music, musical excellence, and a down-home attitude – had a powerful impact on subsequent musicians. A performance by Seeger in Palo Alto, California, in 1956 was viewed by Stanford undergraduate Dave Guard and high school student Joan Baez, both of whom were inspired to turn to folk music in the Seeger mold. It was Guard who had the first success, with a pair of friends, billing themselves as The Kingston Trio. Their three-part harmony singing on the Civil War murder and adultery ballad 'Tom Dooley' resulted in a radio hit that changed the face of American popular music.

'Tom Dooley' was successful in no small measure because of its lyrical complexity. The refrain, 'Hang down your head', was a double-entendre play on the idea of shame at sin and criminality, on the one hand, and, on the other, on the literal fact that the hero is about to be hanged. It was pitched through two viewpoints: the first-person story of the doomed narrator in the verses and the third-person perspective of the chorus, voiced either by Dooley – now alienated from himself – or by some omniscient communal voice. You could enter into the song without inhabiting it too intimately. It told a fragmentary story of a love triangle, punctuated by images of the frontier as a place of escape and small-town life as a place of betrayal and doom.

Two features of the Kingston Trio's approach to folk music are worth noting here. First, and most obvious, they showed that simple music played on traditional instruments (guitar, banjo, tenor guitar) could compete with both the Nelson Riddle–inspired orchestral arrangements of commercial pop and the electric guitars of early rock and roll. They brought to the attention of a mainstream, largely white, record-buying public a kind of music that could be easily followed, if not reproduced. You probably can't sing like Frank Sinatra, but you can sing 'Tom Dooley' yourself. The song made everyone a potential folk singer, breaking down the barrier between professional and amateur. Second, the play with familiarity and unfamiliarity evoked in the distant story of 'the eternal triangle' (as the introduction put it) extended to the Kingston Trio's albums. They set traditional

American folk music in dialogue with songs from around the world usually sung in English or in some blend of English and another tongue. Dave Guard himself had lived in Hawai'i and was attentive to 'exotic' musical traditions – reflected in the name of his group, which hinted at some connection to Jamaica and calypso music. World War II was still a recent memory. It had resulted in tens of thousands of young men and women spending significant time in other countries. The Kingston Trio's song selections reflected that diversity and mediated the differences by recasting everything from Mexican border songs to African chants as 'American Folk Music'. It was music that perfectly caught the blend of a new eclecticism and whitewashed blandness that corresponded to the late-Eisenhower years, in which American military power and economic clout were overtaking the planet – with a period of cultural domination soon to follow. The Kingston Trio brought folk music to the attention of a musical public raised on the big-band music of the War Years, or the post-War pop of Mitch Miller and Doris Day. Folk music, as played by the Kingston Trio, was different, but similarly unthreatening to a status quo of station wagons and suburban ideals.[5]

A Countercultural Public Sphere

The marginality of folk music began to evaporate in 1959 with the first Newport Folk Festival, held in the summer vacation spot of Newport, Rhode Island. The program included the Kingston Trio and Pete Seeger, but also southern white musicians such as the Stanley Brothers, and Black blues and folk musicians such as Memphis Slim, and Sonny Terry and Brownie McGhee. The diversity of programming created the impression that folk music was a kind of universal force that could move from region to region, race to race. The same year, the young Joan Baez, based no longer in California but now in the college town of Cambridge, Massachusetts, made her recording début on an anthology album featuring several singers from her milieu. The following year, 1960, she released her first album, which bore her name as its title, and featured an eclectic selection of songs – English ballads, Scottish songs, a Carter Family tune, an adapted Yiddish folk song, and a song in Spanish.

What is important to note in considering these developments is the function of the folk music album as a kind of space of juxtaposition. Baez took songs from everywhere. The new technology of the long-playing record made possible dialogues between songs that otherwise would never be set together. For a singer like Baez, this strategy of selection and juxtaposition had a show business aspect. It created the persona of the folk singer as a kind of vehicle through which music from all countries could be heard. Through the clever juxtaposition of different kinds of songs the singer was created as a media figure, a star, a celebrity whose talent consisted in bringing different musical examples together through heartfelt interpretations. What do, say, 'Donna, Donna' (a Yiddish folk song) and 'El Preso Numero Nueve' (a prison song by the Mexican composer Roberto Cantoral) have in common? Only the fact that Baez has sung them on a single album. Baez's celebrity, coupled with her status as a solo figure – her striking looks, long black hair and single guitar – presented her as a mediator, a vessel of melodies from times past. This image contrasted with an idea of folk music as a music generated by communities, handed down from generation to generation. In such a communitarian tradition, it would make sense that music should be brought to the public's attention by groups of vocalists, singing in harmony, as did The Weavers and the Kingston Trio. They sang together pleasingly as all well-meaning people should sing together (though perhaps with better pitch). By contrast, for Baez the point of folk music was the generation of sincerity. She stood alone on the stage, facing her audience and carrying the weight of history, like an existentialist hero or a jazz musician embarked on an adventurous solo.

Baez emerged at the precise moment of the encounter between the folk music community and a somewhat different sub-culture – the so-called Beat Generation. Jack Kerouac's 1957 novel *On the Road* had invented a new type of American hobo. No longer refugees from the Dust Bowl (like the singing Woody Guthrie), Kerouac's characters were on an existential quest. College educated, self-conscious, they weren't looking for work, they were looking for kicks, and for the meaning of life. Their music of choice was the Bebop jazz of Charlie Parker and Dizzy Gillespie, with its improvisatory freedom and excesses in both life and art. Thus, superficially, the Beat Generation had nothing in common with folk music traditions. And yet, here again, geography matters. Greenwich Village's history as a space of dropouts and non-conformists placed 'Beatniks' in close proximity to the more focused sub-culture of left-wing folk music. Folk music coffee houses and jazz clubs were often literally across the street from each other. Both cultures shared a disdain for the monochromatic surface of mainstream American culture during the Eisenhower years, and both were looking for forms of revolt. For the Old Left of the folk music culture, it involved collective political action against economic and racial injustice. In the case of the Beats, it involved personal transformation through study,

Figure 3.1 Joan Baez at an anti-draft demonstration in Central Park, New York City, 1968. Photograph by Bernard Gotfryd. Library of Congress.

narcotics, and travel. Yet they lived side-by-side in Greenwich Village, which soon became a theater, of sorts, to which youth from Uptown or the suburban areas around New York would gravitate for an experience of non-conformist freedom. Washington Square Park, on the edge of Greenwich Village, emerged as a space in which young people could congregate to play music. A lively coffee house culture sprang up on MacDougal and Bleeker Streets, where people of all ages could listen to music, consume various stimulants, and, presumably, discuss ideas. Thus, we see the beginnings of a new, sub-cultural version of Habermas's 'Public Sphere'.[6]

The paradoxes that shaped Baez's rise – she sang songs that 'belonged' to everyone but in a voice that no one else could match – were heightened with the emergence of her protégé and partner Bob Dylan. Dylan dropped out of college in Minnesota and travelled to Greenwich Village, ostensibly to meet Woody Guthrie, but, more grandly, to make his way as a folk singer. Dylan took up and developed almost beyond recognition Baez's idea of the folk singer as persona. He presented himself as a man of great mystery, claiming to have been a runaway who had been kicked out of his parents' home and who had ridden the rails and worked in a carnival. None of it was true. He was an upper-middle-class Jewish kid who had discovered folk music in college. But his rough-looking presentation blended the anti-establishment individualism of the Beats with the musical simplicity and proletarian rebelliousness of the left-wing folk music movement. Dylan absorbed features of both of these small cultures and integrated them into his persona.[7]

The truth or falsity of Dylan's self-creation became moot when he began writing his own songs. His earliest songs were in imitation of Guthrie – original lyrics set to melodies by other singers. This was, in a sense, the folk tradition. However, by the time of his second album, 1962's *The Freewheelin' Bob Dylan*, Dylan had developed a character whose voice and appearance made him a star who could bring folk music into the public world in an important way. He quickly moved from writing songs about his 'ramblin'' to songs of social and even political protest.

Yet for folk music to reach a broader public it needed a vehicle that was, like the Kingston Trio, both appealingly hip and non-threatening to the entertainment industry. The breakthrough came with Dylan's 1962 song 'Blowin' in the Wind', which was quickly picked up by Peter, Paul, and Mary, a Greenwich Village folk trio that replaced the Kingston Trio as the darlings of the college-educated listening public. Taken from the melody of an old slave lament, 'No More Auction Block', the song was about racial inequality and war. It spoke poetically about the evils of the world and asked the listener to contemplate his or her own situation. 'How many times can you turn your head away from injustice?' it asked. It offered no answers, but, precisely because of its ambiguity, it became an all-purpose protest song – just as, earlier, the punning 'Tom Dooley' had become an all-purpose song of lost love for the post-Sinatra generation. Peter, Paul, and Mary made Dylan's song into a massive hit. For the first time, folk music entered the public world – not only as entertainment, but as a force for moral and even political change.

Songs such as 'Blowin' in the Wind' took familiar melodies – or melodies that were so simple as to seem familiar – and equipped them with ideas reflecting the controversies of the moment. No less than the ideas of the French Enlightenment that Jürgen Habermas located in the bourgeois public sphere of the eighteenth century, the ideas and attitudes embodied in Dylan's writing offered a vocabulary through which public discussion and debate might take place. His version of 'folk music' both reflected changing attitudes and powered them. Because the music was accessible and easy for even amateurs to produce, it took on a visceral character that the abstractions of political ideology alone lacked. It located politics in the body, and in an exchange of voices.

But the magic of Dylan's appeal and power was only partly linked to the songs themselves. Equally important were his persona and language. The uneasy proximity of the Beatniks and the folk music sub-culture finally found a kind of incarnation in Dylan's voice and self-presentation. And that self-presentation was generational. Woody Guthrie and Cisco Houston had wandered the country in the 1930s. They had lived in labour camps and their songs of protest reflected a solidarity with the working people whom they had seen suffer. But Guthrie and Houston were old, out of date. Dylan offered a role model or mirror to a young, increasingly restless, affluent youth culture invested in the liberal politics of the newly elected president John F. Kennedy. His songs about his travels gave voice to a hunger, not for stability or a job (the preoccupations of the Dust Bowl generation), but for experience, kicks, art – the preoccupations of the Beats. Dylan's songs were political, but they were not about miners' strikes or union solidarity; they were about changing the world in the age of nuclear fear and the Civil Rights movement. His solidarity was with other people in his generation. That generational identity was a new phenomenon in American popular culture.

Central to Dylan's construction of a new song culture that could bring folk music into the public sphere was his curious use of language. His songs often drew on old melodies, so they felt familiar, even as the themes were completely contemporary. The diction, however, was often archaic. He used phrases that were knowingly out of date ('carry yourself back to me unspoiled', 'to tie up the time most forcefully'). This blending of old language and new themes made the songs feel contemporary, but not merely topical or journalistic. Moreover, he drew on regional expressions and vocabulary from a vast range of social groups. His nasal singing voice suggested that he might be from Oklahoma or Texas, and he laced his lyrics with linguistic features that hinted at a rural upbringing. Subject and predicate were often out of agreement in his songs ('by the old wooden stove our hats was hung'), and he bandied about contractions associated with a 'hillbilly' personality—'if'n', 'ain't', 'yes'n'. Yet these ruralisms were counterbalanced with political, poetic, and philosophical pronouncements that suggested someone who was deeply literate and sophisticated in his thinking, more a graduate student than a plowman: 'The land that I live in has God on its side', 'Somebody better investigate soon', 'Like the stillness in the wind before the hurricane begins.'

This linguistic wizardry stands in contrast with the approach of an earlier singer such as Seeger. Across the 1950s and early 1960s, Seeger had been more or less deliberately establishing a canon of 'American' songs, bringing the distinct regions and cultures of the country together with such recordings as *American Folk Songs for Children* (1953), *American Industrial Ballads* (1956), and *American Favorite Ballads* (5 volumes, 1957–62). His response to the cultural conformity of the Eisenhower years and the Red Baiting of McCarthyism had been to build up, brick by brick, an image of America that was both unified and diverse, in song. This contrasted with the tradition of ethnographic field recordings that registered the songs of a specific place or tradition. Dylan rendered this aspect of Seeger's work obsolete by simply taking on the linguistic affectations of the entire country, singing one moment like a Black man from the South and another moment like a cowboy from the West.[8]

Dylan's reinvention of the folk song tradition in a contemporary context helped bring folk music not only into a general 'popular' world, but also into the theoretically defined 'public sphere' imagined by Habermas. His emphasis on contemporary social themes through the manipulation of traditional song forms was soon followed by other singers and songwriters. Singers such as Phil Ochs and Richard Fariña (who worked with Baez's sister, Mimi) introduced songs that drew on traditional folk motifs but pushed their way into a larger popular sphere. These figures, along with the massively popular Peter, Paul, and Mary, targeted a largely white youth audience raised on pop music but concerned about civil rights and the increasing American involvement in Vietnam.[9]

The insertion of folk into the broader popular sphere reached a kind of apotheosis in August of 1963, when 250,000 people assembled in Washington, DC, on the steps of the Lincoln Memorial to listen to the Reverend Martin Luther King, Jr. deliver his famous 'I Have a Dream' speech. There was entertainment at that famous gathering, as well as oratory, and the program offered an emblem of the newly dynamic presence of folk music in American culture and politics. Black singers Mahalia Jackson and Marian Anderson sang spirituals. Peter, Paul, and Mary sang 'Blowin' in the Wind' and Seeger's pacifist anthem 'If I Had a Hammer'. Baez sang 'We Shall Overcome'. Accompanied by Baez, Dylan sang 'When the Ship Comes In', a song about social change, and 'Only a Pawn in Their Game', a controversial song about the power dynamics that shaped southern society and enabled the assassination of the civil rights leader Medgar Evers.

With the March on Washington (officially titled 'The March on Washington for Jobs and Freedom') folk music emerged as a force in shaping the discourse of the public sphere. It was essential to the moment. The ideas being presented in speeches were also present in the songs, in musical phrases that listeners knew by heart. This was quite different from, say, Duke Ellington performing for the president. The songs were a force in the moment, creating the community that shaped the event. The seamless juxtaposition of 'original', composed folk-like songs with traditional tunes such as 'He's Got the Whole World in His Hands' (performed by Anderson), alternating with speeches by important political leaders, reasserted the power of an American folk tradition and its ability to renew itself at a time of political and social change. Rarely has music seemed so old and so new at the same time. The capaciousness of the folk music tradition, its forms and elastic language, disseminated through the new technology of the long-playing record and given pointed messages by writers such as Dylan located the music at the centre of American political and social change.

Beyond the mere thematic importance of folk music as a social force, the social dynamics of the folk movement also played a role. The voices that Seeger had promoted in his own anthology records had a sociopolitical implication. The return by young singers to traditional American music meant a return to the tradition of Black music and, inevitably, to the rediscovery and re-valorizing of the work of many long-forgotten, under-appreciated and, in many cases, exploited Black musicians. Thus in the wings of the folk music boom there came a blues revival that saw figures such as Mississippi John Hurt, Son House, and Sonny Terry and Brownie McGhee playing to white, college-educated audiences. These performances offered a practical demonstration of the importance of the kind of racial integration that the Civil Rights movement was pushing. They offered a public manifestation of the centrality of Black culture to American identity at a time when Blacks were struggling to be heard and noticed. At the same time, of course, by virtue of the medium and the institutions shaping performance, they presented a distanced, nostalgic version of Black music – not urban soul, but rural blues from an agrarian culture that was nearly extinct.[10]

Without attempting to account for the complex and rich history of British folk music (which is beyond the scope of this chapter) we can nonetheless note that something similar took place in the United Kingdom and on the European continent at the same time. The late-'50s vogue for skiffle music had brought to the attention of young people a tradition of uncommercialized, unpolished performance. Lonnie Donegan, the most popular of the skiffle players, brought American folk music to a British public with such songs as Lead Belly's 'Midnight Special'. At the same time, the American blues musician Big Bill Broonzy toured Europe and introduced European crowds to a sophisticated blend of guitar wizardry, dynamic singing, and rich lyrics. As the sixties unfolded, the British scene saw the rediscovery of its own history, as such singers as Martin Carthy and Ewan MacColl emerged to bring the world of traditional English, Scottish, Irish, and Welsh music to a more popular audience. Something similar happened in France, with the work of such regionally identified performers as Alain Stivell, and, later, in Italy with the Nuova Compagnia di Canto Populare. Here, as in the case of the blues revival in the United States, the power of folk music to shape the public world lay less with the thematic content of new 'folk songs' than with the sheer presence of new voices and songs pushing their way into the realm of popular entertainment. European singers, after all, laboured less under the pressure of Vietnam and grew up far from the stain of racism that tainted the United States.[11] Moreover, the geographical density of European spaces and the traditions of pub and café culture made possible the emergence of circuits for folk music performance.[12]

Back in the States, Dylan's discontent with middle-class values and his self-presentation as a rambling, traveling hobo figure opened another front in the popular expansion of folk music. This was a body of writing about disaffected youth, about the alienation of the young from their parents. Dylan's own attacks on the 'Establishment' (in songs like 'The Times they are a-Changin"') were matched and extended in the work of writers such as Paul Simon, whose massively popular composition 'The Sound of Silence' fronted an entire raft of songs about youthful alienation. Simon honed his craft in England, working with traditional musicians who played English folk music. But he made his name by venturing into a zone of middle-class discomfort. Central to his rise was his 1965 reworking of the traditional English song 'Scarborough Fair', which he had learned from Martin Carthy. He skilfully blended the ageless lament about longing and love in an agrarian culture with a counter-melody, called 'Canticle', that offered an anti-war message. The contrast between traditional values and contemporary social upheaval was embodied in the very technique of the recording, which dubbed one melody over the other. Elsewhere, on the same LP, 1966's *Parsley, Sage, Rosemary and Thyme*, Simon and his partner Art Garfunkel sang the Christmas carol 'Silent Night' against a fake newscast that mentioned Vietnam, congressional hearings in Washington, and the drug overdose of the comedian Lenny Bruce. What Dylan achieved through his persona and voice – the alienated rambler who spoke the truth to straight society – Simon did through the technology of the recording itself, which could present different voices and set them in dialogue.

Folk Rock and Fragmentation

This new manipulation of technology to update traditional musical forms was important and influential. For Dylan, the break with a 'folk' format came in July of 1965 at the Newport Folk Festival, when he famously performed with an electric guitar and offered opaque lyrics sung to melodies rooted in the electric Chicago-blues tradition rather than in rural folk music. However, folk music had already been transformed a month earlier, in June, when a California group called The Byrds scored a massive popular hit with Dylan's song 'Mr. Tambourine Man'. They slowed the folky, ballad-like song, which was built on the repetitive structures of traditional music, down from 2/4 time to 4/4 time and backed the vocal with a chiming twelve-string electric guitar. Dylan's version of the song was received as folk music, but the Byrds' version was rock.

Perhaps it is the emergence of the Byrds, more than Dylan's own transformation into an electric blues musician, that recast the role of folk music in the popular space. The first Byrds album, named after their hit song, also featured several Dylan 'protest songs', a Seeger song about a miners' strike, and several self-penned love songs. Their second album, *Turn, Turn, Turn*, released quickly after the first, was named for Seeger's musical setting to the Book of Ecclesiastes, offering age-old wisdom about time and fate, and ending with a plea for peace that could not have been mistaken by listeners in the Vietnam era. It featured Stephen Foster's 'Oh Susanna' (a classic American folk song if there ever was one), Red Hayes's spiritual 'Satisfied Mind', and a set of Dylan tunes. Yet the music was, like Simon's, so cleverly produced that any political messages embedded in the lyrics were bled away into the sonic surface of what was clearly pop music. Journalists called it 'folk rock'.[13]

It is no accident that the advent of folk rock and the triumph of bands like The Byrds came directly on the heels of such high-minded political events as The March on Washington. The liberal politics represented in such large assemblies – to be followed by ever more frequent rounds of demonstrations and marches across the decade – offered an example of a broadly based coalition politics, in which activists of all races could blend their voices and ideals in expectation of a new future. In the realm of music, bands such as The Byrds took songs that had been traditionally circulated by villagers or isolated singers in labour camps and union halls and blended them with the rock-and-roll instrumentation and sensibility that had been popularized by such singers as Elvis Presley and Carl Perkins in the 1950s. Rock and roll, which had always had a rebellious spirit, was now seamlessly intertwined with lyrics and melodies that seemed to come from some much earlier, collective experience. A classic case was Seeger's solemn account of the failure of the 1926 General Strike, 'The Bells of Rhymney', taken from the writing of the Welsh Poet Idris Davies published in 1938 – itself based on an old children's nursery rhyme, but put to an easily singable, anthem-like melody by Seeger. The Byrds made it a tune you could dance to. In this way politically themed folk music, imported from another country, was wound together with American rock-and-roll instrumentation and performed by men whose hair and clothing imitated The Beatles.

But this wasn't folk music as imaged by the Greenwich Village underground. It was a kind of neutralization of the revolutionary creativity and communitarian energy of folk music for a commercial world of rock, enabled by the new technology of the LP and given authority by Dylan's example. Dylan's initial approach of skilfully grafting new lyrics onto old melodies (which both Seeger and Woody Guthrie had been doing for years), had given way to albums that blended original compositions with 'folk songs', and then, finally, to albums consisting only of original compositions. The communitarian values of folk music were subsumed into the massive popularity of rock, which invented a new global village of consumers, even as rock musicians began to drift away from the folk traditions that had powered the rise of folk rock in the first place. Singers such as Baez and Peter, Paul, and Mary continued to record, but often in pseudo-rock settings, featuring collections of songs by different songwriters in a folk-rock vein – Tim Hardin, John Denver, Jackson Browne.[14]

Where, then, did folk music go? It split into pieces. At one level, it evolved into what can only be called a style, a mode of performance that showcased acoustic instruments, unamplified performances and, often, collective 'sing-along' gatherings. As the 1960s came to an end, the political energy emblematized in the 1963 March on Washington was fragmented. The Civil Rights movement for equality among the races was left reeling after the assassination of King. Its claims were complicated by the emergence of other types of groups asking for equality – women's groups, indigenous groups, immigrant groups, gay groups. These groups re-invented the relationship between folk music and the popular world. To the extent that a public sphere of the type envisioned by Habermas continued to exist around music, it was given voice, on the left, by rock music, or, on the right, by a commercialized version of old southern and Appalachian music that was now dubbed 'country and western', and then, simply, 'country'. And yet, within this splintering, paradoxically, folk took on a newly important role as a marker of political and social identity. What you listened to – or sang – became one of the defining characteristics of your relationship to the public sphere. By the middle years of the 1970s, an entirely new body of locally based folk music had emerged, serving small groups of activists with specific goals. The emergence of 'women's music' (Chris Williamson, Meg Christian) or of Native American music (Buffy Sainte-Marie, the poet Joy Harjo), may stand as markers of this newly fragmented but vital musical culture.

At the same time, the deeply historical roots of folk found their reinvention in another form of music that came to be called 'Americana'. It started, again, with Dylan, who holed up in Woodstock, New York, in the late 1960s and began playing daily with a group of mostly Canadian R & B musicians who had backed him during a recent tour. This group, now dubbed The Band, emerged to revolutionize the rock world in 1968 with their album *Music from Big Pink*. The Band sounded 'authentic', even 'folkish', but they were not folk musicians. They performed in a style that recalled early twentieth-century field recordings of ragtime, blues, and country music. But the songs were original, contemporary, composed by the group. In this regard they exactly reversed the approach of the Byrds, who took old songs and recorded them in a new style. The Band took new songs and pretended they were old. It was a marvellously successful approach and spawned an entire wing of the musical field carried on by such later musicians as Gillian Welch and the band Wilco.[15]

Thus, the emergence of folk as a driving force in the public arena has a specific history, linked to the new technology of the LP and to the geographical proximity of diverse sub-cultures in New York at the end of the 1950s. For half a decade, folk was the vehicle through which the discourse of the popular found its vocabulary and sound. In this regard it was operating as 'shared' music, as it had done for decades in traditional societies. It flourished and expanded through the juxtaposition of Beat anti-authoritarianism and left-wing politics. Yet through this expansion the music was swallowed up by the new commercialization of rock. And whereas folk music had stimulated conversation and creativity in small communities early in the 1960s, one might even see a homology between the high-volume sonic chaos of the rock explosion and the chaos that overtook youth culture in the last years of that decade, draining it of its political direction. Folk music, by contrast, was a music of conversation and community and, in its dominant moment, had created a new kind of public sphere. Following the disintegration of this culture of conversation, folk music was displaced by the culture of spectacle that we associate with rock, before finding its current niche on the edges of the public world, in small communities of like-minded listeners.

Within the emerging culture of spectacle, folk made one final statement. In 1967, a duo of comedians called the Smothers Brothers were given a prime-time program on CBS Television. Their approach to comedy involved them presenting themselves as harmonizing folk singers, in the mold of the Kingston Trio. In a typical sketch they would launch into a folk song, only to become derailed by the fumbling member of the duo, Tom Smothers, who would conveniently forget lyrics, or go off topic. As his brother Dick struggled to get the song back on track the two would engage in banter about family, social mores and, increasingly, about politics. In this way, they used comedy to make folk music relevant to a generation being raised on rock. Whereas Paul Simon and the Byrds had used the recording studio as a tool to update folk music, the Smothers Brothers used the vehicle of television – the newly dominant media form. Their 'Comedy Hour' quickly became one of the most watched programmes in America, bringing folk music to millions of viewers and – more importantly – using it as a springboard for the kind of political commentary that singers like Guthrie and Seeger had only dreamed of. As the Vietnam War heated up, they sharpened their pacifist message. A high point came in 1967 when they invited Seeger, who had long been blacklisted from mainstream television, to return to the airwaves and sing a song in protest of the War. Not everyone was happy, however, and the Smothers Brothers soon found themselves at odds with corporate bosses who tried to tone down their political content. Eventually, CBS cancelled the show, censoring the Smothers Brothers and their folk-based entertainment at the height of its popularity.

The Smothers Brothers brought to the fore the paradoxes implicit in Habermas's idea of the public sphere. If the bourgeois public sphere emerged in concert with the new media of the newspaper and the political pamphlet, folk music came to the mainstream of culture in the West through the medium of the long-playing record. As recorded sound became a dominant form of artistic reproduction and circulation, the often-subversive traditions of folk music were placed at odds with the tools of capitalism. When folk exploded onto the scene of television, its disruptive potential became a threat to the very medium through which it was circulated, and it was silenced.[16]

Notes

1. Jürgen Habermas, *The Structural Transformation of the Public Sphere: An Inquiry into a Category of Bourgeois Society*, trans. Thomas Burger and Frederick Lawrence. Cambridge, MA: MIT Press, 1989. Habermas's discussions of 'institutions' in Chapter 5 are especially useful for thinking about music. An excellent expansion of Habermas's ideas is Alan McKee, *The Public Sphere: An Introduction*. Cambridge: Cambridge University Press, 2005.
2. For critiques and appreciations of Habermas, see Mike Hill and Warren Montag, ed., *Masses, Classes, and the Public Sphere*. London: Verso, 2000; of particular interest here is Stanley Aronowitz, 'Unions as Counter-Public Spheres', 83–102.
3. For a good account of this early recording history see Peter Doyle, *Echo and Reverb: Fabricating Space in Popular Music Recording 1900–1960*. Middletown, CT: Wesleyan University Press, 2005, Chapter 3.
4. On The Weavers and the Almanac Singers, see Jesse Jarnow, *Wasn't That a Time: The Weavers, the Blacklist, and the Battle for the Soul of America*. New York: Da Capo Press, 2018, and Robert Cantwell, *When We Were Good: The Folk Revival*. Cambridge, MA: Harvard University Press, 1996.
5. For an account of the Kingston Trio's beginnings see Cantwell, *When We Were Good*, 316.
6. The classic meditation on the intersection of 'beatness' and African American culture, in the context of a post-war search for meaning, is Norman Mailer's 1957 essay 'The White Negro'. *Dissent* 4 (1957): 276–93.
7. For a good discussion of Dylan and the Beat Generation, see Sean Wilentz, *Bob Dylan in America*. New York: Vintage, 2010, Chapter 2.
8. On Dylan's linguistic inventiveness and its social implications, see Timothy Hampton, *Bob Dylan, How the Songs Work*. New York: Zone Books, 2019, Chapter 2.
9. This history and context have been admirably chronicled by David Haidu in *Positively Fourth Street: The Lives and Times of Joan Baez, Bob Dylan, Mimi Baez Fariña and Richard Fariña*. New York: North Point Press, 2011.
10. Also important here is Harry Smith's three-volume *Anthology of American Folk Music*, released in 1952.
11. This is not to suggest that the European scene was free of its own exclusions; see Angeline Morrison's chapter in this volume on the erasure of Black British folk music.
12. On skiffle see Billy Bragg, *Roots, Radicals, and Rockers: How Skiffle Changed the World*. London: Faber and Faber, 2017. On the British folk scene see Jan Leman's film *Acoustic Routes*. London: Leman Productions, 2013. DVD. On the Italian history see Giuseppe Morandi, *Spoleto 1964 Bella Ciao Il Diario*

(cited in Alessandro Portelli, *Bob Dylan, Oral Cultures, and the Meaning of History*. New York: Columbia University Press, 2022, 138).

13. A collection of critics' writing on this transformation can be found in Dave Laing, et al., *The Electric Muse: The Story of Folk into Rock*. London: Methuen, 1975.
14. On the 'myth' of community in rock see Simon Frith, "The Magic That Can Set You Free": The Ideology of Folk and the Myth of the Rock Community'. *Popular Music* 1 (1981): 159–68.
15. On Dylan and The Band see Greil Marcus, *The Old Weird America: The World of Bob Dylan's Basement Tapes*. New York: Picador, 2011. More broadly, see W. J. T. Mitchell, ed., *Art and the Public Sphere*. Chicago: University of Chicago Press, 1992.
16. For the full story of the conflicts between CBS and the Smothers Brothers, see David Bianculli, *Dangerously Funny: The Uncensored Story of the 'Smothers Brothers Comedy Hour'*. New York: Touchstone Books, 2010.

4 | Towards a Critical Folk Music Studies

BRAHMA PRAKASH

The practice of folk music in South Asia in most cases cannot be separated from its embodied song and performance culture; my reference to folk music in this chapter therefore always connotes folk music and song together. We also need to recognize that folk music is very much a part of the active social and cultural life in this region. Elsewhere I have argued how divisions based on dance, music, and theatre create a spatial and temporal hierarchy and perpetuate hierarchical values concerning aesthetic and cultural taste.[1] In most cases, folk and Indigenous performances are discussed using the discourse of ritual and community studies whereas urban elite and middle-class performances are discussed from the perspectives of colonialism, democracy, and citizenship. Folk music always has broader connotations that overspill its boundaries. It is always about music *and . . . something else*: music and ritual, music and dance, music and poetry, music and the social, and so on.

In this chapter, I offer what I would like to term a critical-creative perspective to understand folk music, its meaning, and its affect in India and the South Asian context. Taking a leaf from Antonio Gramsci and Stephen Gencarella, I propose critical folk culture studies (or, in this case, critical folk music studies). Critical, here, 'concerns the active pursuit of emancipation from oppression, the recognition and address of domination and privilege, and the promotion of democratic social change, akin to the intercessory work of, for example, critical cultural studies, critical ethnography and critical pedagogy'.[2] Gencarella has suggested and raised 'the possibility that the production of criticism and critique would be an essential component for robust critical folklore studies'.[3] To take folk music from 'uncritical' and apolitical 'descriptive' studies to critical studies, this chapter seeks to make a few moves that would ask the reader to rethink the conventional relationship through which folk music is understood. Thinking through the examples of performance practices of folk music – ranging from ritual and community-based singing to the songs and music composed by travelling troupes to its mediatized presence in popular media platforms – this chapter examines some key aspects of folk music in India. It also examines the problems with existing scholarship that tend to undermine or idealize the notion of folk music without locating the folk in society. Critical folk music studies would aim to situate folk music in relation not only to social cohesion and integrity but also fracture and erasure.

Is there a performance practice of folk music in India? What makes some performance practices 'classical' and others 'folk'? These questions elicit sharp responses from performers, practitioners, and scholars alike in South Asia. These responses are based on questions of skill, knowledge, rigour, corporeality, genealogy, encounters with modernity, nationality, patronage systems, and various other factors. I examine some of these in what follows. I have discussed the problems of performances described as 'folk' in my previous work on cultural labour.[4] Is folk performance a product of modernity? Is there even a genre called folk music? If so, what was the nature of its practices? Did it exist or is it all a construction? My focus here is on understanding what is special about the practices that differentiate folk from other forms of music making.

The chapter has three broad aims. First, it aims to ground folk music in relation to the socio-cultural and performance practices of South Asia – in a way, provincializing its approach and decolonizing the methods of study. Second, it aims to enter these debates through performance practice. Third, it aims to revisit and undo some of the categories of folk music based on preconceived images. The point is to bring the study of folk music under the spectrum of socio-political and aesthetic understanding. How do we develop categories that provide an emancipatory discourse and also open up the field of study? How do we discuss folk music that moves 'folk' from a descriptive category to an analytical category? Finally, the chapter tries to situate folk as a mode of critique – part of common sense but also a critique of common sense. As social and imaginative practices, folk performances are part of everyday life. Is it possible to think of the practice of folk music itself as critique? The first part of the chapter tries to situate folk music in relation to its performance practice and the second part tries to see it as a body of critique – reversing the gear in which folk music creates a point of difference in relation to classical, popular, and other genres and practices of music. Folk is viewed in direct relation to classical and modern music, and often in opposition. If classical music is about ordering, formalizing, and rationalizing, folk music is seen as a negative formulation or in juxtaposition: it is spontaneous, informal, disorderly, and not standardized and aestheticized enough. The comparisons go further, in which classical becomes a site of rigour and the modern a site of knowledge, with folk bereft, having neither rigour nor faculty of knowledge.

Knowing that geographical and community experiences play a vital role in shaping such perspectives, I locate my analysis in the folk music practices of north India, especially from the regions of Bihar and Uttar Pradesh, where folk music has not been so much part of the statist and nationalist agenda as it has been in other states such as in Rajasthan and Uttarakhand. Although there are increasingly institutionalized notions of folk music and dance, in most cases they remain outside of both the state and the market, which works in parallel but more pervasively than the so-called official 'folk' culture. This becomes one of the vantage points from where one can think about such performance practices. While folk songs, music, and culture at large hint at a conception of the world, any unified understanding of that world would be difficult to arrive at. 'Folk' is not a cohesive identification, but a cultural body full of fractures and erasures. In this chapter, I try to foreground the practice of folk music in relation to labour, embodiment, erasure, and enslavement. In that case, folk is about what is surviving, what is getting erased, and what is getting appropriated and pushed to the boundaries. Beyond the spectacular formations that we see in mediatized spaces, borrowing from anthropological discourse, we can say that folk music remains largely practices of the liminal and marginal in South Asia. Folk is about returning to the community and the 'common' in complicated ways. In contemporary debates, folk is also about the question of labour, service, and dignity.

In my analysis of folk performances in India and South Asia, then, I bring the question of caste to the centre. Indian folk music is deeply intertwined with caste-reflecting social structures and cultural identities. Musicians largely come from two castes: the Dalits and other lower-caste backgrounds (also addressed as *bahujan* communities) and the performing communities. Folk performances can be said to be the cultural practice of *bahujan* communities in India. In other words, it is the Bahujan communities who have been carrying these traditions at large. The question I asked in my previous work was what does a folk performance produce? I have argued that in a caste-based society, folk performance is emblematic of an irony in which most often 'its strength becomes its imprisonment, its aesthetic becomes the reasons for its marginalization and its skills become the shackle'.[5] In other words, we cannot understand the production and values of folk music without understanding the stratification of caste and its embodied manifestation in folk songs and culture. Yet, at the same time, folk remains part of larger unofficial debates. These carry a different conception of the body and the world and therefore differing possibilities. Despite its lineage, folk performance therefore carries an alternative cultural repository in terms of its arrangements of body, language, and ecology.

Scholarship and Criticism

What is folk? What is folk music? Can we have a singular perspective on it? These questions elicit various responses. One faction would argue that folk is a product of colonial modernity and modern institutions, whereas others maintain that it has always been part of the lives of the common people, part of common culture and communities. For some, it is the lost rhythm of the communities; for some, it is still part of their living practices. Many times, folk music is seen in association with rural culture. But the traditions have also been carried out in urban lives. The incorporation of folk cultural elements into industrial and corporate cultures also requires us to see their folk side – what Raymond Williams terms the 'residual experience' in the dominant culture, which can be incorporated despite there being something inherently oppositional and threatening in its very existence.[6] According to Williams, this 'residue culture' represents areas of human experience that the dominant culture neglects, undervalues, opposes, represses, or even cannot recognize. Our understanding of folk music is full of these fuzzy divisions and debates. As the materials of folk music are localized in their specific geographies, histories, experiences, and state policies, we cannot have a common view of what is 'folk'. Perhaps one of the best ways to understand this cultural expression is to examine it through our own locations, histories, and experiences of community, and posit it with all possible flaws and contradictions. There are no perfect and ideal practices of folk music and song that can be reclaimed and revived. Such imaginations only exist in the minds of romantic folklorists or their native elites who hark back to the past for cultural revivals. One of the various ways in which the debate around folk music and practices can be politicized is to talk about their erasure not only in the elite and the nationalist cultural spheres but also within entrenched ritual and cultural hierarchies.

Folk song and music is translated as *lokgeet* or *loksangeet* in many north Indian languages. The *lok* here stands for a world or a conception of the world.[7] We can say that beyond music, song, and dance, folk is also about an alternative conception of the world, an expression of 'unofficial culture', however problematic it can be. It is about basic human desire and sensibility. It is fundamentally about human values. In folk song, there is no separation between art and life, between culture and nature, between body and ecology. The rhythm of the body finds its connection with the rhythm of the land and river. Folklorist Shyam Sundar Dubey argues that the concerns of human relations cannot be separated from the concerns of nature and ecology in folk songs.[8] Perhaps *lok* does not have a similar evocation as *folk* when it gets translated into English. There has been a debate about this term. Stefan Fiol, for instance, locates folk performances in relation to colonialism. He underlines how 'colonial elites understood low-caste, rural, hereditary artisans to be the source of primitive folk culture'.[9] In his view, the forms were later appropriated by high-caste and middle-class individuals. However, we need to understand that not everything was getting appropriated. Appropriation and erasure went together. In other words, folk music has been constructed on the erasure of the materiality of folk performance itself. Therefore, what Aparna Dharwadekar underlines as 'the urban folk drama' cannot be equated with the folk performances embodied in larger social and cultural practices.[10]

Folk songs are mostly organized on the occasions of fairs, festivals, and life cycle rituals. They capture sadness and the celebration of life, changing seasons, sowing of seeds, growing of plants, life stages, and crises. The question can also be asked as to what folk conceptions do to the musical practices *vis-à-vis* what song and music do to the conception of the folk world. Folk music not only celebrates the so-called folk world but also actualizes the conceptions of the common people. The soul of their conception of the world lies in songs. Perhaps no other genres capture the gist of the folk sensibility than the way it gets captured by song and music. Despite all the constructivists' arguments, folk also offers real, practical, and material conceptions of the world for a vast section of society. It is not limited to nostalgia constructed by a postcolonial nation or its institutionalized practices (though that is also true for policymakers and bureaucrats). Folk lies in the field, in homes, with women, and lower-caste communities with all their contradictions. Rather than a construction, folk song and culture is an assemblage of erasure. Yet it is also a repository of what is not erased.

In this regard, Indian folklorist A. K. Ramanujan asks an astute question: who needs folklore? He replies saying that *he* needs folklore as an Indian studying India. He says, 'It pervades my childhood, my family, my community. It is the symbolic language of the non-literate parts of me and my culture'.[11] For me too, the experience of folk is concrete. I cannot think of community life without folk songs and music. It is pervasive. It is material. It is practical. It is part of everyday lives and beyond. Ramanujan says that 'one way of defining verbal folklore for India is to say it is the literature of the dialects, those mother tongues of the village, street, kitchen, tribal hut and wayside tea shop'.[12] The conception of the song and cultural practices also appear through the categories of *margi* (inter-regional) and *desi* (regional). *Desi* connotations of folk lay more emphasis on its local cultural practices, but they also tend to uncritically valorize local knowledge and homogenize its presence based on dominant narratives. Scholars such as

Gopal Guru are critical of the *desi* for its silencing of the marginalized communities in the traditional circle of power.[13] Whatever may be the case, we need to accept that folk is a fractured notion very much like the nation itself.

Indeed, both the nation and the folk have constructed each other, and yet also remain independent in South Asia. In other words, folk is not yet fully appropriated under the ideology of nationalism. Or we can say that it slips the structure of the national culture. In many cases, folk performance allies with the region and can go against the idea of the nation as a unified whole. While the nation gets provincialized, the region acquires a nationalist identification, such as in the case of Tamil Nadu in India. So, the question of folk does not remain about the national or the regional identification but more about whose folk we are talking about – the folk song and music of the dominant or the folk of the marginalized. Most often, the national ideation of the folk and the regional ideation of the folk converge together on ideological grounds even though they differ in their expressions. It is not surprising that every region in India is trying to project their notions of folk in the image of the nation.

The aesthetic question of folk becomes more ethical when one asks the question that Ross Cole has asked in his book *The Folk*: 'Who are "the folk" in folk music?'[14] The question does not elicit any surprising response in Indian and South Asian contexts, where folk performance remains part of the living practices of communities. Though one can see folk music and performance as a modern construction, there are practices where one can find continuity. Sources suggest that *gramyadharma* (literal translation, 'village culture') used to have some inherent characteristics of folk music. Folk is part of the discourse, but it is also about the real practices and concrete facts. Folk music is very much part of the social and cultural construct, and yet it also constructs the very idea of the social and cultural in turn and, for that matter, cosmic worlds and beliefs. The history and historical consciousness of folk music and songs are important; however, the practices of folk music cannot be just a matter of what folk *was*, but what folk music is *doing* in our contemporary time, in our contemporary discourses – its moral and cultural position in relation to consumer culture and the market regime.

What is the practice of folk music and what does folk music practice? What is at stake when folk music emerges not only as a creative field, but also as a perspective that functions as a form of critique? The study of folk music needs to bring in more critical perspectives. The challenge is how to develop what Gencarella calls 'folk criticism as a vibrant, everyday practice' that 'encourages folklorists to embrace critical perspective as a continuation of this essential human activity'.[15] It is to be emphasized that folk music is still largely studied by folklorists. Folklorist Alan Dundes sees a problem with the 'lack of innovation in grand theory by contemporary folklorists'.[16] He has suggested that we should study folklore as performed, and we should be more sensitive to the depiction of women in folkloric texts and contexts.

When it comes to the perspective and study of folk music and song in India and South Asia at large, we find a strange division based on predisposed aesthetic distinctions – something that can be described as aesthetic casteism. In other words, it is a hierarchy based on caste that gives meaning and value to the categories. Such categories maintain instrumental approaches to folk music and performance. For example, there are general tendencies among scholars not to analyse community-based life cycle songs for their aesthetic quality. In the same way, so-called raga-based songs are not analysed for their ritual and ceremonial purpose and, very similarly, we are made to believe that contemporary art practices have completely displaced the traditional elements. As a result, the folk are seen in relation to pastness and in the light of anthropological constructions. Whereas the study of popular and contemporary music has been able to create strong critical scholarships, the study of folk music still uses very conventional categories and conceptual frameworks. It might appear that folk music cannot be critically analysed or does not have the capacity to sustain modern criticism and contemporary critical discourses. As a result, perspectives on folk music have remained in obscurity and resistant to new changes and discourses even though the practice of folk music itself has radically shifted.

Nationalism and Decolonization

Studies of folk music coming from the Euro-American context usually see folk music and performance in relation to predetermined ideas concerning historical pasts that coincide with the end of Romantic rural life. However, the study of folk music developed differently in different countries, influenced by different historical contexts and intellectual perspectives.[17] There are also different experiences of how folk song and music continue and remain in active circulation. If in some parts of Europe folk music is active in festival circuits, in other parts of the world it is moving with migrants and refugees, finding its voice in dislocation and diaspora.[18] Can our perspective on folk music change if we view it through their performance practices? We cannot be sure, but it might complicate some of our simplified understandings of folk music that often create unnecessary binaries. Working on the folk music culture of North India, Peter Manuel makes the observation that 'in contrast to art music, "folk music" is generally defined in negative terms, especially as that traditional or neo-traditional music which is not dependent on elite patronage, and is not grounded in a body of explicit theory'.[19] The question arises, then, how do we positively evaluate folk music? In most of the existing studies on folk song and music in India, folk is discussed from the vantage points of the elite.[20] In those analyses, the folk become somebody's others – the classical's others, the colonialists' others, the modern and contemporary others. This inherent othering and ordering in such approaches strip folk culture of its strengths and potential. In contrast, however, uncritical celebrations of folk music and performances have been questioned by many Dalit scholars and activists.[21] The questions they ask are pertinent: Why do the traditions of folk music remain so ghettoized in India? How do existing culturalist approaches (including decolonial approaches) tend to undermine local power hierarchies? Despite a focus on colonization, some studies remain hesitant about discussing the colonial situation in local contexts and within national boundaries, including aspects such as the dispossession of musical knowledge from Indigenous communities.

The term 'folk' usually comes with problematic usages in India. The idea of folk is very much constituted in the question of the nation and its people. Yet so-called folk music becomes a site of visions that remain critical not only of the colonial past but also of the homogenized idea of the nation and culture. At the same time, a section of performers has been claiming themselves as practitioners of *lok* or *desi* (the genres are usually referred to as *lokgeet, loksangeet,* or *desi sanskriti*), very much like other traditional musics of the many parts of the world, inherently referring to the notion of the 'folk' embedded in community lives beyond rural-urban contexts. To understand this paradox, we need to see folk music in the context of performance practices. Critics who have written about folk theatre, music, and performance have largely directed their criticism against the institutionalized practices of folk performance. Although their criticisms are valid in relation to the institutional framing of folk, these criticisms mostly do not engage with the broader and more complex field of active practice of folk performance.

Aparna Dharwadekar makes a valid distinction between 'urban folk drama' as a revivalist form (part of what is known as the Theatre of Roots project) and community-based folk performances. She rightly points out that urban folk drama is very much part of middle-class urban institutions, whereas folk theatre and performance belong to a specific region, language, ecological cycle, and participating community. Dharwadekar discusses a form of urban folk music in which 'the mediation of authorship, intentionality, textuality imply that the middle-class notion of folk music is different from community-based folk music'.[22] It can be argued that folk music was never revived like either urban folk drama, classical dance and music, or modern theatre. In fact, the nationalist revivalist movement often viewed folk music and performance with disparaging attitudes. For example, the revivalist poet and writer Bhartendu Harishchandra saw it as *bharast kavya* or *Kavyahin* (a corrupt form of poetry).[23]

The question arises as to whether there is another way to think about performance without enquiring first what folk music is and what it is not. Stefan Fiol has traced the changing contours of folk music and its usage in the context of the Indian state of Uttarakhand. He underlines the negative connotations associated with such music:

> The tendency to characterise folk music in negative terms, as an indication of low musical development, or as the antithesis of art music or popular music, has a long history in Indian music scholarship that continues to the present ... nonetheless, most ethnomusicologists researching Indian music continue to use the term 'folk' as a general label to identify musicians and musical styles, either because they demonstrate some combination of qualities normally identified with the term 'folk' or simply because they are using local terminology.[24]

As this passage indicates, folk music exists in dynamic association with a variety of local and community-based practices. Though they show some visible patterns concerning function and value creation, it would be difficult to fix them and find a clear pattern. These fractures and variations lead to difficulty in theorization, unlike in other performance genres. For instance, birth ritual music might have its social function, but many times its aesthetic and entertaining qualities cannot be ignored. The problem with understanding folk music and performance is that it always exceeds, it always leaks; from the point of privilege, it always lacks. It resists categories, analytical lenses, and conceptual frameworks. Folk music needs to be understood in relation to these leaks, lacks, cracks, and associations that move together in resonance and dissonance.

Another problem arises out of the sheer range of performance practices. They remain so vast that any definition of folk music fails to define them or capture them fully. This problem leads to failures of classification and the absence of mainstream discourse informed by scholarship. In other words, it shows the failure of the folk to become objects of analytical enquiry.

Viewed from such a negative perspective, the folk becomes a failure. Its language fails to meet the standard of language, its form fails to meet the standard of form, its skills fail to match the skills and virtuosity of the so-called classical and contemporary performance. In this case, might we need to shift our perspective? For example, what happens when we do not see these qualities as failures but rather as strengths? For example, whereas folk's intrinsic relationship to the body, land, and labour is viewed as a problem, these associations reveal its identity. The decolonization of folk music necessarily asks us to address those failures and change our yardstick to engage with folk music and performances. Decolonialization of folk music also has to go beyond its *idealtypus* approach and pay increased attention to co-production, co-existence, and co-performance.

Moreover, reading folk music or theatre only in relation to the nation and colonization leaves a vast gap concerning folk music not so much impacted by the fervour of nationalism and imperialism. It is possible to think of many practices of folk music that remain outside of such nationalist and post-colonialist constructions. For example, rites of passage (birth, marriage, and death) still play a vital role in community-based society. Most of these occasions are marked by song, music, and dance. These songs relate to existential questions and go against the narrow ideology of the nation and colonization as defined by the West. Indeed, Ania Loomba has argued that too much of the time 'the "Third World" is seen as a world defined entirely by its relation to colonialism. Its histories are then flattened, and colonialism becomes their defining feature'.[25]

In India, it is almost impossible to fulfil the task of decolonization without talking about caste. Decolonization of Indian culture and aesthetic value necessarily entails the decolonization of classical music. To truly democratize Indian art and culture the classical must be decolonized given how much of what is said about classical dance and music today has been constructed on the erasure of the aesthetic and cultural practices of local communities – in other words, the common folk. In this way, the dichotomy of classical and folk music is therefore very much related to issues of nationalism and decolonization. Scholars such as A. K. Ramanujan and Stuart Blackburn have shown interconnections between 'folk' and 'classical'. According to them, 'not only are folk and classical traditions coexistent, they are cooperative ... they complement each other as two ends of a continuum between the control and release of energy'.[26] In their view, the two can be said to have overlapping themes and rhetorical strategies. But, as Kathryn Hansen points out, in their analyses, no specific criteria were used to define 'folk' and 'classical'.[27] In most cases, 'a performance genre is assumed to be "classical" if its verbal texts are in the Sanskrit language (or in Tamil) and predate the modern period; and "folk" is the remainder of what is left'.[28] In order to define 'classical' and 'folk', Hansen has suggested that instead of looking into texts, codes, and themes, we need to give consideration to 'the sources of a tradition's authority, its mode of reproduction, and its relations to dominant social groups'.[29] But these exchanges and continuities do not undermine the privilege of the classical and the marginalization of the folk. In fact, the marginalization we are witnessing is not outside, but very much a part of these exchanges that constitute the classical and the folk. Through such exchanges, the classical is assembled and its others are disassembled.

In this regard, Urmimala Sarkar-Munsi has argued that it is the codes, texts, and references to unbroken tradition that have been constantly assembled to turn many oral, folk, local, and community traditions into assembled 'classical' genres, such as Manipuri dance. In this process, whereas the classical has been hierarchized, 'all other embodied activities are relegated to either the category of "folk" or "tribal"'.[30] Intriguingly, Ramanujan and Blackburn view classical and folk as two different expressions of the same tradition, not different traditions as such. They summarize Indian folklore in terms of two modalities: 'complementary with classical traditions and as a cultural whole'.[31] Although they highlight this complementarity, they tend to overlook the contradictions and conflicts that exist between classical and folk in terms of class, culture, and language. It is not always the case that folk has been under pressure from elite culture. In fact, even *shastra* (classical or textual traditions), as Namvar Singh puts it, under the popular pressure of folk has adopted several of its elements and avoided the emergent conflict.[32] On the other hand, folk has also adopted some norms of *shastra* through acculturation. In this process, both *shastra* and *lok* have shaped each other. Nevertheless, conflicts between the two need to be acknowledged. Singh has also pointed out that the primary debate in medieval India was the conflict between *shastra* (dominant elite) and *lok* (subordinate popular).[33] Even today, the conflict between *shastra* and *lok* is still obvious in the domain of aesthetic and cultural taste.

Krishnadev Upadhyay divides traditional *sanskriti* culture into two categories: *shist-sanskriti* (elite-sophisticated culture) and *lok-sanskriti* (popular folk culture).[34] According to him, whereas the highly educated people in a traditional society – philosophers, scholars, priests, and monks – follow the written rules and laws of the *Vedas*, *Puranas*, and *Smritis*, and represent the *Shist Sanakrirti* (Sankritized elite culture), the beliefs, myths, mores, morals, lifestyles, and personal behaviours of the common people come under folk culture (*loksanskriti*). While Upadhyay's analysis is valid to a certain extent, his ideas of classical and folk are again based on a very homogenous understanding of folk culture. Viewed from these perspectives, folk itself becomes an implicit critique of elitist and nationalist understandings of culture. Indeed, there is a possibility that we need to think of folk itself as a critique of elite and mainstream tastes. For example, folk song and music do not make distinctions between erotic or bawdy songs and sacred or religious songs in various contexts, and yet this division has become a basis of distinction for others.

Critique of Folk Music and Folk Music as Critique

Folk music in South Asia is either viewed as a denigrated practice or gets valorized as an alternative form of knowledge. Both approaches undermine rigour and criticality in the study of folk music and performance. Such approaches have created major hindrances in the progress of study. Recognizing that folk songs and music are full of problems and contradictions, we also need to recognize their potentials. First of all, to develop any critical methodological lens, a critique of folk music is needed. We need to recognize that folk song and music carry aesthetic and cultural practices that often sustain and openly perpetuate hegemonic values of caste, gender, and hierarchy of taste. Operating within the local service economy, they also sustain a culture of obligation and caste-gender subjugation. In most cases, practitioners come from the very lowest rung of society. They are often labelled and called by all sorts of denigrated names such as *bajaniya* (one who plays music), *gawaiyas* (one who sings), *bhand* (one who sings too loud), and so on. To participate in folk music, then, is to produce enslavement and legitimize social and aesthetic hierarchies. For those committed to emancipation, these practices are often viewed as self-defeating for subaltern communities. It is not surprising that many hereditary communities of musicians and singers are now leaving their professions. Political and social activists, moreover, have often appealed to them to move away from such denigrating practices. Practitioners face all kinds of ostracism because of their engagement with folk music – drummers in particular being one of the most ostracized communities in India and South Asia.

But there are various contexts where folk songs and music offer a critical lens. Might we think about the ways in which folk music itself works as critique – against the atomization of life, in defence of the common, against the idea of individual creativity, and also against colonial migration and displacement. For example, Bidesia folk culture emerged against the colonial migration and displacement of the nineteenth century from the Bhojpuri-speaking regions of Bihar and Uttar Pradesh. Migrant labourers created a repository of song culture in the form of *bidesia*. Forced to migrate to the Caribbean as indentured labourers, their songs and music offer us a rich repository of folk performances where folk music takes a critical stance against colonialism and forced migration. It should not pass without notice that most scholars come from upper castes and elite backgrounds, while practitioners of such music largely come from the Dalits and lower castes background. We find the erasure of castes in many of these contexts. Asha Singh has critically examined Upadhyay's role in the construction of Brahminical understandings of folk music and performance in Bhojpuri folk culture. Singh has rightly pointed out the role of early folklorists in creating the ideal image of chaste women, nationalism, and social hierarchy.[35]

Some singer-performers have also developed forms of critique in their own practice, critically engaging with folk traditions while addressing contemporary socio-political issues. Telugu folk singer Gaddar, for instance, transformed patriarchal and misogynist songs into progressive songs, just as a generation of singers including Bhikhari Thakur and Rasul Miyan from Bhojpuri-speaking regions turned folk music itself into a body of critique against caste and colonialism. Songs often become a critique of urban life, capitalism, and forced migration. One of the most popular Bhojpuri songs, 'Reliya na bairi, jahajiya na bairi', goes like this:

> Neither the train is our enemy, nor is the ship our enemy
> Money is the enemy
> Money is the enemy
> That compels our beloved to migrate

These examples show obvious cases of folk song and music acquiring a critical tone. The very peripheral presence of folk music carries traces of bodies, languages, and materiality. These songs and musical performances remain sites of collective creation and dissemination against the growing atomization, artificialization, and individualization of creative practice.

Drawing from the repository of folk song and music, many Bahujan singers have carved out a repertoire of anti-caste and Ambedkarite song. K. Kalyani discusses the emergence of an anti-caste counterpublic through music and song performance.[36] Some of these singers and performers draw

Figure 4.1 Gaddar performing in Hanamkonda district of erstwhile Andhra Pradesh in a programme organized by the All India People's Resistance Forum (AIPRF), 28 December 1997. Photograph by G. D. Satyam, processed and archived by B. Narsing Rao.

heavily from their folk repository to turn the common consciousness of the folk on its head. As Kalyani rightly points out, 'the emerging popular culture develops an alternative worldview, based on the principles of equality and justice to oppressed caste communities'.[37] These singers draw from folk tradition to offer a critique of folk society, in turn developing what can be termed a field of critical folk music culture. While Kalyani draws our attention to the explicit political connections of contemporary folk music culture, folk music also carries implicit forms of embodied agency within subaltern communities. This brings us back to the Gramscian theme at the heart of this chapter. Gramsci's observation is quite apt here:

Folklore should instead be studied as a 'conception of the world and life' implicit to a large extent in determinate (in time and space) strata of society and in opposition (also for the most part implicit, mechanical and objective) to 'official' conceptions of the world (or in a broader sense, the conceptions of the cultured parts of historically determinate societies) that have succeeded one another in the historical process.[38]

Folk songs, for instance, have been acknowledged as reservoirs of women's articulations in South Asia by many scholars.[39] Women across castes and 'lower'-caste men generally script and sing these songs. Life cycle occasion songs such as those for weddings and births are sung by women of all castes. Folk songs accompanying labour processes (especially outside the domestic confines) are sung by women of the 'lower' castes. Likewise, we can find examples of folk songs and music that carry radical elements of religion, culture, and language for the Dalit and subaltern communities in India. The work of Zoe Sherinian has shown how Tamil folk music carries Dalit liberation theology in India and beyond.[40] This is only the beginning of a more thorough acknowledgement of the radical potentials embodied in folk music and song.

Conclusion

Folk songs and music have a strong presence in the socio-cultural life of communities in India and South Asia. These repertoires convey a wide range of practices – from rites, rituals, and festivals to popular dance and entertainment. They are interwoven in the sensibilities of locales and regions. They are part of the life world. For almost all occasions there are songs and music. The music is the marker of distinction and connection: it consecrates spaces, it creates the boundaries of sacred and profane. There is different music for the various stages of marriage and childbirth. There is music for pregnancy and labour pain. There is special music and songs for birth and naming ceremonies. If birth marks a happy occasion, there are also songs and music for death. Mourning and grieving are full of singing. Even when one cries, one sings. Indeed, the practice of crying songs still remains popular. One sings on the occasion of union and separation. In other words, people mourn loss and grieve through music; body and soul are departed through music. From the birth of a child, the separation of lovers, marriage, departure of the bride, ploughing of fields, labour in the fields, leisure from work – all have music. Most migrant workers from north India hear music while working. Folk music and songs cover the entire gamut of their life cycle and beyond. Folk music is so pervasive in the social world of South Asian countries that many times one does not even realize its inescapable presence.

In this chapter, I have offered a broad overview of the spectrum of practices and problems of folk music in India and South Asia. Folk music is usually seen as naïve, ideal, and spontaneous, without much to offer in relation to aesthetics and politics. To offer any perspective on folk music becomes complex as the very category remains contested. Categories based on performance practice remain vital to understanding folk music, but some of them also create unnecessary binaries. For example, Krishnadev Upadhyay only analyses some songs for their aesthetic considerations, whereas *all* music evokes aesthetic and affective meaning.

Anthropologists and folklorists have tried to categorize music under functional and non-functional categories. According to them, functional songs and dance are performed to serve specific social functions, such as marriage or a death ceremony; in contrast, non-functional songs usually have entertainment and aesthetic purposes. Although this division makes some sense, it also carries an inherent connotation of aesthetic hierarchies in which everyday social music is categorized as low. This distinction indirectly hints that music tied to social ritual does not have any meaningful aesthetic qualities. These theoretical divisions drawn along the lines of functional and nonfunctional do not work in practice, as the songs of social occasions can be extremely entertaining and indeed aesthetically appealing. Likewise, music valued above all for its aesthetic qualities is often deeply social and ritualistic (here we could take the example of classical music culture). Folk is often described as regional song or musical tradition in India and South Asia, yet at the same time it maintains its intra-regional presence. Folk performances across cultures are commonly seen as an expression of rural and peasant society. Nevertheless, they also thrive in semi-urban peripheries, in the margins of the metropolis, and with migrant labourers.

Some of these songs are highly ritualized and performed for local patrons as part of service and obligation. Indeed, for many people performing folk music is bound up with providing services to higher castes, and yet one who performs such music is considered inauspicious. Instead of asking *what* folk music is, we should ask *who* the practitioners of folk music are. What do they perform? Do they perform their music or their obligation? What are iterant folk musicians and singers from Rajasthan singing for a global neoliberal audience? How does the Telugu diaspora relate to the songs of Gaddar when he sings 'Mugaboina Gonthulo'? These are questions that not only offer a critique of folk music but also suggest a direction towards what I have portrayed as critical folk music studies. Our field needs to situate its aesthetics as politics and singing in the vernacular not only as an act of resistance, but also a way forward.

Notes

1. Brahma Prakash, 'But We Will Not Give Up the Categories! (De) valuing the Categories in South Asian Performance Traditions'. *Global Performance Studies* 5/1–2 (2022). Online.
2. Stephen Olbrys Gencarella, 'Folk Criticism and the Art of Critical Folklore Studies'. *Journal of American Folklore* 124/494 (2011): 251–271, 251–252. See also Gencarella, 'Constituting Folklore: A Case for Critical Folklore Studies'. *Journal of American Folklore*, Spring 122/484 (2009): 172–196.
3. Gencarella, 'Folk Criticism', 251.
4. See Brahma Prakash, *Cultural Labour: Conceptualizing the 'Folk Performance' in India*. New Delhi: Oxford University Press, 2019.
5. Prakash, *Cultural Labour*, 280.
6. Raymond Williams, *Marxism and Literature*. Oxford: Oxford University Press, 1977, 123–124.
7. *Lokgeet* here stands for लोक (*lok*, 'people') and गीत (*gīt*, 'song'). Although *lok* has other meanings such as 'worldly', it is usually employed by local people and contexts against the grand notion of Hindu Vedic culture. In this sense, *lok* stands against constructions of nationalism.
8. Shyam Sundar Dubey, *Lok: Paramampara, Pahchan and Pravah [Hindi]*. Delhi: Radhakrishna Prakashan, 2003.
9. Stefan Fiol, 'One Hundred Years of Indian Folk Music'. In *This Thing Called Music: Essays in the Honor of Bruno Nettl*, ed. Victoria Lindsay Levine and Philip V. Bohlman, 317–329. London: Rowman & Littlefield, 2015, 326.
10. Aparna Bhargava Dharwadker, *Theatres of Independence: Drama, Theory, and Urban Performance in India since 1947*. Iowa City: University of Iowa Press, 2009, 322.
11. A. K. Ramanujan, 'Who Needs Folklore? Ramanujan on Folklore'. *Indian Literature* (1994): 93–106, 93.
12. Ramanujan, 'Who Needs Folklore', 95.
13. Gopal Guru, 'The Idea of India: Derivative, Desi and Beyond'. *Economic and Political Weekly*, 46/37 (2011): 36–42.
14. Ross Cole, *The Folk: Music, Modernity, and the Political Imagination*. Oakland: University of California Press, 2021.
15. Gencarella, 'Folk criticism', 251.
16. Alan Dundes, 'Folkloristics in the Twenty-First Century'. *Journal of American Folklore* 118/470 (2005): 385–408, 387.

17. See Carole Pegg, 'Folk Music', *Grove Music Online*. www.oxfordmusiconline.com. First published online 2001.
18. See Mark Slobin, *Folk Music: A Very Short Introduction*. Oxford: Oxford University Press, 2011, 116–118.
19. Peter Manuel, *Tales, Tunes, and Tassa Drums: Retention and Invention into Indo-Caribbean Music*. Urbana: University of Illinois Press, 2015, 85.
20. Labelling folk music in negative terms or using it as a form of othering has a long history in India: see Manuel, *Tales, Tunes, and Tassa Drums*; Fiol, 'One Hundred Years'; and Prakash, *Cultural Labour*.
21. See Guru, 'The Idea of India' and Prakash, *Cultural Labour*.
22. Dharwadker, *Theatres of Independence*, 322.
23. Bhartendu Harishchandra, *Bhartendu Granthavali*, ed. Omprakash Singh. Delhi: Anamika Publishers, 2008, 972.
24. Fiol, 'One Hundred Years', 318.
25. Ania Loomba, *Colonialism/Postcolonialism*. London: Routledge, 1998, 18.
26. Stuart A. Blackburn and A. K. Ramanujan. 'Introduction'. In *Another Harmony: New Essays on the Folklore of India*, ed. Blackburn and Ramanujan, 1–37. Berkeley: University of California Press, 1986, 20.
27. Kathryn Hansen, *Grounds for Play: The Nautanki Theatre of North India*. Berkeley: University of California Press, 1992, 43.
28. Hansen, *Grounds for Play*, 43.
29. Hansen, *Grounds for Play*, 43.
30. Urmimala Sarkar Munsi, *Mapping Critical Dance Studies in India*. Singapore: Springer, 2024, 12.
31. Blackburn and Ramanujan, 'Introduction', 22.
32. Namvar Singh, *Doosri Parampara ki Khoj*. New Delhi: Rajkamal Prakashan, 2008, 78.
33. Singh, *Doosri Parampara ki Khoj*, 77.
34. Krishnadev Upadhyay, *Bhojpuri Sahitya Ka Itihaas*. Varanasi: Vishwavidalya Prakashan, 2008, 2.
35. Asha Singh, 'Of Women, by Men: Understanding the "First Person Feminine" in Bhojpuri Folksongs'. *Sociological Bulletin* 64/2 (2015): 171–196.
36. K. Kalyani, 'Music as an Anti-Caste Counterpublic: Notes from North India'. *Social Change* 54/2 (2024): 229–242, 230.
37. Kalyani, 'Music as an Anti-Caste Counterpublic', 230.
38. Antonio Gramsci, 'Philosophy, Common Sense, Language and Culture', in *The Antonio Gramsci Reader*. Delhi: Aakar Books, 2014, 360.
39. See, for example, Gloria Goodwin Raheja and Ann Grodzins Gold, *Listen to the Heron's Words: Reimagining Gender and Kinship in North India*. Berkeley: University of California Press, 1994 and Smita Tewari Jassal, *Unearthing Gender: Folksongs of North India*. Durham, NC: Duke University Press, 2012.
40. Zoe C. Sherinian, *Tamil Folk Music as Dalit Liberation Theology*. Bloomington: Indiana University Press, 2014.

5 | Artist Voice

Fiddler on the Hoof: Reminiscences of an Ethnographer

YALE STROM

In 1981, I attended a klezmer concert and immediately fell in love with the music and the energy it created between the musicians and audience. I had grown up in a Jewish home that celebrated all the Jewish holidays, both major and minor, with plenty of singing in the synagogue and around a dining table laden with an array of known and not so known holiday specialties. But that night, when I heard this music being performed in a nondescript warehouse in downtown San Diego (an area that was just beginning to be gentrified), something touched me. I was so moved I asked the bandleader if I could join the band. The answer was a quick and resolute no. So, as I was driving home after the concert, I decided to form my own klezmer band. Though the revival of klezmer music in America was maybe five years old, I knew I had to make a statement, be different and noticed. And I recognized I couldn't do this with the same old 78 LPs and songbooks others were using. So, I dropped out of law school and bought a oneway ticket to the former Eastern Bloc. I left to look for unknown and unrecorded klezmer melodies and found the one thing missing from the LPs and songbooks: the people who played, danced, and lived with and for this Ashkenazic instrumental folk music.

I thought this would be a two-to-three-month research trek, but it ended up being a little over one year. What struck me the most when meeting these informants – most of whom were Holocaust survivors – was how they still practiced their religious and/or cultural beliefs. This was despite the Eastern Bloc communist governments often making it difficult to practice anything under the rubric of Judaism. Two things made a lasting impression on me during this first trek: first, despite how much Holocaust survivors suffered during WWII and how it also affected their children, Jewish music was their strongest link to their 'Jewishness' (outside of food); and two, how Romani musicians who played in klezmer bands were accepted by their fellow Jewish musicians and for the most part their Jewish patrons.

When I returned to Eastern Europe after I had gotten my master's degree from NYU, I broadened my research from just music to what made these Holocaust survivors return to their former hometowns and create a new life under the oppression of Stalinism. Even if they went back to their actual homes and work, nothing was going to be the same. In addition, I was drawn to learning all I could about Romani culture, and especially their music; just as Romani musicians played klezmer, Jewish musicians often played their music too.

After my first two expeditions I began to lecture about my research and findings. In the audience there was always at least one person who would ask, 'What languages did you speak that enabled you to be accepted by the Jews and Roma?' I do speak Yiddish, which of course endeared me to those Jews who spoke Yiddish, and I spoke some 'street Polish', which helped in the Slavic lands. But the language that connected me most to all the informants was the one I spoke through my violin. The Eastern Bloc was still a precarious place to live and citizens were rightly wary of my intentions. Why would a young American choose to deal with police and border guards always eager to hassle or even arrest a potential spy wandering the East Bloc pretending to be an ethnomusicologist? What better cover to use while spying on military fortifications on the borders and in the countryside than being a folk musician seeking out the local musicians and recording their music? But my music opened hearts.

It was common for different ethnic groups who shared the same co-territorial lands in Eastern Europe for several hundred years before the Holocaust to adopt specific culinary dishes, folk dance melodies, and songs from each other. Long before remote towns and villages were electrified, the most common form of entertainment was enjoying a meal with family and friends while listening to live music being played by a local band. During my travels, I learned several klezmer and Romani folk melodies that both Jews and Roma played. Knowing these specific melodies afforded me immediate entry into their communities as well as their respect.

Despite the constant 'cloak and dagger' experiences I had with military police on the borders and the annoying encounters with police in the cities and villages, these last Iron Curtain years were very fruitful for my research. Here are two stories about informants whom I met that taught me specific things that still inform me today about how to play klezmer, the history of klezmer, and what Jewish music means to the musicians and patrons.

August 1981: Iasi, Romania

On my first trek to the former Eastern Bloc, I met someone who had a profound influence on my klezmer research in Eastern Europe named Itzik Cara Svart. Svart was born in the small town of Podu Iloaiei in the north-eastern region of Romania called Moldavia. He survived the Holocaust by fighting with the Soviet Army. Upon his return to Romania, he married and settled in Iasi, the largest city in the province of Moldavia. For Jews around the world today, Iasi is revered as the birthplace of Yiddish musical theatre (under the inspired leadership of composer-impresario Avram Goldfaden in 1876). Historians have written about how Broadway musical theatre's antecedents are directly linked to Yiddish musical theatre. But back to Itzik Svart. He joined the Yiddish theatre in Iasi in 1949 as the translator and dramaturg, and this remained his primary profession until the theatre closed in 1964. Itzik then began working in the Yiddish Theatre in Bucharest until he retired in the early 1990s. He then became a Hebrew school teacher in Iasi and researcher on the history of Yiddish culture. Over the years, Itzik had collected a lot of archival material on the lives of well-known klezmer bands that traversed the roads throughout Moldavia and Bessarabia during the nineteenth and early twentieth centuries.

Itzik gave me a lot of historical material that I would have never found on my own. But in terms of actual music, his wife Cili was my teacher. Cili was mostly housebound by the time I realized she knew several klezmer melodies, which she had learned from her family and relatives before the Holocaust. However, she was shy and didn't like to sing in front of others. So, it wasn't until 1996 that I first heard her sing, when I visited Cili and Itzik with my then-girlfriend (now wife) Elizabeth Schwartz, whose ancestors were from Iasi. Itzik and Cili invited us over for afternoon tea and conversation. Cili went into the kitchen to make some simple sugar cookies, and Elizabeth joined her. When they eventually reappeared, Cili was singing one of the Jewish melodies she learned as a child from her great-uncle who had lived in Bosnia. She continued to sing several more, and I still play these tunes with my klezmer ensemble, Hot Pstromi.

All too often, ethnographic research focuses on the men – the musicians who played their instruments for a living outside the home, rather than asking the women of the home what songs they sang while they were engaged in their daily domestic chores. The earliest melodies Jews played and transmitted to others were vocal. Similarly, it was natural that many of the *freylekhs*, waltzes and *nigunim* that klezmer musicians first heard was as children in their homes from their mothers and grandmothers.

October 1984: Chisinau, Moldova

During my second trek to the former Eastern Bloc in 1984, I was accompanied by my high school friend Brian Blue. That September, we found ourselves in Chishinau (Kishinev), Moldova, in the USSR. The only connection we had – the address of the Liederman family – had been given by a friend in San Diego. The Liederman family were Jews classified by the Soviet government as 'refusniks', Soviet citizens (primarily Jews) who were refused permission to emigrate. I was given Mrs. Liederman's name because she was a classical pianist who also played Jewish songs. She was a wonderful pianist, but she could see from my reaction that I was not overly captivated. Her playing was lovely, but the repertoire was all Yiddish folk or theatre songs, many of which I already knew. I had been hoping she was going to play some *freylekhs*, *skotshnes*, or *bulgars*. 'Ah Itsik' (my Jewish name), she said, 'you want to hear the very old melodies that were played at Jewish weddings. I know just the person who can teach you these dances.'

She made a call, and a half hour later a short stout man walked in. Mr. Nikolai Radu greeted Mrs. Liederman with a kiss, smiled at me, shook my hand, and then sat himself at the piano. Everyone in the crowded room (which included her husband, her mother, their little daughter, and Brian) sat down and focused their attention on Nikolai. He placed his hands gently on the keyboard. His fingers looked like sausages. He smiled at me and began to play. The music was incredible – spirited and soulful. I wasn't sure what he was playing, but it sounded Jewish. While playing, he turned his head towards me and yelled out in Yiddish: 'Itsik, gib a kik: Rumeynish, Moldavish, Klezmer, Tsigaynish, Rusish, Ungarish! Farshteystu?' (Yiddish: *Itsik, look: Romanian, Moldavian, Klezmer, Romani, Russian, Hungarian! Do you understand?*) I soon realized that by changing the style every two bars, he was demonstrating how simultaneously different and similar klezmer was to all these other ethnic folk music genres. He kept up this frenetic playing for another five minutes then stopped to great applause from everyone in the room.

My first question was, 'Where did you learn to play such a wonderful klezmer *freylekhs*?'

'Well, of course, from my fellow musicians in the band who were all Jewish.'

'You're not Jewish?'

'I'm Roma.'

My next question, of course, was how did he learn to speak such good Yiddish? He laughed and told me that since everyone in the band was speaking Yiddish among themselves and most of their gigs were for Jews who were primarily speaking Yiddish, Nikolai figured it would be useful to be able to converse in Yiddish – especially when it was time to be paid. He

Figure 5.1 Jewish wedding in Roman, Romania with klezmer music from Romani musicians. Photograph by Yale Strom, February 1985.

played some more and then we all retired to the dining room for honey cake and vodka. Over the next several days in Kishinev (as the Jews still today call the city), Brian and I visited the Liedermans to interview and photograph them, and so I could take lessons from Nikolai.

*

Despite having spent so much time with these informants immersed in the very lands where klezmer musicians lived, I have heard over the years from other musicians and the public that my own klezmer compositions and arrangements of 'traditional' klezmer tunes don't sound like the ones heard on a 78 LP (for example) from 1924. This is true. Over the decades I have absorbed many different genres of folk music and performing techniques that have seeped into my consciousness and unconscious. But I can say without any hesitation that the same thing could be said about the klezmer musician who recorded the tune in 1924 and the one who played it 100 years earlier. How could it not have changed? To take this example even further: the Jewish musician of 1524 played that same melody differently from the musician of 1824 and on different instruments from today. Culture is not static. Klezmer musicians from medieval times through to the early part of the twentieth century were often itinerant. Consequently, they listened to and played with many Jewish and non-Jewish musicians they encountered on the roads, inns, and in the taverns. The pillars of culture, food, and language, are not static, so why should music be? Culture is fluid, which means that culture changes all the time, every day, in subtle and tangible ways. To preserve it as a rigid historical document is to deny its ongoing cultivation.

PART II

Elements

6 | Complementary Modalities in Celtic Music

JOSHUA DICKSON

If one looks to the elements that characterize Scotland's traditional music, we find a confluence of *modalities*, or concepts and processes through which music is made, representing both the everyday and the elite in Scottish life, past and present: music that documents (or offers public critique upon) historical events and commemorates someone of a high social stratum; that provides distinctive rhythms for dance and, in the past, group labour such as fulling cloth or rowing boats; music that summons clans to battle (admittedly not since the eighteenth century); that voices grief in mourning; and, increasingly in modern times, music for the sheer exultance of listening.

Taking a leaf from Kenneth Clark's *Civilisation* (though never so grand), what follows in this chapter is a personal view of such modalities that I feel represent a timeless importance to our aesthetic understanding of 'folk' and 'traditional' music. Threading loosely through my exploration is what ethnomusicologist Constantin Brăiloiu called 'the problem of creation' – a phrase he used in relation to Romanian folk music.[1] Brăiloiu's 'problem' serves as a useful way to approach the making of traditional music as a complex interplay of function, acquisition, structure, symmetry, orality, improvisation, variation, literacy, and memory, which I present chiefly through the prism of Scottish music owing to its significance in the historical discourse surrounding our very concept of 'folk'.[2] These modalities are arranged in such a way as to emphasize how they relate to each other: their tension and complementarity, their mutual consonance and dissonance, which before long the reader will recognize as a nod towards the 'sweet and sour' quality of the harmonic structures characterizing much of the traditional music of Scotland, Ireland, and Wales – the so-called Celtic regions of the British Isles.

Function and Change: Prelude

The number three features heavily in Celtic folklore – consider the triskelion of the flag of Mann, or the fact that the monks of medieval Scotland and Ireland referred to the 150 psalms as the 'three fifties'.[3] We are reminded of this symbolism in the Scottish (or rather Shetlandic) ballad 'King Orfeo', which likely predates the Middle Ages and has many variants across the world. It is essentially a re-telling of the myth of Orpheus and Eurydice, in which Orfeo's wife is abducted to Hell while he is out hunting. Orfeo travels to Hell, plays music to her captors and his wife is freed, bringing with her the arrival of spring:

An first he played da notts o noy	And first he played the notes of sadness
Skowan urla grön	The wood greens early,
An dan he played da notts o joy	And then he played the notes of happiness
Whaur giorten han grön oarlak.	Where the hart goes yearly.

The words sung of King Orfeo's performance recall the ancient Celtic division of music into three functional categories: joyful music, sad music, and sleep-music; or to put it another way: dance music, laments, and lullabies. Scottish and Irish folklore is replete with instances in which a highly skilled musician hypnotizes his or her audience with music of either or all three categories.[4] In the ballad, which features fragments of Norn – until the eighteenth century the mother tongue of Scotland's Northern Isles – Orfeo 'played the notes of sadness' and 'the notes of happiness': a direct reference to these Celtic conceptual divisions of the function of music.

These functions can at times be seen to co-mingle almost synaesthetically, as in James Macpherson's use of a phrase drawn from the writings of Edmund Burke – 'the joy of grief' – or when the late celebrated Scots Traveller singer Lizzie Higgins spoke of hearing her father's fingers 'sobbing like a human voice' when playing a lament on the pipes.[5] References to the joy of grief and the sobbing of fingers highlight the cathartic properties of lamentary music, in particular the Gaelic tradition of *caoineadh* (or keening), a type of stylized funerary wailing no longer practiced within living memory in Scotland and Ireland, but of which there are extensive references to wider practice in medieval Europe. Being loosely metered and declamatory in performance, keening often evoked notions of wildness and exoticism among outside observers: early modern writers such as Charles Burney (1776), Alexander Campbell (1815), and William Dauney (1838), for instance, all invoked connections between Scottish music and a supposedly primitive state of nature via references to birdsong in a discourse that has long been considered ideologically outdated.[6] It is ironic therefore that in modern times musicologists like John Purser have begun to revisit the view that certain aspects of Gaelic music such as keening were derived from or imitate birdsong – though not for the same reasons. Where Campbell wrote of the 'melodies of savage nations' like the 'notes of singing-birds' to illustrate

Scottish music's artlessness and simplicity, Purser argues quite the opposite: that the links between keening and birdsong in the Gaelic tradition is evidence of its sophistication, cultivated by skilled practitioners to resemble aspects of the natural world in which the Gael lived and composed.[7]

Song, or verse writ large, has always played an essential role in society in the Gaelic cultural continuum between Ireland and Scotland, and particularly in the panegyric or encomiastic milieu that persisted in the chieftainly halls of Gaelic nobility, providing employment for a professional class of oral poets and musicians whose services passed hereditarily from fathers to sons over centuries.[8] The thematic milieu of Gaelic panegyric music and verse centred around eulogy (praising one's patron) and elegy (lamenting their death), though an important related function in this world was the gathering of men and incitement to battle. Although the world in which these themes served an immediate functional role has long since passed, they remain important markers of continuity and authenticity for many, particularly exponents of pibroch (the art music of the Scottish Highland bagpipe) and singers of bardic poetry, which carry the weight of centuries.

The ways we make and value traditional Scottish, Irish, and other perceived Celtic forms of music have indeed changed over time as these functional pillars shift. In this sense, the modern era of commercial mediation and advancements in communication technology has proved just as transformative to the aesthetics of Scottish and Irish music as was the folk revival of the 1950s through the 1970s. This revival movement ushered in the professionalization of 'folk' singers and instrumentalists, thrusting traditional singers from Scotland's Gaelic and itinerant Traveller communities into a wider national consciousness, continuing a longstanding folkloric fascination with an internal, marginalized Other. This had reciprocal impacts on performers' own style and discourse, which took on decidedly revivalist overtones, including a new distinction between 'source singers' and 'revival singers'.[9] Crucially however – and linked inextricably with this growing professionalization and commercialization – the folk revival brought about a keener willingness among musicians to innovate in instrumental ensemble settings and a greater appetite for it among listeners. In turn, the modern era of digital mediation, communication, the music industry, and related inducements for innovation since the 1980s has seen Scottish and Irish music expand beyond their national borders and encompass a larger consumerist world, creating a market for 'Celtic music' – a scenario, as Simon McKerrell points out, in which 'bands deliberately altered their performative discourse and musical instrumentation to appear more ethnically and authentically Scottish to foreign audiences'.[10]

Inheritance and Bestowal

One day in 1995, in the village of Daliburgh in South Uist, I visited the home of celebrated piper Angus Campbell, then nearly 100, and his wife Bell. Angus is remembered in South Uist as one of the Hebridean community's greatest modern exponents of pibroch – the courtly, ceremonial bagpipe music which by the seventeenth century had begun to overtake the harp as the favourite of the Scottish Highland aristocracy. Pibroch is Gaelic art music: often referred to by pipers and non-pipers alike as the 'classical' music of the pipes, it follows a theme-and-variation format that reflects its Baroque roots. Angus and Bell listened as I played the initial movement of the pibroch *Cumha na Cloinne* ('The Lament for the Children') in their sitting room; they thought it a good performance. 'There must be something in you,' mused Bell, knowing that I was not Scottish. 'My father used to play,' I offered. 'Ah,' she said, as Angus nodded, 'that explains it.'

Despite the metrical and technical sophistication with which musicians have always cultivated their artistry in the Celtic world, and the many pedagogical, transmissive, and social contexts in which this is done, it is nonetheless widely acknowledged that musicality, potential or actualized, is innate in a person: it is 'in' them and their family. This concept manifests itself linguistically in Gaelic: *tha mi 'nam phìobaire* – literally, 'I am in my piper' (meaning I am a piper). A contemporary of Campbell's in South Uist once said, 'If it was in you to be a piper, you would be a piper', while Hebridean poet Donald Allan MacDonald (1906–1992) felt that 'his poetic talents were natural to him and no amount of knowledge or education could substitute for or create that talent'.[11] These sentiments relate to a discernible seam of traditional belief in the Irish and Scottish Gaelic world that reduces the complexities associated with notions of ability, innateness, enculturation, and training to one or the other of two possible ways to acquire musical skill: one's craft is either inherited from family, or it is bestowed by an otherworldly source.

In medieval Ireland, harp music was expected to pass from father to son.[12] We see the same expectation in Scotland's pre-modern panegyric tradition, its composers and performers esteemed artistic professionals who enjoyed high prestige in society and whose offices in service to clan leadership were hereditary in nature. The most celebrated of these families ran 'colleges' – courses of traditional instruction run from their homes – to which gentry from far and wide would send members of their retinue for training.[13] The concept of inheritance relates equally to upbringing and the role of family surroundings in the more demotic, vernacular world of musical transmission in Gaelic rural life up to within living memory. 'The ability to improvise verse', writes the late eminent Gaelic scholar John MacInnes of oral poets in the Hebrides of the 1960s, 'is explained by the composers themselves simply as a hereditary gift. The belief that a poet is born, not made, is extremely strong, and a curious aspect of the belief is that often a bard will stress the fact that his gift comes to him from his mother, or from his mother's people'.[14] The flourishing of traditional Irish and Scottish music in higher education conservatoire settings today – not to mention the rigorous professional training of Irish, Scottish, and Welsh musicians in previous centuries – makes at least one thing clear: acquiring a high standard of musical skill, 'folk' or otherwise, takes nothing less than immersive, conscious, and persistent dedication.[15]

Albert Lord's account of the training of Yugoslavian epic poets in the 1930s recalls this kind of enculturation through family and community in three stages:

1) Listening and immersion in tradition: 'he sits aside while others sing';
2) Imitation and private practice: 'work, work, work';
3) Independence, expansion, and acceptance as a singer by audiences.[16]

This process is comparable with a similarly three-phased schema undergone by village bards and musicians in the Scottish Hebrides within living memory. Around the same time as Lord and his mentor Milman Parry were recording in Yugoslavia in the 1930s, poets like South Uist's Donald Allan MacDonald typically began with a phase of absorption and assimilation in which one would acquire local oral tradition through family and neighbours; like the young Yugoslavian poet who 'sits aside while others sing', Donald Allan would listen voraciously in the home or the *cèilidh* (house parties in which members of the community would gather and pass the evenings enjoyably through music, song, and tales), though in Donald Allan's case he supplemented this by reading any printed texts of Gaelic vernacular works available. A second phase consisted mainly of private practice and still more listening ('I was listening, and listening, and reading old books', he said), and applying knowledge and stylistic understanding through the composition of new songs for family and small local occasions.[17] The final phase saw more public performances of the bard's songs; echoing Lord's account, this phase consolidated the bard's reputation and allowed the songs to be adopted orally into the wider communal repertoire.[18]

The concept of being gifted musical skill from an otherworldly source runs curiously concurrent with these notions of innateness, inheritance, and professional training. Although harp music may have been expected to pass from father to son in medieval Ireland, this did not conflict with a belief that music of the highest quality derived ultimately from the otherworld, and we see this perpetuated in Scottish Gaelic folklore describing pipe music as a gift bestowed to mortals from the fairies.[19] An example can be found in the reminiscences of Calum Beaton (1931–2009), a popular piper for dances in the local *cèilidhs* of 1950s–70s South Uist. One day at the turn of the twenty-first century as we talked of tunes, Beaton played for me a reel he called *Port Bean Aonghuis Ruaidh* – 'the tune of the wife of red-haired Angus' – which he had learned in his youth from a neighbour. According to Beaton, the neighbour had learned it from the wife in question, an elderly woman who, she claimed, had been 'given' the tune by the fairies, suggesting that belief in the supernatural as a source – perhaps the ultimate source – of musical knowledge and skill was still to be observed until well within living memory in Gaelic tradition.[20]

Structure, Symmetry, and Sonority

Scotland's role in the emergence of the idea of a 'folk modality' began with popular reactions to the publication of *The Poems of Ossian* in 1761 and 1763 by James Macpherson, which coalesced into a discourse that suggested a paradox: great value being placed on folk music and poetry's supposedly oral origins – a perception of unlettered purity – co-mingling with great scepticism about the ability of the oral society that produced said music and poetry to maintain it 'intact' over successive generations.[21] This led to 'tradition' being defined as unlettered knowledge corrupting over time, a discourse referred to as the 'Macpherson paradigm' by historian William Donaldson.[22]

Charles Burney, writing in his *General History of Music* in 1776, promoted what he saw as links between Scottish, Chinese, and ancient Greek scale types – a discourse revolving around the concept of a scale defined by its 'gaps': a universal, primitive, early-Man 'folk modality'. In consequence, ideas of universalism, monolithic and abstracted, accreted around Scotland's music as the central impetus for and focus of discourse in the late eighteenth century, gradually and fancifully associating it with Chinese, ancient Greek, and purportedly even more ancient Egyptian musical traditions – against which any empirical evidence of stylistic and scalar differences between musical cultures cast widely through space and time was seen as an inconvenience.

However fanciful this notion of a universal folk modality, it relates nonetheless to an essential question of structure. Prevailing theories on structure in oral poetics and music in both Western and non-Western traditions recognize the mnemonic functions they serve in predominantly oral societies, and a closer look at these structures tells us much about the role they play in conceptualizing and composing through practice. This was the central thesis of Lord's *The Singer of Tales* of 1960, which introduced his 'oral-formulaic theory' based on the singing of Yugoslavian oral poets whom he and Parry had recorded in the 1930s. Lord's theory has long since been subject to critical review (as we shall see later), but a search for the 'paradigmatic rules of deep structure', as Ardis Butterfield puts it, has been the object of many a scholarly analysis of oral poetics ever since.[23] Susan Wittig, in her *Stylistic and Narrative Structures in the Middle English Romances*, seeks to 'go beyond the simple linearity of the surface order to a deeper structural examination in which the infrastructure of formal oppositions is revealed'.[24] In Scottish, Irish, and Welsh instrumental music, Wittig's 'infrastructure of formal oppositions' reveals itself as a scaffold involving an oscillation between two modal centres, or sonorities.

To wit: an unlikely congruence took place between two eighteenth-century writings on Scottish music from the pens of two very different people: on the one hand, Joseph MacDonald, in his early twenties, born and raised in the far north of Scotland, a classically educated musician but a piper steeped in his native Gaelic tradition and a keen observer of the music surrounding him; and on the other, the American-born patriot and statesman Benjamin Franklin. Writing to a friend in Europe in 1765, Franklin attributes the modal quality of many Scottish airs to having been composed by minstrels playing harps and, supposing they had no means to dampen the strings, reasoned that stressed notes thus needed to be harmonically consonant with those that immediately followed. He called these consonances 'emphatical notes'.[25] Five years earlier and ship-bound for India, young Joseph MacDonald busied himself writing a treatise on Highland pipe music in unprecedented detail, in which he described the way a pibroch's variations (which he termed 'allegros' or 'runnings') typically related to its theme ('adagio' or 'ground'):

Their Allegros are for the most Part . . . regularly built upon the Ground, to which it Commonly Keeps very Closs, taking in the Heads of the Ground, at Such and such

Particular Notes where the Taste of the Adagio Seems to lay ... & thus by taking in the Heads or *Emphatick Notes* of the Ground the whole Scope is perceived in the runnings.[26]

MacDonald thus described a superstructure or tonal skeleton made up of the ground's stressed notes on which the variations are based. These 'emphatick notes' produce either consonance or dissonance against the drones of the bagpipe, and it is the oscillation or shuttling between these binary harmonic centres in formulaic patterns that contributes to pibroch's characteristic sound. Robin Lorimer in 1962 was the first to publish a theory of the tonal and metrical structures of pibroch that explicitly foregrounded notions of symmetry and the oscillation of these binary phrase patterns in highly formulaic and consistent structures across the repertoire.[27]

In 1760 MacDonald had referred to an 'Antient Rule for regulating Time & Composition' indicating that the ground of any 'regular' pibroch must consist of four quarters each consisting of the same number of phrases (typically spanning four bars, e.g. 4:4:4:4).[28] However, conventional wisdom in succeeding generations of pipers came to dictate that a typical ground be represented as three lines, with bars distributed unevenly (e.g. 6:6:4) as in Figure 6.1.

Drawing on the writings of MacDonald, Lorimer recognized that pibroch's metrical structure consisted of phrase patterns characterized by oscillation between two distinct sonorities, and discovered that a pibroch's typical phrase pattern could be schematized as an oscillation divided into two reciprocal, inverted halves.[29] Figure 6.2 represents these oscillating sonorities.

In this schematization the rounded binary form AABA is instantly recognizable. So too is the structural basis of what many term the Scottish 'double-tonic' effect: that is, melodic phrases that alternate a whole step apart. George Thomson was the first Scot to discuss this

	(two bars)	(two bars)	(two bars)
Line 1:	A	A	B
Line 2:	A	B	B
Line 3:	A	B	

Figure 6.1 A 'primary' pibroch ground as it has been most commonly conceptualized since the 1890s.

A	A	B	A
B	B	A	B

Figure 6.2 The phrase pattern in Figure 6.1 reconfigured by Lorimer to reveal its structural reciprocity.

double-tonic in his published writings of the early nineteenth century, but his contemporary Finlay Dun was the first to describe it as an 'essential ... property of Scottish music'.[30] In re-discovering the harmonic and structural basis of this 'essential property' of Scottish music, Lorimer had in effect uncovered a Gaelic musical worldview, symmetrical and cyclic, 'more Ptolemaic than Newtonian' and long hidden under the surface of a vast repertoire.[31] 'One harmony is the light', posits piper and scholar Barnaby Brown, 'the other the shadow cast by the presence of the drones'.[32]

The phrase pattern AABA|BBAB (and other formulae in pibroch of a similar nature) began to assume further significance in later decades thanks to research by Peter Greenhill into the Welsh *cerdd dant* ('string craft') tradition, in which a vocal improvisation is performed over an established harp or lute melody. His examination of a manuscript written around 1613 by the Welshman Robert ap Huw, harper and lutist to the court of King James VI of Scotland and I of England, shed further light on the meters upon which medieval Welsh harpers composed, defined by the same quality of symmetrical binary harmonic oscillation between consonance and dissonance, or tension and resolution, as are the meters of pibroch.[33] Figure 6.3 illustrates *Alban hyfaidd*, the 'bold Scottish measure', one of 24 measures outlined in ap Huw's manuscript, in which the harmonic units are represented as Is and Os rather than As and Bs:

In more recent times, this oscillation between centres of opposing harmonic quality has been observed in a considerable number of traditionally unaccompanied Scottish Gaelic songs (where such harmonies are merely implied); Brown, moreover, has written extensively on the role played by this bi-modal patterning as a range of compositional blueprints undergirding the character of much Indigenous music of the British Isles – both 'art' and 'folk', from panegyric compositions to the strathspeys and reels played for dancing.[34] Although ap Huw's manuscript provides evidence that such bi-modal structures were once explicit

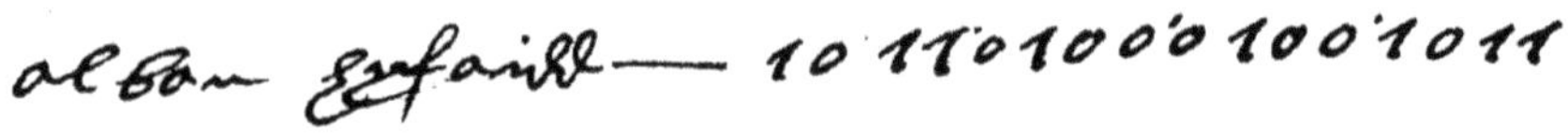

Figure 6.3 The 'Scottish Measure', one of twenty-four outlined in Robert ap Huw's manuscript of c.1613.

to the professional elite, they now exist under the surface and, if written out, tend not to be recognized at sight. Some might ascribe this invisibility in the Scottish context to a loss of traditional knowledge in the changing economic and cultural landscapes of the late eighteenth century, but the structures' continuity as implicit or tacit knowledge through practice is a testament to their tenacity as a defining characteristic.[35]

Theme, Variation, and Improvisation

The idea of variation as characteristic of traditional or folk music lent support to notions of collective origin (held by the likes of Cecil J. Sharp and Béla Bartók) and went hand-in-hand with suspicion of individual creativity. Brăiloiu had followed in the footsteps of Bartók, who was a major influence on his thinking and devotion to fieldwork – but he rejected such collectivist views. Indeed, Brăiloiu offered a critique of the prevailing debates of the nineteenth and early twentieth centuries wherein 'romantics' believed in communal creativity – as Grimm put it, 'folk songs emanate in silence from the tranquil strength of the whole' – and 'realists' upheld Hans Naumann's *gesunkenes Kulturgut*, positing that folk music and song is by definition the trickle-down detritus of society's educated elite, the 'come-down cultural goods' comprising an 'impoverished echo of fashionable art'.[36] These views of variation in oral tradition defined by decline and corruption echo the paradoxical 'Macpherson paradigm' we encountered earlier.

A collectivist zeitgeist was further shaken by Lord's revolutionary insistence in 1960 on the agency of the oral poet as a creative artist.[37] This agency, in Lord's view, was founded on the Yugoslavian epic singer's mastery of orally transmitted poetical structures and their toolkit of 'formulaic expressions' that could be deployed to recreate a song-tale in infinite ways displaying spontaneous yet conscious artistic decision-making. This resonates with Leo Treitler's remarks on improvisation and composition occupying much the same space in medieval European chant.[38] Something like this was observed in action during a 2016 workshop with a celebrated Irish traditional fiddler, in which he taught the group a traditional tune, repeating it around two dozen times over the course of the workshop – each iteration differing melodically, rhythmically and/or ornamentally. An observer, Mats Johansson, thereafter determined that:

Improvisation within traditional fiddling typically comprises minor melodic and rhythmic transformations, the patterning of bowing figures, rhythmic and dynamic phrasing, and a variety of ornaments ... Clearly, in this case the concept of improvisation could easily be replaced by that of variation. Improvisation, then, refers to the spontaneous and emergent nature of the variations observed.[39]

However, Irish and Scottish traditional music is pluralistic enough in its manifestations that variation and improvisation are not always synonymous, nor subject to one set of rules. Even in the context of oral transmission, not all variations are improvised, and not all improvisation is spontaneous. The late Irish musicologist Breandán Breathnach regarded melodic variation as 'undoubtedly the most important characteristic of Irish dance music', but warned that although not predetermined, 'in performance, the traditional player is largely refashioning elements of embellishment he has already developed himself or acquired from other players'.[40]

The lyrics and airs of *òrain luaidh* – Gaelic songs once sung by women in the Scottish Hebrides to accompany the waulking of cloth – were subject to constant spontaneous variation, just as melismatic and rhythmical variation is an intrinsic quality in Irish and Scottish Gaelic *sean-nós* songs, conferring 'an individual distinction' among their singers.[41] However, the refrains of waulking songs (made up of non-lexical vocables) are entirely fixed and immutable.[42] Pibroch, meanwhile, is based fundamentally on the performance of variations upon a piece's ground, or initial theme. These variations are not spontaneous, but they might once have been: as noted earlier, the earliest musical evidence relating to pibroch and similar panegyric instrumental music of the British Isles, like *cerdd dant*, suggests that its earliest composers and performers improvised on tonal frameworks involving a binary oscillation between centres of opposing harmonic quality. That being said, today's average Scottish Highland piper most often learns music from notation and performs these fixed scores from memory without intended deviation, owing primarily to a competition and adjudication culture that has developed since the late eighteenth century.

Significant aspects of Scottish and Irish music as we know it today owe much to the Baroque era, for a variety of reasons. In Baroque music, frameworks for improvisation and variation were fundamentally harmonic, which we see in Wittig's 'infrastructure of formal oppositions' at work in pibroch and *cerdd dant*.[43] Even earlier, the European *basse danse* tradition (a principal court dance during the late Middle Ages and Renaissance) gave rise to musical practices that, as noted by *Grove Music Online*, served as 'a proving ground for many early instrumental techniques such as improvisations over a ground, variations and the forming of suite-like combinations' – again, resonating strongly with the traditional instrumental music of Gaelic and Welsh noble classes.[44] Others have noted the cosmopolitan Baroque setting in which high-caste musicians of the British Isles and continental Europe were likely subject to mutual influence: Brown points out that the *basse danse* and its successors were fashionable in French and Italian courts, and that in the time of James V, 'there were no shortage of Italian and French musicians permanently employed in the royal palaces at Stirling and Holyrood, and the dancing of the Scottish Gaelic aristocracy would have been modelled on that of the Stuart king'.[45]

The advent of mid-eighteenth-century and Enlightenment figures such as Oswald and Dow compounded the impact of Baroque Italianate fashions for musical filigree and variation on Lowland and North-east Scots fiddle music, leading to flights of musical fancy rivalling even the Gaels' penchant for patterning and cyclicity. The variations arranged on the traditional strathspey 'Tullochgorm' by James Scott Skinner (1843–1927) illustrate these heights of deft exuberance. Tunes in Scottish and Irish music are commonly composed of two parts, sometimes four, each part being eight bars in duration, and each tune 'genre', as it were, defined by its rhythmic idiom, which in turn is associated with a particular dance form. The Scotch reel, for instance, was the supreme social dance of Scotland for centuries, and tunes called reels involve common-time legato rhythms that drive the characteristic whirling of the dancers. A strathspey is a uniquely Scottish rhythmic variation on the reel-tune in which the rhythms are divided into more or less binary couplets – long-short, long-short – and often accented with the 'scots snap', in which a couplet's rhythm is inverted to short-long, producing a more staccato effect.

'Tullochgorm' is traditionally a tune of two parts of eight bars each. Skinner's arrangement produces six variations that depart from or reprise the initial theme in a manner reminiscent of verse-and-refrain, evoking a kind of consonance and dissonance: in Figure 6.4, Variations 1, 2, and 4 might be deemed 'consonant', each one remaining close to the familiar melody while increasing rhythmic density; being 'dissonant', Variation 3 departs from the familiar melodic thread for a new contour at a lower octave. One might therefore be tempted to see in Skinner's variational scheme another manifestation of the ubiquitous sonata form AABA:

Figure 6.4 Variations 1–4 of J. S. Skinner's 'Tullochgorm' from *The Scottish Violinist*, 1900.

Pibroch likewise must have drawn a great deal from Baroque fashions, not only with regard to harmonic frameworks, but also to rhythm. Rhythmic elasticity was a natural bedfellow of ornamentation in the Baroque French and Italian courts and their cultivation of a dynamic cadence idiom. Virginal and viol players were known to grace noble Highland residences in the early seventeenth century – a milieu in which pibroch's expressive economy must have been cultivated among a cosmopolitan class of musicians who performed and co-created in an international setting.[46] In this sense, the medieval Gaelic harpers of Ireland and Scotland, the piping dynasties of the seventeenth- and eighteenth-century Highlands, and later master fiddlers like Skinner were influenced as much by the sensibilities that gave rise to the *basse danse* and Baroque French cadential traditions as by what Purser called 'the Celtic love of formal patterning, immensely sophisticated but far from rigid in fact or effect'.[47] Their music manifests in sonic terms the fractal visual embroidery of the Book of Kells, evoking a scenario in which, far from the isolated backwater on which nineteenth-century notions of the preservation of unlettered 'folk' music depended, Gaelic instrumental musicians employed by the noble classes in the pre-modern era were well-travelled, respected as elite artists, and informed by broadly understood European musical and expressive fashions – including that in which improvisation and variation upon a theme shared a common space.

Orality, Literacy, and Memory

The relationship between orality and literacy in Scottish and Irish traditional music has long been characterized by a kind of consonance and dissonance mirroring the binarism of harmonic structures undergirding much of the music itself. Just as poets such as the aforementioned Donald Allan MacDonald supplemented their oral learning in the home and community milieu by the reading of printed collections, so too did pipers acquire repertoire and rhythmic understanding aurally within one social context (traditional *cèilidh* or dance gatherings) while concurrently acquiring a separate-but-related canon and stylistic idiom through printed notation in another (piping competitions pervading the Scottish Highland games circuit). Pipers in South Uist would refer to music learned aurally in the dance context as *ceòl cluais* ('ear-music') and to music associated with competition and its printed sources as *ceòl farpais* ('competition-music'), contributing to a musical bi-lingualism that informed a piper's holistic skillset.[48]

Lord's assessment of the impacts of literacy and the memorization of fixed texts on oral transmission was brutal: he decried the popular 'folk singer' of the 1960s as a mere performer, a fraud who has 'deceived us and robbed the real oral poet of credit'; he dismissed singers who memorize from printed collections (thereby implicating more or less the entire Scottish folk revival generation) as 'lost to the oral traditional process'.[49] Brăiloiu, who contended that variation was 'annihilated by writing', most probably would have agreed.[50] However, perspectives such as Lord's lacked the nuance outlined by the likes of musicologist Ruth Finnegan, who problematized various musical cultures' oral and literate aspects, interwoven and mutually supportive, in modern times.[51] We see these overlaps in the co-mingling of *ceòl cluais* and *ceòl farpais* in the making of Hebridean pipers; similarly, Scotland's long tradition of print collections – from the publication of Thomson's *Orpheus Caledonius* in 1725 to the compiling of the Greig-Duncan Folk Song Collection prior to the First World War – can be understood as an important contributor to the variability, re-composition, and oral circulation of Scottish ballads, comparable to the relationship between ballads and print culture in seventeenth-century England.[52] Turning the clock further back, we see this overlap in the oral–written continuum in the compositional methods practiced in medieval Irish bardic schools as described by the Earl of Clanricarde in 1722 ('each by himself on his own bed, the whole next day in the dark, till at a certain hour of the night, lights being brought in, they committed to writing') and by the elite bards of Gaelic Scotland in the seventeenth century as observed by Martin Martin.[53] Turning the clock forward, we see it today in Scottish piping, which is often learned from printed sources, but performed from memory.

These overlaps and interweavings are not unprecedented. As Treitler has shown, our medieval forebears regarded memory 'not as an alternative to creativity but the route to it. It is the basis of *extempore* performance, but not in the sense of parroting what has been learnt by rote'.[54] Taking also into account the Baroque-era expectation 'that the performer be both literate and aurally trained to know the style conventions', this describes well the process of learning and performing pibrochs today, of which memorization is a key component.[55] To paraphrase Treitler, the same melodic or motivic properties that facilitated *composing* pibrochs facilitate *remembering* them. 'Remembering', he continues, 'is an active process of construction or reconstruction on the basis of formal schemes, salient details, and cues'.[56] This is an accurate description of the performance of both pibroch and traditional balladic song in Scotland and elsewhere, whose performers may have learned material from a range of printed and recorded sources, from tutors in a more or less formal setting, and via 'situated learning' in the home and community.[57]

Lord's oral-formulaic theory has some resonance here. As has been discussed, it relates to the binary harmonic formulae at the deep structural level of much Scottish, Irish, and Welsh instrumental music. The use of thematic formulae in Gaelic songs for waulking cloth and in Scots ballads – what MacInnes regarded merely as 'rhetorical techniques that employ an inherited store of imagery' – suggests that stability in Scottish traditional song is to be found primarily in narrative and content.[58] The subject matter of many older traditional waulking songs suggests origins in the sixteenth or seventeenth century and covers everyday Hebridean life from women's perspectives. Motivic analysis by J. L. Campbell and Francis Collinson suggests that a wide variety of these subjects, from the hospitality of the clan chief to a lover's gifts, references to musical instruments, success in hunting, and feelings towards the aristocratic class, were expressed in highly formulaic ways.[59] Formulaic imagery can also be seen in Scots ballads, for instance, as when a protagonist calls for a horse to be saddled, signalling the start of a journey. 'These formulas convey meaning at the level of deep structure,' writes Emily Lyle, 'so that even when the surface details differ the same fundamental meaning comes through'.[60] Such expressions appear to recall Lord's view that stability in oral traditional songs was to be found in the songs' essential stories, not their texts – though Lyle is careful to distinguish Scots balladry as 'affected by the context of literacy' and therefore not in quite the same category as Lord's epic singers.[61]

MacInnes, like Lyle, argues against the oral-formulaic theory's relevance to Scottish oral tradition.[62] To support his view 'that Gaelic oral poetry is not markedly formulaic and that what is represented as *ex tempore* composition is perhaps the least formulaic of all', he points to the body of songs composed by Duncan Bàn MacIntyre (1724–1812), who could neither read nor write but who composed and dictated over 6,000 lines, few of which showed evidence of formulaic expressions.[63] In relation, however, to instrumental Scottish music, melodic and rhythmic motifs play a strongly formulaic role: 'older material is present in newer musical material through the motivic re-use of canonical rhythms, melodic patterns and motifs', writes McKerrell, 'and it is in this sense that musical tradition can be understood to perform the past in the present'.[64]

Function and Change: Reprise

The 'problem of creation', as Brăiloiu put it, has been a convenient thread with which to cohere the range of modalities that I have drawn together in this chapter. Brăiloiu problematized the creative impulses in Romanian folk music in the early twentieth century, asking what were heretical questions for his time: is the oral poet not a creative agent rather than a mindless drone? Is variation a mere accident or rather an act of conscious artistic decision-making? Such questions were taken up in time by the likes of Lord and others, as we have seen. Inevitably, the sounds, representations, and perceptions of traditional Scottish, Irish, and other perceived Celtic forms of music have changed over time in tandem with the drifting of their functional loci. But where Scottish music is concerned, no change has made as significant an impact on the nature and functions of traditional music as the distance that has developed since the Scottish and Irish folk revival of the 1950s and 1970s between traditional dance forms, on the one hand, and the compositional aesthetics and practices of modern traditional musicians on the other. Since the 1980s, as McKerrell writes, we have witnessed 'the gradual dissolution of dance music forms and structures' in commercial music alongside forms such as jigs and reels being 'transformed into exciting new musical structures'.[65] Among bands and highly skilled soloists whose musicality is increasingly eclectic, this functional separation between dance forms and the types of tune traditionally performed to accompany them has afforded greater artistic opportunities to explore musical meaning through compositions that have stretched the boundaries of what is regarded as 'traditional'.[66]

Pipers no longer summon clans to battle and Highland women no longer keen at funerals nor sing to the waulking of cloth, except as self-conscious recreations of past custom. Although many maintain a belief that one's craft is in some way a family inheritance, few regard musical talent as a gift from the Otherworld. The professional class of musicians serving in the retinues of seventeenth-century nobility has given way to a professional class of freelance folk musicians operating in a tonal, rather than modal, world.

Some modalities nevertheless remain steadfast: the paradigmatic rules of deep structure and the harmonic frameworks of the Baroque era persist in pibroch, in the canonical rhythms and melodic motifs of Scottish and Irish dance music, and in the variational and improvisational toolkits of today's practitioners, for whom memorization aids (rather than hinders) creativity. The relationship between orality and literacy remains mutually supportive in the acquisition and transmission of music. Nationalist and labour movements related to the revival era found their most visceral expression through song, and traditional song still plays a role in commemorating historical events today, projecting an overt sense of belonging and an appeal to commonality. When the Scottish Parliament was resurrected in 1999 after a lapse of nearly 300 years, it opened to the sound of Sheena Wellington singing Robert Burns' 1795 'A Man's a Man for A' That', a statement on the common worth shared by a people – indeed, by all people:

> What though on hamely fare we dine,
> Wear hoddin grey, an' a that;
> Gie fools their silks, and knaves their wine;
> A man's a man for a' that:
> For a' that, and a' that,
> Their tinsel show, an' a' that;
> The honest man, tho' e'er sae poor,
> Is king o' men for a' that.

Notes

1. Constantin Brăiloiu, *Problems of Ethnomusicology*. Cambridge: Cambridge University Press, 1984, 103.
2. See Matthew Gelbart, *The Invention of 'Folk Music' and 'Art Music': Emerging Categories from Ossian to Wagner*. Cambridge: Cambridge University Press, 2007 and Simon McKerrell, *Focus: Scottish Traditional Music*. New York: Routledge, 2016.
3. John Purser, *Scotland's Music: A History of the Traditional and Classical Music of Scotland from Early Times to the Present Day*. Edinburgh: Mainstream Publishing, 1992, 145.
4. For example, see E. C. Carmichael, 'Never was Piping so Sad, Never was Piping so Gay'. *Celtic Review* 2 (1905): 76–84, 78.
5. Gelbart, *The Invention*, 62; Ailie Munro, 'Lizzie Higgins, and the Oral Transmission of Ten Child ballads'. *Scottish Studies* 14/2 (1970): 155–88, 157.
6. Gelbart, *The Invention*, 132.
7. Gelbart, *The Invention*, 132; Purser, *Scotland's Music*, 23–25.
8. Derick S. Thomson, 'Gaelic Learned Orders and Literati in Medieval Scotland'. *Scottish Studies* 12/1 (1968): 57–78, 70; John MacInnes, 'The Oral Tradition in Scottish Gaelic Poetry'. *Scottish Studies* 12/1 (1968): 29–43, 33.
9. See Ailie Munro, *The Democratic Muse: Folk Music Revival in Scotland*. Aberdeen: Scottish Cultural Press, 2006; Tamara Livingston, 'Music Revivals – Toward a General Theory'. *Ethnomusicology* 43/1 (1999): 66–85, 69; and Joshua Dickson, 'Tullochgorm Transformed: A Case Study in Revivalism and the Highland Pipe', in *The Highland Bagpipe: Music, History, Tradition*, ed. Joshua Dickson, 191–219. Aldershot: Ashgate, 2009, 193.

10. McKerrell, *Focus*, 124.
11. Alexander MacAulay, 'The MacKenzies of Lochboisdale'. *Piping Times* 13/10 (1961): 5–9, 6; John Angus MacDonald, 'The Songs of Donald Allan MacDonald'. MLitt thesis, University of Aberdeen, 1983, 91.
12. J. F. Nagy, 'Oral Tradition and Performance', in *Medieval Oral Literature*, ed. Karl Reichl. Berlin: Walter de Gruyter, 2011, 287.
13. Hugh Cheape, 'Traditional Origins of the Piping Dynasties', in *The Highland Bagpipe*, ed. Dickson, 97–126, 100–101.
14. MacInnes, 'The Oral Tradition', 40.
15. See Joshua Dickson, 'The Changing Nature of Conceptualisation and Authenticity among Scottish Traditional Musicians: Traditional Music, Conservatoire Education and the Case for Post-Revivalism', in *Understanding Scotland Musically: Folk, Tradition and Policy*, ed. Simon McKerrell and Gary West, 81–92. London: Routledge, 2018, and Jessica Cawley, 'The Musical Enculturation of Irish Traditional Musicians: an Ethnographic Study of Learning Processes'. PhD thesis, University College Cork, 2013.
16. Albert Lord, *The Singer of Tales*. Cambridge, MA: Harvard University Press, 2000, 20–25.
17. John Angus MacDonald, *Òrain Dhòmhnaill Ailein Dhòmhnaill na Bainich / The Songs of Donald Allan MacDonald: 1906-92*. Benbecula: Comann Eachdraidh nan Eilean mu Dheas, 1999, 60.
18. Joshua Dickson, *When Piping Was Strong: Tradition, Change and the Bagpipe in South Uist*. Edinburgh: John Donald, 2006, 232.
19. Nagy, 'Oral Tradition and Performance', 287; Carmichael, 'Never was Piping so Sad', 78.
20. Dickson, *When Piping Was Strong*, 26.
21. Gelbart, *The Invention*, 156–61.
22. Donaldson, *The Highland Pipe and Scottish Society, 1750–1950*. East Linton: Tuckwell Press, 2000, 19.
23. Ardis Butterfield, 'Repetition and Variation in the Thirteenth-Century Refrain'. *Journal of the Royal Musical Association* 116/1 (1991): 1–23, 11.
24. Susan Wittig, *Stylistic and Narrative Structures in the Middle English Romances*. Austin: University of Texas Press, 2014, 8.
25. Gelbart, *The Invention*, 116.
26. Roderick D. Cannon, *Joseph MacDonald's Compleat Theory of the Scots Highland Bagpipe (c. 1760)*. Glasgow: The Piobaireachd Society, 1994, 74.
27. Robin Lorimer, 'Studies in Pibroch'. *Scottish Studies* 6 (1962): 1–30. For a much earlier attempt, see C. S. Thomason, *Ceol Mor*, 1975.
28. Cannon, *Joseph MacDonald's Compleat Theory*, 64.
29. Robin Lorimer, *Pibroch: Classical Music of the Scots Highland Bagpipe*. Edinburgh: Waverley Press, 1964, 1.

30. Gelbart, *The Invention*, 142.
31. M. Wesseling, 'Structure and Image in the "Altus Prosator": Columba's Symmetrical Universe'. *Proceedings of the Harvard Celtic Colloquium* 8 (1988): 46–57, 51.
32. Barnaby Brown, 'Scottish Traditional Grounds, Part 1: Tullochgorm'. *Piping Today* 38 (2009): 44–47, 47.
33. Peter Greenhill, 'Author's Note to the Present 2010 Edition'. *The Robert ap Huw MS – An Exploration of its Possible Solutions*. www.cl.cam.ac.uk/~rja14/musicfiles/manuscripts/aphuw/.
34. Peter Cooke, 'Some thoughts on the song melodies in Elizabeth Ross's Collection of "Original Highland Airs", 1812', in *'A Guid Hairst': Collecting and Archiving Scottish Tradition: Essays in Honour of Dr Margaret A Mackay*, ed. K Campbell, W Lamb, et al., 103–23. Masstricht: Shaker Publishing, 2013. 107–8, 115; Brown, 'Scottish Traditional Grounds, Part 1', 47; Barnaby Brown, 'Scottish Traditional Grounds, Part 3: Bonnie Annie'. *Piping Today* 42 (2009): 38–41, 39; Barnaby Brown, 'The Craft of Pibroch: A Study of the Technical Language of Scottish Gaelic Pipers in Sources 1751–1838'. PhD thesis, University of Cambridge, 2021, 60.
35. For example, Simon McKerrell, 'Scottish Competition Bagpipe Performance: Sound, Mode, and Aesthetics'. PhD thesis, Royal Conservatoire of Scotland and University of St Andrews, 2005.
36. See Gelbart, *The Invention*, 160; Brăiloiu, *Problems of Ethnomusicology*, 6, 103.
37. Lord, *The Singer of Tales*, 4, 5, 13.
38. Leo Treitler, *With Voice and Pen: Coming to Know Medieval Song and How It Was Made*. Oxford: Oxford University Press, 2003, 58.
39. Mats Johansson, 'Improvisation in Traditional Music: Learning Practices and Principles'. *Music Education Research* 24/1 (2022): 56–69, 57.
40. Breandán Breathnach, *The Use of Notation in the Transmission of Irish Folk Music*. Cork: Cumann Cheol Tradisiúnta Éireann, 1986, 9.
41. J. L. Campbell and Francis Collinson, *Hebridean Folksongs III: Waulking Songs from Vatersay, Barra, Eriskay, South Uist and Benbecula*. Oxford: Oxford University Press, 1981, 223; MacInnes, 'The Oral Tradition', 32.
42. Campbell and Collinson, *Hebridean Folksongs*, 200.
43. Wittig, *Stylistic and Narrative Structures*, 8.
44. Daniel Heartz and Patricia Rader, 'Basse danse (Fr.; It. bassadanza)'. *Grove Music Online* (2001). DOI: https://doi.org/10.1093/gmo/9781561592630.article.02242'.
45. Brown, 'The Craft of Pibroch', 313; see also John MacInnes, 'Allan MacDonald', in *Dastirum* ed. Barnaby Brown, 55–57. Cambridge: Siubhal.com, 2007, 56.
46. Barnaby Brown, 'Making Sense of Pibroch', in *Donald MacPherson: a Living Legend*, 19–25. Cambridge: Siubhal.com, 2004, 20.
47. Purser, *Scotland's Music*, 44.
48. Dickson, *When Piping Was Strong*, 234.

49. Lord, *The Singer of Tales*, 13, 137.
50. Brăiloiu, *Problems of Ethnomusicology*, 57.
51. Ruth Finnegan, *Literacy and Orality; or, Studies in the Technologies of Communication*. Milton Keynes: Callender Press, 2014 and Ruth Finnegan, *Oral Poetry: Its Nature, Significance and Social Context*. Cambridge: Cambridge University Press, 1977.
52. See Adam Fox, *Oral and Literate Culture in England, 1500–1700*. Oxford: Oxford University Press, 2000.
53. Finnegan, *Oral Poetry*, 19; Martin Martin, *A Description of the Western Islands of Scotland Circa 1695*. Edinburgh: Birlinn, 1999, 79.
54. Treitler, *With Voice and Pen*, 136.
55. Patricia Shehan Campbell, 'Orality, Literacy and Music's Creative Potential: A Comparative Approach'. *Bulletin of the Council for Research in Music Education* 101 (1989): 30–40, 37.
56. Treitler, *With Voice and Pen*, 134.
57. Jean Lave and Etienne Wenger. *Situated Learning: Legitimate Peripheral Participation*. Cambridge: Cambridge University Press, 1991.
58. MacInnes, 'The Oral Tradition', 40; Lord, *The Singer of Tales*, 138.
59. See Campbell and Collinson, *Hebridean Folksongs*.
60. Emily Lyle, *Scottish Ballads*. Edinburgh: Canongate, 1994, 17.
61. Lyle, *Scottish Ballads*, 16.
62. MacInnes, 'The Oral Tradition', 40.
63. Douglas Young, 'Never Blotted a Line? Formula and Premeditation in Homer and Hesiod.' *Arion* 6/3 (1967): 279–324, 284.
64. McKerrell, *Focus*, 147.
65. McKerrell, *Focus*, 123.
66. See Lori Watson, 'The New Traditional School in Scotland: Innovation, Beyond-Tune Composition and a Traditional Musician's Creative Practice'. PhD thesis, Royal Conservatoire of Scotland and University of St Andrews, 2012.

7 | Thinking About the Words to Folks' Songs

DIANNE DUGAW

In 1939, Phillips Barry defined a folk song as one 'most people – or most *folks* – are fond of singing' – a commonsensical definition avoiding the mystifications that often weigh down folksong scholarship.[1] Instead, Barry points us towards inclusive parameters that shape the familiarity and singing of certain songs over time as they circulate and remain 'alive' to people. Consistently remembered, shareable, and re-voiced in informal performance, folk songs are the ones that remain widely known by people who sing them from memory and hear them and keep them sung and heard across swaths of space and time. What are the words of such songs like? How do they work? What can we say about them?

From the outset, let's admit that commentary on the lyrics of folk song as a general category, the world over, is an impossibly broad topic. My remarks will draw the majority of examples from and focus attention on my areas of familiarity and expertise, primarily Anglo-American and British traditions from the early modern era to the present. I offer particular songs for, I hope, a broadly useful, inclusive, and illustrative sense of how people's singing and song traditions work, pulling especially from one illustrative context of vibrant song-making. Any of the examples from other contexts could be explored with similar range and detail. Recurring characteristics that I identify in these examples are not limited to the categories of songs in which they appear here; they occur widely across song types.

Cultures, Communities, and Songs

Folk songs come from an arena that might be called *unofficial* culture – what we adopt, as if by osmosis, because we live 'here' and 'now', among people who show us what to do next, how to do it, and (sometimes) why. This domain does not heed the divisions of orality and literacy, popular and elite, folk transmission and commercial exposure or formal instruction that much scholarship has insisted upon. Such songs represent one way that people maintain cultural expression and participation on their own, taking up, holding onto, and reshaping aspects of culture alongside those official and commercial elements that are maintained and sanctioned 'from above'. Important to the formation and transmission of this level of culture are orality and collectivity: learning 'by ear', and passing along 'by word of mouth' in a process of adopting and adapting songs to serve people's lives and spirits. Mysterious and not altogether predictable, orally transmitted and traditional songs are part of a complex, ongoing process of borrowing, re-creation, and reciprocity among all levels of culture.

People sing and rely on songs that fulfill emotional, calendrical, ritual and other purposes. The ubiquitous 'Happy Birthday to You', originally composed at the turn of the twentieth century by Kentucky school teachers Patty and Mildred Hill, is sung across the United States and many other countries in some twenty languages – a marker for birthday celebrations almost worldwide.[2] Indeed, for many calendrical occasions people remember and sing songs, whatever their origins and without regard to possible copyright restrictions – for example, the carols 'Jingle Bells' and 'Silent Night' at Christmas, often sung to mark the season with little or no attention to religious tenets.[3]

Shared place and time, as well as language and ethnicity, establish communities of people who create and may then re-create songs in continuing traditions – sometimes over centuries. For instance, some eighteenth-century Scots sang ballads that were published by collectors of that time. In 1802, author and literary figure Walter Scott published *Minstrelsy of the Scottish Border*, a collection of such songs. Some had already long been known and continue to be sung today, as is the case with what is known in English as 'The Two Sisters', in Danish 'Hørpu rima', in Norwegian 'Dei tvo systar', and in Swedish 'De to Søstre' or 'De talende strenglelag'.[4] Many songs have similarly crossed borders of language, geography, and culture, spread by contacts of trade, emigration, diaspora, and colonization as well as by media networks. Variants of a particular song might be sung in English-speaking Britain and Gaelic Ireland, as well as in the French, German, Italian, Spanish, and Slavic languages of Europe and the Mediterranean Basin, and beyond.[5]

A note about ballads, which for many people may be a first or primary association with the term *folk song* and its study: in scholarly discourse since the eighteenth century across the disciplines of literatures, languages, musicology, and folklore, a ballad is a narrative song set to a stanzaic tune, thus distinguishing it from nonnarrative or lyrical song. Focusing on a single episode and a small cast of characters, a ballad usually tells of catastrophe – death, defeat, stolen love, shipwreck, destruction. In all European languages since the medieval period, anonymous popular ballads representing a collective cultural sensibility have been widely studied, displaying recognizable links and parallels across regions.[6]

Characteristics of the Words to Folk Songs

Recognizable traits characterize the diverse songs that persist in people's traditions. For example: simplifying repetitions enhance memorability. Formulaic openings and framings make and keep songs readily familiar and accessible. Conventional images and phrases likewise make a song seem 'recognizable' on first acquaintance and easy to sing and remember thereafter, ensuring a deeper familiarity and emotional resonance for a community that shares the conventions. Responsorial forms and improvisation engage audience participants and prompt on-the-spot re-creation. Rhetorical voice enlivens a song and shapes its relevance as a keepsake: third-person narration for storytelling songs; a first-person speaker – a heartfelt 'I' – to convey personal feeling and identifiable experience; or second-person address to heighten dialogic interest and tension, at times bringing us face-to-face with fearsome disaster or supernatural and larger-than-ordinary experience. Recurrent patterning in the overarching narrative structure of songs can ensure collective relevance, especially as people pass songs along over generations to re-make the predictable frame narrative, allowing room for the diversity of everyone's experience to find a place.

Of course, formulaic elements of music and song differ from one community to another across shifts wrought by time as the functions of songs and their words mutate. For example, popular songs held different and more various functions in the culture of eighteenth-century London than in the present-day city. There, the pre-modern world fashioned songs that were more integrally tied to topical events, with narrative ballads supplying 'coverage' not unlike contemporary journalism: 'Of fire, fire, fire, I sing' opens 'London mourning in Ashes', a ballad of 1666 detailing the devastating blaze that levelled the city in September of that year.[7] While informing about the news of the day, such ballads often satirically commented on it as well. Songs widely sung in that cultural milieu combined aspects that more recently have operated as separate arenas: vehicles for entertainment or expression of sentiment; news journalism now in print, broadcast, and on-line sources; political satire, cartoons, and memes to lampoon people and happenings; and comedy routines that likewise ridicule, rail, and humorously comment on public matters. As we'll see, some have continued to circulate as folk songs long after the passing of their original pre-modern context. Today, by contrast, songs function primarily as entertainment or ceremonial forms, more likely lyrical than narrative, and often more imaginative than documentary. Diverting us from the 'real business' of our daily lives, songs in present-day Anglophone tradition, rather than relaying the news, bring us together in communities of taste and heritage.[8]

The basic modern structures of the dynamic of commercial and non-commercial reciprocity have remained in place since Shakespeare's era, when the emergence of print media – single-sheet broadsides – first allowed the cheap, street-level marketing of popular songs. As folk-song scholar D. K. Wilgus observed in the 1950s, the earlier Phillips Barry included ballad printers among the folk 'keepers of tradition'.[9] If to Barry's 'printers' and 'broadsides' we add newer commercial media – in Wilgus's time radio, tape, and vinyl recordings, and more recently, CDs, downloads, YouTube clips, streaming, and whatever is coming next – only then can the depth and dimensions of singers' traditions and the ongoing recreation and singing of folksongs be understood.

The folk songs of any culture that I have sampled entail a range of fertile and paradoxical tensions and interplay: between the individual and the collective; unity and diversity; invention and convention; topicality and tradition; novelty and familiarity; professional and amateur; public and private. As Mark Booth has observed, people hear and then choose to sing any song as an imaginative absorption. Experiencing a performance of the song, maybe even singing along, brings a listener into 'the interior of a shared image' with the singer.[10] Folk songs – especially, those songs that, in a given cultural context, 'most folks are fond of singing' – shine with an exhilaratingly familiar imaginative resonance that engages and unites their listeners and singers.

Childhood Remembered over Centuries

Childhood is marked by singing in myriad ways: lullabies, game and counting songs, teaching tools, ritual markers, and entertainments. As adults, many people across cultures and social levels can summon up songs from early life, remembered years later in the voices of parents, grandparents, aunts and uncles, siblings, companions, or social gatherings of various sorts.

Lyrics to children's songs usually display two general and frequent features, which keep these and many folk songs readily singable and memorable: simplifying repetitions and formulaic openings and framings. Interspersed burdens and refrains – for children, often involving repeated nonsense syllables with vivid and enjoyable sounds – invite an interweaving response from listeners: a 'chorus' answers the principal singer, in the kind of patterned-repetition-with-variations that humans (probably among other creatures) love and find satisfying. Orally circulating folk songs, and especially children's songs, focus tightly on a few images or actions if the song has a narrative arc. To interest children, these are often startling and exaggerated, while the pace is likely slowed and farcically abbreviated.

Green Berry Horton, a fifth-generation banjo-picker and farmer, lived down a twisty, beautifully wooded 'holler' in the Ozark Mountains of Arkansas, where I visited him as a young music and song enthusiast in the mid-1970s. He reported that his Granny sang a song called 'Bangston' to him as a child, the youngest of a large family living on that farm at about the time of World War I. Children love a good grotesquing of adult activities, and 'Bangston' delivers this with gusto. Rollicking yet deadpan, it mock-heroically touts an Arkansas woodsman riding along a river with his 'slide', that is, a nineteenth to early twentieth-century logging rig.

'Hit's jes a silly ol' kids' song', Green Berry Horton chuckled to me as we sat on his porch looking across the tomato field of that high summer. His pale-blue eyes widened mischievously as he drew on his pipe, then sang a capella:

Bangston rode that river side.	*Diddle-i-do-dum.*
Bangston rode that river side.	*Quiddle-i-quo-qum.*
Bangston rode that river side	
With two horses and a slide.	*Diddle-i-do-dum, quiddle-i-quo-qum.*

The song continued in the formulaic mode typical of folk songs, with easy-to-remember repetitions, and startling yet spare specificities:

Bangston rode around that wild hog pen.	*Diddle-i-do* &c. (3x)
And he spied the bones of a thousand men.	*Diddle-i-do* &c.
Bangston drew his wooden knife.	*Diddle-i-do* &c. (3x)
And he swore he'd take that wild hog's life.	*Diddle-i-do* &c.
He drew his bugle to his mouth.	*Diddle-i-do* &c. (3x)
Blew east and west, both north and south.	*Diddle-i-do* &c.
Bangston rode that river side.	*Diddle-i-do* &c. (3x)
With two horses and a slide.	*Diddle-i-do* &c.[11]

In the paradoxically fenced-in 'wild hog pen', Bangston spies 'the bones of a thousand men', just the right note of hyperbolic grisliness (think of the old lady 'who swallowed a fly', followed by successively larger insects and animals until she choked on 'a horse' and 'died, of course'). Green Berry Horton's absurd hero responds with a flourish of his 'wooden knife', a toy weapon wielded amid the laughably mock-Latin *quiddle-i-quo-qums*. In a final parodic military move, Bangston draws 'his bugle to his mouth' – always amid the framing *diddles* and *quiddles* – to blow magisterially in all four directions, 'east and west, both north and south'. Whereupon horses, hero, and slide continue their sashay down 'that river side'. where it all began – with little to nothing done about the threatening pen of wild hogs.

In fact, Green Berry Horton's 'Bangston' has a history longer than his Granny's time. As students of folk traditions appreciate, individual songs that 'catch on' in singers' oral traditions seem to take on lives of their own through time and space, often traversing social strata and intersecting realms of oral tradition and print, amateur and professional. A textual and melodic ancestor to 'Bangston' is 'Sir Eglamore', a farcical ballad found in 1680s London songbooks popular at the court of King Charles II. Sir Eglamore, 'a valiant Knight', vanquishes a 'Dragon ... that had slain God knows how many Men', in a narrative punctuated throughout by a *'fa la, lanky down dilly'* refrain. After flourishing among the high and mighty (undoubtedly freighted with political innuendo), a reworked 'Sir Eglamore' then circulated lower down the social scale. Over time, the fanciful name becomes 'Sir Rylas' or 'Sir Robert Bolton', the song shrinks to a handful of verses, and the fearsome dragon turns into a monstrous pig.[12] By the 1800s, settlers from the British Isles brought the ballad with them to America, where it continued to be part of oral traditions with various titles: 'Wild Boar', 'Bangum and the Boar', 'Brangywell', 'Old Bang 'em', and as Green Berry Horton's toy-wielding logger, 'Bangston'.[13]

Themes of Lost Love

Another hallmark of folk-song lyrics is vivid yet conventional images that render a song both memorable for the singer and familiar to the audience. In 1973, Laurence Hightower of Bee Branch, Arkansas, sang for me 'Bring Me Back My Blue-Eyed Boy', a mournful first-person lyric in the voice of a maid bereft of her beloved who has gone to sea without her – learned, he said, 'from wonderful old friends a-way back yonder'.[14] Besides repeated phrases and images, repetition occurs in alliterative sounds: 'Bring me back my blue-eyed boy', sings the chorus after each verse; 'Bring my darling back to me, / Bring me back the one I love, / And Oh, how happy I shall be.' The stanzas present the speaker's lovelorn grief in a simple image – a bird who can fly away to the desired: 'I wish I was a little bird,' she sings, then laments that she must instead 'sit and moan, and pass the weary hours by', repeating after each stanza the plaintive, pleading chorus: 'Bring me back my blue-eyed boy'.

In many popular songs and hymns a speaker longs to fly as a bird to a distant lover or a homeland or even heaven. In the eighteenth-century 'Maid of Bedlam', the 'maid' expresses this desire, as does the abandoned girl-speaker of 'The Sparrow / Come All You Fair and Tender Ladies', another song long-remembered by Anglo-American singers that echoes the stanzas of Laurence Hightower's 'Blue-Eyed Boy'.[15] Formulaic images about having wings and taking flight appear in songs of various types – especially blues, spirituals, and widely popular hymns such as 'Some Glad Morning' ('I'll fly away to glory').[16] This commonplace yet powerfully emancipatory image of people yearning and potentially becoming able to fly away notably weaves throughout African American songs, hymns, and stories. As Leslie Dunn and Nancy Jones observe, 'flight is a recurrent image in ... African American songs ... a symbolic opportunity for oppressed slaves to free themselves.'[17]

'Bring Me Back My Blue-eyed Boy', as encountered in Arkansas, also shows how an individual singer's life can resonate with and determine the choice and function of songs. Laurence Hightower (animated, wiry, and well along in his seventies when I met him) sang mournful songs whose words filled a neatly handwritten notebook with lyrics about vanished lovers. When asked about his repertoire, he told me that when he was young his promised bride took sick and died shortly before the wedding day. He never married. That love doesn't work out is a ubiquitous theme; for Hightower, it had particular poignance.

In addition, 'Blue-Eyed Boy' reveals the consistent back-and-forth between popular commercial versions of songs and the so-called 'traditional' forms of people's songs. In Laurence Hightower's youth, variants of 'Blue-eyed Boy' were being sung as folk songs and noticed by collectors, primarily in the southern United States. In addition, versions had appeared in print in *Wehman Brothers' Good Old-Time Songs, No. 2* (1910) as 'My Love is a-going across the sea', and on commercial recordings in 1929, by Arthur Tanner and Riley Puckett in Atlanta, and the Carter Family in Virginia.[18] Radio shows, barn dances, traveling performers, recordings, and the like contributed to and gained from the repertoires of ordinary singers like Laurence Hightower. Over time, most songs that people sing circulate within a complex, reciprocal, and mutually reinforcing matrix of commercial and non-commercial dissemination; written and oral; and professional and non-professional artistry.

This interplay of commercial songs, the singing of ordinary people, and the links such familiarity have to the time of one's youth stood out recently in my hometown. Jake Martini, a young professional songwriter and singer/musician now centred in Nashville, Tennessee, returned to Oregon for a visit. During his week in Eugene, Jake played a night at Sam Bond's Garage, a longstanding venue of the local music scene. A standing-room-only crowd, loudly good-spirited, jammed the pub as servers squeezed through dispersing beer, fries, and burgers to parents and siblings, aunties and uncles, cousins and comrades from Jake's earlier life, before relocation to seek his fortune in 'Music City'. In general, the fans represented two generations: proud parents, former teachers, employers, and mentors on the one hand, and on the other, cheering friends, cousins, former bandmates, and the like.

Onstage with an acoustic guitar, Martini affectionately bantered and sang in an array of pop modes – folk, country, hip-hop. Midway, he treated the audience to well-chosen, sing-a-long 'call-back' songs, appropriate to the generational split. At the first words of 'Sweet Caroline', older fans in particular joined at the top of their voices: 'Good times never seemed so good'. In rising crescendos, Neil Diamond's cult oldie of 1969 was bellowed to the rafters. A song or two later, the venue burst into a similar eruption as the crowd's younger half sang to Martini's deft cover of 'Just a Friend' by Biz Markie (Marcel Theo Hall). The chorus to this 1989 pop hip-hop ballad, notably and comically more sceptical about love than Diamond's, filled the bar: 'You, you got what I need / but you say he's just a friend / And you say he's just a friend, oh baby'. With all the gusto of the older song, 'Just a Friend' wailed and boomed, many singers even rhyming along by memory in the extended rap narration of Markie's rueful first-person tale of (almost wilfully naive) romantic self-deception. Members of each generation leapt eagerly at the chance to sing familiar songs of their youth – with most of the words intact. Will 'Sweet Caroline' or 'Just a Friend' remain known to future singers? That question will have to be answered in a hundred years or so.

Responses to Catastrophe

Rhetorical voice shapes the experience of any song. The solemn third-person narrator relating Bangston's farcical hero-mongering, for example, prompts our laughter and engagement with ridiculous scenes and images. The lovelorn first-person speaker of 'Blue-Eyed Boy' moves singer and hearer to emotional sympathy with the song's bereft 'I' and its familiar topic of lost love. With similar effect, invocational second-person framing frequently governs the creation and experience of songs. As Thomas Dubois notes,

> second-person address in an unambiguously stylized and predictable manner ... foregrounds its distinctiveness from an ordinary utterance in every way. It is associative in that it powerfully underscores both an inscribed speaker and an inscribed recipient, be it a lover, an absent friend, or a powerful supernatural entity.[19]

Songs on topics of devastating loss and remembrance, cataclysmic and deadly events, and human confrontation with enormity and inexplicability frequently direct their lyrics to an addressee. Seemingly universal is the linking of song to elegiac feeling and expression, and second-person address may serve the rhetorical heightening that Dubois calls 'a mystical understanding', expanding a song's scope of gravity and grief to underscore the collective function of songs in the face of mysterious and fearsome enormities.[20]

Across cultures, people have responded to disaster and loss with songs recounting misfortune and lamenting the costs of storms and earthquakes, fires and floods, shipwrecks and train wrecks, and calamities of every kind – as already noted earlier with regard to 'London mourning in Ashes'. Following the massive volcanic eruption in 1980 of Mount Saint Helens in the Pacific Northwest corner of the United States, locals in this sparsely populated area generated songs, their regionally produced recordings on 7-inch vinyl phonograph 'singles' could be purchased at markets, gas stations, pharmacies, and tackle shops.

'Mighty Mount Saint Helens' by Jeanie Bigbee of Mossyrock, Washington, is one such response. A prolific and recognized songsmith in her small town, Bigbee described some years later being asked for a song about the eruption: '[People] said "You know how we all feel. Put it down."' She recounted her rapid creation of tune and lyrics, pointedly personifying and speaking to the volcano: 'It didn't take me any time ... it tells about [the erupting mountain's] raving ... her [earlier] beauty, and ... how could anything so absolutely beautiful turn to something so wicked?'[21] Her song opens with striking direct address:

> We listened to you rumble. We listened to you roar.
> We watched the smoke roll from your top like we'd never seen before.
> You'd given us fair warning that where there's smoke there's fire.
> O, Mighty Mount Saint Helens you've left nothing to admire.[22]

People living near volcanoes have typically personified them – perhaps a response to their singular form and dominance over a landscape, perhaps because of their changeable activity, producing intermittent tremors, steaming crevices, lava leaks, hot springs, rumblings, smoke plumes, and ash-rains. As traditional stories of the Cowlitz, Chehalis, and Klickitat peoples attest, this personifying predated the coming of Europeans. Fraught tensions run through depictions of the volcanic triangle that settlers dubbed Mount Saint Helens and her 'suitors': Mount Rainier (Tahoma) to the north, Mount Adams (Pahto or Klickitat) to the east, and Hood (Wy'east) to the south. Respectful of possible harm (or 'wickedness', to use Jeanie Bigbee's term), the Indigenous peoples warned Euro-American newcomers of the threatening spirits randomly spooking Lawetlat'la – 'The Smoker', as Mount Saint Helens was known to the Cowlitz – prompting her fiery and destructive outbursts.

Direct address and personification characterize a further sampling of songs from the region that, like 'Mighty Mount Saint Helens', were created and sung in connection with the 1980 eruption. Rick Bartlett's 'Ballad of Harry Truman', written just before the explosion, achieved wider – even national – airplay, echoing local authorities and news outlets at the time in pleading with an 'old timer named Harry', who lived at the base of the pluming and quaking mountain, to see reason and evacuate his home:

> Harry, won't you come down offa that mountain.
> There isn't nothing you can do.

In response, and directly addressing the personified Saint Helens, the song's defiant codger refuses, as indeed the much-interviewed and ultimately lava-interred Harry Truman did:

> Harry looked straight up at the mountain.
> He said, 'Mountain, I'm not afraid of you.'[23]

As the final stanza ends, the volcano has, as the speaker predicted, 'come down on you'.

Similarly facing natural disaster and its terror, Bessie Smith's 1927 'Homeless Blues' (Columbia 14260-D), one of many songs about the devastating Mississippi flood of that year, opens with an address to the river:

> Mississippi River, what a fix you left me in.
> Lord, Mississippi River, what a fix you left me in.
> Mudholes of water clear up to my chin.

Stanzas of 'Homeless Blues' recount details of the flood experience:

> 'Homeless, yes, I'm homeless, might as well be dead (2x)
> Hungry and disgusted, no place to lay my head.

The speaker concludes with a rueful longing to fly away from the destructive waters:

> Wished I was an eagle, but I'm a plain old black crow. (2x)
> I'm gonna flop my wings and leave here and never come back no more.[24]

The still widely sung blues 'Titanic (Fare Thee Well)' (1948) by Lead Belly (Huddy Ledbetter) interrupts third-person narration with recurring second-person invocation, as a heightening tag-line to each stanza as events of the infamous wreck are recounted:

> It was midnight on the sea,
> The band was playing 'Nearer my God to Thee,'
>   *Fare thee, Titanic, Fare thee well. (2x each stanza)* ...
> Titanic was comin' around the curve
> When she ran into that big iceberg,
>   *Fare thee, Titanic, Fare thee well.* &c.[25]

In 1999 Gail Branum and Louise Beckman responded in a similar way to a contemporary shipwreck and oil spill off the northwest Pacific coast of the United States. Exemplifying the popular-culture matrix for people's song-making, 'The Tale of the New Carissa' guaranteed sing-ability by borrowing the tune of the theme song from a widely re-aired US TV show of the 1960s, the cult favorite *Gilligan's Island*.[26]

> Just sit right back and you'll hear a tale,
>   A tale of a fateful trip
> That started from this tropic port
>   Aboard this tiny ship.[27]

'The New Carissa' uses this matrix for a new saga:

> That started on a Thursday morn
>   Aboard a cargo ship, aboard a cargo ship.

Americans of all ages tend to recognize the hornpipe-like ditty, one repeatedly used to set satirical songs. With the gusto of familiarity, listeners could thus join in with each stanza's repeating tag-lines as 'The New Carissa' recounts the ship's breaking apart, its two halves drifting along the coast leaking fuel (despite attempted interventions), its hulks eventually washing ashore and then floating off again – even as the lambasted Coast Guard 'told reporters,/ 'This time we'll get it right, This time we'll get it right.'"[28]

Second-person address occurs in disaster songs in other languages as well. For example, with elegiac grief the Asturian/Spanish 'Santa Barbara Bendita' responds to a tragic mining accident, invoking both Santa Barbara (Saint Barbara), patron of lightning, explosion, dynamite – and therefore miners – and also the first-person speaker's beloved, Maruxina. From the province of Asturias, in the north of Spain, the text quoted here is in Asturian dialect, but the song is sung throughout Spain in the generally spoken Castilian (often titled 'El pozo de María Luísa'). Set to a tune with the haunting rhythm of a funeral march, each stanza includes a stirring, easily sung non-lexical refrain (of the sort we saw in 'Bangston'): *'Trailarai larai, trailarai'*. The song's speaker, wounded in a deadly blast in the María Luisa coal pit, returns with 'cabeza rota' (fractured head) and shirt 'roxa ... De sangre d'un compañeru' (red with a comrade's blood). With implicit denunciation, he cries 'Mirái, mirái Maruxina, mirái' (Look, look Maruxina), 'mirái como vengo yo' (look how I'm coming home).[29] A well-known anthem, 'Santa Barbara Bendita' still accompanies protests, especially of miners as well as workers more generally, and remains widely sung in Spain.

Making Space for Marginal Experience

Beyond conventional phrases, images, refrains, forms of address, and other characteristics mentioned earlier, a frequent feature of folk songs that 'catch on' over centuries is recurrent narrative patterning. We see this in an extensive group of ballads about gender nonconforming female warriors – fighting and sailing women who cross-dressed and passed as men. These songs rose to popularity as the equivalent of pop hits from Shakespeare's time through to the Victorian age, when they were widely sung, printed, and sold. Some remained in oral traditions as folk songs. Hundreds of variants of well over a hundred of these songs existed in English from the sixteenth century to the present; a few dozen continue in singers' repertoires. Many are found in other languages.[30]

In the 1970s Ozarks, another acquaintance-informant named Ollie Gilbert sang two such ballads for me in her home in Mountainview, Arkansas: 'Pretty Polly' and 'Cruel War'. She identified them as songs 'from the American Civil War' that she had learned from her mother and grandmother. Subsequent research in archival collections of English broadsides revealed that singers and printers had known versions of 'Pretty Polly' and 'Cruel War' in the early 1700s, well before the mid nineteenth-century lifetime of Ollie Gilbert's grandmother.[31]

A model of daring and pluck, 'Pretty Polly' dons male disguise to inhabit a highly conventionalized narrative that has spanned centuries. In the opening stanzas:

> Way down in the valley Pretty Polly did dwell,
> Who was courted by a captain who loved her so well.
> Her father and mother came this for to know
> And parted Pretty Polly and her own true love.
>
> One night she was musing on the bed
> A very strange notion came through Polly's head.
> She went through her father's stables and viewed them around
> And picked out a horse to travel the ground.
>
> Then first a vest coat she put on,
> And in every degree, she seemed like a man.
> With a brace and a pistol swung by her side,
> Like a United States soldier Pretty Polly did ride.

Predictable elements of this story-type arrive in a standard sequence: the heroine conjoins her inclinations to what the culture categorizes as on the one hand 'womanly' love, on the other 'manly' courage; in most cases, separation from her lover prompts her disguising and adventuring; journeying as a soldier or sailor, usually to combat, she overcomes tests of both prowess and love; eventually, discovery of her disguise brings about, not disgrace or condemnation, but reunion with her lover and celebration of her and her achievement.

Although elements of the story ring predictably, the pattern governing these ballads in fact overturns and thus exposes long-standing systemic concepts of gender and heroism as these contribute to and create each other. Across the time-span of these ballads' wide circulation, socially constructed and transmitted binary gender norms – 'man' OR 'woman' – posit 'manliness' as necessary to most stories of honour, action, and heroism. *Doing* characterizes the male role; while passive *undergoing* typifies the predominant female role. By contrast, in these ballads, the disguising woman performs an active role that undermines the fixity of this binary. Further, this female heroism unseats paradigms about women's supposed 'natural' frailty, whether psychological or physical.

After flourishing in singing and print for centuries, the female warrior waned in commercial popularity; modern folk singers like Ollie Gilbert nevertheless remembered and performed dozens of these long-ago songs for collectors. Many such singers – though not all – were women, who may well have been heartened by the challenge to cultural restrictions that the female hero offered in this song pattern. In 1941, the folklorist Alan Lomax asked Nova Scotia singer Carrie Grover – who recorded a number of these songs – if she ever had 'daydreams of being such a woman soldier'. 'I sure did,' replied Mrs. Grover. 'I had daydreams about a good many of these songs ... I imagine things like this happened in the days gone by ... but now they've got laws, so they couldn't get away with it'.[32]

Despite literary instances of disguising women (for example in Shakespeare's *Twelfth Night*) being long assumed to be a fanciful literary trope, historical women did in fact disguise as men and fight in many wars over the centuries, as Grover astutely surmised. Documentable women who went to sea or soldiered as men, occupying 'manly' social contexts as well as narratives, and receiving 'manly' pay – to which women otherwise had no access – were certainly one significant motive for such lived histories.[33]

Female-warrior ballads illustrate another way that folk songs may become long-lasting: when they encompass and represent not just dominant norms, but edges and reversals, questionings and re-imaginings of culturally predominant standards. Offering success stories about (to use earlier terms) a hermaphroditic 'masculine-feminine', or an androgynous 'tomboy', these songs parallel what today we term non-binary, transgender, or trans identity. Furthermore, they make space for often strikingly queer implications of same-sex desire. Although the overarching structure of these ballads typically fashions, and closes with, a heterosexual love story, along the way the gender-disguising guarantees homoerotic innuendo in the telling and creates a queering space, which many ballads steer directly into. Men are sexually attracted to these 'Pollys' and 'Nancys', while thinking they are men; and women are as well. A song from the 1700s proclaims: 'In soldier cloaths she look'd so smart, / She captur'd many a virgin's heart.'[34] Deliberately foregrounding homoeroticism, the ship's captain in another song 'sighs' over his cabin boy and declares: 'Your ruby lips and cherry cheek have so enticed me / That I do wish with all my heart you were a maid, said he'.[35] Each time the song is sung and heard, it opens to imaginative exploration of alternative desires – as transgender writer-activist Leslie Feinberg recognized in the 1990s.[36] In the past, just as much as now, genders and sexualities were and have always been various and performative rather than innately fixed or essential. As the centuries-long singing of female-warrior ballads attests, 'folks' have been glad to acknowledge and recount this fact.[37]

Call and Response and the Re-creative Spirit

Discussions of folk song often elide the vast arena of religious and spiritual songs found in every culture. Such songs reach people through officially produced and institutionally overseen channels; however, they can remain vital and revisited in personal and collective repertoires long after their official sanction and fashion wane. At their home on Canaan Mountain, Arkansas, in the 1970s, Noni Ward and her husband David performed the song 'Workin' on a Building'. As Noni on guitar led with her ringing soprano, David joined with growly, low, overlapping responses, then united in harmony on the final line:

> Noni: I'm a-workin' on a building,
> David: I'm a-workin' on a building, (repeat)
> Both: For my Lord, for my Lord.[38]

Widely performed in America for generations, this song comes from African American ring-shout traditions of sacred song and dance. Sung by a leader and an answering chorus, ring-shout song originally accompanied a highly stylized counter-clockwise circular dance performed with hand clapping and other percussion.[39] 'Workin' on a Building' made its way to modern repertoires through nineteenth- and twentieth-century camp-meeting revivals, church singings, song- and hymn-books, popular recordings, and other modes of transmission.

After the chorus, Noni sang solo stanzas to the melody's second phrase:

> If I was a singer, tell you what I would do,
> I would just keep on singing,
> Working on a building too.

Then together, the two singers returned with the chorus:

> I'm a-workin' on a building, (3x)
> For my Lord, for my Lord.
> There's a Holy Ghost building, (3x)
> For my Lord, for my Lord.

Improvising each subsequent verse solo, Noni inserted successive occupations, each followed by the jointly sung chorus: 'If I was a preacher', 'a teacher', 'a sailor' (variants of the song by other singers often add to the list wastrels who say they'll *stop* drinking, gambling, and so on). As folklorist John Greenway observed of 'Workin' on a Building' in the 1950s: 'the music is strong and the stanzas simple and open to endless expansion.'[40]

Both call-and-response and direct address flourish the world over, especially in oral traditions. Among the Shona people of Zimbabwe, for example, the grieving song 'Ndoenda Zvangu Kumandega' ('For my part, I go to a place to be alone') varies its address to the departed ancestral spirit in each line of the lead singer's call, followed by a consistently stable answering response: 'Nyarara Baba' ('Be quiet now, respected one; don't cry; be at peace').[41]

Lead:	Mudzimu wangu Baba (My ancestral spirit [respected one]')
Answer:	Nyarara Baba (Be quiet now, respected one; don't cry; be at peace)
Lead:	Wakandisiya ndiri ndega (You have left me all alone)
Answer:	Nyarara Baba (Be quiet now, respected one; don't cry; be at peace)
Lead:	Ndoenda zvangu kumundega (For my part, I go to a place to be alone) (2x)
Answer:	Nyarara Baba (Be quiet now, respected one; don't cry; be at peace)[42]

While prevalent across Africa, responsorial singing has parallels in other traditions. It is the Latin responses of medieval European liturgical chant, for instance, that Green Berry Horton's 'Bangston' parodically mimics with its '*Diddle-i-do-dums*' and '*Quiddle-i-quo-qums*'.

Improvisation pervades traditional African music, both instrumentally and vocally. With its strong African American roots, 'Workin' on a Building' reflects this lineage with its interjections of diverse occupations – preachers, teachers, gamblers, and so on. Improvisation is a driving force in traditions that centre on the mbira, a small keyboard held on the lap. Each player holds the instrument, flicking with fingers the steel keys, which ring within an amplifying gourd to create 'a buzzy sonority something of a cross between marimba and harp', as Paul Berliner describes it.[43] Shona mbira music is a transformational interplay: in a ritual context, the musicians improvise together with singers, dancers, drummers, and other percussionists, as well as ancestral spirits called forth by the music. Such music-making is fully participatory, with everyone present understood to be engaged in the event.[44]

Lyrics to a version of the widely known Shona piece 'Nhemamusasa' (Cutting msasa branches for a temporary shelter) illustrate improvisatory interjections similar to those in 'Workin' on a Building'. The sung message of 'Nhemamusasa' is 'prepare for trouble and be ready to meet it when it comes.' As performed by the singer Linda Nemarundwe (Mai Chi) Maraire, each repetition of the sung lead line ends with direct address to particular listeners:

Nhemamusasa nhamo ichauya ... **vakomana**
(Building a temporary shelter, trouble comes if you are not prepared ... **boys**)

As the song continues, each successive repetition modifies its addressees:

Nhemamusasa nhamo ichauya ... **vasikana**
(Building a temporary shelter, trouble comes if you are not prepared ... **girls**)
            ... **babavangu** (my father);
            ... **amaivangu** (my mother);
            ... **vanavangu** (my children).[45]

With her interjections of particular addressees, Mai Chi Maraire engages listeners in a fashion similar to Noni Ward's substitutions in 'Workin' on a Building'. Both songs show how singers, instrumentalists, and audience members collectively re-voice, affirm, and inhabit together the 'sheltering buildings' of their song traditions.

Vibrantly memorable, singable, and improvise-able, both 'Workin' on a Building' and 'Nhemamusasa' remind us of the mysteriously lasting processes of the manifold traditions of songs that 'most folks are fond of singing'. The shaping and governing conventions of folk song lyrics – repetition and familiar imagery, rhetorical framing, parodic echoing and interjection, evocation of childhood and youth, meeting catastrophe and voicing grief, formulaic yet flexible structural patterning, and call-and-response engagement – these reaffirm belonging and cultural community. People feel known by and within their folk songs, an experience not just of carrying the songs onward, but also being carried by them. As Elf, a character in David Mitchell's rock-music novel *Utopia Avenue* says: 'Art is memory made public. Time wins in the long run .... But as long as the art endures, a song ... that someone once thought worth keeping is saved and stays shareable. Others can say, "I feel that too".'[46] Consistently remembered, shared, and re-voiced in unprofessional and professional performance, folk songs are the ones that remain widely known by people who re-create them from memory and improvisationally, to and with others who, in turn, hear them and keep them singing and heard, across vast swaths of space and time.

Notes

1. Helen Hartness Flanders, Elizabeth Flanders Ballard, George Brown, and Phillips Barry, *The New Green Mountain Songster*. New Haven: Yale University Press, 1939, v.

2. Robert Brauneis, 'Copyright and the World's Most Popular Song'. *Journal of the Copyright Society of the U.S.A.* Legal Studies Research Paper No. 392, 56 (2–3) (2010): 335–426.
3. On 'Jingle Bells', see Ray Browne and Pat Browne, *Guide to United States Popular Culture*. Madison, WI: Popular Press, 2001, 171; on 'Silent Night', see Jason Daley, 'A Brief History of "Silent Night".' *Smithsonian*, 17 December 2018.
4. Walter Scott, *Minstrelsy of the Scottish Border*, 3 vols. Kelso: Ballantyne, 1802, 2:143.
5. See William Entwistle, *European Balladry*. Oxford: Clarendon, 1939.
6. See Dianne Dugaw, 'Ballad', in *The New Princeton Encyclopedia of Poetry and Poetics*, ed. Roland Greene. Princeton: Princeton University Press, 2012, 114–18.
7. *The Pepys Ballads*, ed. Hyder Rollins, 8 vols. Cambridge, MA: Harvard University Press, 1929–32, 3:3–10; also, English Broadside Ballad Archive, http://ebba.english.ucsb.edu/ballad/21888/citation.
8. See Roger Abrahams and George Foss, *Anglo-American Folksong Style*. Englewood Cliffs: Prentice-Hall, 1968; Mark Booth, *The Experience of Songs*. New Haven, CT: Yale University Press, 1981; Thomas Dubois, *Lyric, Meaning, and Audience in the Oral Tradition of Northern Europe*. Notre Dame: University of Notre Dame Press, 2006; Lars Eckstein, *Reading Song Lyrics*. Amsterdam: Rodopi, 2010; and Kip Lornell, *Exploring American Folk Music*, 3rd ed. Jackson: University Press of Mississippi, 2012.
9. D. K. Wilgus, *Anglo-American Folksong Scholarship Since 1898*. New Brunswick: Rutgers University Press, 1959, 284 and 430.
10. Booth, *The Experience of Songs*, 21.
11. For a recording, see Dianne Dugaw, with Amanda Powell and Dorothy Attneave, *The Aunties' Song Kettle: Songs for Kids of All Ages*, 2007.
12. See Bertrand Bronson, 'The Interdependence of Ballad Tunes and Texts,' *California Folklore Quarterly*, 3 (1944): 185–207 and F. J. Child. *The English and Scottish Popular Ballads*, 5 Vols. New York: Dover, 1965 (republication of Houghton, Mifflin and Co., 1882–98), 1:208–15. See also www.vwml.org/roudnumber/29.
13. See Bertrand Bronson, *The Singing Tradition of Child's Popular Ballads*. Princeton: Princeton University Press, 1976, 70–74.
14. Dianne Dugaw, '"Dreams of the Past": A Collection of Ozark Songs and Tunes'. *Mid-America Folklore*, 11 (1983), 10–11; Roud 4308 for variants.
15. Roud 968 and 451.
16. Roud 18437. On conventions, see Mary-Ann Constantine and Gerald Porter, *Fragments and Meaning in Traditional Song*. Oxford: Oxford University Press, 2003.
17. Leslie Dunn and Nancy Jones, *Embodied Voices: Representing Female Vocality in Western Culture*. Cambridge: Cambridge University Press, 1994, 202; see also Virginia Hamilton, *The People Could Fly: American Black Folktales*. New York: Alfred Knopf, 1985.

18. See Roud 4308.
19. Dubois, *Lyric, Meaning, and Audience*, 65.
20. Dubois, *Lyric, Meaning, and Audience*, 66.
21. J. Revell Carr, III, 'Disaster Songs: A Continuing Tradition in American Folksong' (MA Terminal Project in Folklore, University of Oregon, 1998), 77. See https://nwmusicarchives.com/artist/bigbee-jeanie. For a recorded version, see Dugaw, *The Aunties' Song Kettle*.
22. Carr, 'Disaster Songs', 58.
23. Carr, 'Disaster Songs', 59.
24. *Bessie Smith, vocals; with other musicians*, https://lccn.loc.gov/96705587.
25. Roud 11693. See Charles Wolfe and Kip Lornell, *The Life and Legend of Leadbelly*. New York: HarperCollins, 1992.
26. https://en.wikipedia.org/wiki/Gilligan%27s_Island. On the shipwreck, see www.oregonencyclopedia.org › articles › new_carissa.
27. https://lyricsondemand.com/tvthemes/gilligansislandlyrics.html, lyrics by G. Wyle and S. Shwartz.
28. *The Columbian* (8 March 1999), 13.
29. https://en.wikipedia.org/wiki/Santa_B%C3%A1rbara_bendita. See Fernando Klein, *Canciones para la memoria: La Guerra civil Española*. Barcelona: Edicions Bellaterra, 2008, 66; and https://guerracivilespanolabdx.wordpress.com/cancion-de-la-guerra.
30. See Dianne Dugaw, *Warrior Women and Popular Balladry, 1650–1850*. Cambridge: Cambridge University Press, 1989; also Dianne Dugaw, 'Heroines Gritty and Tender, Printed and Oral, Late-Breaking and Traditional: Revisiting the Anglo-American Female Warrior' in *Ballads and Broadsides in Britain, 1500–1800*, ed. Anita Guerrini and Patricia Fumerton. Aldershot: Ashgate, 2010; and Dianne Dugaw and Simone Chess, *The Warrior Women Project* (https://s.wayne.edu/warriorwomen/). See also Rudolf Dekker and Lotte van de Pol, *The Tradition of Female Transvestism in Early Modern Europe*. London: Macmillan, 1989.
31. Roud, 367 and 401 (65 and 23 in Dugaw and Chess). Ollie Gilbert's 'Pretty Polly' can be heard on *Banjo Songs, Ballads, and Reels from the Southern Mountains* (Prestige/International 25004).
32. Archive of Folksong, US Library of Congress, Tape 4463A-2, B1, 2.
33. See Julie Wheelwright, *Amazons and Military Maids*. London: Pandora, 1989; Fraser Easton, 'Covering Sexual Disguise: Passing Women and Generic Constraint', *Studies in 18th-Century Culture*, 35 (2006): 95–125 and 'Gender's Two Bodies: Women Warriors, Female Husbands, and Plebeian Life', *Past and Present*, 180 (2003): 131–74; D. Blanton and L. Cook, *They Fought Like Demons: Women Soldiers in the Civil War*. Baton Rouge: Louisiana State University Press, 2002; and Lauren Cook Burgess, ed., *An Uncommon Soldier: The Civil War Letters of Sarah Rosetta Wakeman, alias Private Lyons Wakeman, 153rd Regiment, New York State Volunteers*. New York: Oxford University Press, 1994.

34. *The Life and Extraordinary Adventures of Susanna Cope*, London: J. Pitts, c.1800, 8.
35. 'The Constant Female' (Dugaw and Chess, 68; Roud 231 and V3304).
36. See 'The Handsome Cabin Boy' (Dugaw and Chess, 105; Roud 239); Pauline Greenhill, '"Neither a Man nor a Maid": Sexualities and Gendered Meanings in Cross-Dressing Ballads,' *Journal of American Folklore*, 108 (1995): 156–77; and Leslie Feinberg, *Transgender Warriors*. Boston: Beacon Press, 1996.
37. See *The Warrior Women Project*: https://ebba.english.ucsb.edu/page/24.
38. Dianne Dugaw, 'Collection of Ozark Folksongs' (M.Mus. Thesis, University of Colorado, 1973), Vol. 2, 55–56; Roud 4276.
39. See Katrina Dyonne Thompson, *Ring Shout, Wheel About: The Racial Politics of Music and Dance in North American Slavery*. Urbana: University of Illinois Press, 2014; Samuel A. Floyd, *The Power of Black Music: Interpreting Its History from Africa to the United States*. New York: Oxford University Press, 1995; and Maria Leach, ed., *Funk and Wagnalls Standard Dictionary of Folklore, Mythology, and Legend*. New York: Harper and Row, 1984, 944–45.
40. John Greenway, *Workin' on a Buildin'*. Wattle Recordings-C-1, 1957, liner notes.
41. 'Baba' literally means 'father'; in this context, it connotes 'respected one' or 'ancestor'.
42. I thank Mudavanhu Magaya (Shona Gwenyambira [mbira master] and teacher) for translations and consultation and Dennis Urso (Kutsinhira Cultural Arts Center, Eugene, Oregon) for these lines.
43. Paul Berliner, *The Art of Mbira: Musical Inheritance and Legacy, Featuring the Repertory and Practices of Cosmas Magaya and Associates*. Chicago: University of Chicago Press, 2020, vii.
44. See Berliner, *The Art of Mbira*; Paul Berliner and Cosmas Magaya, *Mbira's Restless Dance: An Archive of Improvisation*, 2 Vols. Chicago: University of Chicago Press, 2020 (Nonesuch: www.nonesuch.com/albums/zimbabwe-shona-mbira-music).
45. I thank Mudavanhu Magaya and Dennis Urso for translation and text. On Linda Nemarundwe (Mai Chi) Maraire and her husband Dr Dumisani Maraire, see https://pan-african-music.com/en/dumi-maraire-tichazomuona/ See also *Tichazomuoana* (1986) reissued as https://pan-african-music.com/en/mbira-dumisani-maraire.
46. David Mitchell, *Utopia Avenue* New York: Random House, 2020, 98.

8 | Folk Instruments

MAEVE CAREY-KOZLARK

At the core of folk music lies an intrinsic connection with the instruments that not only carry its melodies but also perpetuate its enduring sociopolitical resonance. These instruments transcend materiality, serving as living witnesses to history while embodying multiple, sometimes contradictory, cultural narratives. A comprehensive exploration of musical instruments categorized as 'folk', then, demands a multidimensional approach whose methodology attends to critical facets of material culture otherwise marginalized in conventional musicological analyses.

Categorizations of musical instruments have historically been approached through Western 'top-down' methods of taxonomy. In many cases, these have resulted in the marginalization of certain instruments and the perpetuation of inaccurate or incomplete narratives surrounding their origins and usage.[1] By categorizing instruments solely based upon their construction and method of sound production, the Hornbostel–Sachs system, for instance, ignores the diversity of ways in which an instrument might be described or played – the very elements that are central to understanding folk instruments. Ethnomusicologists Margaret Kartomi and Victor Kofi Agawu have (among others) advocated instead for a 'bottom-up' methodology that centres the agency of makers and users of musical instruments in their categorization.[2] This emphasis on vernacular tradition lends itself particularly well to the study of folk music as it sheds light on the ways in which instruments are not mere objects, but rather living embodiments of cultural identities and histories.

Several scholars have taken a postcolonial approach towards specific instruments and musical contexts, and many have further argued for studying the embodied affect and symbolic or affective meanings of musical instruments more broadly.[3] Applying this lens to the study of folk instruments allows for a more inclusive and representative body of knowledge to emerge. Although attuned to specific dynamics within sub-Saharan Africa, Agawu's work in particular is pivotal within this discourse. The four groups of organological questioning he proposes are best positioned to address this challenge as they allow for categorization and attention to the nuances inherent in folk traditions. To that end, Agawu's approach allows us to unpack the essence of folk instruments beyond their physical construction or place of origin: from the craftsmanship responsible for their creation, maintenance, and dissemination to the social and historical contexts that have intertwined them within their stewards' broader cultural landscapes. Ultimately, the aim of this chapter is not to create a rigid taxonomy of instruments categorized under the rubric 'folk', but rather to attempt to move beyond the limitations of traditional schools of organological thought to provide a more inclusive and representative understanding of folk instruments and all they embody.

The first of four groups outlined by Agawu centre around the intricate processes involved in the manufacture of musical instruments, prompting an investigation into their compositional properties and engendering a deeper inquiry into the provenance of their materials. This encompasses an assessment of whether these materials derive from natural sources or are synthetically manufactured, as well as an examination of the processes and techniques employed in the construction of specific instruments. Agawu's second mode of inquiry is more historiographical, necessitating not only an attempt at determining the origins of each instrument (where possible) but also untangling the complex interplay between potential contributing factors including migration, trade, political hegemony, and cultural exchange. The third mode delves into the formal and informal pedagogies surrounding these instruments, the contexts in which they are typically performed, and artistic conventions or belief systems held within particular communities. The fourth and final mode addresses how compositional processes and musical aesthetics are embodied within an instrument's physical construction, and how these may allow one to differentiate between sounds accepted as 'music' against those that fall beyond this classification.[4]

In their roles as repositories of tradition and narrative, folk instruments epitomize the intricate relationship between musical expression and physical construction that defines Agawu's fourth mode. The fiddle and the violin are emblematic of this distinction between different ways of performing and receiving music. Physically, they are indistinguishable, sharing the same basic body shape, bridge, bow, and four strings. However, their transformation into either a (folk) fiddle or a (classical) violin hinges entirely on the musical context and stylistic traditions they are utilized within. The violin finds itself firmly ensconced in the canons of Western art music; its construction – a testament to centuries of standardized craftsmanship and devotion to tonal norms – typically adheres to stringent principles of design and material selection. The fiddle, by contrast, embodies an ethos where compositional processes and musical aesthetics are inextricably intertwined with vernacular heritage. Its construction is typically identical to that of a classical violin, although its ethos allows for local particularities to emerge – be it hardwoods native to Appalachia or adornments and additional strings in the case of the Scandinavian Hardanger fiddle, each instance underscoring the fiddle's adaptability and capacity to assimilate regional nuances.[5] This, I shall argue, is a defining feature of folk instruments: their shifting patterns of use and reuse over time.

The demarcation between sonorous elements deemed to be 'music' and those relegated beyond the confines of this classification acquires heightened significance in the context of folk instruments. The traditional hurdy-gurdy – potentially dating back to the Moorish invasion of Spain and the subsequent spread of similar instruments across Europe via pilgrim routes – was initially relegated to church settings (then known as the organistrum) and limited to slow-paced sacred melodies.[6] However, the thirteenth century saw it redesigned for solo musicians, becoming the *vielle a roue* with the addition of rhythmic drone accompaniment that rendered it ideal for dance music.[7] In the modern era, the hurdy-gurdy's resurgence, including electronic adaptations and extended techniques, is a sign of its enduring significance. Its physical form and operation underscore the dialectical tension between conventional tonal hierarchies and unconventional sonic expressions. Within its intricate wheel and resonator assembly lies an inherent ambiguity, challenging normative aesthetic dichotomies by encompassing conventional sounds together with ephemeral, non-linear tonalities. This in particular exemplifies how folk instruments, through their unique physical configurations, often blur the boundary between the musical and the non-musical, inviting discourse on the ontology of sound and the perception of music within specific cultural contexts.

Building on Agawu's modes, I propose that folk instruments can be divided across three strata. At the most foundational level, we encounter instruments intimately associated with early Western traditions such as stringed lutes, percussive devices, and flutes or other basic wind instruments. These instruments – characterized by their presence across generations and resilience against morphological, symbolic, and functional transformations – convey an extraordinary historical depth. This complements Agawu's historiographical mode of inquiry, encouraging an exploration of the origins and complex interplay of factors shaping the evolution of these instruments. Next, we encounter instruments such as fiddles and banjos that can trace their origins to specific cultural contexts yet have earned a sense of permanence within the general populace that marks them as 'traditional'. This finds resonance in Agawu's pedagogical mode, as instruments often carry different artistic conventions and practices within particular communities. The third and final stratum provides a platform to examine the embodied aesthetics Agawu describes in his fourth mode, shedding light on how compositional processes and musical aesthetics evolve alongside changes in cultural landscapes. This category encompasses instruments introduced over the past century or two, covering a wide variety of instruments ranging from electrified guitars to cajons and handpans. Several instruments within this layer have gradually assimilated local accents and are poised to establish themselves – if they have not already – as integral components of the 'folk' classification, even in instances where tradition long predates the instrument itself or already has first- or second-strata instruments associated with its practices. Rather than ascribing a distinct temporal origin to each strata, an analysis adopting a concurrent perspective must be employed to draw attention to their simultaneous existence in the present. Following this scheme, we can map out the ways in which tradition and modernity, antiquity and novelty, rural and urban, and local and foreign intersect, mutually influencing one another while retaining a certain degree of autonomy.

Production and Sustainability

Instrument-making is, at its most basic level, a process of place making and economy building. By emphasizing the role of materials in the physical production of these instruments, one becomes conscious of the fact that folk instruments are inextricably intertwined with people and places and are shaped by particular periods and technologies. Instruments also have an intrinsic ability to (re)connect us to the natural world through the materials from which they are made, as is being increasingly explored in ecomusicological spheres. Kevin Dawe, for example, argues that all musical instruments can best be understood as products of nature and culture in which knowledge of exploiting the acoustic and aesthetic properties of materials is developed.[8]

Animal by-products have long been a prominent material in the construction of folk instruments owing to their resonant properties and rich tonal characteristics. This is particularly the case with percussive instruments, which serve as some of the earliest forms of historical record: Sumerian relief carvings dating to 2100 BC depict at least four distinct types of clay and animal-skin drums; ancient Babylonian art depicts ritual drums made of bull hide; and Neolithic alligator-skin drums have been found at Taosi archaeological site in Xiangfen, Shanxi, China.[9] 'Gut' or animal intestines used as strings have been utilized since at least the Eighteenth Egyptian dynasty, and have more recently played a central role in comparatively modern folk traditions, with banjos, fiddles, and lutes turning to them for their warmth and tonal characteristics.[10] It thus follows that folk instruments, whether originating from indeterminate sources or repurposed from an existing form or function, are intimately connected to the transmission of ancestral knowledge. Natural materials serve as repositories of these histories, fostering a connection to the past and acting as vessels through which cultural memory is preserved and transmitted. This contrasts sharply with contemporary practices in mainstream or commercial convention that increasingly favour synthetic materials – typically metals, plastics, and specialized polymers – in aiming to provide greater control over tonal consistency, projection capability, and durability. This shift reflects both the influence of Western modernity and the desire for standardization as instruments came to be mass-produced and consumed.

The depletion of natural resources used in the traditional production of folk instruments nevertheless poses a significant threat to the sustainability of this craft. The overexploitation of tonewoods such as rosewood and mahogany utilized in guitar construction has led, for instance, to the endangerment of several species, and the production of animal hide for drum-making has come under scrutiny owing to environmental and ethical concerns, necessitating the development of more sustainable alternative materials and synthetic substitutes.[11] This adoption of alternative materials brings with it its own complexities: the cultural significance and emotional resonance attached to traditional craftsmanship must be carefully considered, as a shift away from natural materials has the potential to be construed as an inauthentic departure from established practices. The dilemma in folk music instrument-building spheres hence revolves around finding a delicate balance between ecological sustainability and cultural authenticity, viewing them as complementary objectives rather than mutually exclusive paradigms. Likewise, recent technological advancements have had an impact on the production and consumption of folk music. As recording technology improves, the ability to capture and distribute music has become increasingly widespread. As such, existing associations between folk music and specific instruments may become less relevant in certain contexts as musicians are able to challenge convention by experimenting with new sounds and textures, lessening their dependence on physical instruments. In examining the role of technology in folk music, scholars have noted the potential for technology to both democratize and homogenize musical traditions; the future of particular instruments designated as 'folk' may therefore depend on how and whether they are utilized to reinforce or subvert these associations.[12]

A Case Study: The Banjo

Migration, cross-cultural transaction, and fluctuations in political dominance have left behind a wide array of traditions and tangible artefacts, revealing the intricate imprints of colonial powers, shifting intellectual paradigms, and negotiations between universalism and localized identity. Within such processes, musical instruments have come to embody unique tensions. The Enlightenment's advocacy for universal tolerance paradoxically coincided with the rise of racial hierarchies wherein cultural expressions were specifically moulded to further European dominance.[13] In Germany, philosopher Johann Gottfried Herder's argument that the purest form of a nation's culture could be found among *das Volk* – the common people – was subverted by burgeoning pseudo-science that further delineated superiority along class and racial lines.[14] These dialectics set the stage for musical instruments to carry lay cultural authenticities and colonial imprints simultaneously.

The era of colonization bore witness to the strategic deployment of folk instruments as localized musical expression alongside repression by imperial bodies involving bans and confiscations. In Britain, the seventeenth century was characterized by increasing migration among the Irish and Ashkenazi Jews, the latter of whom had been banned from Britain since their expulsion by Edward I in 1290. Given long-standing anti-Irish and anti-Semitic sentiment and the centrality of the fiddle to Irish music and the emerging klezmer style (*fidl*), it comes as no surprise that King Charles II's 1657 'Act against Vagrants and wandering, idle dissolute persons' outlined the following:

and be it further Enacted by the authority aforesaid, That if any person or persons commonly called Fidlers ... shall at any time after the said First day of July, be taken playing, fidling and making musick in any Inn, Alehouse, or Tavern, or shall be taken proffering themselves, or desiring, or intreating any person or persons to hear them to play, or make musick in any the places aforesaid, that every such person and persons so taken, shall be adjudged, and are hereby adjudged and declared to be Rogues Vagabonds, and Sturdy Beggers, and shall be proceeded against and punished.[15]

Colonial powers sought to quell Indigenous musical forms to assert dominance resulting in a strained coexistence between native practices and imposed cultural norms.[16] Queen Elizabeth I's alleged 1603 decree to 'hang the harpers, wherever found, and destroy their instruments' is particularly emblematic, although similar practices persisted well into modernity: the Nazi regime contained at least two divisions, Sonderstab Musik and Einsatzstab Reichsleiter Rosenberg, specifically charged with the confiscation of Jewish musical instruments and cultural property.[17]

The banjo is an emblematic source of solace and agency, revealing the adaptive capacity of folk instruments amidst colonial subjugation. Tracing a lineage from its roots in Africa to the Caribbean and the United States via the Atlantic slave trade and its eventual admittance into the twentieth-century traditional Irish music zeitgeist, serves as a compelling illustration of these intricacies. Its earliest origins on the African continent are difficult to pinpoint as the multitude of peoples, languages, and musics there has rendered it difficult for scholars to associate the banjo with a single specific prototype; however, today's musicological consensus is that its precursors travelled from West Africa to the Americas via the West Indies.[18] One potential ancestor of the banjo is thought to be the *ekonting*: a three-stringed spiked lute belonging to the Jola people of Gambia, Senegal, and Kaabu, or modern-day Guinea-Bissau. When compared with early plantation and minstrel banjos in the American South, both the *ekonting* and its early equivalents on the opposite side of the Atlantic were constructed from dried-gourd bodies and stretched animal skin, and its practitioners shared a number of similar techniques, particularly in their treatment of the drone string.[19]

Several narratives in banjo scholarship have suggested the instrument's rise to popular prominence was achieved by white instrument makers and performers during the nineteenth century.[20] Recent scholarship has countered this by turning to the extensive material archive surrounding banjos to emphasize their African origin, and a number of initiatives and research guides making a similarly concerted effort to undo the whitewashing of musicologists past have since emerged in prominent collections.[21] The use of the banjo in Irish music as a case study in this chapter, then, does not aim to undo or counter this work. Instead, it aims to demonstrate how the banjo's incorporation into Irish tradition demonstrates how folk instruments and their living, dynamic practices are able to accommodate innovation and change under varying conditions of power.

A variety of historical references demonstrate that early versions of today's banjo – the *banjar, banjie, banjer, banza,* or even *banjeaux* – were first crafted and played sometime in seventeenth-century America by enslaved peoples who constructed their instruments from gourds, wood, and tanned skins, using hemp or gut for strings.[22] In the United States, the banjo was considered essentially exclusive to African American culture until it entered a phase of mass production in the late eighteenth and early nineteenth centuries. By the 1920s, the banjo had become almost synonymous with white Appalachia in a total (re)invention of tradition as part of a conscious effort to define and promote a distinct cultural identity in the region.[23] In the decades preceding this, however, these strong associations with African American culture made banjos the perfect fodder for parody in blackface minstrelsy. Many of the earliest and largest names in minstrelsy were Irish-born or first-generation Irish-American, owing to the 'elbow-rubbing' between Irish and African Americans as described by Eric Lott.[24] These groups often lived side-by-side in working-class communities and early minstrel performances incorporated elements of Irish folk culture – dances, in particular, often combined elements of Irish jigs and reels with African-American styles.[25] For the then politically powerless and economically disenfranchised Irish-American diaspora, minstrelsy provided a means by which to elevate their social standing and carve out a covert forum of cultural representation.

Given the high quantity of Irish minstrel performers and the international popularity the genre achieved, minstrelsy can realistically be labelled as Ireland's first formal introduction to the instrument.[26] The first known public performances of the banjo in Ireland took place between 1843 and 1845 in Belfast, Dublin, and Cork when the Virginia Minstrels – an American minstrel group composed of at least two Irish-Americans, Daniel Emmett and Joel Walker Sweeney – toured in Europe.[27] The two presented themselves in blackface as 'Ethiopian delineators' and claimed to play the authentic music and instruments of the plantation slaves; yet, as documented in period sheet music, the music they played was markedly more Irish than African in melodic and rhythmic structure.[28] The overwhelming likelihood is that the iteration of the banjo introduced to Ireland at this time was slightly more advanced – likely a five-stringed, fretless descendant of the three or four-string variety commonplace on plantations. Some scholars credit Joel Walker-Sweeney with adding the banjo's fifth

Figure 8.1 Banjo by William Esperance Boucher, Jr., Baltimore, United States, c.1845. Metropolitan Museum of Art.

string, allegedly because he was dissatisfied with the rhythmic and melodic limitations of the then-popular four-string banjo.[29] While there is no definitive evidence that this was the case, the banjo having reached this stage in its evolution in Ireland is supported by an 1887 sketch of another Irish-American minstrelsy-adjacent touring group in Captain Francis O'Neill's 1913 book *Irish Minstrels and Musicians*, which features Uilleann piper Richard 'Dick' Stephenson and John Dunne playing a banjo upon which the fifth string and peg are clearly visible.[30]

Following its initial introduction to Ireland by way of returning emigrants – whether permanently, or as visitors – banjos occupied a largely sub-cultural role in musical tradition and society more broadly. Until the turn of the nineteenth century, Irish banjos were used primarily as a rhythm or accompanying instrument in songs or tunes, with the occasional rudimentary plucking of simpler melodies. Because the minstrel banjo brought by returned migrants and visiting Irish-American performers was likely fretless, playing above the fifth string position would have posed intonation issues and rendered the instrument unsuitable for the complex melodic tradition that by then had been well established in Irish traditional instrumental music.[31] This placed individuals in a unique position to develop their own technique completely independent of the two worlds they straddled. Without the African American frame of reference they were accustomed to, the banjo provided a means to continue the negotiation of identity inherent in many contemporary folk traditions alongside the process of reconciliation with a rapidly changing world. Frets were added to the Irish iteration of the instrument sometime in the 1880s, followed by the installation of steel strings. Banjo players in Ireland increasingly began experimenting with different plectral playing styles and tunings, particularly influenced by the plectrum in mandolin playing technique. Soon, a number of individual styles and variations of the instrument came to co-exist among the modest fraternity of banjo players in Ireland, bolstered further by the rise of the American dance hall scene in the 1920s. However, these stylistic variations would remain largely disparate until the more widespread move towards standardization during the folk revival of the 1950s and 1960s.[32]

By the turn of the twentieth century, the banjo had been wholly claimed by White culture in the United States and was rising in the socioeconomic ranks of its consumers. However, this peak was short-lived, as changing musical tastes and the development of arch-top (and eventually electrified) guitars made the tenor banjo obsolete in many American popular music circles by the mid 1930s, and they came to be regarded largely as an object of nostalgia or novelty until regaining prominence during the folk revival.[33] The bands that played the once-ubiquitous Irish dance halls in New York City were increasingly required to perform American music alongside Irish tunes, so a tenor banjo or banjo player was sometimes added to the ensemble. English dance bands tended to emulate the American groups, and in the process banjos (and banjo techniques) from the United States and Britain eventually found their way back to Ireland, continuing the cycle of exchange.[34] A number of other 'cross-contaminations', as Irish music historian Mick Moloney occasionally refers to them, occurred both as a result of increased return migration to Ireland from the United States that followed the onset of the Great Depression as well as from the cultural imperialism that the United States was enacting during this period, intent on shaping popular consciousness and establishing hegemony.

Under first-generation Irish-American (Catholic) mayor Jimmy Walker, New York passed its Cabaret Law of 1926 – a law which on paper prohibited music and dancing in food-selling public places without a special cabaret licence, but in practice was arbitrarily enforced and weaponized against marginalized groups. Ireland, itself in a period of intensifying Catholic rule under Fianna Fáil's government, is thought by some scholars to have been inspired by Walker in introducing its Public Hall Dance Act in 1935.[35] In some areas, this led to a ban on dances held in private homes, which the clergy regarded as 'occasions of sin'.[36] Partly for this reason, but also because of the influence of popular music from England and America, traditional dancing in Ireland had virtually no choice but to move from farm outbuildings and cottage kitchens into public village or parochial halls.[37] The need for an ensemble loud enough to be heard in these larger environments led to the rise of the 'ceili bands' with a lineup that added the much louder accordion, piano, bodhran, Uilleann pipes, and – for the first time – the banjo, to the established instrumental lineup.[38]

In sum, folk instruments are not static entities, and the banjo's journey from Africa to its assimilation into Irish traditional music exemplifies complex negotiations between tradition and modernity while underscoring the impact of migration, cultural exchange, and colonial power on the evolution of musical traditions. There is, therefore, an intrinsic connection between folk instruments and the broader sociopolitical landscapes they inhabit. As living witnesses to these historical shifts and cultural negotiations, banjos challenge rigid taxonomic classifications and emphasize the need for a more inclusive, dynamic, and representative understanding of musical instruments.

Tradition, Invention, and Authenticity

Much like the banjo, the Appalachian lap dulcimer, or 'mountain dulcimer', is bound up with invented tradition – the process by which cultural practices perceived as traditional are legitimized in the present with reference to a carefully crafted or imagined past.[39] Folk musical instruments provide concrete examples of deliberate efforts to rewrite or reshape cultural heritage for sociopolitical, economic, and symbolic purposes. The Appalachian dulcimer was consciously promoted as an emblem of American folk tradition during the mid twentieth century. The folk revival underway in Britain and the United States engendered a resurgent fascination with instruments such as the lap dulcimer. Today, it is regarded as one of the few (and potentially only) wholly American instruments, and certainly the only uniquely American addition to the fretted zither family.[40]

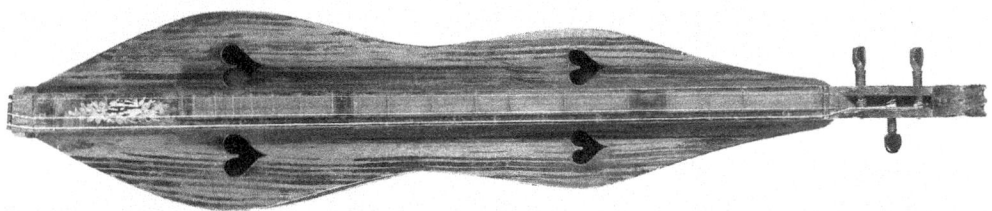

Figure 8.2 Appalachian Dulcimer by Charles Napoleon Prichard, United States, late nineteenth century. Metropolitan Museum of Art.

The mountain dulcimer emerged from a number of cultural confluences among the settlers of the Appalachian frontier. The constraints of this environment, particularly the scarcity of wire, led to pragmatic adaptations of existing European lap zithers such as the German *Scheitholt* or French *Epinette*.[41] In practice, this typically meant reducing its string count to just three or four – a simplification that enhanced its portability and practicality while opening doors to a more accessible (and thus disseminatable) repertoire.[42] The introduction of a raised fingerboard further expanded the instrument's expressive capabilities, enabling the nimble execution of Scots-Irish jigs and reels with the aid of a plectrum. Records also point to the possibility that the name dulcimer to describe this particular instrument is a recent development. The English word and its cognates, Italian *dolcemela* and middle French *doucemelle* are derived from the Latin dulce melos, or 'sweet melody'. To most Americans from the eighteenth through to the twentieth centuries, the term 'dulcimer' was exclusive to the hammered dulcimer – a percussive string instrument trapezoidal in shape descended from the medieval psaltery. Writing in 1925, folklorist Josiah Combs was one of the first to describe the Appalachian dulcimer, emphasizing that 'it must not be confused with the classical or traditional dulcimer, to which it bears no resemblance'.[43] Terms such as 'lap harp' and 'music box' to describe the Appalachian dulcimer were used with more regularity by Appalachian musicians until the early twentieth century. Some practitioners further suggest that the shift towards referring to it as a type of dulcimer despite differing considerably in form, sound, evolution, and manner of playing 'seems [to be a product] of media-encouraged tendencies for folk to adopt proper, standardized names'.[44]

Unlike other instruments that followed a linear path to their present form, the dulcimer existed as a dynamic entity, constantly evolving and being reinvented. Most of the dulcimers that emerged in the late eighteenth century were not commercially produced and were instead built by the players themselves or a member of their community. Makers turned to poplar wood as their material of choice as it was readily available, easy to work with, and not subject to significant warping from extremes of temperature and humidity. This lack of standardized manufacture allowed their shapes and sounds to vary widely across the Appalachian region. In the heavily German-populated Shenandoah valley, dulcimers typically assumed a Scheitholt-like triangular or teardrop shape; Kentucky and Tennessee dulcimers, in contrast, were known for their hourglass-shaped and rectangular boxlike instruments, respectively.[45] Appalachian dulcimer music of the late nineteenth and early twentieth centuries was primarily functional in that it typically accompanied work or religious practice, although it was also used as a pastime and form of entertainment. Rural settlement schools and localized folk music traditions kept such practices active and visible on a regional level until Jean Ritchie helped bring them to wider, national attention in the early years of the folk revival.

Born into a family of musicians in Kentucky, Ritchie grew up surrounded by mountain folklife. Prior to her birth in 1922, English song collector Cecil Sharp had used her community's settlement school as a home base during his trip to Knot County, Kentucky.[46] Two of the songs he transcribed during this time are attributed to members of Jean's family: her older sister, Una, and second cousin, Sabrina.[47] Another sister, May, is mentioned in Sharp's diary.[48] Ritchie, a lifelong Appalachian dulcimer player, eventually left Kentucky in the 1940s to pursue a career in social work in New York City. There, her teaching of traditional Appalachian music to children on the Lower East Side caught the attention of the growing folk revivalist community including Pete Seeger, Alan Lomax, and Woody Guthrie. By 1951, she had become a leading documentarian of folk tradition and was operating as a full-time musician song collector. Later that same year, Ritchie was recorded by Lomax for the Library of Congress Archive of American Folk Song.[49]

The following decades saw more concerted efforts to modify the instrument's design, construction, and playing techniques in order to align it with the emerging needs and preferences of the era. This process largely revolved around standardization, whereby specific dimensions, tuning systems, and playing techniques were established towards the formation of a single coherent and readily identifiable dulcimer 'tradition'. Although Ritchie estimates the Appalachian dulcimer to have been present in the region since the mid-to-late nineteenth century, until this time it bore no singular representative style, context, or repertoire. The standardization introduced to the dulcimer's design not only facilitated an ease of learning and enhanced its appeal to a wider audience, but also aimed to foster a sense of historical continuity by positioning it as an integral facet of Appalachian musical heritage.[50] Developments surrounding the instrument's physical construction were followed by a push to establish a universal 'traditional' practice specifically associated with the dulcimer. Ritchie's subsequent publication of *The Dulcimer Book* created for the first time a formal Appalachian dulcimer technique, tuning, and repertoire, curating a new canon from a multifaceted musical ecosystem.[51]

The Appalachian dulcimer's reshaping during the mid twentieth-century folk revival holds a number of parallels with the construction of the bagpipe tradition in Scotland. In both cases, revivalists played a pivotal role, seizing upon the resonances of cultural identity to perpetuate a sense of heritage, tradition, and continuity. The entrance of both of these instruments into national consciousness – from local musics to emblematic portraits of cultural resilience – exemplifies how the folk concept emerges at the intersection of efforts to shape and legitimize cultural practices in the present while anchoring them to elements of the (often imagined) past. The origins and arrival of the bagpipe on Scottish soil remain largely undetermined; scholars generally suggest they made their way to the British Empire by way of the Romans, who in turn brought them from Egypt.[52] In Scotland, bagpipes were long romanticized as instruments of war, as they always accompanied soldiers into battle and as such were thought to have been included in the 1746 Act of Proscription that banned 'highland dress' and the possession of arms under threat of exile:

And be it further enacted by the authority aforesaid, that if ... any arms, or warlike weapons, shall be found hidden or concealed in any dwelling house, barn, out-house, office, or any other house whatsoever ... the Tenant or possessor of such ... shall suffer the penalties hereby above enacted against concealers of arms ... and be it further enacted by the authority aforesaid, that if any person who shall have been convicted of any of the above offences ... shall thereafter presume to commit the like offence a second time, that he or she ... shall be liable to be transported to any of his Majesty's plantations beyond the seas, there to remain for the space of seven years.[53]

While this was not the case in practice – the Falkirk Tryst, Scotland's first formalized bagpipe competition, was held in 1781 and followed by several in the decades thereafter – the bagpipes earned themselves elevated standing as a symbol of resistance to imperial cultural repression. The rapid expansion of the British Empire that followed this period spurred an undercurrent of localized nationalism manifested in the fabrication of the bagpipes as a symbol of Scottish national pride. The fervour for nationalist agendas coalesced with the revivalist impulse, creating an environment conducive to the construction of invented traditions. The Scottish bagpipes became an ideal canvas upon which the narrative of Scottish cultural resilience and lineage could be painted. In this pursuit, the modern Scottish bagpipes – alongside other deliberately manufactured cultural mainstays such as tartan – emerged not merely as instruments of musical utility but as resonant symbols of a distinct, rekindled identity.[54] The narratives surrounding both the Appalachian dulcimer and the Scottish bagpipes highlight the extent to which cultural entrepreneurship, revivalist movements, standardization, and association building work to establish conceptions of authenticity.

Canons and Archives

Distinctions drawn by cultural anthropologist Aleida Assman between 'active' versus 'passive' forgetting and 'canon' versus 'archive' offer a valuable framework for examining our understanding of what is or is not considered a folk instrument. 'Active forgetting' manifests when communities – including state, colonial, or religious authorities – deliberately discard, destroy, or criminalize certain instruments and/or the traditions associated with them. Conversely, 'passive forgetting' occurs when these are naturally lost, neglected, or relegated to the periphery of public attention over time – in many cases as a by-product of colonization. Assman describes this as a process of cultural memory:

> Nation-states produce narrative versions of their past which are taught, embraced, and referred to as their collective autobiography ... Cultural memory, then, is based on two separate functions: the presentation of a narrow selection of sacred texts, artistic masterpieces, or historic key events in a timeless framework; and the storing of documents and artefacts of the past that do not at all meet these standards but are nevertheless deemed interesting or important enough to not let them vanish on the highway to total oblivion. The tension that exists between these two poles can be further illustrated by two different approaches to literary criticism ... One adopts the strategy of the canon, investing the text with existential meaning and framing it with an aura; the other adopts the strategy of the archive, aiming at destroying the aura.[55]

Musical instruments enshrined in a canon, then, have made it into working cultural memory through rigorous processes of selection, enjoying a status that often transcends historical change and fluctuations in taste. In contrast, the archive encapsulates instruments consigned to the periphery, awaiting reclamation and reinterpretation. They have lost their 'immediate addressees'; they are de-contextualized and disconnected from their former frames that had authorized them or determined their meaning. As part of this archive, they are hence open to new contexts and lend themselves to new interpretations that, in some cases, may allow them to transcend the mechanisms of power that originally defined them or cast them aside.

Any number of colonial projects throughout history might serve to illustrate this process. The 1969 declaration by then prime minister of Israel Golda Meir that 'there was no such thing as Palestinians ... they did not exist' is representative of a longstanding process of active forgetting in an effort to rewrite a place-based cultural canon.[56] Today, scholars note that Palestine before the Nakba was on a par musically and culturally with the rich traditions of its Arab neighbours; from the 1936 advent of Palestinian broadcasting onward, the music scene was regarded as lively and progressive.[57] The partitioning of Palestine by the United Nations in 1947, the events of 1948, and the resulting mass exodus of 750,000 Palestinian refugees to neighbouring countries created a chasm in musical life on all levels, dismantling both the professional music scene and extant folkloric repertoires, as songs, instruments, and performers were transplanted into refugee camps across the region. In essence, nearly all growth towards a cohesive and distinct Palestinian musical canon was disrupted, both through deliberately constructed mechanisms of state power and as a by-product of occupation.[58]

Folk instruments in Palestine were not only physically removed from the landscape, but also from the airwaves. The Nakba of 1948 brought the removal of Radio Jerusalem's Arabic music ensembles from the air, and soon thereafter the dissolution of the station itself; all broadcasting equipment, tapes, and recordings left behind were confiscated or destroyed.[59] According to the Israeli archive Akevot, settlers and military personnel alike looted Palestinian belongings during the depopulation and resettlement of towns and villages – musical instruments among them.[60] Music and arts festivals Nabī Mūsá and Nabī Ṣāliḥ were dismantled, and by the First Intifada in 1987 all public music performances were strictly banned in both Gaza and the West Bank for fear that such displays of Palestinian national identity would incite an uprising.[61] Performance had become an 'essential force in propelling and sustaining uprisings, generating national sentiment, and forging the indexical linkages between the political goal of ending the occupation and the cultural goal of preserving a sense of the historic Palestinian nation against colonial erasure'.[62] Many Palestinians were arrested or had their instruments confiscated for composing and performing songs of resistance, in effect positioning them as a mechanism just as threatening to the new Israeli cultural and geopolitical canon as rebel forces.[63] An underground network of cassette distribution – whose recordings were largely composed of Indigenous folk songs layered with contemporary political messages and imagery – emerged to keep traditional Palestinian music alive in response to these conditions of censorship and confiscation; in effect, an act of radical active remembering under a strictly enforced policy of active forgetting.[64]

In the West, the idea of folk music as a separate repository of traditional forms and techniques is itself a relatively recent development, emerging in the nineteenth century as a reaction against the industrialization and urbanization of Europe and North America.[65] By valorizing the music of rural and remote communities, intellectuals and cultural nationalists sought to counter the homogenizing effects of modernity and to reaffirm the authenticity and value of local practices. This romantic idealization of the past, however, was always tempered by the present and a desire to shape the future. By rescuing and archiving songs and practices, collectors hoped to ensure their survival and continued relevance. Similarly, the folk revival of the mid twentieth century was as much a response to the political and cultural ferment of the times as it was a nostalgia for a bygone era. The venues and festivals that proliferated during this period across the Atlantic were not simply showcases for traditional music, but rather sites of resistance against dominant cultural norms. One of the most striking features of the folk revival was its willingness to adapt and innovate by using traditional forms as a launching pad for new creative expression. The 1960s saw a surging revival of interest in instruments such as the banjo, the mandolin, and the fiddle that had largely fallen out of favour. Rather than simply reproducing old styles and techniques, however, musicians increasingly experimented with new tunings, rhythms, and tonalities, creating a hybrid form that was both traditional and modern. This creative tension between past and present, tradition and innovation, was at the heart of the revival and it continues to animate the contemporary folk scene.[66]

The study of folk instruments is more than a merely preservationist venture. Instruments categorized as 'folk' and their associated repertoires play a pivotal role in understanding history, shaping contemporary realities, and fostering visions of what the future might hold. It is increasingly evident that these instruments – whether canonized or relegated to the archive – embody collective memory. They stand as testaments to the enduring significance of cultural heritage, offering a unique lens through which one can examine what it means to bear witness to history. In this simultaneous embodiment of past, present, and future, folk instruments invite us to explore the creative possibilities arising at the intersection of tradition and innovation.

Notes

1. Stéphanie Weisser and Quanten Maarten, 'Rethinking Musical Instrument Classification: Towards a Modular Approach to the Hornbostel-Sachs System'. *Yearbook for Traditional Music* 43 (2011): 122–146, 129.
2. Margaret Kartomi, 'The Classification of Musical Instruments: Changing Trends in Research from the Late Nineteenth Century, with Special Reference to the 1990s', *Ethnomusicology* 45/2 (2001), 283–314; Kofi Agawu, *The African Imagination in Music*. New York: Oxford University Press, 2016, 65–66.
3. Regula Qureshi, 'How Does Music Mean? Embodied Memories and the Politics of Affect in the Indian Sarangi'. *American Ethnologist* 27/4 (2000): 805–838, 821; Kevin Dawe, 'People, Objects, Meaning: Recent Work on the Study and Collection of Musical Instruments'. *Galpin Society Journal* 54 (2001): 219–232, 220.
4. Agawu, *The African Imagination*, 65–66.
5. Arne Bjørndal, 'The Hardanger Fiddle: The Tradition, Music Forms and Style'. *Journal of the International Folk Music Council* 8 (1956): 13–15; Paul F. Wells, 'Fiddling as an Avenue of Black-White Musical Interchange'. *Black Music Research Journal* 23/1-2 (2003): 135–147, 136.
6. Francis Baines, 'Introducing the Hurdy-Gurdy'. *Early Music* 3/1 (1975): 33–37.
7. Rebecca Baltzer, 'Ecclesiastical Foundations and Secular Institutions' in *The Cambridge Companion to Medieval Music*, ed. Mark Everist, 263–275. Cambridge: Cambridge University Press, 2011, 269.
8. Kevin Dawe, 'Materials Matter: Towards a Political Ecology of Musical Instrument Making' in *Current Directions in Ecomusicology*, ed. Aaron S. Allen and Kevin Dawe, 109–120. New York: Routledge, 2016, 110.
9. Marcelle Duchesne-Guillemin, 'Music in Ancient Mesopotamia and Egypt'. *World Archaeology* 12, no. 3 (1981): 287–297, 294; W. K. Loftus, *Travels and researches in Chaldaea and Susiana; with an account of excavations at Warka, the 'Erech' of Nimrod, Shush, 'Shushan the palace' of Esther, in 1849–52*. New York: Robert Carter & Brothers, 1857, 257; Li Liu, 'Ritual and Hierarchy in the Longshan Culture'. *Early China* 21 (1996): 7–9.
10. Asymmetrical low-lyre, ÄM 10247, Egyptian and Papyrus Collection, The Egyptian Museum of Berlin; Banjo, 2013.639a, The Metropolitan Museum of Art.

11. José E. Martínez-Reyes, 'Timber to Timbre: Fijian Mahogany Plantations and Gibson Guitars' in *Audible Infrastructures: Music, Sound, Media, Critical Conjunctures in Music and Sound*, ed. Kyle Devine and Alexandrine Boudreault-Fournier, 93–132. New York: Oxford University Press, 2021, 4.
12. Kenneth S. Goldstein, 'The Impact of Recording Technology and British Folksong Revival' in *Folk Music and Modern Sound*, ed. William Ferris and Mary L. Hart, 3–13. Oxford, MS: University Press of Mississippi, 1982; A. L. Lloyd, 'Electric Folk Music in Britain' in *Folk Music and Modern Sound*, ed. Ferris and Hart, 14–18, 16.
13. Edward W. Said, *Orientalism*. New York: Pantheon Books, 1978, 2–3.
14. Philip V. Bohlman, 'Folk Song at the Beginnings of National History: Essay on Alte Volkslieder (1774)' in *Song Loves the Masses: Herder on Music and Nationalism*. Oakland: University of California Press, 2017, 32, 36; Markus Dirk Dubber, 'The German Jury and the Metaphysical Volk: From Romantic Idealism to Nazi Ideology'. *American Journal of Comparative Law* 43/2 (1995): 227–271, 255.
15. 'An Act against Vagrants and wandring, idle dissolute persons', in *Acts and Ordinances of the Interregnum, 1642–1660*, ed. C. H Firth and R. S. Rait, 1098–1099. London: His Majesty's Stationery Office, 1911; Eric Richards, *Britannia's Children: Emigration from England, Scotland, Wales and Ireland since 1600*. London: Hambledon, 2004, 143; Todd M. Endelman, 'The Jews of Great Britain (1650–1815)' in *The Cambridge History of Judaism*, ed. Jonathan Karp and Adam Sutcliffe, 949–971. Cambridge: Cambridge University Press, 2017, 963.
16. Moses Chikowero, '"Our People Father, They Haven't Learned Yet": Music and Postcolonial Identities in Zimbabwe, 1980–2000'. *Journal of Southern African Studies* 34/1 (2008): 145–160, 152.
17. W. H. Grattan Flood, *The Story of the Harp*. London: Scott, Scribner, 1905; Jonathan Petropoulos, 'The Polycratic Nature of Art Looting: The Dynamic Balance of the Third Reich' in *Networks of Nazi Persecution: Bureaucracy, Business and the Organization of the Holocaust*, ed. Gerald D. Feldman and Wolfgang Seibel, 103–117. New York: Berghahn Books, 2005, 110.
18. Laurent Dubois, *The Banjo: America's African Instrument*. Cambridge, MA: Harvard University Press, 2016, 85.
19. Greg Adams and Chuck Levy, 'The Down-Stroke Connection: Comparing Techniques Between the Jola Ekonting and the Five-String Banjo' in *Banjo Roots and Branches*, ed. Robert B. Winans, 83–110. Urbana: University of Illinois Press, 2018, 90.
20. Shlomo Pestcoe and Greg Adams, 'Changing Perspectives on the Banjo's African American Origins and West African Heritage' in *Banjo Roots and Branches*, ed. Winans, 3–18.
21. Joseph Johnson, 'African-American Banjo Music: Resources in the American Folklife Center', Library of Congress. https://guides.loc.gov/African-american-banjo/?loclr=blogflt, Library of Congress (2023); Paul Ruta, 'Black

Musicians' Quest to Return the Banjo to Its African Roots', https://folklife.si.edu/magazine/black-banjo-reclamation-project-african-roots. Smithsonian Center for Folklife and Cultural Heritage (2020); Black Banjo Reclamation Project (2023).

22. Dubois, *The Banjo*, 1, 109.
23. Dubois, *The Banjo*, 236.
24. Eric Lott, *Love & Theft: Blackface Minstrelsy and the American Working Class*. New York: Oxford University Press, 1993, 49.
25. Marshall Stearns and Jean Stearns, *Jazz Dance: the Story of American Vernacular Dance*. Boston: De Capo Press, 1968, 84, 325–327; Lott, *Love & Theft*, 98–99.
26. Dubois, *The Banjo*, 266.
27. *New York Clipper*, 4 June 1854 and 28 April 1860.
28. Fortifisco, M1.A12I vol. 9, 'Dandy Jim from Caroline', Library of Congress (1844), billed as a 'traditional Ethiopian song', demonstrates several aural hallmarks of a traditional Irish reel, for instance.
29. Dubois, *The Banjo*, 195–196; Philip F. Gura and James F. Bollman, *America's Instrument: The Banjo in the Nineteenth Century*. Chapel Hill: University of North Carolina Press, 1999, 48–49, 161.
30. Francis O'Neill, *Irish Minstrels and Musicians: With Numerous Dissertations on Related Subjects*. Chicago: The Regan Printing House, 1913, 21.
31. Dubois, *The Banjo*, 234.
32. Mick Moloney, 'Lecture: Banjo in Irish Music' (undated), AIA.031.003, Series III: Academic, 1889–2011, inclusive, Box: 22, Folder: 2, Mick Moloney Irish-American Music and Popular Culture Papers, Tamiment Library and Robert F. Wagner Labor Archives, New York University; Mick Moloney, 'Ceol Traidisíunta: Traditional Music: Irish Dance Bands in America'. *New Hibernia Review / Iris Éireannach Nua* 2/3 (1998): 127–137, 146.
33. Dubois, *The Banjo*, 306.
34. Moloney, 'Lecture'.
35. Moloney, 'Lecture'.
36. 'Public Dance Halls Act, or, An Act to Make provision for the Licensing, Control, and Supervision of Places Used for Public Dancing, and to Make Provision for Other Matters Connected with the Matters Aforesaid', 19 February 1935.
37. Jim Smyth, 'Dancing, Depravity and All That Jazz: The Public Dance Halls Act of 1935'. *History Ireland* 1/2 (1993): 51–54.
38. Moloney, 'Lecture'.
39. Eric Hobsbawm, 'Introduction: Inventing Traditions' in *The Invention of Tradition*, ed. Eric Hobsbawm and Terence Ranger. Cambridge: Cambridge University Press, 1983, 1–14.
40. Charles Seeger, 'The Appalachian Dulcimer'. *Journal of American Folklore* 71/279 (1958): 40–51, 46.

41. Scheitholt zither – wood (date undetermined), 1993.0569, Smithsonian National Museum of American History – triangular shape, eight strings; Épinette des Vosges. 89.4.991, The Metropolitan Museum of Art – angled rectangular shape, five strings.
42. Arthur D. Tyler, Appalachian Dulcimer, 1996.0276.23, Smithsonian National Museum of American History – hourglass shape, reduced to three strings.
43. Josiah Combs, *Folk-Songs of the Southern United States*. Austin: University of Texas Press, 1967, 95.
44. Nancy Gross and J. Scott Odell, 'Interview with J. Scott Odell, Washington D.C., 1978' in *Smithsonian Studies in History and Technology no. 44: The Hammered Dulcimer in America*. Washington: Smithsonian Institution Press, 1983, 2.
45. Seeger, 'The Appalachian Dulcimer', 8.
46. Stephen Winick, 'Jean Ritchie, 1922–2015', *Folklife Today*. https://blogs.loc.gov/folklife/2015/06/jean-ritchie-1922-2015.
47. 'Nottamun Town' and 'The Little Devils' in Cecil J. Sharp and Olive Dame Campbell, *English Folk Songs from the Southern Appalachians*. New York: G. P. Putnam's Sons, 1917.
48. Sharp, 1917 Diary, 215. Kentucky Pine Mountain Settlement, 30 August, 215. Vaughan Williams Memorial Library.
49. Margalit Fox, 'Obituary: Jean Ritchie, Lyrical Voice of Appalachia, Dies at 92', *New York Times*, 2 June 2015.
50. R. Alvey, *Dulcimer Maker: The Craft of Homer Ledford*. Lexington, University of Kentucky Press, 2003, 16.
51. Jean Ritchie, *The Dulcimer Book*. New York: Oak Publications, 1963.
52. R. D. Cannon, 'English Bagpipe Music'. *Folk Music Journal* 2/3 (1972): 176–219, 201.
53. 'Act of Proscription' (1747).
54. Hugh Trevor-Roper, 'The Highlander Myth'. *The Wilson Quarterly* 8/3 (1984): 104–120, 111.
55. Almeida Assman, 'Canon and Archive', in *A Companion to Cultural Memory Studies*, ed. Astrid Erll and Ansgar Nünning, 97–108. Berlin: De Gruyter, 2010, 101.
56. Frank Giles and Golda Meir, 'Interview: Who Can Blame Israel?' *Sunday Times*, 15 June 1969.
57. N. Jalal et al., 'A Musical Catastrophe: The Direct Impact of the Nakba on Palestinian Musicians and Musical Life' in *Palestinian Music and Song: Expression and Resistance since 1900*, ed. Heather Bursheh, Moslih Kanaaneh, Stig-Magnus Thorsén, and David A. McDonald, 37–52. Bloomington: Indiana University Press, 2013, 51–52.
58. Jalal et al., 'A Musical Catastrophe', 51–52.
59. Jalal et al., 'A Musical Catastrophe', 46.

60. Adam Raz, ביזת הרכוש הערבי במלחמת העצמאות / أدم راز نهب الممتلكات العربية [Looting of Arab Property During Israel's War of Independence]. Jerusalem: Carmel, 2020, 54–56, 92.
61. Jalal et al., 'A Musical Catastrophe', 50; David A. McDonald, 'Performative Politics: Folklore and Popular Resistance during the First Palestinian Intifada' in *Palestinian Music and Song: Expression and Resistance since 1900*, ed. David A. McDonald, Moslih Kanaaneh, Stig-Magnus Thorsén, and Heather Bursheh, 123–140. Bloomington: Indiana University Press, 2013, 137.
62. McDonald, 'Performative Politics', 137.
63. Andy Morgan, Mu'tasem Adileh, and Bill Badley, 'Palestinian Music: Sounds for a New State' in *The Rough Guide to World Music: Africa and Middle East*. New York: Rough Guides, 2006, 580–88.
64. Morgan, Adileh, and Badley, 'Palestinian Music', 138.
65. On this history, see Ross Cole, *The Folk: Music, Modernity, and the Political Imagination*. Oakland: University of California Press, 2021.
66. Dick Weissman, *Which Side Are You On? An Inside History of the Folk Music Revival in America*. New York: Continuum, 2006, 60.

9 | Folk Dance in a Global Frame

THERESA JILL BUCKLAND

The concepts of dance, ritual, and embodiment typically coalesce in classic characterizations of folk dance, often sharing a conceptual trajectory, history, and literature with that of folk music. As a performative practice, folk dance has accrued a diverse range of meanings and values across the globe, signifying identities and evoking connections to a shared rural and often ethnic past which – even if sometimes imagined rather than historically accurate – often resonates with its twenty-first-century practitioners. In a globalized world where cultural heritage seems to face continual threats from ever-growing processes of modernization as well as from critics who have chipped away at nineteenth-century certainties about the nature and value of the folk, people maintain, revive and take up folk dancing, finding relevance and reward in their involvement. This chapter offers some reflections on lingering conceptual assertions about folk dance, its relationship with ritual, and how these older claims resonate in contemporary embodied performance.

Historically, folk dance has been identified as a repertoire that stands in opposition to both classical and popular/commercial dance forms, or by an identifiable set of processes that include factors such as continuous embodied transmission, gradual choreographic evolution, and faithfulness to a supposed original form or manner of execution. However, what counts as folk dance – as the historiography of identification, collection, and subsequent performance of dances labelled as 'folk' demonstrates – is not and has never been a rarefied debate restricted to academic circles.[1] Those people contributing to debate on its definition may themselves be both folk dancers and scholars drawing upon their own participatory experience. Consequently, ontological issues concerning folk dance exert practical implications on performance and reception for a wider public. Definitions shift when applied to new forms and contexts; yet older and often discredited claims for the distinctiveness and value of folk dance often underlie current discourse on its nature. Expanding the frame towards a global perspective, the following reflections and examples serve not only to interrogate conceptual and performative diversities in folk dance; they also highlight the persistent yet pliable allure of folk dance as ancient pagan ritual, its enduring imbrication with nationalist and colonialist ideologies, and its proclivity (despite oft-cited laments of ephemerality) to assert ongoing testimonial significance to embodied collective memory and intangible cultural heritage.

Conceptual Dilemmas

Eurocentric interest in dance and ritual expanded around the turn of the twentieth century when the notion of folk dance was attributed import in understanding the cultural evolution of humankind. In this discourse, folk dance was positioned as inseparable from national and ethnic land rights, atavistic sentiment, and pagan ritual. Such performative testimonies to a supposed lingering and perhaps threatened *Volksgeist* were to be uncovered in rural communities, recorded, and revived often in new performance and social contexts. Central to the concept of folk dance was an emphasis on relational continuities of sound, space, time, and moving human bodies. Such elements are, of course, hardly exclusive to this performative activity, and there was little consensus surrounding a definition of folk dance.[2] Since at least the mid-twentieth century, scholars and folk dancers alike have often struggled to align a nineteenth-century European appellation with its referent's diverse and changing performers, forms, environments, and practices. Many have abandoned attempts to be convinced of its conceptual validity, offering alternative labels such as traditional, ethnic, popular, vernacular, or cultural dance.[3] Research into the historical and contextual circumstances in which folk dance was first identified as a distinctive phenomenon has cast doubt on its veracity, while growing knowledge and understanding of globally diverse dance practices have revealed its limitations and even irrelevance as a cross-cultural concept.

Difficulties with respect to consensus on the meaning of folk dance were brought to the fore in a proposed survey of folk dance by the International Folk Music Council (IFMC) Dance Commission in the early 1960s, led by the German ethnomusicologist and folklorist Felix Hoerburger. Their principal aims were to facilitate global comparative study and to create an international introductory 'kind of guidebook' for the study of folk dance.[4] To circumvent potentially confusing and inaccessible terminology, Hoerburger argued for a definition of folk dance that would guarantee its discussants were 'referring to the same thing'.[5] He thus identified and proposed three distinct categories of folk dance: those 'still transmitted by oral tradition', those 'deliberately cultivated', and those manifesting 'an explicit tendency to stage presentation'.[6] At the time he was writing, environments for folk dance had shifted considerably from rural contexts to urban folk dance clubs, stage ensembles, exhibitions, and competitions evidencing increased engagement by people with little direct connection to those involved when the dances were first collected. Furthermore, the aspirational global reach of the IFMC brought together, broadly speaking, European folklorists and North American ethnomusicologists whose intellectual histories, experiences, and world views differed substantially.[7]

In many cultures outside Europe, the concept of folk dance was neither used nor relevant – an absence that could have indicated to the Folk Dance Commission the limitations of its conceptual framework. Such divergences and misalignment were already evident in American dance scholar Gertrude Kurath's earlier attempt at a global survey of the emerging discipline of dance ethnology published in 1960.[8] Not only did the mapping exercise of the IFMC reflect the globally nascent state of dance studies of any kind in the mid twentieth century, it also resulted in a focus on Europe, largely as a result of the geopolitical realities of the decades immediately following the Second World War. The members of the IFMC Dance Commission (which gave rise to the IFMC Subgroup on Folk Dance Terminology, later to become the Study Group on Ethnochoreology) comprised scholars from the Eastern Bloc whose states sponsored folkloric research in pursuit of nationalist goals but, at the same time, restricted communication and contact with scholarship that did not reflect Soviet ideology.[9] The experiences and expertise of the IFMC Dance Commission therefore shaped the conceptual direction of classification, focusing on dances of the people conceived as the artistic products of peasant culture. Anthropological approaches to the study of dance developing initially in the United States, which would interrogate etic conceptualizations such as folk dance, were yet in their infancy.[10]

In 1964, initial results from the IFMC Dance Commission survey prompted Hoerburger to urge further clarification on definitional aspects, distinguishing between what he termed 'first existence' (denoting 'original tradition') and 'second existence' (denoting 'revival, or even arrangement').[11] Nearly all respondents, he noted, employed the term 'folk dance' to include both situations. Emphasizing that the difference between the two was factual rather than evaluative, he designated so-called first existence folk dances as 'a field of folklore research' and second existence as 'the field of cultivation'.[12] This binary division was in fact a modification of fellow German musicologist Walter Wiora's notions of *erstes und zweites dasien* (first and second existence).¹³ Hoerburger's adaptation indicates how the emergent academic study of folk dance drew upon and closely paralleled theoretical perspectives from the more established field of music. Hoerburger regarded 'the greatest problem in any talk on *folk* dance' to be that (much like in music) the one term 'is used to mean *different things*'.¹⁴ His characterization of first and second existence folk dance was explicitly designed not to be exhaustive or final, and he was aware that in practice there were many 'intermediate stages'.¹⁵ Yet these terms now recur in the literature without due critical or contextual interrogation of his original text, at the root of which is the often overlooked commitment to the hallmarks of a classical folk paradigm: authenticity, religious origins, and remote rural community.¹⁶

Subsequent folk dance scholars – influenced by developments in anthropology, folkloristics, and contemporary dance forms and practices – have enlarged the investigative field to include study of diasporic dancing and revivalist practices.¹⁷ In this case, Hoerburger's concept of second existence has proved suitably flexible to application and revision – notably, for example, in the work of Canadian folk dance scholar Andriy Nahachewsky on Ukrainian folk dance.¹⁸ Expanding upon Hoerburger's scheme, Nahachewsky introduced the idea of 'vival' and 'reflective' dance – vival dance signalling 'dance traditions with a focus solely on the present', and reflective dance those dances 'in which the participants make conscious reference to their tradition's past'.¹⁹ This dichotomous scheme has echoes of the folk paradigm, a potential criticism which Nahachewsky addresses from his adopted position as 'outsider' to the cultural practice, cautioning that experiences of reflective dance should be viewed as 'tendencies and processes'.²⁰

Comparably sophisticated engagement with the concepts of first and second existence dance occur in the work of American scholar Anthony Shay.²¹ Dissatisfied with a lack of subtlety in Hoerburger's characterizations and the 'faintly derogatory' language of second existence, Shay proposes the concept of 'parallel traditions' to embrace at least five contextual and often inter-related practices recognized by their participants as folk dance. In his 2006 monograph concerned primarily with the folk dance practices of immigrant communities in North America, Shay discerns the following porous categories: the social sphere of dances performed within the community; those dances displayed to a public, notably at international folk festivals; the repertoire of theatricalized versions performed by national state companies, frequently from the country of origin; dances adopted by the communities often from state companies' repertoire and which are believed to be indicative of the community's ethnicity for outside audiences; and performances by professional and amateur groups, along with the wider recreational folk dance movement that might involve individuals from outside the specified ethnic community.[22] In both Shay's and Nahachewsky's deliberations on the nature of folk dance, emphasis is placed on identifying the exact sociocultural, temporal, and geographic contexts of the examples in which their theoretical suggestions are grounded, as well as the role of emic perspectives.[23]

The importance of bringing emic perspectives into the discussion is also given weight in ethnochoreologist Egil Bakka's work on differing attitudes towards folk dance (and costume) within the Norwegian organized folk movement.[24] Bakka distinguishes between those who believe their primarily regional inheritance to be directly from past performers with whom they self-consciously share a strong and continuous bond of kinship or close neighbourhood (heirs); those who less self-assuredly assert their connection to regional 'source' materials, seeing folk dance and costume as resources to serve a wider purpose such as professing identity or wider societal goals (users); and those who aim for faithful re-enactments based upon detailed study of past performances (researchers). These ideal types are not mutually exclusive in Bakka's model which, however, fundamentally follows Hoerburger's distinctions of first and second existence.

Circumventing the problematic qualifiers of ethnic, popular, vernacular, and traditional as alternatives, a new category of 'cultural dance' is employed by Australian folk dance scholar Jeanette Mollenhauer. 'Cultural dance' designates the dancing of diasporic communities within Australia whose geographical origin does not necessarily align with national boundaries nor do its practitioners necessarily claim 'ancestral exclusivity'.[25] Mollenhauer argues that given the relative positioning of elitist genres such as ballet in Australia as universal and hence 'acultural', it follows that those genres not credited with this status can be described in her study as 'cultural'. Aside from likely objections to the dichotomous reasoning (and to the fact that *all* dance genres are cultural), Mollenhauer's consideration of traditional dancing within diasporic and first people communities in Australia uncovers and critiques issues of orientalism, eurocentrism, racial essentialism, and colonialism that have inevitably generated structural imbalances of privilege and value across the dance field.[26] Many factors play into this dominant cultural hierarchy, the manifestation of which is not the preserve of Australia alone – especially where the dancing practices are within the domain of the amateur rather than the professional dancer.

Undoubtedly, folk dance's aesthetically arresting character facilitates its symbolic valency as a cultural identity marker deployed for political purposes. What cannot be denied is the rich potential of productively indeterminate concepts such as 'the folk' employed in tandem with performance for nationalist purposes. Witness, for example, the Vienna Ritualist School's pan-Germanic interpretations of sword dances in Nazi Germany, the gendered nationalist ideology of the Sección Femenina's enactment of folk dance in Franco's Spain, the performance of the men's dance *zeibekiko* during elections in Greece by politicians of the Panhellenic Socialist Movement between the 1980s and the first decade of the twenty-first century, and (perhaps best known) the professional folk dance ensembles from Soviet-dominated countries during the Cold War period.[27] Politically motivated issues of ownership and authenticity often rise to the fore in nationalist discourse and practice, with dance and ritual claimed as belonging solely to one ethnic group. Over the last two decades, for instance, Hindu nationalist extremists have claimed exclusive ownership of the dance ritual *garba* of Gujarati even though it is also practised by Christian and Muslim communities within the region.[28] I also recall when adjudicating at a folk dance festival during the 1980s a dispute over the name Macedonia and issues surrounding ownership of dances between a Greek folk dance group and diasporic Macedonian competitors from Canada.[29] Folk dance represents not only cultural, but also political capital; in consequence, folk imaginaries have material impact. A striking instance of this is the conscious creation of a folk dance repertoire in the founding of the Israeli nation state.[30] Initially, Jewish communities outside Israel seeking to affirm their connection to the homeland through dance preferred the supposed 'authenticity' of folk dance creations by choreographers within Israel, though in the twenty-first century the imperative of this criterion drawn from the folk paradigm has lessened.[31]

Although consensus on definition is impossible to reach when exploring the diverse dance activities to which the label 'folk' has been applied, it is important to recognize that in the heyday of European folk dance collection there was frequently a rural repertoire in existence that was notably distinct or differently performed from that seen in urban, courtly, and institutional contexts. So too were there often distinct processes of transmission and enactment. This historical phenomenon was not an entire misapprehension or chimera, even if later revisionist scholarship has rightly drawn attention to issues surrounding class, race, and political ideology that facilitated such a construct. Viewed in the light of present-day knowledge and sensibilities, the motivations, recording techniques, and taxonomic conceptualizations of earlier folk dance collectors and revivalists might be found wanting in scholarly rigour and/or to be ethically moribund. Be that as it may, through their efforts there now exists a corpus of choreographic and ethnologic materials that affords a degree of insight into past dance cultures that also proffers a range of aesthetic and creative opportunities for contemporary practice.

Ritual

If the European 'folk' of the nineteenth and twentieth centuries did not conceive of themselves as such, neither did they label their customary dance practices as 'ritual'. Scholars and folk dance collectors of the time, however, categorized dances associated with the calendar, with religion, or with healing and purification strategies as relics of pagan religious rites in accordance with the dominant intellectual paradigm of unilinear cultural evolution.[32] This nineteenth-century social theory, influenced by Darwinism, postulated a single chronological line of stages of societal development through which all societies progressed, though at differing rates. Non-Western societies were positioned as remaining in an early developmental stage of pagan primitivism – whereas Western urban societies, standing at the top of the evolutionary tree, were seen as civilized and increasingly secular. The folk appeared to exist at an intermediate stage somewhere between the two. Cultural and artistic practices were deemed to follow an equivalent developmental process. Thus, it was believed that the folk lying midway in this evolutionary process from pagan to modern performed traditional actions such as dancing unreflectively, an activity considered (if at all) by contemporary anthropologists, ethnologists, and scholars of religion as the most unsophisticated of expressive art forms. This positioning reveals much about Victorian male academic attitudes towards dance, which were steeped in centuries of logocentrism and Christian antagonism towards dancing.[33] Rational thought, a prerequisite of advanced civilization, required skill in verbal language, whereas bodily arts were construed as irrational and lower in the artistic hierarchy of Eurocentric culture, typically privileging the mind over the body in a gendered binary. The body in most Judeo-Christian religious traditions was the seat of sin and temptation, particularly with respect to sex and seduction: activities that involved men and women dancing together or dancing exhibitions in which women were subject to the male gaze were especially frowned upon by religious authorities. In the eyes of Christian puritans during the European Reformation, dancing was thus the work of the devil and an undesirable relic of paganism.

Late-nineteenth-century anthropologists, fascinated by the idea of pagan origins and the idea of a mysterious 'other', as the historian Ronald Hutton has astutely examined, believed dance to be an essential element in the foundations of pre-Christian religious activity, and that all dancing stemmed from this originary purpose.[34] In line with Tylorian survivals theory, European peasant agricultural customs, as collected in a pioneering survey by German mythologist and ethnologist Wilhelm Mannhardt, furnished comparable source material for many scholars.[35] The most notable and profoundly influential for much of the twentieth century was British anthropologist James Frazer, whose bestseller *The Golden Bough* (1890) was referred to in support of the belief that folk dancing was inextricably bound in origin and function with pagan sacrifice and fertility rites.[36] Frazer's later wife, Lilly Grove, made clear her debt to him in linking dancing and its origins to pagan religious rites in her world history of dance.[37] It is also perhaps no accident that around the same time there was a conceptual shift from historical understandings of ritual as script to that of ritual as symbolic behaviour and universal phenomenon.[38]

Ritual dances thus came to enjoy special status over social dancing as repositories of often unfathomable meaning related to ancient pagan fertility rites. It was not until the later twentieth century that this unfounded interpretation began to release its hold on academic studies of folk dance. A well-known example is that of English morris and sword dancing, which in the early 1900s were categorized by Cecil J. Sharp as ritual dance.[39] Numerous scholars have challenged the evolutionist basis of Sharp's attribution, contesting his interpretations with scholarly source criticism of actual historical records that indicate a rather shorter history of practice of some five hundred years, rather than the mythic origins theory of being lost in the mists of time.[40] And yet the mystical pull of unknowable ritual pasts in relation to folk dancing continues to enchant.[41]

From the 1990s, the increasing popularity of 'dark border morris' with its punk-, gothic-, and pagan-inspired aesthetic has presented an alternative vision to that of the quiet rural idyll of dancing on the village green.[42] Reformulating morris for modern sensibilities, a new generation of dancers has emerged, several of whom refute academic dismissal of pagan origins theory, preferring to feel a spiritual connection between nature, people, landscape, and history. Such atavistic cravings often intersect with environmentalism, modern paganism, and the creative arts. Eschewing nationalism, this new wave of morris, it is declared, 'looks back to a pre-industrial time, largely untainted by England's sticky colonial legacy'.[43] A high-profile example of this new approach is the all-female morris team Boss Morris established in 2015, whose website proclaims their inclusion in 'a wider movement which is reclaiming the narrative around our culture and past and how we feel about "England" and "Englishness"', and who describe themselves as 'a group of female creatives supported by professional musicians who share an artistic and progressive vision of morris dancing as a means to increase social engagement and interest in this unique and ancient folk dance'.[44] Not all participants in contemporary morris dancing claim to be pagans, although some acknowledge that it *feels* pagan or that it makes them feel connected with the Earth.[45] Much of the foundation of such thinking echoes nineteenth-century evolutionist ideology and chimes with ideas that thrive in environments of rapid social and technological change.

This search for spirituality in an increasingly secular Western world had earlier in the twentieth century inspired interest in folk dancing in the genre known as 'circle' or 'sacred dancing'. This composite repertoire of mainly European traditional circle dances and modern choreographies was taught from the 1970s by German ballet master Bernhard Wosien at the Findhorn Foundation in Scotland, a centre dedicated to spiritual living.[46] Now a worldwide movement, circle dancing is not held by all participants to be sacred in character, but the wider aim of well-being to be achieved through dancing together is acknowledged to be beneficial in therapeutic circles, especially for older people. Leading figures in the movement extol the circle as both a natural and ancient formation that occurs across cultures and thus by implication pre-dates nationalistic affiliations.[47]

A clear thread running through these re-envisioned practices of morris and circle dancing is a deeply held belief in the age-old relationship between people dancing together and the natural environment. As elements of past rituals and dances are brought together acts of bricolage create new rituals – whether regarded as sacred or secular in function. This has not always met with approval from the more puritanical guardians of tradition. During the 1980s, for instance, some members of the Society for International Folk Dance (a UK-based organization founded in 1946 for amateur participation) complained that the sacred circle dancers had scant regard for the 'original' choreography and context.[48] For leading advocates of circle dancing, however, their purpose lies in 'reclaiming ... ancient awareness and wisdom' through dancing in the 'natural circle', moving back to 'oneness' away from the individuation of modern living.[49] These pliable beliefs of land, culture, moving bodies, and spirit are evident in both fascist and left-leaning visions of folk dance. Post–Second-World-War cultural movements such as circle dancing and the Californian-initiated 'dances of universal peace' share more in common with the hippy movement, for example, than with extreme right-wing nationalism in their use of folk dances from across the globe to promote peace, love, and intercultural unity. The latter's repertoire – made up of 'simple folk movements drawn from the world's traditions' and generated from chanting sacred phrases from a diversity of languages – has commonalities with modern paganism, which in the search for spiritual expression often turns to widely disparate practices of shamanism, folk costume, sound, and imagery from various cultures.[50]

In these eclectic practices, remnants of ancient pagan rituals become both sources and strategies for spiritual communication and harmony between people, conducted in kinetic dialogue with diffuse concepts of nature, the earth, and the environment. As noted earlier, the significance of tying distinctive archaic dances classed as folk to cultural and historic geographies is muted in the discourse. Suspicious of past imperialist and nationalist investment in imaginaries of folk culture, these contemporary proponents of folk dance eschew older nationalist clarion calls that assert the legitimacy of primal ethnic identity in relation to specific territory.[51]

For marginalized and oppressed peoples, however, this linking of land, people, and the interpretation of folk dance as former pagan ritual may be deployed to unify and make visible their existence in a volatile global world. Although arising from European Romantic nationalism, this ideology has been deployed for similar purposes elsewhere in non-Christian communities and in comparatively recent times. In the twentieth and twenty-first centuries across the contested territories known from an occidental perspective as the Middle East, one widespread dance form in particular has been interpreted as a cultural activity remaining from agrarian, pre-Islamic times.[52] Known as *dabkeh*, *dabke*, or *dhabka* among other spellings, its performance has often been repurposed from recorded localized practice as a celebratory rural dance in order to express and consolidate national unity and identity, notably in Syria and Palestine.[53] During the 1970s, Palestinian nationalist folklorists, influenced by European scholarship, posited *dabkeh*'s origins in ancient Canaanite fertility rites – an interpretation which pre-dated other regional peoples' claims to ownership of the dance.[54] Such attributions of antiquity, stability, and resilience to a dance that was once practised at joyful peasant gatherings resonated with nationalist claims relating to the Palestinian people at large. The performance of *dabkeh* became 'a new cultural ritual, proclaiming collective identity through repetitive enactment'.[55] Purposefully re-cast to override potential barriers of age, class, gender, or religion, whether resident in town, country, the diaspora or in refugee camps, *dabkeh* as the Ministry of Culture proclaims in a 2022 video 'gives Palestinians a sense of pride, identity, and belonging to their homeland'.[56]

However, not all origin narratives for folk dance rituals are bound to paganism or claims of immutable ethnicity and land entitlement. Nor indeed are such rationales necessarily known or foremost in all participants' minds. Nonetheless, the theory of cultural survivals and pagan ritual origins has served to underpin, as in the nineteenth century, contemporary aspirations and interests. Whether political or spiritual, or indeed both, the notion of *Volksgeist* as an unassailable bond between the earth, land, and people remains a malleable and vital force in the contemporary world.

The Body

Since the later twentieth century, studies of 'the body' and 'embodiment' in performance have proliferated, mapping such features as gender, race, sexuality, class, religion, and age.[57] In genres conceived of as traditional or folk, the supposed authenticity of the body has been deeply valued in the eyes of some participants and scholars, leading to acts of exclusion in spite of the oft-professed idea that folk dancing is for all. In the folk revival movement of the 1970s and 1980s in England, for example, several male morris dance teams cited the authority of 'authenticity' to deny rights of participation to women and to men from outside their locality.[58] Notable among these were several dancers in north-west England who identified with a re-envisioning of the folk as urban working-class rather than as the rural poor. These neotraditionalists chose to emphasize the nineteenth-century existence of adult male morris dancers in the region, obscuring the fact that some of the sources for their reconstructed dances evidenced early twentieth-century participation by women and children. The record of the past was thus used selectively to support present practice. This revivalist insistence on male exclusivity in morris dancing was drawn from Cecil Sharp's then largely uncontested demarcation of English ritual performance – a definition that also highlighted localized provenance in claims to authenticity.[59]

Fiercely protective of their newly collected repertoire, several north-west morris dancers condemned its performance by southern English dancers.[60] The local dances differed in form and style from the more widespread

Cotswold or south midlands morris, which had formed the basis of the national morris revival by Sharp and his followers. The revivalists' antagonism mapped onto long-held perceptions of a north–south divide in which the latter appropriated the resources and embodied industry of the north. Leading north-west morris dancers – resident in a region formerly regarded as an industrial powerhouse of the British Empire, but in post-imperial times slipping yet further into impoverishment under the government of Margaret Thatcher – employed a rhetoric of regional cultural embodiment to assert exclusive performance rights. One influential individual believed local residence to be an essential criterion for authentic performance, arguing that each person, 'is a product of where you live, and your own area is ingrained in you, as part of your character'.[61]

A long-standing dichotomous relationship between the supposed innate character of northerners and southerners, moreover, was identified in the repertoire. North-west morris dances were said to embody regional attributes of strength, power, stamina, endurance, discipline, teamwork, and above all working-class masculinity. Cotswold morris was considered by die-hard north-west morris dancers to embody the opposite. Comparing the grace, flow, melody, and light elevation of men waving handkerchiefs as they danced in the southern style, north-west dancers perceived the grounded power, uniform precision, and noisy rhythm of dancing in clogs to reflect industrial male strength.[62] The straight lines of the latter's spatial pathways and arm movements, as contrasted with the curves of the former, were seen as indicative of character, gender, and associated sexuality for the 'straight lads' of the north. Subsequent decades have seen a lessening in such chauvinist attitudes as changing societal values and realities became reflected in the morris dance revival movement's wider acceptance of the national dissemination of localized dances and especially of women's participation.[63]

This shift in the performance of dances previously the sole domain of one particular gender to meet changing gender expectations in contemporary society is visible in other folk dance genres. For example, the Norwegian virtuoso solo male dance *halling* is also danced by women in the twentieth century; gender-free calling in American contra dancing has become the norm; and in diasporic Chinese communities, women and young girls are increasingly performing the traditional lion dance previously reserved for men.[64] Most of these transitions in performance have been towards women taking on men's repertoire rather than the other way around. The growing inclusion of women, however, is by no means a global phenomenon. Indeed, in Afghanistan, Iran, and Saudi Arabia strict interpretations of Islamic law prevent women from dancing in public.[65]

Embodied gender norms typically profile kinetic expressions of power, strength, and stamina for men and those of grace and modesty for women. This nineteenth-century vision of gender appears in the staging of most national folk dance ensembles, where the distinction between male and female movement is a deliberately choreographed feature. It is particularly evident in ensembles influenced by Soviet choreographer Igor Moiseyev, who created a 'parallel tradition' of ballet-inspired folk dance companies.[66] The professionalized bodies of these state ensemble folk dancers reflected an idealized view of the peasantry as predicated on the tradition of homogeneity for the *corps de ballet*. Slender, highly trained, technically uniform, and youthful dancers portrayed an image to the world: 'all-smiling, all-happy, all-working – all the time'.[67] It was an image often critiqued in folk dance competitions, where authenticity is a crucial criterion extending to authenticity of the body. From personal experience in the 1980s, folk dance scholars on juries in Hungary held fast to notions of peasant authenticity in their desire to shift dancers' and audiences' understanding of folk dancing from theatrical, balleticized, and choreographed performances to the more amateur and improvisational renditions recorded on field trips to the villages. The adjudicators expected to see older people and children on stage and, above all, variation between dancers in the execution of steps and groupings. Such adherence to ideals of authenticity establishes forms of essentialism, as some dancers professed that only those by birth might truly execute their Indigenous dances; those born elsewhere of a different ethnicity, it was claimed, could offer only approximations. Similar attitudes can also be found among audiences watching the performances of visiting folk dance troupes at festivals. I well remember from 1989 some audience members at the Sidmouth International Folklore Festival in England complaining about the slender, blonde woman in the California-based group 'Dances of the Pacific', whose body type did not conform to their expectations of women performing Hawaiian repertoire.

The notion of happy dancing peasants was roundly criticized by the American cultural anthropologist, musician, and activist Charles Keil in 1978, who proclaimed the field of folk and its academic study to be 'a grim fairy tale', created as an act of oppression and appropriation by the bourgeoisie.[68] As Keil indicates, this 'playing at' and 'make-over' of the expressive culture of dispossessed or subordinate peoples for the commodified consumption of the powerful has a long history. One might be tempted to argue, following this Marxist line of reasoning, that false consciousness has encouraged acceptance of the concept of folk dance to such an extent that marginalized peoples readily participate in this labelling. An interesting case is that of African American novelist and choreographer Zora Neale Hurston, whose 1930s staged depictions of Black expressive culture – drawn from her fieldwork in the Bahamas and southern Florida during the late 1920s – largely complied with a view of its 'folk' roots in the poor rural South.[69] Her promotion of 'untampered-with Negro folk material' collected from Black migrant workers emphasized authenticity.[70] However, this claim to legitimacy must also be seen, as American dance scholar Anthea Kraut has sensitively and persuasively argued, in the contemporaneous context of dominant theatrical images of Black dancers – most notably those in blackface minstrelsy and Black musical theatre, where the choreography fed White racist stereotypes of the exuberant 'natural' Black dancer.[71] This essentialist trope, current even in the twentieth century alleges that all peoples of African ancestry possess innate dance ability. Such a belief lies in racist and evolutionist notions of the perceived child-like, spontaneous, and unstructured dancing among so-called primitive peoples, coupled with the low value of dance in Eurocentric hierarchies of art.[72] Breaking down barriers of body types physiologically and/or racially identified in order to facilitate access to dance can therefore be double faceted. Outsiders might not see themselves reflected in the models of dancing presented to them, whereas dancers, especially the colonized, whose embodied culture may feel the last bastion of ownership and autonomy, might regard inclusion as cultural appropriation by another name.[73]

Even when offensive and distorted images of persecuted and marginalized peoples are not operative within a dominant colonial culture, the play of memory may bear less resemblance to lived historical experience than to projected cultural memory. A powerful imaginary is often at work in the re-enactment of folk dances by diasporic communities, whose sense of dislocation and disempowerment may activate a nostalgic vision of a static rural past – one that cultivates a shared sense of memory when dancing together in an unfamiliar land. But the cultural practices and politics of the homeland also undergo change, of course, occasioning accusations of cultural deterioration and protestations of cultural purity from diasporic communities who profess to have maintained 'the tradition' or sense of national identity.[74] Where a common political purpose exists, however, between residents of the homeland and diasporic communities, social media has helped to promote a unifying embodied vision of national resistance, as in the case of *dabke* noted earlier.[75] Through the internet, dancers can give embodied expression to their sense of solidarity and togetherness, making new memories through a virtual performance of a cultural and politicized heritage.

In contrast, the symbolic power of place brought into being through the embodied collective performance of cultural heritage in actual time and space is of especial significance for the displaced inhabitants of the Department of Ayacucho in Peru. For these Andean communities, fleeing the twenty years of political violence (1980–2000), their new home in the city of Huamanga provides a safe space in which to enact embodied memories of their homeland through customary yet formerly forbidden dances. The choreography of weaving pathways, movement of ribbons tied to the men's legs, and hopping movements evoke for these displaced people not only bodily sensations of traversing the mountainous terrain where they once lived, but also emotional connections with the flora and fauna of home, with their ancestors, and with those friends, neighbours, and relatives who disappeared in the recent persecution. A 'lost place', Michaela Callaghan argues, is thus 'danced into being through collective participation'.[76]

In twenty-first-century scholarship, the dancing bodies of imperially conquered or displaced peoples are deciphered less as bearers of mythic pagan pasts than as testimony to traumatic histories of migration and enslavement, which continue to be recognized creatively in dance performance.[77] Treated as living archives, the moving bodies of dancers become witnesses to material events. Indeed, the act of performing traditional dancing has been employed as a research methodology to elicit embodied memories of migration among British Bangladeshi women.[78] Often dispossessed of the ability to record and maintain experiences verbally, dancers may embody and transmit collective memories as forms of intangible cultural heritage.

Old Claims and New Trajectories

In 2003, the Convention for the Safeguarding of the Intangible Cultural Heritage was ratified by UNESCO, incorporating dance within its remit. On its website can be found those dance forms granted UNESCO status from across the world, such as the polonaise of Poland, the Kalela dance of Zambia, the kolo of Serbia, the rumba of Cuba, and the lad's dance of Romania.[79] The procedure is not without controversy, and UNESCO's definition of intangible cultural heritage as 'traditional, contemporary and living at the same time', 'inclusive', 'representative' and 'community-based' is at odds with some dance practices long considered to be 'folk'.[80] On the one hand, the convention enshrines outdated concepts related to the folk paradigm and on the other might be found to be too interfering in expecting older attitudes to be dispelled. Conceptual parallels between intangible cultural heritage and folk have not gone unnoticed by critics.[81]

However, an erroneous categorization of a dance or indeed dismissal of the taxonomic class of folk has little bearing on the pleasure experienced by those who choose to practise activities classed as folk or traditional dance. What is so often overlooked in scholarly debates on ideological issues, important though they are, is the visceral pleasure experienced by folk dancers of moving in certain codified ways to particular musical rhythms, dynamic textures, and sonorities. As American ethnomusicologist Gibb Schreffler has argued in discussing bhangra dance, there has been a preponderance of academics discussing issues of identity when participants are often most concerned with 'matters of aesthetics and logistics'.[82] Intellectual scrutiny of enjoyment and the reasons why people are attracted (or not) to particular forms of dancing have tended to lag behind cultural and political studies of folk dance. It is also time for a return of attention to issues of choreographic structure and composition as well as aesthetic considerations in order to more roundly understand the continuing appeal of folk dancing.

Listening and giving value to the embodied experiences as well as the beliefs of people who practise(d) and observe(d) phenomena labelled as folk dancing lies at the heart of ethnographic and historical research. So too does attempting to understand the manifold, complex, sometimes paradoxical, and always situational reasons for participation. The symbolic potentiality of communal dance forms for the expression, suppression, and arrogation of identity politics of various hues cannot be denied; nor can individual and often co-existing motivational rewards: sociality, spirituality, physical exercise, opportunities for travel, financial recompense, heritage maintenance, nostalgia, and well-being. The designation of dances as 'folk' and their potential relation to ritual requires ongoing critical examination through both non-presentist historical inquiry and systematic anthropological scrutiny that aims to uncover emic attitudes, terminology, and appraisal. In laying bare old claims and forging new trajectories, the choreological, the sensate, and the aesthetic deserve to be brought more firmly into the frame.

Notes

1. See, for example, Petri Hoppu, 'National Dances and Popular Education – the Formation of Folk Dance Canons in Norden'. In *Dance and the Formation of Norden. Emergences and Struggles*, ed. Karen Vedel. Trondheim, Norway: Tapir Academic Press, 2011, 27–56, and Peter Harrop, 'Morris, Sword and Northern Soul: Grappling with "Folk"'. *Folk Music Journal* 12/5 (2025): 32–45.
2. For overview, see LeeEllen Friedland, 'Folk Dance History'. In *International Encyclopedia of Dance*, ed. Selma J. Cohen. Oxford: Oxford University Press, 1998.
3. For discussion see Joann W. Kealiinohomoku, 'Folk Dance'. *Encyclopaedia Britannica* (2008); Sherril Dodds, *Dancing on the Canon: Embodiments of Value in Popular Dance*. London: Palgrave Macmillan, 2011, 45–65; Andriy Nahachewsky, 'A Folklorist's View of "Folk" and "Ethnic" Dance: Three Ukrainian Examples'. In *The Oxford Book of Dance and Ethnicity*, ed. Anthony Shay and Barbara Sellers-Young. Oxford: Oxford University Press, 2016, 297–318.
4. Felix Hoerburger, 'Proposals for the Work of the IFMC Dance Commission'. *Journal of the International Folk Music Council* 14 (1962): 161.
5. Hoerburger, 'Proposals', 161.
6. Hoerburger, 'Proposals', 161.
7. For a history of the IFMC, until 2023 called the International Council for Traditional Music, see Svanibor Pettan, Naila Ceribašic and Don Niles, ed., *Celebrating the International Council for Traditional Music: Reflections on the First Seven Decades*. Ljubljana: International Council for Traditional Music and University of Ljubljana Press, 2022.
8. Gertrude Prokosch Kurath, 'Panorama of Dance Ethnology'. *Current Anthropology* 1/3 (1960): 233–254.
9. Anca Giurchescu, 'A Historical Perspective on the Analysis of Dance Structure in the International Folk Music Council (IFMC)/International Council for Traditional Music (ICTM)' in *Dance Structures: Perspectives on the Analysis of Human Movement*, ed. Adrienne Lois Kaeppler and Elsie Ivancich Dunin. Budapest: Akadémiai Kiadó, 2007, 3–18, and Catherine E. Foley and Elsie Ivancich Dunin, 'ICTM Study Group on Ethnochoreology'. In *Celebrating the International Council for Traditional Music*, ed. Pettan, Ceribašic, and Niles, 245.
10. See Adrienne L. Kaeppler, 'American Approaches to the Study of Dance'. *Yearbook for Traditional Music* 23 (1991): 11–21.
11. Felix Hoerburger, 'Folk Dance Survey'. *Journal of the International Folk Music Council* 17 (1965): 7–8, 7.
12. Hoerburger, 'Folk Dance Survey', 7.

13. Felix Hoerburger, 'Once Again: On the Concept of "Folk Dance"'. *Journal of the International Folk Music Council* 20 (1968): 30–32, 30.
14. Hoerburger, 'Once Again', 30.
15. Hoerburger, 'Once Again', 30.
16. See as an example Sarah Whatley, 'Embodied Cultural Property: Contemporary and Traditional Dance Practices'. *International Journal of Cultural Property* 29/2 (2022): 171–181; for critical responses see Theresa Jill Buckland, 'Definitions of Folk Dance: Some Explorations', *Folk Music Journal* 4 (1983): 315–32 and the following all by Andriy Nahachewsky: 'Participatory and Presentational as Ethnochoreological Categories', *Dance Research Journal*, 27/1 (1995): 1–15; 'Once Again: On the Concept of "Second Existence Folk Dance"', *Yearbook for Traditional Music* 33 (2001): 17–28, and *Ukrainian Dance: A Cross-Cultural Approach*. Jefferson, NC: McFarland, 2011, 234–235.
17. Nahachewsky, 'Participatory and Presentational' and 'Once Again'.
18. Nahachewsky, 'Participatory and Presentational' and *Ukrainian Dance*.
19. Nahachewsky, *Ukrainian Dance*, 24, 26.
20. See Theresa Jill Buckland, '"Th'Owd Pagan Dance": Ritual, Enchantment, and an Enduring Intellectual Paradigm', *Journal for the Anthropological Study of Human Movement* 11/4, 12/1, (2001/2002): 418–419; Nahachewsky, *Ukrainian Dance*, 275, 28. See also his discussion, 234–235.
21. Anthony Shay, 'Parallel Traditions: State Folk Dance Ensembles and Folk Dance in "the Field"'. *Dance Research Journal* 31/1 (1999): 29–56; *Choreographic Politics: State Folk Dance Companies, Representation and Power*. Middletown, CT: Wesleyan University Press, 2002; *Choreographing Identities: Folk Dance, Ethnicity and Festival in the United States and Canada*. Jefferson, NC: McFarland, 2006.
22. Shay, *Choreographing Identities*, 9–14.
23. Shay, *Choreographing Identities*; Nahachewsky, 'A Folklorist's View'.
24. Egil Bakka, 'Heir, User or Researcher: Basic Attitudes within the Norwegian Revival Movement'. *Proceedings of the 17th Symposium of the Study Group on Ethnochoreology 1992*, Nafplion: Peloponnesian Folklore Foundation, 1994, 117–126. See also Egil Bakka, 'Whose Dances, Whose Authenticity?' in *Authenticity. Whose Tradition?* ed. László Felföldi and Theresa Jill Buckland. Budapest: European Folklore Institute, 2002, 60–69 and compare Sille Kapper, 'Estonian Folk Dance: Terms and Concepts in Theory and Practice'. *Folklore. Electronic Journal of Folklore* 54 (2013): 73–96.
25. Jeanette Mollenhauer, *Cultural Dance in Australia: Essays on Performance Contexts Beyond the Pale*. Sydney: Palgrave Macmillan, 2022, 17.
26. Compare Joann W. Kealiinohomoku, 'An Anthropologist Looks at Ballet as a Form of Ethnic Dance'. *Impulse* 20 (1970): 24–33. Republished in *Moving History/Dancing Cultures: A Dance History Reader*, ed. Ann Dils and Ann Cooper Albright, 33–43. Middletown, CT: Wesleyan University Press, 2001

and Theresa Jill Buckland, 'All Dances are Ethnic but Some Are More Ethnic than Others: Some Observations on Dance Studies and Anthropology'. *Dance Research* 17/1 (1999): 3–21.

27. See Stephen D. Corrsin, '"One Single Dance Form Like the Sword Dance Can Open Up a Whole Lost World": The Vienna Ritualists and the Study of Sword Dancing and Secret Men's Unions'. *Folklore* 121/2 (2010): 213–233; Daniel David Jordan, *Coros y Danzas: Folk Music and Spanish Nationalism in the Early Franco Regime (1939–1953)*. Oxford: Oxford University Press, 2023; Irene Loutzaki, 'Greek Politicians' Dancing: Theatrical Representations of Political Power'. In *Perspectives in Motion: Engaging the Visual in Dance and Music*, ed. Kendra Stepputat and Brian Diettrich. Oxford: Berghahn Books, 2021, 197–213; and Shay, *Choreographing Politics*.
28. Jessica Falcone, 'Dance Steps, Nationalist Movement: How Hindu Extremists Claimed Garba-raas'. *Anthropology Now* 8 /3 (2016): 50–61.
29. For the geopolitical context, see Demetrius A. Floudas, 'Pardon? A Conflict for a Name? FYROM's Dispute with Greece Revisited'. In *The New Balkans: Disintegration and Reconstruction*, ed. George A. Kouvetaris and Victor Roudometof, 87–115. Columbia: Columbia University Press, 2002.
30. See, for example, Judith Brin Ingber, *Seeing Israeli and Jewish Dance*. Detroit: Wayne State University Press, 2011.
31. Dina Roginsky, 'Relativism of Authenticity: Consumption and Production of Israeli National Dances Outside of Israel'. *Israel Affairs*, 23/6 (2017): 1148–1168; Rebecca Pappas, Avia Moore, and Eileen Levinson, 'Unfixing Folk Dance: Community, Continuity and Reinvention'. In *The Oxford Handbook of Jewishness and Dance*, ed. Naomi M. Jackson, Rebecca Pappas, and Toni Shapiro-Phim, 650–675. Oxford: Oxford University Press, 2022.
32. See Alan Barnard, *History and Theory in Anthropology*, 2nd ed. Cambridge: Cambridge University Press, 2022.
33. For a fuller discussion, see Theresa Jill Buckland, 'Disciplining Terpsichore: Moves towards the Study of Dance in Victorian Britain'. In *Victorian Culture and the Origin of Disciplines*, ed. Bennett Zon and Bernard Lightman, 4–68. New York: Routledge, 2019 and 'Dance, Ritual and Religion'. In *A Cultural History of Dance in the Age of Romanticism and Industrialisation*, ed. Stephanie Schroedter. London: Bloomsbury Academic, forthcoming.
34. See Ronald Hutton, *The Triumph of the Moon: A History of Modern Paganism*. Oxford: Oxford University Press, 1999.
35. See Edward Burnett Tylor, *Primitive Culture: Researches into the Development of Mythology, Philosophy, Religion, Language, Art, and Custom*. London: John Murray, 1871 and Tove Tybjerg, 'Wilhelm Mannhardt – a Pioneer in the Study of Rituals'. In *The Problem of Ritual*, ed. Tore Ahlbäck, 27–37. Stockholm: Almqvist and Wiksell International, 1993.

36. See Theresa Jill Buckland, 'Dance and Evolutionary Thought in Late Victorian Discourse'. In *Evolution and Victorian Culture*, ed. Bernard Lightman and Bennett Zon, 173–195. Cambridge: Cambridge University Press, 2014.
37. Lilly Grove, *Dancing*. London: Longmans, Green and Co., 1895, 67.
38. See Talal Asad, *Genealogies of Ritual: Discipline and Reasons of Power in Christianity and Islam*. Baltimore, MD: John Hopkins University Press, 1993, 55–80.
39. See the Introduction to Cecil Sharp, *The Sword Dances of Northern England, together with the Horn Dance of Abbots Bromley*, 3 vols. London: Novello, 1911–13.
40. John Forrest, *The History of Morris Dancing, 1458–1750*. Cambridge: James Clarke & Co, 2000, 3–27; Michael Heaney, *The Ancient English Morris Dance*. Oxford: Archaeopress, 2023.
41. For further discussion, see Buckland, '"Th'Owd Pagan Dance"'.
42. See Chloe Middleton-Metcalfe, *The History and Development of Dark Border Morris*. Morris Federation Digital Publication, 2021, www.morrisfed.org.uk/wp-content/uploads/2021/10/The-History-and-Development-of-Dark-Border-Morris.pdf and Andy Lechter, 'Paganism and the British Folk Revival' In *Pop Pagans, Paganism and Popular Music*, ed. Donna Weston and Andy Bennett. London: Routledge, 2014, 91–109.
43. Genevieve Marks, 'In England, Morris Dancing Is Loved, Mocked and Getting a Makeover'. *New York Times*, 25 August 2023.
44. www.bossmorris.com/about
45. For a wider context see Fergal Kinney, 'How Folk Culture Made a Comeback in 2023'. *The Face*, 21 December 2023.
46. June Watts, *Circle Dancing: Celebrating the Sacred in Dance*. Sutton Mallet: Green Magic, 2006, 3, 19–26; https://findhornsacreddance.com/about/.
47. Watts, *Circle Dancing*, 19–24; https://circledancegrapevine.co.uk/.
48. Watts, *Circle Dancing*, 3–4.
49. Watts, *Circle Dancing*, 3, 19–26.
50. www.dancesofuniversalpeace.org.uk/the-dances/history/. See, for example, Weston and Bennett, ed. *Pop Pagans* and Ethan Doyle White, *The Visual Culture of Pagans, Myths, Legends and Rituals*. London: Thames and Hudson, 2023.
51. See, for example, Maria Malone, 'Global Folk in a Global World'. *Animated*. Leicester: People Dancing, The Foundation for Community Dance (Summer, 2023): 38–42.
52. See Shayna M.Silverstein, *Fraught Balance: The Embodied Politics of Dabke Dance Music in Syria*. Wesleyan University Press, 2024; Nicholas Rowe, *Raising Dust: A Cultural History of Dance in Palestine*. London: I. B. Tauris, 2010.
53. Silverstein, *Fraught Balance*; Nicholas Rowe, 'Dance and Political Credibility: The Appropriation of Dabkeh by Zionism, Pan-Arabism, and Palestinian Nationalism'. *The Middle East Journal*, 65/3 (2011): 363–80.
54. Rowe, *Raising Dust*, 120–122.

55. Rowe, *Raising Dust*, 118.
56. https://youtu.be/VBQx3BXZ_74.
57. For an overview, see Helen Thomas, *The Body, Dance and Cultural Theory*. London: Palgrave Macmillan, 2003.
58. Heaney, *The Ancient English Morris Dance*.
59. Cecil J. Sharp, *Country Dance Book*, Part 1. London: Novello, 1909, 9–10.
60. Theresa Jill Buckland, 'Being Traditional: Authentic Selves and Others in Researching Late-Twentieth Century Northwest English Morris Dancing'. In *Dancing from Past to Present. Nation, Culture, Identities*, ed. Theresa Jill Buckland, 199–227. Madison, Wisconsin: University of Wisconsin Press, 2006.
61. MM, 'Garstang Morris. "Straight Lads from Lancashire"'. *Morris Matters* 7/2 (1984): 8–12.
62. Theresa Jill Buckland, 'Dancing Northernness in a Global Context: Reflections on Embodied Concepts of Identity'. *Proceedings of 8th International NOFOD Conference.* Stockholm: NOFOD, 2006, 21–30.
63. Theresa Jill Buckland, 'Liberating Tradition: Gender Politics in Late Twentieth Century English Revivalist Morris Dancing'. In *Folklore Revival Movements in Europe post 1950: Shifting Contexts and Perspectives*, ed. Daniela Stavělová and Theresa Jill Buckland, 305–324. Prague: Institute of Ethnology, Academy of Sciences, 2018, 325–326
64. Anne Fiskvik, 'Renegotiating Identity Markers in Contemporary Halling Practices'. *Dance Research Journal*, 52/1, (2020): 45–57; Andrew Snyder, 'Contraculture: Bird Names and the Degendering of Contra Dance'. *Yearbook for Traditional Music* 51 (2019): 187–215; Casey Avaunt, *Claiming Ritual: Female Lion Dancing in Boston's Chinatown*. Doctoral dissertation, University of California, Riverside, 2018.
65. www.youtube.com/watch?v=UjlIY69kmz0 ; Ida Meftahi, *Gender and Dance in Modern Iran. Biopolitics on Stage*. London: Routledge, 2016; www.dancemagazine.com/dance-in-iran/#gsc.tab=0; Shay, 'Parallel Traditions', 38; archive.aramcoworld.com/issue/200702/saudi.folk.music.alive.and.well.htm.
66. See Shay, *Choreographic Politics*.
67. Shay, *Choreographic Politics*, 81.
68. Charles Keil, 'Who Needs the Folk?' *Journal of the Folklore Institute* 15/3 (1978): 263–65, 263.
69. Anthea Kraut, *Choreographing the Folk: The Dance Stagings of Zora Neale Hurston*. Minneapolis, MN: University of Minnesota Press, 2008, 17–24.
70. Cited in Kraut, *Choreographing the Folk*, 25.
71. Kraut, *Choreographing the Folk*, 28–38.
72. Buckland, 'Dance and Evolutionary Thought', 188–189.
73. As an example, see Matthew Krystal, *Indigenous Dance and Dancing Indian: Contested Representation in the Global Era*. Denver, CO: University of Colorado Press, 2012.

74. See, for example, Sau-ling C. Wong, 'Dancing in the Diaspora: Cultural Long-Distance Nationalism and the Staging of Chineseness by San Francisco's Chinese Folk Dance Association'. *Journal of Transnational American Studies* 2/1 (2010): 1–35.
75. See for example, www.tiktok.com/@ajplus/video/7329589434796576043; www.instagram.com/writtenbyshay/reel/C2dRZIQvAV5/; Zeana Hamdonah and Janelle Joseph, 'Indigenous Dance, Cultural Continuity, and Resistance: A Netnographic Analysis of the Palestinian Dabke in the Diaspora'. *Media, Culture and Society* (2024): 1–17.
76. Michaela Callaghan, 'Dancing Embodied Memory: The Choreography of Place'. *M/C Journal* 15/4 (2012).
77. See, for example, Elina Djebbari, 'Archive and Memory in Cuban Dances: The Performance of Memory and the Dancing Body as Archive'. In *Cultural Memory and Popular Dance: Dancing to Remember, Dancing to Forget*, ed. Clare Parfitt. London: Palgrave Macmillan, 2021, 193–209.
78. Julia Giese and Emily Keightley, 'Dancing Through Time: A Methodological Exploration of Embodied Memory'. *Memory Studies* 17/2 (2024): 444–457.
79. https://ich.unesco.org/en/home.
80. See, for example, Valeria Lo Iacono and David H. K. Brown, 'Beyond Binarism: Exploring a Model of Living Cultural Heritage for Dance'. *Dance Research* 34/1 (2016): 84–105; Egil Bakka and Gediminas Karoblis, 'Decolonising or Recolonising: Struggles on Cultural Heritage'. *Dance Research*, 39/2 (2021): 247–263, and Jane Carr, 'The Tangible and the Intangible: Dance and the Safeguarding of Intangible Cultural Heritage'. *Dance Research* 41/1 (2023): 66–78.
81. See, for example, Vladimar Tr. Hafstein, 'Intangible Heritage as a Festival: or, Folklorization Revisited'. *The Journal of American Folklore* 131/520 (2018): 127–149.
82. Gibb Schreffler, 'Situating Bhangra Dance: A Critical Introduction'. *South Asian History and Culture*, 4/3 (2013): 384–412, 386.

10 | Artist Voice

An Introduction to Introductions

JON BODEN

Within a 90-minute performance of traditional song, most professional performers will spend up to 30 minutes speaking to the audience – and yet this area of performance is rarely discussed or analysed. It would be perfectly possible to perform folk songs without spoken introductions, and yet it is difficult to think of a successful folk performer who is (or was) not also a skilled introist. It is not too difficult to think of performers whose commercial success owes as much to their oratorical flair as it does to their musical abilities. Clearly the institution of 'The Introduction' is providing some sort of benefit to the audience, otherwise the natural selection of the entertainment industry would have seen it die away. So, what is it offering to the audience and the performer, and how do introductions influence the way traditional songs are received?

Humour

Why is it that comedic intros seem to be so entrenched in the performance of traditional folk song – so much so that they have spawned the comedy careers of Billy Connelly, Jasper Carrot, and several others? Were a classical soprano to intersperse a programme of Schubert Lieder with humorous anecdotes it would cause, at best, surprise and, at worst, consternation. The subject matter of folk song is often no less dark and yet performers who *don't* use humour are the outliers. Banter with the audience in rock and jazz gigs is less uncommon, but even a skilled raconteur such as Bruce Springsteen will spend far less time talking than the average folk performer.

Perhaps the underlying dynamic at play here is that folk song, like humour, is by its nature a conversational, everyday, informal art form. The murder ballad is the tabloid front page of its day; the plaintive love song the Tinder doomscroll; the agricultural seasonal song barroom small talk about the weather. Thus, conversational humour and folk song remain natural, comfortable bedfellows in a way that is less the case with other more formal or more 'showbiz' art forms.

But introductions (even long ones) do not necessarily need to be funny to work within a folk performance. More important than offering light relief is the introduction's ability to allow the performer to curate the audience's experience of a song. This is done in a variety of ways for a variety of aims and can be a profound element of the performance.

Framing Stories

Good ballads tell their story in a clear, concise, complete manner, and some audiences are very used to listening out for these stories. But it is also true that many ballads can be difficult to follow. They may use archaic language or regional dialect. The action of the story may be implied rather than stated, particularly if it's sexual in nature. The folk process may have led to verses being lost and the narrative becoming disjointed. More significantly, whereas the seasoned folk audience member may be accustomed to the level of active listening required to follow a story, the average non-specialist listener is more likely to listen passively, letting the lyrics wash over them rather than actively trying to process the narrative or form mental images of the characters.

Although it can seem counterintuitive to *tell* the story before *singing* the story, doing so can improve the audience's engagement. With narrative ballads it can work well to simply tell the complete story so the audience knows what to listen out for. A more subtle and often more potent approach is to use the introduction to steer the audience's imaginative engagement. This can be done through pre-characterization – planting images of the protagonists' physical, social, and behavioural characteristics. It is unusual for an introduction such as this to be in any way theatrical. For example, an introduction to 'Tam Lin' that begins 'the mist is rolling in across the darkening combe as Janet enters the ancient forest' is likely to alienate the average folk audience. In contrast, something more conversational, even off-hand such as 'Janet is a head-strong, spoilt rich kid with hippy tendencies who would be played in the film by Helena Bonham-Carter' might get a laugh, while also planting a strong sense of the character in the audience's mind. Of course, if that characterization doesn't chime with an individual's perception of Janet, they may experience some temporary cognitive dissonance while they 're-cast' her to their own directorial taste. But unlike in actual film, the introduction is merely suggesting an interpretation at the outset rather than continually imposing it throughout the narrative.

Historical Context

Another common type of introduction is concerned with contextualizing the song itself rather than supporting the narrative it contains.

A good introduction will place the song in its historical and authorial context for the listener. For example, 'this next song "The Seeds of Love" was collected by Cecil Sharp in the summer of 1903 from a gardener called John England in the village of Hambridge' tells the audience that (a) this is NOT an original song written by the performer (as many non-specialist listeners might assume), (b) this is an OLD song, and (c) that the song was collected in the field. Even if this latter point is a novel and unfathomable concept to the green listener, it points them in an interpretive direction that is helpful to how they receive the subsequent performance.

The less helpful version of this type of introduction is that which serves only to display the performer's knowledge rather than to enhance the listener's experience. 'This next song has the Roud Index number 3,' for example, does nothing to enhance the listeners' experience – it merely demonstrates that the performer has memorized the Roud number. A good contextual introduction will instead take the audience into the historical world in which a song was collected and sung.

Taking Sides

Perhaps the most powerful aspect of the introduction is how it allows a performer to steer the audience towards a particular emotional or moral understanding of a song. For example, I will often suggest that the sinking of the *CSS Alabama* in the nineteenth-century song 'Roll Alabama' is a celebratory moment as it marks a victory of the North over the South in the American Civil War. The text of the song, however, is entirely neutral on the subject of which side are 'the goodies' and 'the baddies', so that a Confederate apologist might just as easily present the song as 'the tragedy of the loss of the heroic *Alabama*'. My curation of the audience's perception, though not directly at odds with the song, is certainly pushing the song into a moral box that it does not inherently inhabit. In doing so I have not changed the song, but I have steered the audience towards my preferred interpretation. I am using the introduction to influence the twenty-first-century audience's perception of a nineteenth-century song, much as I might use an emotive chord modulation or a pointed rallentando to encourage the audience to empathize in a particular direction. The latter approach is certainly more subtle, but that doesn't necessarily make it any more legitimate than attempting the same via a spoken introduction.

Distancing

With a song like 'Roll Alabama' the moral standpoint is ambiguous enough to allow a performer to steer the audience's ethical perception one way or another. In other songs the tone is explicit and may well be at odds with the moral instincts of performer and audience alike, as the moral assumptions of the 1720s or the 1820s are not those of the 2020s. In general, performers will be disinclined to perform songs whose moral framework they find to be problematic or objectionable – but there are so many songs that contain (for example) the misogynistic and imperialistic assumptions of bygone times that it's difficult to avoid these completely without abandoning the entire genre. In such cases the introduction can serve to distance the performer (and by extension the audience) from such morally objectionable elements. For example, one light-hearted line I find myself using quite regularly in introductions is 'we found this next song in the Penguin Book of Misogynist Folk Ballads'. Whilst not absolving a song of problematic elements, an introduction such as this at least distances the performer from the song's dubious morality and encourages the audience to do likewise.

The Fourth Wall

Whereas a well-structured, informative, and humorous introduction can elevate a sub-par performance, a badly delivered, rambling, or boring introduction can lose the audience and undermine the musical content of a show. However, there are cases when a good introduction can have a detrimental effect and a bad introduction a positive impact. In both cases this relates to the positioning of the fourth wall between performer and audience.

On the one hand, a good introduction can have a negative impact when it serves to turn a social-singing environment into a performance environment. 'The Introduction' is part and parcel of the professional performance of folk song as it has evolved since the 1950s – but it is not an inherent part of folk music in origin. Songs sung in pub, kitchen, and field would not have involved protracted, polished, multi-layered, curatorial introductions. The imposition of such an approach upon a genuinely social singing environment in the present day (free-for-all pub singing, campfire singing, pre-match football sings, pub carol sings, impromptu singing on busses, etc.) will often cause a form of contextual dissonance by imposing a fourth wall onto a collective experience. In this case even an informative, articulate, witty introduction ultimately serves to debase the experience of the listener as it destroys a precious and vanishingly rare experience of communal singing.

Conversely, the performer operating in the professional realm is often balancing the folk audience's desire for a sense of personal accessibility and communality with the equally necessary demands of entertainment professionalism. A band that creates a successful polished set-piece moment for a particular section of their show may pay for it with a feeling that the audience have become more distant – that the fourth wall between them has become more impenetrable. In this case, a deliberately off-hand, even clumsy introduction can be beneficial by breaking down the fourth wall and giving the audience a sense of communality and accessibility.

*

'The Introduction' has evolved to become a powerful tool for the performer to curate and influence the audience's experience of folk music. A performer can use the introduction to impose their own interpretation of a song upon an audience. This might seem objectionable (particularly to an egalitarian-minded folk audience), but stage-based performance is by its nature an autocratic undertaking in contrast with communal singing environments such as pub singarounds. The performer can use the introduction to play with the positioning of the fourth wall between them and their audience, allowing them to engage with the inherent tension of folk song as communal activity versus folk song as performance art. The introduction can encourage an audience to approach the material with a strong sense of historical context. They can be helped to follow an obscure narrative, to find poetry within the prosaic, to distance themselves from outdated morality, or to step into the shoes of a character and appreciate a song within its own environment. If done badly, introductions can fundamentally undermine the whole performance; if done well, they can be a central and vital part of an audience's experience of traditional song.

PART III

Imaginaries

11 Folk Music and Nationalism

KATHARINE ELLIS

To frame the argument of her book *The Creation of National Identities*, Anne-Marie Thiesse muses on the inherent internationalism of the national identity projects that characterized the period from the later eighteenth century onwards in Europe.[1] The makers of nations needed to know who they were, but also who they were not, and for that very reason interior questions of national identity morphed easily into comparative questions allied to nationalist rivalry. Moreover, the foregrounding of 'an identitarian heritage' for each nation was as crucial as geopolitical and legal questions that cemented the rights of a modern nation-state.[2] Shared national origin stories, however artificial, brought a sense of belonging and community, while nation-statehood rendered communities national subjects or citizens, their sense of belonging leveraged into active loyalty to the flag via public service ranging all the way from local administration to military duty overseas. In an age of anti-monarchical and anti-imperial revolutions, these social structures and expectations were progressively middle-class phenomena emanating from the intelligentsia of capital cities that showcased a nation's modernity while curating its past through new modes of civic education. Public museums and art galleries displayed the national story – in international context via the spoils of war and empire – and they operated alongside public monuments, history-writing, literature, commemorations, and education policies to create a multi-media national image whose import was disseminated in the approved national language. It is for this reason that Joep Leerssen has argued that 'All nationalism is cultural nationalism.'[3] Intangible though it was, the music that middle-class collectors called 'folk music' became part of this identity-building process, underpinning the enacting of both nation and nationalism. Folk music, in various forms, became its soundtrack.

In any account of musical nationalism within Western modernity, folk music is all but unavoidable; but it is also slippery. Among Western writers and musicians of the (very) long nineteenth century, the appeal to Indigenous folk culture as a marker of place, community belonging and imagined heritage, was widespread. Having invented the genre of folk music as something akin to a repository of national oral history, these writers and musicians – with all the social and cultural capital of literate elites – deployed it in defence of the idea of the nation itself, and of the home nation in contradistinction to others. The shadow of Johann Gottfried Herder looms large, in other words, whether we talk about the collection of folk song and dance music from its traditional peasant guardians, the publication of folk-music collections, the use of folk music in national hymnody, or the inclusion of folk music as the primary ingredient in pieces of art music performed in opera houses, concert halls, and domestic salons.[4] For this reason, in countries where folk music is officially disparaged or downplayed as nationalist raw material, the situation is noteworthy enough to prompt the question why.

As to folk music's slipperiness: If we look closely, even defining it as 'national', and therefore as raw material for nationalist use, is fraught. This is not only because, to place Thiesse and Matthew Gelbart in parallel, we are dealing with two 'inventions' – the modern nation and the concept of folk music – piled on top of each other, but because 'inventing' folk music for the nation cannot fully control a genre that is informal and mobile in its natural habitat. Ostensibly local musical tropes and markers often signify in international and intercultural ways (pentatonicism, for instance), and although in the name of national unity local dialects can be suppressed and folk lyrics translated, their melodies can travel faster and more freely, attached to multiple texts. Slipperiness is also present because folk music relates to communities at both national and sub-national (ethnic or regional) levels and can accordingly represent either a celebration of the nation-state or an expression of resistance to it. Finally, folk music is slippery because the act of rendering it politically powerful for nation-building entails streamlining it and thereby distorting the 'pure' national essence that folk music has so often been claimed to transmit. Beyond freezing this inherently mobile and often improvisatory genre into written versions of a single performance, industrial modes of print dissemination brought with them simplification, standardization, and commodification. Microtones disappeared; elasticity of rhythm was curbed; earthiness and political incorrectness were censored; geographically specific texts were sometimes changed beyond all recognition.

The original community owners of what became 'folk music' lacked political agency in nineteenth-century society and were bystanders in the world-building of their social superiors while also being cultural agents presaging nothing less than a redrawing of the world map. Gelbart characterizes them as representing both 'relics' and 'roots' – but never the fully formed and civilized nation.⁵ A duality exists here between the nineteenth century as the century of the genius composer and the growing cultural importance of a hidden, primitive, and anonymous musical foundation on which such genius might rest. More troublingly, because of folk music's fabled characteristic of collective, bottom-up authorship and its status as a pre-modern yet timeless expression of its home community, its local performers rubbed up against the pseudo-scientific claims of social Darwinism in England and racial theory internationally, their performances metaphorically pinned like butterflies to the boards of hierarchical human classification. Folk music – as invented by the colonizer rather than as practiced in everyday life by the colonized – could in this guise serve empire as much as it served nation.

Thus far I have prioritized the use of folk music by musicians in a position of power. However, this same cadre of musicians frequently used folk song as a vehicle for nationalist resistance. In fact, the most common understanding of Romantic nationalism in music involves the co-option of folk music into art music as the triumph of the underdog, premised on the usually unspoken idea that throwing off of the yoke of empire by smallish European states in the late nineteenth and early twentieth centuries constituted a series of liberations joyously anticipated via folk-inflected protest music – a mode emblematized by Smetana's *The Bartered Bride* of 1866. In this scenario, which accords with Thiesse's theory of internationalism and nationalism being symbiotic, nationalism and folk music usually exist in charmed anti-imperial alliance. It remains the case that audiences in the West are guided via programme notes and radio broadcasts alike to interpret Romantic nationalist music from one side only: presenting Sibelius's *Finlandia* as an affront to the dignity of the Russian Empire was unthinkable even before Russia's 2022 invasion of Ukraine. Historiographically, our optics have to be carefully calibrated to local circumstances: resistance can be aesthetic or political, metaphorical or real, and related to external or to internal colonies (including the provinces of centralist nations). In respect of individual pieces of music, teasing out the musicological relationship between dominant and subaltern status becomes indispensable, as does recognition that thinking in terms of 'resistance' or even 'identity' might be to bark up the wrong tree.

A propos the more general history of nationalism, separatism, and civil war, Richard Taruskin posed a fundamental question about the legitimacy of Romantic nationalism in a 1993 essay on American Dvořák celebrations that was short but explosive. How, he asked, can the continued celebration of Romantic nationalist art music be defensible, given the colonialist nature of its composers' elevation of folk music, and the lessons of recent civil wars sparked by ethnic nationalism?[6] These issues have lost none of their urgency, and it is for that reason that this chapter references examples that remain contested – including Scotland, Corsica, and Catalonia – alongside discussion of nationalism occurring within their current nation-states. In addition, this chapter foregrounds the perennial distinctiveness of Celtic nations and Celtic ethnic nationalism, whether within the British Isles, France, or the United States.[7]

National, Nationalist, and Local Colour

Many accounts of the European folk imaginary start, as I have done, with a reference to Herder; but as Gelbart points out, Herder's coining of the term *Volkslied* took place within an essay on Ossian, the mythical third-century Scottish bard who took Romantic Europe by storm as an emblematic folk 'primitive', courtesy of James Macpherson's 1760s poetry.[8] The Ossian phenomenon spawned art music aplenty, from Beethoven to Massenet, but it also put both Gaelic song and pibroch-style bagpiping on the pre-Romantic musical map, inspiring tourism to a still-wild landscape and helping baptize the musical tropes of Scotland as the archetypal primal folk music of the entire European continent – a vestige of ancient practice conserved in the Highlands and Islands.[9] In a turn that Gelbart ascribes to the Republicanism of the French Revolution, it took little time for the idea of bardic authorship to transform into that of a peasant, collective origin story for Scottish music, which usefully distinguished it from the more confected and stuffy style of English songs.[10]

Political events, notably the failed Jacobite Rebellion of 1745–46 (including the Battle of Culloden and the flight from Scotland of the Stuart pretender, the Catholic Bonnie Prince Charlie), also helped portray Scotland as a seat of political resistance. Jacobite-themed songs cemented its reputation as a Romantic nation par excellence, but a nation denied the full expression of its identity by the integrationist actions, post-Culloden, of a hostile government in London. That does not mean that all songs about Bonnie Prince Charlie are Scottish in origin or that they date from the time of the rebellion. From the perspective of an invented tradition of folk memory, the case of the famous 'Skye Boat Song' is instructive. The melody can be traced to a published collection of 1782, setting an apolitical Gaelic text of love and rejection. By contrast, lyrics relating the escape of Bonnie Prince Charlie from the island of Benbecula to the Isle of Skye came as late as 1870, from Sir Harold Boulton, an Englishman with an interest in Celtic folk song.[11] However, despite its hybrid origins and its English-language text, the song's status as a totem of Scottish national identity remains unshakable because of the way the lyrics indicate both place and Jacobite sympathies. There is no question, then, of its being an 'English' folk song, and if folded into the idea of British folk song more broadly it retains its identity as a part of specifically Scottish history.

Nevertheless, it would be a stretch to view it as 'nationalist' in the sense I have outlined above. That label is much better attached to the tune 'Hey, Tutti Taiti', reputedly played by Robert the Bruce's pipers at the Battle of Bannockburn (1314). In this battle of the First Scottish War of Independence, Scottish forces repelled the invading English armies of Edward II. In different forms, the tune was printed in several eighteenth-century collections of traditional Scottish airs and given a new spin in 1793 when the poet Robert Burns, himself a collector of folk song, sealed the connection with Bannockburn by writing lyrics, in both Scots and English, that evoked Robert the Bruce's rousing pre-battle speech. The resulting song was 'Scots Wha Hae' [Scots who have].[12] That other lyrics attached to the same tune also reference the Jacobite uprising ('When you hear the trumpet-sounds/Fill up your bumpers high') merely reinforces the associative connection.[13]

'Scots Wha Hae' was an unsurprising choice as an unofficial national anthem and, in the twentieth century, as the Scottish National Party's official song: it combines anonymity of musical authorship, layers of ancient history, inspirational memories of military victory, and, as the final touch, the poetry of a national literary hero. In the nineteenth century the song also found its way into what we might call third-party Romantic nationalism within art music – where ethnic-national songs become mere 'local colour'. Berlioz used a version of the melody for his overture *Rob Roy*, and although 'Hey Tuttie Taiti' was apparently played as Joan of Arc led her Scottish supporters into Orléans, its use in *Rob Roy* is unlikely to constitute a statement of French-Scottish solidarity on Berlioz's part.[14] Rather, the tune is simply a Scottish melody well known in France and eminently suitable for depicting a rebellious folk hero with whom Berlioz might well have identified on a personal level, much as he identified with the struggles of the sculptor Benvenuto Cellini. For Berlioz, 'Hey Tuttie Taiti' is part of a heroic but generalized Celtic imaginary that also included Thomas Moore's *Irish Melodies*, whose tunes he ignored and whose most revolutionary text (the Elegy for Tom Emmet) he used to underscore personal, rather than political, aspirations for a connection to Ireland.[15]

Taking a wider historical view, this adoption of folk music for local colour can be seen as typical of early and even mid nineteenth-century practice; it is in the later nineteenth century, after the turmoil of Italian and then German unification (1861 and 1871 respectively), that the nationalist movement in music gathers real momentum. In line with the 'resistance' trope, and despite studies on the very different nationalist trajectories of Germany, Italy, and France, standard musicological narratives of Romantic nationalism have focused the majority of their attention on composers from smaller and emerging nations on Europe's peripheries (Bohemia, Finland, Spain), and on the tensions between a 'universalist' or a 'folk-music' approach to composition within those spaces.[16] The Russian Empire, with all its ethnic-national territories, has emerged as at once a model of and counter-example to this process.[17] Stretching into the first decades of the twentieth century, these are the instances of folk-based musical nationalism that are most familiar within European art music. Yet even in this later period a nuanced distinction between national, nationalist, and exoticist uses of folk music is required: an eclectic magpie such as Saint-Saëns might seem no more politically invested in the Breton folk melodies within his *Three Rhapsodies on Breton Sacred Songs* (1863) than he is in the 'Nubian' melody he quotes (alongside Spanish and Indochinese evocations) in the second movement of the Fifth Piano Concerto (1896). Both are the products of a composer's touristic experience of exotic music. After a trip to watch the traditional religious 'pardon' of Sainte-Anne de Palud, during which he heard a boat captain playing Breton folk melodies, Saint-Saëns described these melodies in typically primitivist terms: 'at once so savage and so charming, that are such a welcome change from our too refined music, and refresh the soul like a salty breeze'.[18] Nevertheless, Jann Pasler argues that we should take the Nubian melody, alongside Saint-Saëns's *Africa* of 1891, more seriously as part of the composer's complex and trans-Mediterranean understanding of his own French identity, which included folk music of the colonized encountered during his regular escapes to North Africa.[19]

This French example brings with it the related question of how the art-music composers of established nation-states used their folk music. It is perhaps indicative that despite the deep heritage of Herder and the collecting activity of the brothers Grimm, nineteenth-century German nationalism of the post-1871 era shows few folk traces: indeed, Barbara Eichner laments that the customary musicological definition of nationalist music as requiring folk traces renders German musical nationalism 'inaudible' because German nationalism is instead predicated on abstract connotations of seriousness, on the tradition of 'absolute' music, and on subject markers of myth and national heroism, rather than being predicated on sonic markers – however imprecise or invented – of place.[20] This expectation is what makes the early symphonies of Mahler stand out in transgressive relief, not only in respect of his quotations from his own folk-like settings of *Des Knaben Wunderhorn* poetry, but, in the First Symphony (completed 1896), because of his use of klezmer music as a disruption to the already folk-inspired 'Bruder Martin' material of the third movement. Here, the presentation of folk musics represented a double provocation to national norms from a composer whose Jewish identity in an anti-Semitic environment meant that his sense of national belonging would be angst-ridden throughout his career.[21]

Attitudes in France were different because of the centralizing afterburn of the 1789 Revolution, which meant that the unity of the secular nation had to take precedence over the old diversity of provinces. Folk music, some of it in local languages, some of it overtly Catholic or counterrevolutionary (especially in Brittany and the Vendée regions), was problematic. As in Germany, but for different reasons, there is no French pendant to the popular Romantic nationalism of Smetana or Sibelius; rather, in a newly nationalist context following defeat by Prussia in 1870, composers who used folk-based or folk-like material tended to use it either as local colour (an internal exotic, especially in opera), or as an indication of personal investment in the region – a case of sub-national nationalism often compared proudly to the situation of the Russian 'Five'. Vincent d'Indy's *Symphonie cévénole* of 1886 is the most cited case, though it is sometimes erroneously described as a French nationalist piece in the sense of nation-state nationalism.[22] By contrast, French-nationalist attention of the late nineteenth century tended to be focused on finding a strong musical voice for France's own version of the 'universal' – its Latinité – which entailed looking outwards towards the classical inheritance of ancient Greece and Rome, rather than towards the rustic particularism of the old provinces, unless these latter two musical strands could be fused into a genteel *couleur historique*.

Collecting and Publishing for the Nation

The Scottish and Irish melodies I have discussed thus far were never actively collected in the sense of being recorded live from the performance of a particular singer or piper. Rather, they were gathered with other well-known tunes, forming part of an eighteenth-century tradition of published anthologies for use at home. The same was true of Welsh songs during this period; English anthologies were conspicuous by their absence. The Celtic antiquarian collections might, again, be described as national but not nationalist. The latter kind of heft came from a sense of urgency, sometimes reaching the level of government ministries, about collecting the dying vestiges of a national pre-industrial culture, winnowing out the impurities of later use, preserving precious and 'authentic' artefacts for future generations, and (frequently) inserting them into school curricula. The 'Fourtoul Project' (1852–57) in France was emblematic but ill-fated: a plan, decreed by the future Napoleon III, to collect folk songs by region, using over 200 local volunteers spread across the country and overseen by a ministerial committee in Paris.[23] The goal – a series of geographically specific collections that would demonstrate the richness and distinctiveness of French folk poetry (and where possible its music) – resulted in the publication of just one, belated, collection (Provence).[24] In this context the publication, in 1860, of *Chansons populaires des provinces de la France*, a joint effort by the poet Jules Champfleury and the Conservatoire librarian Jean-Baptiste Weckerlin, stands as a melancholy trace of the ambition of the Fourtoul project: twenty-seven provinces covered, and referred to by their pre-Revolutionary names, with just three folk songs each and no regional languages represented. A few songs were carols, reflecting Champfleury's conviction that folk song was equally at home inside and outside church, and others were wry ballads of peasant guile; but none was in any way historical, ethnic-nationalist, or political – which suggests a particular kind of selectivity on the part of the editors.[25] Had the Alsatian Weckerlin helped compile this collection a decade or so later (by which time Alsace had been lost to Germany), one wonders whether its levels of sensitivity to ethnic nationalism might have been higher, not least because Alsatian difference was the obvious permissible exception to the 'unity in uniformity' principle in France.

Subsequent, more centralist, governments in France made no attempt to resurrect the Fourtoul project: instead, folk song collection in France returned to being a matter of private and local enthusiasm on the regional model of Viscount Hersart de la Villemarqué's celebrated and infamously inauthentic *Barzaz Breiz* of 1839. Composers such as Vincent d'Indy, Charles Bordes and Joseph Canteloube – all closely connected with the private Parisian conservatoire, the Schola Cantorum – continued in this vein, including, in 1903, launching a nationwide competition for folk song collection that bore a striking resemblance to the Fourtoul Project in its ambitions and modest levels of success.[26] Where folk music broke into the 'national' domain was in occasional competitions and pageants. The most extraordinary of these was the 'Concours des Musiques Pittoresques' at the 1889 Paris World's Fair, timed to celebrate the French Revolution's centenary, where in a display of calculated Republicanism, folk song was cast aside (problematic texts and languages) and folk dance presented in a concert hall in the same building as France's ethnographic museum – as though its wax mannequins had come to life and wandered in with their instruments. Although several French regions were represented, in what appears to have been a tactical move the organization of the competition by organological category served to downplay the regional in favour of the universal/scientific.[27]

The situation in Britain was different: there was no government buy-in, however fleeting, to the idea of financing a national collection of folk music. Instead, as far as collecting was concerned, private enthusiasts such as Lucy Broadwood, Frank Kidson, or Sabine Baring-Gould ploughed their own furrows, publishing collections based on their own work in individual counties and banding together in the national learned organization that started life as the Folk-Song Society (1898), with a mission to preserve folk song from across Britain and Ireland. This London-based organization split in two in 1911 (the formation by Cecil Sharp of the English Folk Dance Society) before the two societies merged in 1930, six years after the death of the indefatigable but divisive Sharp and under the presidency of Ralph Vaughan Williams. Under this latter title the Society still exists, and the dissemination of historical collections of folk music continues to be a part of its activity.

Apart from the breadth of its original mission, which encompassed both England and its Celtic neighbours, there were two important strands to the 'national' activity for which this society formed a metaphorical centre of gravity: the educational dissemination of folk song collections together with its nationalist rationale; and the insertion (or re-insertion) of folk music into the music of the Established Church, the Church of England. The first places Cecil Sharp in the spotlight; the second, Vaughan Williams.

Sharp's somewhat belated arrival within the Folk-Song Society in 1901, and his subsequent initiatives in collection and publication, bear the hallmarks of the fundamentalism of the converted. For him, the folk music of a small corner of the south-west of England stood not only for England, but for Britain.[28] In his work, which despite contestation by Kidson, Vaughan Williams, and others, became increasingly paradigmatic of anglophone folk ideology, the claims of Celtic folk music withered in favour of his conception of English folk dance and song: as early as 1902, just three years into his collecting odyssey, his *A Book of British Song for Home and School* was noted, in the opening salvo of a dusty and anonymous *Musical Times* review, to contain sixty-six English melodies against just ten – these included reluctantly – from Scotland and Ireland.[29]

In 1905, when a Board of Education report recommended that elementary schoolchildren sing British national or folk songs, Sabine Baring-Gould and Sharp rushed into print their cheap and cheerful *English Folk-Songs for Schools* (1906, including songs for sale individually, and a mass-market edition with tonic sol-fa notation). They claimed in their Preface that the volume accorded with the Board of Education's 'requirements' and noted that they were avoiding 'foreign models'; but here they neatly sidestepped the issue of the absence of Britain's Celtic nations from their work.[30] An alternative view came from the Dublin-born Charles Villiers Stanford and his *National Song Book* (also 1906, and also a response to the Board of Education report), which covered Ireland, Wales, and Scotland as well as England, and pointedly drew attention to the rhythmic superiority of Celtic melodies, a superiority which Stanford attributed to their continuing an ancient spirit of dance that English folk songs had lost at the time of the Commonwealth.[31]

For all their ethnic-nationalist differences, both Sharp and Stanford (and Baring-Gould) were convinced of the utility of folk song, presented in a form suitable for the classroom, to educate children into a sense of national belonging. However, where Stanford included all the Board's suggested music, Baring-Gould and Sharp presented almost nothing but folk songs they had themselves collected from deepest rural England. This approach gave the two books another contrasting feature. The Stanford collection acknowledged something of anti-English history within the British Isles (though without explanation): it included ethnic-nationalist songs such as 'Scots Wha Hae' and the Irish 'O'Donnell's March' alongside 'Rule, Britannia!', and it presented Welsh songs bilingually. By contrast, the Baring-Gould and Sharp collection treated English history both more whimsically and as a proxy for Britain, through a dream ballad about Agincourt ('Henry V and the King of France') and via a mother's home-front lament about sending her menfolk to the Great Northern War of 1700–21 ('High Germany'). This latter song was followed by 'Sweet England', the ballad of an orphaned girl adrift in America and dreaming of the roses around her aunt's cottage door. In this context of love songs, chivalric songs, and seafaring songs, nationalist intent might appear attenuated; reading the Preface, however, reveals the opposite.

As Ross Cole notes, given that Sharp managed to cover so many bases, issuing a treatise on folk song and patriotism – *English Folk Song: Some*

Conclusions – in 1907, and as part of his breakaway English Folk Dance Society, training teachers to evangelize the approved message among diasporic communities, it was no wonder that his voice became unavoidable and, eventually, predominant.[32] This voice was stridently in favour of the 'pure' and collective authorship of a rural populace rooted in their own locality and untainted by industrialization or city life, as though the ideologically necessary rootedness of the music could be guaranteed by the restricted horizons of often remote rural communities for whose members travel to the nearest market town constituted a major event. The route taken by Vaughan Williams was different, though not always by design. His folk collecting ranged wider, geographically and demographically, and although he still focused on England, he acknowledged the hybridity (including Celtic influences) of the folk music he collected from Northumberland to Essex.[33] He also – which Sharp would never have done – collected songs from mining and industrial communities, bringing working-class tunes into the sphere of what he termed, after Herder, 'national music'.[34] Politically at odds with Sharp, he represents a less tribal and 'blood and soil' face of folk song collecting for the nation, and the unorthodox nature of his practice indicates the levels of contestation in play.

Nevertheless, he too shared a strong sense that folk music could and should represent the nation. His own pendant to the collections of Stanford, and of Baring-Gould and Sharp, and published the same year, was *The English Hymnal* (1906), for which he accepted a 1904 commission from the Christian Socialist parson Percy Dearmer to provide the music. The vast majority of hymn tunes he selected came from old psalters or other historical sources, or else they were folk tunes collected by himself, Lucy Broadwood, Sharp and others, that he labelled 'traditional melodies'; very little was newly composed (there were four of his own tunes, labelled 'Anon.'). Among 656 hymns, a little under ten percent were folk melodies, and half of these were English.[35] Nevertheless, he wrote in his Preface that 'No particular country, period, or school has been drawn upon to supply material', and his listing of musical sources indicates cosmopolitanism via international reach across Europe and even the Atlantic, and considerable ecumenism (Luther rubs shoulders with old French carols and Welsh Methodism). Ideologically, the agnostic Vaughan Williams saw as his primary task a moral one: to purge the Anglican Church of its mawkish musical Victoriana, replacing 'the miasma of the languishing and sentimental hymn tunes that disfigure our services' with something more robust.[36] There are faint echoes of muscular Christianity here, with its fear of the effete male and its concomitant elevation of physical fitness allied to patriotic duty at home and (crucially) across the empire, and indeed Dearmer's Christian Socialism has been traced back to one of the origins of the term, the writer and social reformer Charles Kingsley.[37] In this sense, a streamlined form of European folk song fitted well alongside sacred congregational music – as straightforward and free of decadence – and in any case Vaughan Williams saw such melodies as passing freely between sacred and secular domains in centuries past. An element of childlike artlessness akin to Sharp's preferred type of folk song (and its utility) is also present in the *English Hymnal*: the highest concentration of English folk melodies occurs in the section 'At Catechism', devoted to hymns for children.[38] Not for nothing did Vaughan Williams link the spirit of folk song to that of the Christmas carol, often pastoral, and reflective of the innocence of the Nativity scene.[39]

In terms of the relationship between folk music and national identity, however, there is more to add. If Stanford, following the Board of Education's recommendations, prioritized the bodily movement of march rhythms as a way of instilling solidarity in children, Vaughan Williams homed in on tessitura for the same purposes. His choice of low keys responded to the overtly congregational nature of his concept.[40] Where altos and basses were pushed below their comfort zones in his four-part harmonizations, it was to prioritize the collective force of the unison hymn sung by untrained voices.[41] Vaughan Williams himself said in public education lectures in 1902: 'The collector of folk songs gives them back again to the world … Will they not, perhaps, once more make their way back to the mouths of the people?'[42] The *English Hymnal* was a way to do precisely that, across the nation, every Sunday. Yet in this hymnic guise, with rhythms streamlined, and some pitches and phrasing recast, what Vaughan Williams gave to the people of the Established Church as the folk music of a new national hymn book lay at some distance from the fluidity he tried to record when collecting performances of folk song.[43] Just as this was folk music returned to the nation but also adopted for the nation from foreign sources, so was it necessarily repackaged, simplified for its new function of collective singing, and refashioned to mirror its editors' aim of stiffening the nation's moral backbone.[44]

Whose Folk Music?

During the French Third Republic, the 'national' collection, publication and display of folk music was more tightly controlled than across the

Channel. Amid the frenzy of folklorism happening elsewhere in Europe, regionally specific repertoire never gained the unequivocal acceptance of French governments unless its identitarianism could be mitigated as part of gentrified fusion with early dance music, 'national' or multi-region competition, or pageant, for example at the World's Fair of 1889 or as sponsored by the leftist Popular Front at the World's Fair of 1937.[45] It was eventually welcomed with rapture as part of an anti-industrial philosophy of commitment to (rural) 'work, family and nation' under Pétain's Vichy regime of the early 1940s, at which point several decades-worth of private folk collection, publication, and dance-group activity were leveraged – including by established figures such as Canteloube – into propaganda for a fascist national religion. At the same time, French folk music served as an emotional crutch and as a vehicle of national solidarity for the captives in at least one Nazi prisoner of war camp.[46]

The case of France and its long history of official ambivalence with regard to its own folk musics is itself extreme, though the landing point I have indicated earlier, of wholehearted governmental embrace by the Right, is detectable elsewhere in Europe. Notably, it is present at the outset of the Franco regime in Spain, where the collection, co-option, and international display of national folk music was administered in a patriarchal and Catholic moral context via government-sponsored female groups presented as keepers of the flame.[47] There are other links with Spain: the Spanish parallel to Brittany was Catalonia, a region with its own language, folklore, ethnic-nationalist aspirations, and cross-border identification with neighbouring parts of France on the other side of the Pyrenees – including folk music. From as early as the 1920s, during the Primo de Rivera dictatorship, those political aspirations, fuelled by cultural nationalism, would be suppressed. Franco merely continued the policy, his attempt to circumscribe folk music as a one-nation phenomenon acting as a mechanism of control. These tensions were in turn the legacy of a nineteenth-century struggle between regionalism and centralization whereby the choice of which region's folk music might best represent Spain was hotly contested, not least between the 'historic nations' of Catalonia, the Basque country, and Galicia. Overarching these debates was the sense that Spain needed to build a national music from folk roots as a way to escape cultural degeneracy.[48] Spain, too, wrestled with tensions between 'backwardness' and exotic, touristic, distinctiveness: the troubled emergence of flamenco as a sonic marker of Spain that never ceased to signal Andalusia and never quite lost its taint of vulgarity, is emblematic.[49]

The situation was even more troubled in America, where the options for choosing a 'home' folk music were multiple and immediately racialized.

The composer who blundered into the fray and proffered advice on a national solution for a folk-based American music was none other than the Romantic nationalist Antonín Dvořák, newly arrived in Washington in 1892 to direct Jeannette Thurber's National Conservatory of Music, which as part of its progressive policy offered tuition, sometimes free of charge, to African Americans, to women, and to disabled musicians. Drawing on his own practice of folk-based composition, he wrote in two newspaper articles of African-American spirituals as America's true folk music, conflated their melodies with Native American music, and drew attention to the relative lack of interest in old Irish and Scottish melodies among 'English' musicians.[50] Finally, he offered America a sonic masterclass in the form of the Symphony 'From the New World', premiered in Carnegie Hall in December 1893. To act thus, even outside the South, almost thirty years after Emancipation, was to light a fuse. The debate that ensued was partly manufactured, international, and, especially on the American side of the Atlantic, steeped in assumptions about the relative evolutionary stages of different races, the relative status of the descendants of white settlers as opposed to other immigrant groups, and the suitability of a Black folk music to represent the American nation.[51] It resulted in Dvořák's work being called his 'African' Symphony; equally, and consonant with the problem of musical codes being shared across cultures, at least one critic preferred to hear in it a host of European influences, from Slav to Scandinavian to Celtic.[52]

Alongside the journalistic storm, however, there was a musical rejoinder to Dvořák's prescription and his symphonic modelling of its implications. That rejoinder came from a member of the New England school, Amy Beach, who had argued in print that Dvořák's folk sources, though beautiful, were 'not fully typical of our country' and that American composers —'We of the North'—would be more likely to look to Celtic sources for folk inspiration.[53] Whether she had read Dvořák's articles is unclear, but she started work on her First Symphony less than a month after hearing the Ninth. Beach had Irish ancestry on her mother's side, and the resultant 'Gaelic Symphony' took its folk music inspiration from Irish sources, both real and imagined. Adrienne Block writes that she might have had exposure to folk and traditional music at the recent World's Fair in Chicago but is more confident that she did library research to choose her melodies, possibly drawing on an Irish nationalist magazine of the 1840s published in Dublin – *The Citizen* – which published Irish melodies.[54] Beach's view of their value is significant. She wrote that they 'sprang from the common joys, sorrows, adventures and struggles of a primitive people. Their simple, rugged and unpretentious beauty led me to take my pen in my hand and try to develop their ideas in symphonic form'.[55]

These ideas of undeveloped primitivism that also underlie Dvořák's journalism, however sympathetically expressed, make assumptions about races and linear evolution because the aim is to elevate the primitive to the rank of the civilized via the synthetic power of art music. For both, folk music is 'marked' regionally, but also in terms of under-development in a context of civilized culture. Hence it is perennially childlike and artless in the most literal sense. Once racial theory is overlaid on such pronouncements, the moral is all too clear: European folk music is superior to that of other races. To skip back across the Atlantic, a cursory glance at C. Hubert H. Parry's *The Evolution of the Art of Music*, whose text was completed in 1893, reveals a chapter on folk music organized from the 'savage' and unintellectual (Aboriginal) to a higher folk music of pleasing pattern and design, containing implications for harmony and signs of emotional sensitivity. Racial hierarchy is glued firmly to the musical.[56] The folk music Parry designated as 'probably the most human, most varied, most poetical, and most imaginative in the world', was Irish folk music, with the 'Anglo-Scotch border folk-music not far behind'.[57] Beach is not on record as having made racist comparative claims of this kind, but the speed and nature of her musical rejoinder to Dvořák's call nevertheless give pause.

Coda

It is one of the ironies of folk music that whereas its markers of place and identity are both vague and permissive, its uses nevertheless often narrow to a nationalist point. Gapped scales, modality, pentatonicism, dance rhythms or mixed meters, and instruments with drones or plucked strings are ubiquitous, and yet each group – increasingly, in the nineteenth century, comprising those who help create the culture foundational to the idea of the modern nation – claims the resulting music as its own distinctive property and gathers it into bundles labelled 'national music'. Some of that irony can be explained as musicological short-sightedness – that in the case of folk song it is the texts that are 'national' in the first instance, rather than the music. But the inclusion of folk song into hymn-singing and into children's education suggests otherwise: that despite all its implications for distortion, translation from the individual performer to the collective grouping of choir or congregation is necessary to the success of nationalist projects because it presents embodied ways of institutionalizing the repertoire. The rise of folk dance societies reinforces that emphasis on embodied participation as part of a group. These reflections leave me aware that emphasis on folk music's receivers, rather than on those who practised their community music regardless of the presence or absence of roving collectors, is at risk of sidelining yet again those closest to the metaphorical coal face. It is, however, to acknowledge that the study of folk music in its nationalist guises entails engagement in a meta-study of folk music. And it is in so doing that the full range of that music's power – from nostalgic melancholy to political protest, to triumphalism – reveals itself.

Notes

1. Anne-Marie Thiesse, *The Creation of National Identities: Europe, 18th–20th Centuries*. Leiden: Brill, 2022, 1. The French original dates from 1999.
2. Thiesse, *Creation of National Identities*, 6.
3. Joep Leerssen, 'Nationalism and the Cultivation of Culture', *Nations and Nationalism* 12/4 (2006): 559–578.
4. On Herder and national song, see Philip V. Bohlman, *Song Loves the Masses: Herder on Music and Nationalism*. Oakland: University of California Press, 2017 and Matthew Gelbart, *The Invention of 'Folk Music' and 'Art Music': Emerging Categories from Ossian to Wagner*. Cambridge: Cambridge University Press, 2007.
5. Gelbart, 'Romanticism, the Folk, and Musical Nationalisms', In *The Cambridge Companion to Music and Romanticism*, ed. Benedict Taylor, 74–91. Cambridge: Cambridge University Press, 2021, 78.
6. Richard Taruskin, '"Nationalism": Colonialism in Disguise?', *New York Times*, 22 August 1993, reprinted with 2008 postscript in Richard Taruskin, *The Danger of Music, and Other Anti-Utopian Essays*. Berkeley: University of California Press, 2009, 25–29.
7. Martin Stokes and Philip V. Bohlman, ed., *Celtic Modern: Music at the Global Fringe*. Lanham, MD: Scarecrow Press, 2003, 2.
8. Gelbart, *Invention of 'Folk Music'*, 11.
9. Discussed in James Porter, *Beyond Fingal's Cave: Ossian in the Musical Imagination*. Woodbridge: Boydell & Brewer, 2019; see Gelbart, *Invention of 'Folk Music'*, 64.
10. Gelbart, *Invention of 'Folk Music'*, 95.
11. Boulton also popularized the Welsh and Breton song 'Ar Hyd y Nos' in English translation as 'All Through the Night'. This song, too, first appeared in print in the 1780s (Edward Jones, *Musical and Poetical Relics of the Welsh Bards*. London: The Author, 1784, 56).

12. The version quoted in George S. Emmerson, *Rantin' Pipe and Tremblin' String: a History of Scottish Dance Music*. Montreal: McGill-Queen's University Press, 1971 (16) comes from Oswald's *Caledonia Pocket Companion* of c.1751.
13. Emmerson, *Rantin' Pipe and Tremblin' String*, 15.
14. Emmerson, *Rantin' Pipe and Tremblin' String*, 16.
15. The song was inscribed 'F.H.S.' (For Harriet Smithson, the Irish actress Berlioz would eventually marry). David Cairns, *Berlioz: The Making of an Artist*. London: Andre Deutsch, 1989, 321–322.
16. See Matthew Riley and Anthony D. Smith, *Nation and Classical Music: From Handel to Copland*. Woodbridge: Boydell and Brewer, 2018. By contrast, on France, see Annegret Fauser, 'Gendering the Nations: The Ideologies of French Discourse on Music (1870–1914)', in *Musical Constructions of Nationalism: Essays on the History and Ideology of European Musical Culture, 1800–1945*, ed. Harry White and Michael Murphy. Cork: Cork University Press, 2001, 72–103; on Germany after 1871, see Barbara Eichner, *History in Mighty Sounds: Musical Constructions of National Identity, 1848–1914*. Woodbridge: Boydell and Brewer, 2012, 27–29; and on post-*Risorgimento* Italy, see Alexandra Wilson, *The Puccini Problem: Opera, Nationalism and Modernity*. Cambridge: Cambridge University Press, 2007.
17. See Richard Taruskin, *Defining Russia Musically: Historical and Hermeneutical Essays*. Princeton: Princeton University Press, 1997; and Marina Frolova-Walker, *Music and Russian Nationalism: from Glinka to Stalin*. New Haven, CT: Yale University Press, 2007.
18. See Brian Rees, *Saint-Saëns: A Life*. London: Chatto & Windus, 1999, 131–132 and Stephen Studd, *Saint-Saëns: a Critical Biography*. London: Cygnus Arts, 1999, 63, who cites Saint-Saëns's words from his *Portraits et souvenirs*.
19. See Jann Pasler, 'Saint-Saëns and the Ancient World: From Africa to Greece'. In *Camille Saint-Saëns and this World*, ed. Jann Pasler. Princeton: Princeton University Press, 2012, 253–256.
20. Eichner, *History in Mighty Sounds*, 30.
21. On the hostile reception in Vienna, versus enthusiasm in Lviv (then Lemberg), see Leah Batstone, 'Mahler's Symphony No, 1 in the Centre and on the Periphery', *Music & Letters*, 105/2 (2024): 202–221; even in Lemberg, Mahler's folk 'borrowings' appeared problematic (208–209).
22. See Katharine Ellis, *French Musical Life: Local Dynamics in the Century to World War II*. New York: Oxford University Press, 2022, 324–326.
23. See Ruth E. Rosenberg, *Music, Travel, and Imperial Encounter in 19th-Century France: Musical Apprehensions*. London: Routledge, 2015, chapter 3.
24. Damase Arbaud, *Chants populaires de la Provence*, 2 vols. Aix: Makaire, 1862, 1864.
25. Jules Champfleury and Jean-Baptiste Weckerlin, *Chansons populaires des provinces de la France*. Paris: Bourdilliat, 1860.

26. Discussed in Peter Asimov 'Arbitrating "Authenticity": the Schola Cantorum's *Concours de chant populaire* (1903–04) and its Losers'. In *European Musical Competitions, 1700–1940: History, Context and Meanings*, ed. Charles Edward McGuire. Turnout: Brepols, 2025, 253–287.
27. Ellis, *French Musical Life*, 301–304.
28. Ross Cole, *The Folk: Music, Modernity, and the Political Imagination*. Oakland: University of California Press, 2021, 134.
29. Cole, *The Folk*, 134. *Musical Times*, 1 January 1903, 28.
30. Sabine Baring-Gould and Cecil Sharp, *English Folk-Songs for Schools*. London: J. Curwen and Sons, 1906, iii–iv.
31. Charles Villiers Stanford, *The National Song Book: a Complete Collection of Folk-Songs, Carols, and Rounds Suggested by the Board of Education (1905), Edited and Arranged for the Use of Schools*. London: Boosey & Hawkes, 1906, iii.
32. Cole, *The Folk*, 143.
33. Georgina Boyes, 'The English Folk Revival'. In *Vaughan Williams in Context*, ed. Julian Onderdonk and Ceri Owen. Cambridge: Cambridge University Press, 2024, 124–125.
34. Boyes, 'The English Folk Revival', 125.
35. Eric Saylor, *Vaughan Williams*. New York: Oxford University Press, 2022, 45; Julian Onderdonk, 'Folk-Songs in *The English Hymnal*', In *Strengthen for Service: 100 Years of the English Hymnal, 1906–2006*, ed. Alan Luff. Norwich: The Canterbury Press, 2005, 191–216.
36. Ralph Vaughan Williams, 'Preface' to *The English Hymnal with Tunes*. London: Oxford University Press, 1906, xi.
37. Katie Palmer Heathman, 'Christian Socialism and *The English Hymnal*'. In *Vaughan Williams in Context*, ed. Onderdonk and Owen, 127–134, 128.
38. Noted in Michael Kennedy, *The Works of Vaughan Williams*. London: Oxford University Press, 1971, 68.
39. Lecture series of 1902 given in Bournemouth, cited in Kennedy, *The Works of Vaughan Williams*, 32–33.
40. Heathman, 'Christian Socialism', 130.
41. Vaughan Williams, 'Preface', xii.
42. Cited in Kennedy, *The Works of Vaughan Williams*, 74.
43. Saylor, *Vaughan Williams*, 45–46.
44. See Onderdonk, 'Folk-Songs', esp. 195–205.
45. See Ellis, *French Musical Life*, 301–304; 310–312; 349–355.
46. Ellis, *French Musical Life*, 312–316.
47. See Daniel David Jordan, *Coros y danzas: Folk Music and Spanish Nationalism in the Early Franco Regime (1939–1953)*. New York: Oxford University Press, 2023.
48. For an excellent summary of these concerns, see Matthew Machin-Autenrieth, Salwa El-Shawan Castelo-Branco, and Samuel Llano, ed., *Music and the Making of Portugal and Spain: Nationalism and Identity Politics in the Iberian Peninsula*. Urbana: University of Illinois Press, 2023, 9–12.

49. Machin-Autenrieth, Castelo-Branco, and Llano, ed., *Music and the Making of Portugal and Spain*, 12–13.
50. Articles in *New York Herald*, 21 May 1893 and 15 December 1893.
51. Douglas Shadle, *Antonín Dvořák's New World Symphony*. New York: Oxford University Press, 2021, 102–107; also Adrienne Fried Block, *Amy Beach, Passionate Victorian: the Life and Work of an American Composer, 1867–1944*. New York: Oxford University Press, 1998, 87.
52. Shadle, *Antonín Dvořák's New World Symphony*, 108; 130–131.
53. Block, *Amy Beach*, 87.
54. Block, *Amy Beach*, 88.
55. Block, *Amy Beach*, 88.
56. C. Hubert H. Parry, *The Evolution of the Art of Music* [1896], 8th edition. London: Kegan Paul, Trench, Trubner & Co. Ltd, 1923, 48–81. This edition was published as volume 80 of the publisher's 'International Scientific Series'.
57. Parry, *Evolution*, 79.

12 | Colonialist Hierarchies

ERIN JOHNSON-WILLIAMS

Folk music discourses have long held a deep-seated, if multifaceted, relationship to colonialism. When invited to write this chapter, I was eager to have the opportunity to draw attention to an issue that is often the elephant in the room in colonial music studies: where, exactly, does folk music fit in? There appeared, at first, no clear way to answer this question aside from noting a general sense in music scholarship that there is a gap in the literature requiring attention. In her *Grove Music Online* article on 'Folk Music', for example, Carole Pegg points out that 'the extent to which the use of "folk music" outside of Europe and America is a colonialist construction needs to be further explored'.[1] Many longstanding academic definitions of folk music were formulated explicitly in dialogue with acts of Western colonialist extractivism and racialized cultures of collecting. As I explore in what follows, moreover, the idea of folk music as a 'safe alternative' to recent 'trending' conversations about decolonization and cancel culture continues to reinforce colonialist assumptions about folk music's origins and identities. Definitions of colonialism – or the occupation and exploitation of one land by a dominant power – have usually been formulated through the voices of Western colonizers (or those educated within their intellectual traditions), rather than created dialogically by embedding the perspectives of the musicians whose repertoires are being 'collected'.[2] Discourses on folk music have likewise shied away from postcolonial studies, reinforcing Victorian ideas of folk music as a natural art form that somehow exists separately from other, less static or rooted, musical ecosystems.[3]

This chapter encourages a timely conversation about the intersections between folk music and colonialism. My own positionality is that I come to this topic as a scholar of music colonialism rather than folk music. Nevertheless, many of my family's ancestors migrated from England to the southern Appalachians in the United States over the last 300 years and were part of (or adjacent to) the communities that Cecil Sharp and Maud Karpeles travelled from Britain to collect from in the early twentieth century. I grew up with a sense of unease at the ways in which, as Rebecca Scott puts it, 'constructions of whiteness' in Appalachian culture are often racialized as a kind of 'pure' Englishness that collapses into racial nostalgia for an imagined settler colonial homogeneity.[4] The perpetuation of essentialist constructions of settler colonial whiteness can still be seen in current populist discourses like J. D. Vance's *Hillbilly Elegy*.[5] Although there is starting to be a degree of pushback against such stereotypes, Vance's ideologies continue to hold sway in the populist imagination.[6] My own experience of ballad-singing culture in the Appalachians – which nearly died out in my family three generations ago – is that Appalachian musicians are deeply implicated in the colonial process because they too occupy Indigenous land and space. And yet Appalachian communities themselves are victims of a racialized processes of colonial extractivism. Indeed, Karpeles and Sharp collected folk song in an explicitly colonialist fashion, not *for* the folk communities they visited, but rather to contribute to an idealized notion of the folk they believed might shape and strengthen England's future. In Sharp's formulation, folk music was intrinsically related to upholding the idea of an untainted, white, English race: as he notes with regard to white Appalachian communities, 'their language, wisdom, manners, and the many graces of life that are theirs, are merely racial attributes which have been gradually acquired and accumulated in past centuries and handed down generation by generation'.[7]

In response to the ongoing legacy of colonialist understandings of folk music that pervade contemporary ways of conceptualizing traditional music, this chapter is structured around three themes: (1) folk music as a postcolonial alternative to 'cancel culture', (2) folk music as a racialized category, and (3) strategies and possibilities for folk music's decolonial futures. Focusing on British ideologies around the folk – and acknowledging that nineteenth-century discourses relied on privileging racialized notions of 'Englishness' – I advocate for placing folk music into a critical dialogue with decolonial and Indigenous systems of knowledge that have the capacity to shift the power dynamics of these discussions away from outmoded colonial hierarchies.

Folk as Postcolonial Alternative

First, let us start in the present day, where folk music is often branded as a 'pure' or 'safe' retreat from 'woke' discussions about postcolonialism and decolonization – a classification that only reinforces many of the Victorian assumptions that fuelled folk song collecting in the first place. As Elizabeth Bennett notes, nostalgic or politically reductive discourses 'do not create an inclusive space' in folk music culture.[8] This 'pure white' branding of folk music has a long history. Take, for example, the ways in which discourses of 'plain white' folk music set up by the likes of Sharp have fed into the gendered norms of 'plain white' American country music. As Jeffrey Manuel argues, colonialist racial stereotyping of white folk music as being more melodically innovative and adaptive than Black oral traditions has shaped American music historiography.[9] The explicit segregation of musical genres in the United States – what Karl Hagstrom Miller has described as the 'musical color line' – led to deeply entrenched ideas about folk and popular traditions being inherently racial categories.[10] Miller reminds us that 'academic folklore and the music industry are rarely discussed in histories of segregation', yet both were 'enamored with the South and developed their own definitions of southern music' that made little room for the diverse experiences of southern musicians.[11] Consequently, 'white' folk and country repertoires are often branded as being a retreat from the commercial and political world based on notions of their deeply rooted musical or melodic purity – despite the long association of American folk music with radical left-wing politics.[12] Although various interventions are now being made concerning how folk songs can be used as part of decolonial and anti-racist pedagogies, the road forward is still muddied by unchallenged assumptions about folk music sitting 'apart' from the more problematic hierarchies of colonial history.[13] Add to this the strategic associations in the music industry of folk music with white bodies – what Miller refers to as the 'firm correlation between racialized music and racialized bodies' – then the idea of folk music emerges as a deeply colonialist framework, ripe for critical decolonial engagement.[14]

I write this chapter as an American living in Britain in 2024, reading and thinking about these issues within a political and ideological climate that struggles with its colonial past and the implied racialized, hierarchical baggage that is attached to its musical cultures – from music education syllabi to the way that concerts of 'British music' are programmed at the BBC Proms. It therefore seems fitting to start this discussion in the present because it is in contemporary Britain where, as William Fourie notes, an 'amnesiac condition' concerning the former empire often limits productive discussions about music's cultural work in contemporary society.[15] This 'amnesiac condition' is particularly the case when it comes to discussions of folk music. Over the past few years I have been following trends surrounding colonialism, postcolonialism, and decolonialism in British music scholarship, particularly following the Black Lives Matter protests during the summer of 2020. The watershed moment of mid-2020 meant that most areas of academic music studies were affected in some way by conversations around decolonization, increasing public awareness of colonial history, racism, and authorial positionality. Yet English-language discourses on folk music have, by and large, stayed relatively separate – if not, by implication, 'exempt' – from many of these difficult conversations. Despite the fact that the English Folk Dance and Song Society reassessed its archives in 2021 owing to the prevalence of overtly racist language in Sharp's personal writings and his quest for 'pure Englishness', wider conversations about the colonial legacies of what 'folk' music means in Britain have often remained separate from public conversations about decolonizing British music.[16] When I did a quick search through *The Guardian* newspaper's online archives with the key words 'folk music', 'racism', and 'coloniality', it brought up an article entitled 'Segregation Blues' as the top hit, written nearly twenty years ago.[17] Certainly, a rise of more recent reporting and documenting on the whiteness of folk music culture has helped to evidence the systemic racism and whitewashing of folk music traditions, although many of these conversations focus more on racism than colonialism.[18] In other words, conversations about decolonizing folk music's racial history as a legacy of colonial power structures have yet to be initiated in any sustained way.

In a 2024 interview, British cellist Sheku Kanneh-Mason suggested – picking up on rising conversations about decolonizing the BBC Proms following the Black Lives Matter movement – that perhaps the explicitly imperialist song 'Rule, Britannia!' (often programmed at the Last Night of the Proms) could be replaced with British folk music: 'There is so much wonderful British music, the wealth of folk music from this country is astonishing . . . I think that would be [a] wonderful thing to take its place'.[19] Kanneh-Mason's statement exposes several conflicts that are inherent to public debates concerning what I have discussed elsewhere as the 'presumed innocence' of retreating from the difficulty of decolonial discussions to what might (on the surface) appear to be safer or less politically fraught alternatives.[20] First, there is the timeworn opposition between folk music and Western art music – as if such music is a logical step away from a bombastic piece such as 'Rule, Britannia!' towards something more innocent, gentle, and traditional. Second, there is the implication that folk music is distinctly less divisive and/or racist than 'Rule, Britannia!', and that it would therefore make minoritized musicians feel less uncomfortable. Yet the notion that folk traditions might be an alternative to the postcolonial discomfort felt towards mainstream Western art music only reinforces new kinds of hierarchies and assumptions about the racial innocence of British folk traditions, which scholars such as Ross Cole have recently worked to unpack.[21] That a BBC Proms concert entitled 'Songs and Dances with the Kanneh-Masons' was scheduled for 4 August 2024 (including a range of classical arrangements of 'folk' music in compositions by Béla Bartók and Antonín Dvořák) raises more questions than it answers about ideas of Indigeneity, nationalism, and the branding of folk traditions as something that British musicians of colour can access (or not).[22]

The idea that folk melodies are a style of music musicians of colour might turn to as a relief from pompous imperialist works alleviates the burden of decolonization from folk music. The overwhelmingly negative reactions in the conservative British press to the UKRI recently awarding £1.5 million to a research project at the University of Sheffield to decolonize and diversify folk music is evidence of a reticence to accept that decolonization and anti-racist theories are relevant to folk music practices.[23] We could even go so far as to suggest that folk music tacitly replicates white supremacy: as Caroline Lucas argues, British folk music 'can be understood as encoded with racialized meanings which reproduce whiteness' – meanings replicated within both far-right and left-liberal political discourses.[24] Unwittingly, therefore, Kanneh-Mason's advocating for British folk music reinforces Victorian discourses that positioned folk traditions as a 'primitive' alternative to Western art music. Such ideas have been around since composers such as Bartók promoted the idea of effectively 'purifying' Western art music by basing it on the 'spirit' of 'authentic' folk music, which in turn meant that Western art music based on folk elements carried a more pure and authentic national character.[25]

Following this perpetuation of folk music's supposed neutrality, the relative slowness of folk music organizations in Britain to engage with debates around colonialism and decolonization has received more attention over last five years. Public-facing institutions such as Cecil Sharp House and the English Folk Dance and Song Society have taken the track of working hard on diversity, with images on their website of racially diverse musicians attending their events. In 2021, the Vaughan Williams Memorial Library Conference (hosted by Cecil Sharp House) focused on 'Diversity in Folk', with a welcome array of papers on race and diversity, though no papers specifically addressing colonialism.[26] Cecil Sharp House has also fostered strategic relationships with collectives such as the 'Black Singers and Folk Ballads' project, which promotes folk musicians of colour – but, through their public resources, does little to address the question of *why* folk music has historically focused on privileging white musicians, and what colonialist baggage this assumption might carry. A recent BBC

Travel article by Zoey Goto rightly claims that on many levels 'Cecil Sharp House has been questioning the very notion of what traditional British music means in the multicultural 21st century'.[27] Her article goes on to note that Cecil Sharp House puts on dancing workshops that combine 'folk' influences from Bollywood and hip hop, and places strong emphasis on inclusivity within traditional song lyrics.[28] The role of Sharp himself as a problematic figure is acknowledged, although his explicit racism against Black musicians is significantly downplayed, if not altogether erased:

> Joining me in the main hall at the Cecil Sharp House beneath a whimsical mural of folkloric creatures and abstract dancing figures, Katy Spicer, the chief executive and artistic director at EFDSS, pointed out that it is, however, a work in progress making the English folk scene truly inclusive. 'In terms of diversity, ethnicity has been the hardest challenge' she said.
>
> Somewhat ironically, it's possible to trace the roots of this reluctance back to the late 19th- and early 20th-Century folk music collectors, including Cecil Sharp himself. Their cannon of work focussed on the white, rural working-class dances and ballads, marking the genre out as a white heritage space and overlooking the cross-cultural exchanges that have always existed.[29]

This article diverts what might be a more incisive discussion about the broader ideology of race with ideas of diversity, ethnicity, and cultural exchange. What goes unmentioned is that while there are, indeed, many instances of cultural exchange in the songs that Sharp collected, the power dynamics across many of these sites of musical exchange occurred in the context of racism, settler colonialism, slavery, and the displacement of Indigenous peoples.

A more challenging conversation about how an institution like Cecil Sharp House – or the BBC Proms programming the Kanneh-Masons playing Western 'folk songs' to largely white classical music audiences – fits into wider debates about cultural repatriation and the colonial systems that have maintained such musical traditions in the first place has yet to enter into public consciousness. Folk music is still frequently lauded in Western 'classical' discussion boards on the internet as a way to showcase and demonstrate national and ethnic purity, unintentionally echoing nineteenth-century politics of race and nation.[30] Simultaneously, many professional British folk musicians talk openly about how folk music is not a 'political tool' and should not be viewed as such, thereby diminishing discussions of the political force of ideologies surrounding folk music as 'neutral'.[31] In order to have sustainable, open conversations about folk music's cultural work in the present day, the enduring cultural baggage around the (racialized) purity of the genre – and its indelible links to colonial thought and activity – needs to be unpacked more explicitly.

Folk Music as a Racial Category

In the late nineteenth and early twentieth centuries, connections between folk music, nationalism, and colonialism were central to European justifications for song collecting. Whereas it goes without saying that every community in the world has its own traditions, it is noteworthy that the most influential uses of the word 'folk' were applied by nineteenth-century European writers to European rural musics, forging links with the rise of Western nationalism and leading to the separation of 'folk music' from other 'world' traditions. As Philip Bohlman reminds us, the earliest and most well-known definitions of the folk – coming via Herder and the Grimms – projected a fantasy of non-literate white culture that was the purview of nationalist-minded European artists and musicians to draw inspiration from as 'their own'. Bohlman continues:

> This is why historically folk music scholars tended to neglect the traditional music of American Indians or black Africans, among others, arguing that such musical heritages should be left for the anthropologist or ethnomusicologist to study. This view is intellectually indefensible insofar as it reflects a nineteenth-century ethnocentric, racist evolutionary bias in which 'savages' were presumed to evolve through a stage or stages of barbarism (= peasants) before finally achieving 'civilization', the culture of the scholars doing the classifying!
>
> Because of the tenacious persistence of a nineteenth-century classification of the peoples of the world, one finds to this day that folk art refers to European peasant art while 'primitive' or 'non-Western' art refers to the art of New Guinea, aboriginal Australia, North and South American Indigenous populations, etc.[32]

In this formulation, a separation of 'the folk' from 'the colonial' was sealed into the history of the term from its earliest incarnations. This separation has always tended to run along racial lines: 'folk' implies music that is from a less educated or rural strain of white, European civilized culture, whereas 'primitive' refers to music from non-Western and non-white countries.[33] To that extent, folk music has always been both linked to, and cut off from, discussions of the colonial, because an artificial separation of folk music as 'ours' (from Europe) versus 'theirs' (from outside of Europe) was embedded into early ethnological scholarship and music criticism.

Discourses that take for granted the ways in which nationalist ideologies about folk music have been embedded into state educational programmes therefore have an excuse for not framing the folk as explicitly colonialist, because the implication is that folk music comes from a European or formerly imperial home rather than from the colonies. Yet these are potentially dangerous assumptions, particularly when considering the significant role that imperial constructions of folk music played in settler colonial music education practices. Early British graded exam syllabi excluded 'folk' from 'proper' musical examination repertoires when these systems were exported around the colonial world from the late nineteenth century onwards.[34] However, a limited amount of British folk music was nevertheless taught in settler colonial schools throughout the twentieth century, with the implication that this would be a way for the children of white settlers to connect with the musical heritage of the colonizer – rather than to learn the Indigenous repertoires of the countries that they were now living in.[35] Today, the legacies of these assumptions persist. Many countries around the world, including former British colonies, now include 'folk' music from their own countries within school curricula as a way to foster a sense of national identity.[36] Notably, however, nationalist rhetorics around what counts as folk music still uphold Eurocentric assumptions and definitions, distancing 'the folk' from notions of musical Indigeneity and complicating projects of inclusion and decolonization.[37]

Some of the most vocal proponents of the incorporation of folk music in education as a form of uncritical nationalism came from imperial Britain: most famously, Sharp went in search of English folk songs and lobbied for British music educational policies on the use of folk singing in schools. The composer Hubert Parry also popularized singing in schools, arguing for a curriculum that prioritized 'Englishness' in singing for English school children. His motivations for including folk music as a substantial component of his 1896 publication *The Evolution of the Art of Music* was because such music supposedly revealed racial characteristics:

Racial differences, which imply different degrees of emotionalism and imaginativeness, are different degrees of the power of self-control in relation to exciting influences, are shown very strongly in the folk-music of different countries ... The natural music of a demonstrative people is rhythmic and lively; of a saturnine people, gloomy; of a melancholy and poetical people, pathetic; of a matter-of-fact people, simple, direct, and unelaborated; of a savage people, wild and fierce; of an earnest people, dignified and noble.[38]

Within the context of nineteenth-century scientific racism often described as social Darwinism, Bennett Zon has explored how Victorian thinkers such as Parry and Herbert Spencer placed folk music into a Victorian doctrine of survival, where folk music 'corresponds to preliminary stages in intellectual development'.[39] Folk material, Zon argues, 'engenders hereditable traits'.[40]

This idea helps to make sense of why Sharp believed folk songs should be collected for future generations of school children in England. As he states in *English Folk Song*, 'above all, [the songs] must be of the same nationality as that of the children, English folk-songs for English children, not German, French or even Scottish or Irish'.[41] Without the legacy of British colonialism, figures such as Sharp and Parry would have had neither the cultural framework for idealizing the notion of folk 'purity' in music, nor the infrastructure of contexts of settler colonial 'isolation' like the southern Appalachian region of the United States. The case of Appalachia was relatively unique in this regard, at least insofar as attention given to the music of a settler colony, partly because of the earlier white settlement of the thirteen colonies of the United States prior to the nineteenth century. In the case of other British colonies such as India, South Africa, and Australia, by contrast, white folk traditions have – or at leave have been perceived to have – grown up in tandem with more cosmopolitan and popular influences at the height of empire.[42]

Sharp went out of his way to remove himself from encountering Black and Indigenous music in the United States, seeing this as unworthy of collection and describing African Americans as exemplars of a 'lower race'.[43] Sharp's collecting methods, moreover, were explicitly colonialist inasmuch as he invested in extracting the songs and taking them in notated form back to England for the direct benefit of English society, rather than preserving them for the next generation of Appalachian children. As he writes in *English Folk Song*, 'Tune is the natural foundation of musical education. The world made tunes for centuries before it made harmony, and the wise educationist, bearing this in mind, will prescribe melody, and melody only, for the musical education of very young children'.[44] If these English 'tunes' were implemented into schools, Sharp argued, the national character of his country would be reinforced:

We may look, therefore, to the introduction of folk-songs in the elementary schools to effect an improvement in the musical taste of the people, and to refine and strengthen the national character. The study of the folk-song will also stimulate the growth of the feeling of patriotism ... There are many ways of stimulating the feeling of patriotism. Education is one of them. Our system of education is, at present, too cosmopolitan; it is calculated to produce citizens of the world rather than Englishmen. And it is Englishmen, English citizens, that we want. How can this be remedied? By taking care, I would suggest, that every child born of English parents is, in its earliest years, placed in possession of all those things which are the distinctive products of its race.[45]

The reification of national or racial character through English folk song worked well even for late Victorian nationalists who were not in favour of colonialism, as it kept the musical focus inwardly on England (Spencer, for instance, was an anti-imperialist).[46] Indeed, Sharp's suggestions for taking English folk song into elementary schools was not a 'returning' of Indigenous repertoires comparable to postcolonial contexts of repatriation. It was, rather, quite the opposite. English children at the time were growing up with an international mix of art and popular songs, but these repertoires were becoming too stylistically diluted for the likes of Sharp. Understanding the Appalachian communities that he visited to represent a pure, lost white English lineage, Sharp collected their music specifically for its traces of racial character.

The history of British folk song collecting, therefore, became a form of a colonialist construction of sonic knowledge that replicated extractivist and hierarchical ideas about music and race. It is important to remember, here, that these hierarchies reflected colonialist constructions of knowledge regardless of whether the folk song collectors themselves supported colonialism: rather, nationalist epistemologies of Western folk song relied on the existence of an empire in the first place in order for notions of 'the folk' to take on such political significance. Knowledge of English folk song, in England, would therefore further nationalist populism of both colonialist and anti-colonialist persuasions. Such ideas, for example, are evident in an 1897 editorial in the *Musical News*, which reported on complaints that 'the music performed at the review of the Colonial troops by the Grenadier Guards shows a lamentable disregard for British music' as there were too many numbers with French and German titles. As a solution, the article concluded that 'there is, however, an enormous wealth of [English] folk-music which is not sufficiently used'.[47] The following year, the *Musical News* even went so far as to suggest that, just as in Boston, Massachusetts, perhaps street musicians in England could pass a Music Commission audition to gain a performance licence from the Police – the benefit being to encourage street musicians to sing folk melodies 'instead of spreading the knowledge of worthless music hall melodies', which both

Sharp and Parry greatly disliked.[48] In both these examples, folk music is being valued as a way to encourage patriotism and create forms of political exclusion far more than upholding the interests of rural communities.

Perhaps because of the entrenched nature of colonialist hierarchies within music studies, the academic study of folk music has a lot of catching up to do in terms of acknowledging this history, particularly in comparison with folklore studies more generally. While Cole notes that 'the discourse of folklore was formulated under the influence of colonialist epistemology', very few music scholars have risen to the task of examining the parallel colonialist epistemologies between folk music and folklore.[49] Indeed, there is far more literature linking the field of folklore to coloniality and postcolonialism than there is linking these domains to folk song. Consider, for example, the following definition put forward by Sadhana Naithani:

> The history of folklore as a subject and object of research is traced back to the early nineteenth-century romantic-nationalist movement in Germany ... The global history of folklore research is Eurocentric in its approach to the extent that it is based on nineteenth-century European folklore collectors *within* Europe, although it is well known that in the same century a large number of Europeans collected folklore of countries on other continents much of this work outside the European continent was accomplished in the context of colonial relations and done by non-folklorists, yet oral narrative and poetic expressions of peoples of other continents were collected, transcribed, translated, published, and discussed internationally. Folklore studies have not taken into consideration a major phase in the history of the discipline: folklore collection and scholarship in the colonial Empires, including the British Empire.[50]

In other words, the state of folklore as a discipline is explicitly open to decolonial questions, perhaps in a way that is less obvious for folk music, which has so many active stakeholders today. As Naithani continues, 'theories in the humanities have since the 1970s stressed that colonial hegemony is not only about establishment of political systems, but also about its acute implications in the cross-cultural perceptions of peoples and societies'.[51] Naithani stresses that the impetus for the rise of folklore across the British empire was about building an imperial identity that would stand up on a global stage: 'In Great Britain, the Empire was the locale for folklore collection and identity building – a space not within the nation, but outside it'.[52]

It is worth considering what music studies today could take from Naithani and Charles Brigg's call in 2012 for a more structural understanding of the 'coloniality of folklorists', which involves understanding the very *idea* of folklore as being inherently colonial – exposing the structural (and hierarchical) ways in which folklore collecting as a form of colonial power has long shaped academic discourses and constructions of modernity.[53] Bohlman's 1988 book *The Study of Folk Music in the Modern World* exposed many of these tensions almost three decades ago, reminding us to shy away from universalizing definitions and to think about power dynamics and cultural context.[54] Although the links between modernity and colonialism have been well established by scholars such as Paul Gillen and Devleena Ghosh, Olúfémi Táíwò, and Saurabh Dube and Ishita Banerjee-Dube, these connections are generally less explored in music studies.[55] Notably, explorations of the intersections of modernity, coloniality, and music such as Viet Erlmann's *Music, Modernity, and the Global Imagination* have tended to focus on 'colonialism' and the Global South (South Africa) rather than 'the folk' as a powerful racial category.[56]

One of the less-cited reasons for why academic scholarship on folk music has such entrenched roots in Western colonialist thinking is that extractivist difference is written into the history of the term. There is often no equivalent Indigenous word for 'folk music' in, for example, sub-Saharan Africa or the Pacific, and it is recognized as a recent importation in non-Western contexts.[57] There is now more emerging scholarship detailing, for example, the role of folk music traditions within colonial contexts, such as Anastasia Hasikou's work on how British colonialism impacted local folk music traditions in Cyprus; Roald Maliangkay's study of Korean folk song, which opens the door to more discourses about how certain nationalist folk movements become heightened under colonial and postcolonial power structures; and Brian L. Moore's work on cultural hybridity and Afro-Creole folk culture in colonial Guyana.[58] Revisiting Andrew Blake's influential 1996 essay 'Re-Placing British Music' and *The Land Without Music*, it is also worth reframing just how central constructions of folk have been to the development of British musical nationalism; links between folk song collecting and colonialism are relatively underexplored despite being integral components of the story he is narrating.[59]

In considering where we can now turn, it might be useful to reflect upon how the racializing of folk music as white historically separated 'the folk' from non-Western traditions of 'world music' that have usually been considered more obvious examples of sonic coloniality.[60] Within academia, one of the first steps forward will be to explicitly acknowledge the adjacency of colonialist epistemologies to the emergence of folk music as a racial construction, accepting that the history of folk song collecting would not have been possible without the ideologies of preservationist collecting that evolved from imperial mindsets. Indeed, as Miriam Piilonen has recently written, 'colonial narratives about musical conquest and domination, how people and societies should be, and whether human and animal expressions may be read like a musical score' are intrinsically related to the history of music, evolution, and empire.[61] The Victorian systems of classification and 'collecting' that were the foundation of the early discipline of ethnomusicology relied on the same ideologies that informed Sharp's travels in Appalachia – a settler colony long framed as a site of colonialist 'capture'.[62] As I explore in the next section, nevertheless, the future of folk music as a site of inclusion in the twenty-first century will depend upon whether these older epistemologies of colonial capture and racial stereotyping can be engaged with productively.

Folk Music's Decolonial Futures

In this third and final section I want to consider the possibilities for folk music's decolonial futures. As mentioned at the outset, there has been a marked rise in conversations about decolonizing musical repertoires and creating space for Indigenous voices over the past few years. I suggest that only by acknowledging the relationship between colonialism and folk music that pervades contemporary ways of conceptualizing the 'traditional' in academic discourses can it be feasible to advocate for placing folk music into a critical dialogue with decolonial and Indigenous systems of knowledge that would, in turn, shift the power dynamics of 'folk' discussions away from racialized hierarchies that have their roots in nineteenth-century Europe.

Recent decolonial publications that foreground Indigenous music traditions such as Craig Harris and Stephen Butler's *Rise Up!* celebrates how 'Indigenous fingerprints are all over North America's music'.[63] In Amanda Minks' *Indigenous Audibilities* she acknowledges the hierarchies that have long placed categories of 'art music, folk music, and commercial music in separate spheres'.[64] Landmark publications in decolonial studies including Dylan Robinson's *Hungry Listening* and his edited volume, with Keavy Martin, *Arts of Engagement*, have largely focused on bringing Indigenous voices into dialogue with Western traditions of art and popular music.[65] However, little space in decolonial music scholarship is given over to the role of so-called 'white' folk music and how its historiography and definition went hand in hand with the very divisions that reinforced racialized hierarchies around other musical genres. Perhaps a colonialist undercurrent within nineteenth and early twentieth-century music historiography linking folk genres to racial groupings, rather than the diversity of a specific context, has only reinforced these limitations. Miller, for example, begins from the 'premise that people's music worlds were less defined by who they were – in terms of racial, class, or regional identity – than by what music they had the opportunity to hear'.[66] In other words, white Appalachia was always more musically diverse than folkloric historiography would have us believe, and yet the incorporation of Indigenous, African American, and popular or commercial genres within Appalachia have long been discredited.

There is wide scope, going forward, for bringing folk music into dialogue with decolonial theory in more sustained ways. The first and most obvious benefit of doing so – from a historiographical standpoint – would be to raise awareness of the colonial history of definitions of folk music as a (predominantly white) racial category with its roots in nationalist European movements that are themselves inextricably linked to extractivist cultures of collecting. Second, there is the issue that folk music currently sits outside of scholarship pertaining to decolonization and Indigenous studies, which in turn means that the settler colonial contexts of, say, Sharp's collecting – and the ways in which the songs that he heard were directly impacted by the Indigenous and African American musics that permeated these areas – have yet to be placed into sustained dialogue with decolonial approaches. Finally, combining the previous two points: I suggest that 'the folk' as a musical construction that emerged directly out of longer colonial epistemologies is *particularly* ripe for decolonial analysis. Initiating decolonial conversations would enable folk musicians and academics to take ownership of the history of their traditions and to work through some of the Victorian baggage they inevitably still carry. Folk song collecting, moreover, might also find a space for critique as part of a rising body of work on the colonial values written into extractivist cultures of collecting and ethical ownership.[67]

Imagining possible decolonial futures for folk music is challenging. To be productive, it will rely heavily on dialogical approaches to listening and understanding. As Linda Tuhiwai Smith writes in her Foreword to *Decolonising Methodologies*, 'The intellectual project of decolonizing has to set out ways to proceed through a colonizing world. It needs a radical compassion that reaches out, that seeks collaboration, and that is open to possibilities that can only be imagined as other things fall into place'.[68] Nevertheless, she continues 'the process of decolonizing can be extremely "messy", often leading to extreme violence; and ... in a political sense it can fail miserably, replacing one corrupt elite with its mimics'.[69] Though published in 1999, Tuhiwai Smith's words bear relevance today, particularly when calls for decolonization as open, dialogical collaboration soften the project of decolonization into a social justice catchphrase for equality, diversity, and inclusion rather than acknowledging decolonization's attendant violences. As the landmark 2012 essay by Eve Tuck and K. Wayne Yang 'Decolonization is Not a Metaphor' maintains, decolonization is about repatriating the extractivist violences of colonialism and should not be metaphorized into a buzzword for other kinds of social justice.[70]

Decolonization, in music studies, is 'messy and always situational', as Shzr Ee Tan maintains at the outset to a special issue on decolonizing music studies.[71] It remains to be seen whether, and how, the category of folk music will enter into these debates. Sharp, after all, did little to repatriate his song collections to the settler colonial communities of Appalachia. At the same time, these singers were from settler communities that occupied Indigenous land, adjacent to plantations that had relied on slave labour. The extent to which 'pure English folksong' in the Appalachians is in dialogue with Indigenous and African American musical traditions cannot be explored fully without acknowledging their problematic contextual adjacencies. These questions become even more potent when considering the colonialist implications of folk music collecting and field recording in the non-Western world. It has been increasingly possible, since calls from within folk music studies from the 1970s and 1980s, to conceive of a more contextually aware future in which folk music, sound recording practices, and colonial power are integrated into discussions of cultural ownership.[72] Folk music has, undeniably, been used as a tool for totalitarian propaganda in contexts such as Nazi Germany and Soviet Russia, to name but two.[73] We need, now, to ask the uncomfortable question of whether totalitarian uses of folk music are so successful precisely because of the colonialist ideologies – and essentialist constructions of race and place – that were inscribed into European formulations of 'the folk' in the first place. This question might intersect with understanding why governments at times react strongly to the 'danger' of folk music that is censored for having too 'much' political content.[74]

We might also think more carefully and critically about the ways in which the terms 'Indigenous' and 'folk' are conflated or used interchangeably, undermining the colonial, racialized, and extractivist power structures that have long persisted around the idea of 'folk'. Bohlman has noted that many constructions of folk music 'express Indigenous understanding[s] of the complexity of musical culture', but does not distinguish at length between the two terms.⁷⁵ In decolonial studies there is a rise in scholarship that employs the term 'Indigenous folk', but it would perhaps be useful to bring this work into dialogue with the colonial history of how folk song collecting has often conflicted with preserving or honouring Indigenous cultures.⁷⁶

Can folk music discourses exist alongside critical decolonial explorations of Indigeneity? Moving beyond Sharp, it might be useful to remember that songs can only be 'collected' within an ontological mindset that there is 'folk' material out there to collect – as opposed to a more intersectional study of the creative processes, meanings, and hybridities of music in the culturally diverse climate of any community (settler/colonial or otherwise). In this more reflexive construction, the act of programming folk music at the Last Night of the Proms might be the start of larger conversations around the history of musical gatekeeping: *what* 'British music' has previously embraced and discounted, *who* has been allowed to make these decisions, and what these decisions *imply* about the institutions that have historically excluded certain types of music from places like London's Royal Albert Hall. It will remain to be seen whether political futures can embrace folk music for its often-problematic complexities, rather than to fall back into idealizing the folk as a politically nostalgic space resistant to decolonial responsibilities. At the time of finishing this chapter, former Shadow Secretary of State for Culture, Media and Sport Thangam Debbonaire recently backed Kanneh-Mason's suggestion that 'Rule, Britannia!' should be replaced with British folk music.⁷⁷ If, over the next decade, these kinds of questions can be embraced contextually, and if the intersections between folk music as a category and colonial history can be more readily admitted, then it might be possible for folk music to enter the potentially redemptive decolonial spaces of disruption, resistance, and reconciliation. Yet to move towards a more nuanced understanding of folk music's colonial history, a more critical, global conversation about what 'the folk' means – who it excludes and includes – needs to begin.

Notes

1. Carole Pegg, 'Folk Music', *Grove Music Online*. www.oxfordmusiconline.com. First published online 2001.
2. Neil Larsen, 'Imperialism, Colonialism, Postcolonialism', in *A Companion to Postcolonial Studies*, ed. Henry Schwarz and Sangeeta Ray, 23–52. Malden: Blackwell Publishers, 2005.

3. Joseph Williams, *England's Folk Revival and the Problem of Identity in Traditional Music*. London: Routledge, 2022, 3.
4. Rebecca R. Scott, 'Appalachia and the Construction of Whiteness'. *Sociology Compass* 3/5 (2009): 803–810.
5. J. D. Vance, *Hillbilly Elegy: A Memoir of a Family and Culture in Crisis*. Ashland: Blackstone, 2016
6. See Anthony Harkins and Meredith McCarrol, *Appalachian Reckoning: A Region Responds to Hillbilly Elegy*. Morgantown: West Virginia University Press, 2019.
7. Cecil J. Sharp and Olive Dame Campbell, *English Folk Songs from the Southern Appalachians*. New York: G. P. Putnam's Sons, 1917.
8. Elizabeth Bennett, *Performing Folk Songs: Affect, Landscape, and Repertoire*. London: Bloomsbury Academic, 2023, 208.
9. Jeffrey T. Manuel, 'Sound of the Plain White Folk? Creating Country Music's "Social Origins"'. *Popular Music and Society* 31/4 (2008): 417–431.
10. Karl Hagstrom Miller, *Segregating Sound: Inventing Folk and Pop Music in the Age of Jim Crow*. Durham, NC: Duke University Press, 2010, 3.
11. Miller, *Segregating Sound*, 3.
12. See Dick Weissman, *Which Side Are You On? An Inside History of the Folk Music Revival in America*. New York: Continuum: 2006 and Richard A. Reuss with JoAnne C. Reuss, *American Folk Music and Left-Wing Politics, 1927–1957*. Lanham: Scarecrow Press, 2000.
13. Ian Cicco, 'Elementary Music Educators' Use of Folk Songs with Racist Origins and Anti-Racist Pedagogical Practices'. *Journal of Research in Music Education* 72/1 (2023): 28–47.
14. Miller, *Segregating Sound*, 4.
15. William Fourie, 'Musicology and Decolonial Analysis in the Age of Brexit'. *Twentieth-Century Music* 17/2 (2020): 197–211, 200.
16. 'English Folk Dance and Song Society Reassessing Its Archives Due to Racist Language', *The Journal of Music* (1 July 2021). https://journalofmusic.com/news-uk/english-folk-dance-and-song-society-reassessing.-its-archives-due-racist-language.
17. Hugh Barker and Yuval Taylor, 'Segregation Blues'. *The Guardian* (4 May 2007). www.theguardian.com/music/2007/may/04/folk.
18. Garth Cartwright, 'Angeline Morrison'. *The Guardian* (7 October 2022). www.theguardian.com/music/2022/oct/07/angeline-morrison-i-can-count-on-one-hand-the-times-ive-been-in-a-folk-club-with-other-people-of-colour; Sophie Alvarez Boyd, 'Breaking Down the Legacy of Race in Traditional Music in America'. *NPR* (25 July 2020). www.npr.org/2020/07/25/895112760/breaking-down-the-legacy-of-race-in-traditional-music-in-america; Zakia Sewell, 'My Albion'. *BBC Radio 4*. www.bbc.co.uk/programmes/m000pffy.
19. Noor Nanji and Steven McIntosh, 'Sheku Kanneh-Mason'. *The Guardian* (21 January 2024). www.bbc.co.uk/news/entertainment-arts-68034779.

20. Erin Johnson-Williams, 'Valuing Whiteness: The Presumed Innocence of Musical Truth'. *Current Musicology* 109/110 (2023): 43–73.
21. See Ross Cole, *The Folk: Music, Modernity, and the Political Imagination*. Oakland: University of California Press, 2021.
22. BBC Proms Website, 'Proms 20: Songs and Dances with the Kanneh-Masons'. www.royalalberthall.com/tickets/proms/bbc-proms-24/prom-20/.
23. Charlotte Gill, '"White-Centricity" of Folk Music' Investigated in £1.5 m Academic Study'. *The Telegraph* (22 June 2024). www.telegraph.co.uk/music/news/folk-music-study-sheffield-race/.
24. Caroline Lucas, 'The Imagined Folk of England: Whiteness, Folk Music and Fascism'. *Critical Race and Whiteness Studies* 9/1 (2013): 1–19.
25. Julie Brown, 'Bartók, the Gypsies, and Hybridity in Music'. In *Western Music and Its Others: Difference, Representation and Appropriation in Music*, ed. Georgina Born and David Hesmondhalgh, 119–142. Berkeley: University of California Press, 2000, 134.
26. 'Diversity in Folk'. Vaughan Williams Memorial Library Conference (13 November 2021). www.efdss.org/images/present/Docs/Library/DiversityConference2021ProgrammeWWW.pdf
27. Zoey Goto, 'The London Venue Reimagining British Music'. *BBC Travel* (8 May 2023). www.bbc.com/travel/article/20230507-the-london-venue-reimagining-british-music.
28. Goto, 'The London Venue'.
29. Goto, 'The London Venue'.
30. Talkclassical.com, 'Classical Music vs European Folk Music'. www.talkclassical.com/threads/classical-music-vs-european-folk-music.60505/.
31. Dave Simpson, 'Shirley Collins'. *The Guardian* (18 May 2023). www.theguardian.com/music/2023/may/18/shirley-collins-is-folk-music-a-potent-political-tool-i-would-say-my-arse
32. Philip V. Bohlman, *The Study of Folk Music in the Modern World*. Bloomington: Indiana University Press, 1988, ix–x.
33. Bohlman, *The Study of Folk Music*, ix–x.
34. Erin Johnson-Williams, 'The Examiner and the Evangelist: Authorities of Music and Empire, c.1894'. *Journal of the Royal Musical Association* 145/2 (2020): 317–350.
35. See, for example, Robert Amos Chanunkha, 'Music Education in Malawi: The Crisis and the Way Forward'. PhD dissertation: University of Pretoria, 2005; Emmanuel James Flolu, 'Re-Tuning Music Education in Ghana: A Study of Cultural Influences and Musical Developments, and of the Dilemma Confronting Ghanaian School Music Teachers'. PhD dissertation: University of York, 1994; and Eric Charry, 'Music and Postcolonial Africa'. In *The Palgrave Handbook of African Colonial and Postcolonial History*, ed. Martin S. Shanguhyia and Toyin Falola. New York: Palgrave Macmillan, 2018, 1231–1261.

36. Göran Folkestad, 'National Identity and Music'. In *Musical Identities*, ed. Raymond A. R. MacDonald, David J. Hargreaves, and Dorothy Miell. Oxford: Oxford University Press, 2002, 151–162.
37. Caitlin Oberhofer, 'Decolonization and Indigenization in Music Education'. *The Canadian Music Educator* 62/1 (2020): 48–53.
38. Hubert Parry, *The Evolution of the Art of Music*. New York: D. Appleton and Company, 1896, 59.
39. Bennett Zon, *Evolution and Victorian Musical Culture*. Cambridge: Cambridge University Press, 2017, 131.
40. Zon, *Evolution and Victorian Musical Culture*, 132.
41. Cecil J. Sharp, *English Folk-Song: Some Conclusions*. London: Simpkin & Co., 1907, 134.
42. See, for example, Christopher Daniel Sullivan, 'The Case for an Australian Folk Music Tradition'. PhD: Southern Cross University, 2020.
43. See Cole, *The Folk*, 144.
44. Sharp, *English Folk-Song*, 134.
45. Sharp, *English Folk-Song*, 135.
46. See Michael W. Taylor, 'Herbert Spencer: Nineteenth-Century Politics and Twentieth-Century Individualism'. In *Herbert Spencer: Legacies*, ed. Mark Francis and Michael Taylor. New York: Routledge, 2015, 40–59.
47. Arthur Watson, 'Neglect of British Music'. *Musical News* 13/335 (31 July 1897), 105–106, 105.
48. 'Comments on Events'. *Musical News* 15/388 (1898), 121.
49. Cole, *The Folk*, 8.
50. Sadhana Naithani, *The Story-Time of the British Empire: Colonial and Postcolonial Folklorists*. Jackson: University of Mississippi Press, 2010, 1–2.
51. Naithani, *Story-Time*, 2.
52. Naithani, *Story-Time*, 6.
53. Charles L. Briggs and Sadhana Naithani, 'Coloniality of Folklore: Towards a Multi-Genealogical Practice of Folklorists'. *Studies in History* 28/2 (2012): 231–270, 231.
54. Bohlman, *The Study of Folk Music*.
55. Paul Gillen and Devleena Ghosh, *Colonialism & Modernity*. Sydney: University of New South Wales Press, 2007; Olúfẹ́mi Táíwò, *How Colonialism Preempted Modernity in Africa*. Bloomington: Indiana University Press, 2010; Saurabh Dube and Ishita Banerjee-Dube, ed., *Unbecoming Modern: Colonialism, Modernity, Colonial Modernities*, 2nd ed. London: Routledge, 2024.
56. Viet Erlmann, *Music, Modernity, and the Global Imagination: South Africa and the West*. New York: Oxford University Press, 2008.
57. Pegg, 'Folk Music'.
58. Anastasia Hasikou, 'Music and Society in Cyprus: British Colonialism and the Emergence of European Music Traditions'. *Athens Journal of Humanities & Arts* 2/3 (2015): 177–190; Roald Maliangkay, *Broken Voices: Postcolonial*

Entanglements and the Preservation of Korea's Central Folksong Traditions. Honolulu: University of Hawai'i Press, 2017; Brian L. Moore, *Cultural Power, Resistance, and Pluralism: Colonial Guyana, 1838–1900.* Montreal: McGill-Queen's University Press, 1995.

59. Andrew Blake, 'Re-Placing British Music', in *Modern Times: Reflections on a Century of English Modernity*, ed. Mica Nava and Alan O'Shea, 208–239. London: Routledge, 1996, 226; and Andrew Blake, *The Land without Music: Music, Culture and Society in Twentieth-Century Britain.* Manchester: Manchester University Press, 1997.
60. Jeff Roy, 'Towards Decolonial Pedagogies of World Music'. *Ethnomusicology Forum* 31/1 (2022): 50–69.
61. Miriam Piilonen, *Theorizing Music Evolution: Darwin, Spencer, and the Limits of the Human.* New York: Oxford University Press, 2024, 139.
62. Bill McClanahan, 'Capturing Appalachia: Visualizing Coal, Culture, and Ecology'. PhD dissertation: University of Essex, 2017.
63. Craig Harris, *Rise up! Indigenous music in North America*; foreword by Stephen Butler. Lincoln: University of Nebraska Press, 2023, 1.
64. Amanda Minks, *Indigenous Audibilities: Music, Heritage, and Collections in the Americas.* New York: Oxford University Press, 2023, 19.
65. Dylan Robinson, *Hungry Listening: Resonant Theory for Indigenous Sound Studies.* Minneapolis: University of Minnesota Press, 2021; and Dylan Robinson and Keavy Martin, ed., *Arts of Engagement: Taking Aesthetic Action in and beyond the Truth and Reconciliation Commission of Canada.* Waterloo: Wilfrid Laurier University Press, 2016.
66. Miller, *Segregating Sound*, 7.
67. See Emily Hansell Clark, 'Audibilities of Colonialism and Extractivism'. *The World of Music* 10/2 (2021): 5–20.
68. Linda Tuhiwai Smith, *Decolonizing Methodologies: Research and Indigenous Peoples*, 2nd ed. London: Zed Books, 2012, xii.
69. Tuhiwai Smith, *Decolonizing Methodologies*, xii.
70. Eve Tuck and K. Wayne Yang, 'Decolonization is Not a Metaphor'. *Decolonization: Indigeneity, Education & Society* 1/1 (2012): 1–40.
71. Shzr Ee Tan, 'Special Issue: Decolonising Music and Music Studies'. *Ethnomusicology Forum* 30/1 (2021): 4–8, 6.
72. See, for example, William Ferris and Mary L. Hart, ed., *Folk Music and Modern Sound.* Jackson: University of Mississippi Press, 1982, and more recently Anette Hoffmann, *Listening to Colonial History: Echoes of Coercive Knowledge Production in Historical Sound Recordings from Southern Africa.* Basel: Basler Afrika Bibliographien, 2023.
73. See Erik Levi, *Music in the Third Reich.* Macmillan: Basingstoke, 1994; Yang Mu, 'Erotic Musical Activity in Multiethnic China'. *Ethnomusicology* 42/2 (1988): 199–264; Neil Edmunds, *Soviet Music and Society under Lenin and Stalin: The Baton and Sickle.* London: Routledge, 2004.

74. For example, see Sofia Erickson, 'This Paper Kills Fascists: The US Government's Persecution of Folk Singers, 1930s–1950s'. *TimePieces* 24 (2023): https://studentjournals.lib.unb.ca/timepieces/article/view/12.
75. Bohlman, *The Study of Folk Music*, 90.
76. For example, see Hong-Key Yoon, 'Indigenous "Folk": Geographical Ideas and Knowledge'. *Advances in Anthropology* 7/4 (2017): 340–355.
77. Harriet Line, 'Rule, Britannia is "Alienating" to Others'. *Daily Mail* (4 March 2024). www.dailymail.co.uk/news/article-13156647/Rule-Britannia-alienating-Labour-culture-spokeswoman-claims.html.

13 | Reviving the Folk

BRITTA SWEERS

When the English electric folk band Fairport Convention released their fourth album *Liege & Lief* in 1969 it caused a major stir. Featuring Child Ballads such as 'Matty Groves' (or 'Little Musgrave and Lady Barnard'), 'Tam Lin', and other traditional songs like 'Reynardine', the album presented this repertoire in an amplified rock-folk fusion. Celebrated by rock journalists, its approach was partly met with criticism within the British folk club scene (the primary site of the so-called second English folk revival) that valued acoustic and unaccompanied performance.[1] The criticism occurred despite the band having undertaken meticulous research in the main archive of the English Folk Dance and Song Society (EFDSS), the Vaughan Williams Memorial Library at Cecil Sharp House—a site built in 1929 emerging from the first English folk revival.[2] The album's inner sleeve likewise contained images and informed descriptions of a variety of esoteric English musical traditions, including Pace-eggers, the Padstow hobby-horse, Burry Men, morris dancing, and traditional singers, as well as song collectors such as Cecil J. Sharp and Francis James Child. Not least due to the need for larger rooms that accommodated rock amplification, Fairport Convention increasingly shifted into the world of British progressive rock. This scene revolved around performance spaces including the UFO club (which also featured Pink Floyd) and the Roundhouse in Camden Town, as well as university auditoria.

Fairport Convention were not the only electric folk band caught up in such multi-layered discourses in which voices from what we might call the 'reference' traditions were rarely included. Although the significant gap between reference traditions and revival cultures might appear to be specific to England, similar debates occurred not only in Scotland, Ireland, and the United States, but also in Baltic Countries such as Latvia. Rather than dwelling on divergences from reference traditions, disputes tended to occur between acoustic and electric revivals – the latter being perceived as a modern contrast to 'the tradition' itself. These discourses revolved around issues of authenticity, performative accuracy, and the violation of specific rules and political, sociocultural, and moral ideals espoused by acoustic folk music movements.

Although change and transformation have always been part of living tradition, such processes have often been perceived as a threat to original tradition bearers by folk music revivalists. This theme is apparent within the field of ethnomusicology itself, which was slow to accept studies on hybrid fusion forms (including my own book *Electric Folk*). It took until well into the new millennium to establish studies on revivalism and global fusion forms firmly within the academic canon through texts such as *The Oxford Handbook of Music Revival*. This new subfield responded to what has been characterized as 'thick globalization' – major changes yielding unprecedented forms of instant communication, digitalization, and access to multiple musical genres, styles, and fusion processes.[3] On the one hand, these developments have contributed new forms and contexts for traditional music genres. On the other hand, musical traditions have indeed been disappearing at an unprecedented rate in the twenty-first century – or have, as a counter-reaction, run into the danger of ending up in museum-like formats of preservation.

As my introductory example indicates, discovery and revival in folk music have been inseparable acts for many collectors and performers. What are the effects and legacies of this process? How can modern folk music revivals be approached from a broader, less biased perspective? Are processes such as revival, fusion, and interaction with new forms of (mass) media an exception, or have they always been part of traditional contexts? Revival processes seem to be a central element of folk musics across different cultural and national traditions. Consequently, rather than perceiving revival as the exception, folk music might be described as consisting of several revival waves that create new 'microcultures' interacting beyond their initial historical and cultural contexts.[4] Given the impassioned nature of these debates, the act of revival is unquestionably entangled with ideals of authenticity and cultural value. Following scholars such as Svetlana Boym, these waves of revivalism might be described as a defensive mechanism against eras of accelerated global change.[5] This chapter suggests that folk revivalism can be understood as an act of imaginative investment in the past and future, a nexus where nostalgia and utopia – as a counterpoint or solution to this sentiment of loss – meet.

Revivals in Theory

Music revivals emerged as a central theme in ethnomusicological research during the late 1990s, evident from various publications by Neil Rosenberg,

Max Peter Baumann, Linda Fujie, and Ove Ronström.[6] This was followed by a growing theoretical debate influenced by Tamara Livingston's structural conceptualization of revivalism that eventually resulted in *The Oxford Handbook of Music Revival* in 2014.[7] As the editors, Caroline Bithell and Juniper Hill, argue in the introduction to this book, revivals are 'almost always motivated by dissatisfaction with some aspect of the present and a desire to effect some sort of cultural change'.[8] This could include a political or social agenda even if aesthetic aspects or simply a search for alternative repertoires are at the foreground. Paradoxically, as Bithell and Hill point out, although a revival gives great value to historical elements it 'often involves selecting or reinterpreting history and establishing new or revised historical narratives'.[9] A revival process is thus never neutral, but is shaped by a selective use of history that frequently in turn becomes a fixed referential object.[10] Moreover, revival processes are intertwined with gestures and related discourses of legitimization, which explains why the issue of authenticity has played such an important role in many related debates.[11] For a deeper understanding of revival processes, these conceptions of authenticity need to be understood as relative and relational, rather than being taken as absolute and fixed.[12]

An almost constant process of revival and re-discovery appears to be characteristic of folk music, particularly in the twentieth and twenty-first centuries. However, revivalism – especially when integrating electric instruments – has most often been perceived as a distortion rather than a continuation of musical tradition. Before turning to the concepts of nostalgia and utopia that have been a primary motivation behind folk revivalism, what follows is a theoretical overview focusing on England as an archetypal case study. A potential pattern (one that can be transferred to other European contexts to a greater or lesser extent) can be sketched as such:

1. **The development of a systematic approach to printed collections in the nineteenth century.** Although song collections appeared in the seventeenth and eighteenth centuries (for instance, John Playford's *The English Dancing Master*, 1651), they tended to focus on texts. A change towards a more systematic approach only occurred in the nineteenth century, evident from Svend Grundtvig's *Danmarks gamle volkeviser* (begun in 1853) and Francis James Child's *The English and Scottish Popular Ballads* (1882–98), although tunes to the Child Ballads were, like many central German folk song collections, added later.[13] These collections often drew on pre-existent printed documents. As the

case of Scotland illustrates, these early activities were often intertwined with adaptation of the repertoires into art music.[14]

2. **A revival outside the original ('reference') tradition from the late nineteenth century onwards.** Utilizing then-new recording technologies alongside more simple methods of documentation, activities started to include direct encounter with traditional singers and resulted in larger bodies of musical material. Known as the first English folk revival, this process was pioneered by professional musicians, academics, and other figures from outside the original traditions they were documenting. Many English collectors (such as Lucy Broadwood, Cecil Sharp, Maud Karpeles, and Ralph Vaughan Williams) were either middle or even upper class. Their activities included conscious revival attempts – for example within school music curricula or by the foundation of specific societies that attempted to revive performance practices – as well as publications such as the *Journal of the Folk-Song Society*. In England, this movement was represented by the Folk-Song Society (founded in 1898) and the English Folk Dance Society (founded in 1911) that were later merged into the English Folk Dance and Song Society in 1932.

3. **A further revival after the Second World War.** The acoustic second English folk revival, pioneered by core activists including Ewan MacColl, Peggy Seeger, and A. L. Lloyd, not only drew on previous collections, but also integrated further repertoires (such as sea shanties, urban workers' songs, and mining songs) and undertook new collecting work. It established its own performance sites that deviated from the previous revival – most notably folk clubs that developed their own set of rules, such as only permitting unaccompanied singing of songs from one's own home region. Independent record labels such as Topic Records were central to this revival, as was journalistic coverage in specialist folk music magazines and popular periodicals like *New Musical Express* or *Melody Maker*. Key artists included the singer Shirley Collins and the singer-guitarist Martin Carthy.

4. **Folk rock or electric folk fusions in the late 1960s.** These approaches emerged from the search for new expressive means as many artists perceived the rules of the second revival to be too restrictive. Drawing again on previous activities (such as material from the first revival, evident on *Liege & Lief*) and folk club performers of the second revival (such as violinist Dave Swarbrick and singer Sandy Denny), this new microculture shifted the repertoires into a different sociocultural context. This became apparent in Fairport Convention's collaborations

with rock musicians, as well as in a shift to performance venues of the progressive music scene and contracts with commercial record labels.
5. **A third major revival in the new millennium.** As can be observed in Britain, Switzerland, and Finland, performers of these contemporary revivals are mostly conservatory-trained and thus technically more versatile than their predecessors, but appear comparably egalitarian regarding earlier rules and implicit customs. Many artists have also appeared in the so-called 'world music' scene. Although still based in a Western cultural sphere, these revivals are indicative of shifting forms of globalization.[15]

These revivals have all been shaped in different ways by modern conceptions of national identity. Another example would be Latvia, where folk music played a major role in the recreation of society after the end of the Soviet Union.[16] Although the later revivals follow a similar pattern to England, these processes were specific to a Latvian political context. During the Soviet period, for example, folk music activities were dominated by mass cultural movements. Performing acoustically and with untrained voices was hence less a reference to original tradition than a deliberate statement made against the presence of highly polished Soviet culture mass choirs. Likewise, the fusion with electric instruments – as undertaken by 'postfolklore' band Iļģi, for instance – can be read as a reaction against restrictive Soviet politics. Iļģi was nevertheless criticized by the broader acoustic movement for its deviation from established rules.

These are just selected examples, yet it seems that European folk music revivals can be identified by a series of recurring features: early collection activities and preservation attempts connected with nationalist politics, acoustic revivals with increasing restrictive rules, rebellion, the embrace of electric instruments, and finally more open and experimental approaches today. Such revivals often result in specific musical cultures or networks with distinctive aspects that have been termed 'post-revival'.[17] These can be described using the following terminology:

- Revival cultures feature what Livingston calls *core revivalists*.[18] Examples might include Lucy Broadwood and Cecil Sharp, who became reference figures of the first revival, or A. L. Lloyd and Ewan MacColl who, partly supported by American folk music collector Alan Lomax, were the central activists of the second revival. This core or authority position is evident in collecting activities and theoretical publications, as well as in recordings and organizational activities. MacColl, for instance, founded clubs and shaped performance rules while Lloyd brought marginal repertoires into circulation again.

- Revival cultures encompass *revival informants and/or original sources*, often defined by their regional and social backgrounds. Singers of the early collections and recordings in particular became references ('learnt from the singing of . . . '), and, if still alive, were celebrated as stars, such as Scottish Traveller singer Jeannie Robertson. Later revivals in turn took second revival singers and even electric folk performers as reference models.
- *Revivalist ideology and discourse* are particularly evident in publications and performance-related rules. The latter were already apparent in some first revival publications that emphasized unaccompanied singing; this was partly for pragmatic publication and recording reasons, but was also due to instruments being regarded as a sign of modernity and, thus, a potential distortion of the original tradition. This later became an absolute concept in second revival folk clubs – notwithstanding actual traditional practices.
- A group of followers forming the basis of a *revivalist community* including amateur singers, club organizers, journalists, and audience members. The latter is difficult to separate fully from the musicians, as repertoire knowledge and the ability to join in choruses was often expected, as well as specialist knowledge of individual artists, songs, and their histories.
- Each revival culture has developed its own *format of activities*, be it dance and singing within the confines of the EFDSS, club singing events of the second revival, festivals such as the Cambridge Folk Festival, or publications, such as song collections. One prominent example is *The Penguin Book of English Folk Songs* (1959), edited by Vaughan Williams and Lloyd, that became a central reference for second revival performers.
- Revivals have also tended to involve non-profit and/or commercial *enterprises catering to the revivalist market*, such as niche record labels (e.g. Topic Records), specific magazines (e.g. *fRoots*), regular features in newspapers, and dedicated sections in record stores.

We might speak of these as 'microcultures' that emerge after each revival and exist alongside, and yet interact with, the original reference tradition.[19] This perception helps to locate tradition and revival as activities that exist along a spectrum rather than as entirely separate domains.

Authenticity and Change

Revivals often contribute to the broader revalorization of a genre, an individual artist, or even an entire community. Whereas folk music revivals are centred on historical repertoires, they are thus intertwined with change on multiple musical, sociocultural, and political levels. Each revival has resulted in a sociocultural or (if occurring only within one culture) generational shift. In the case of the English folk revivals, we can observe a sociocultural shift away from rural or industrial communities into folk clubs and universities. In other words, although English referential traditions were mostly related to rural or urban working classes, the first revival was strongly upper-middle class, while the second revival was strongly educated middle class.

These social changes were interwoven with contextual and functional changes, such as from participatory support of labour work (farming, fishing, waulking, or weaving) to entertainment and from personal or individual experience to broader political ideologies and groupings. We can likewise observe a shift in audience relations, from intimate, informal contexts (the home or public house) to performer-audience separation and more formalized behaviour or towards professional performance with a full-time music-based income. Other changes include pedagogical shifts from informal and autodidactic to institutionalized contexts with formalized degree recognition – examples being the BA in Folk and Traditional Music at Newcastle University or the folk music programmes at the Sibelius Academy in Helsinki. The music, its transmission, and performance are likewise altered in the process. This includes altered formats of transmission, from oral or semi-oral transmission to notated and printed formats, which leads to a fixation on a smaller variety of texts and melodies. Notated versions and their collectors thereby obtain authority status, as the *Liege & Lief* sleeve cover demonstrates.

However, access to documented repertoires can also result in new fusion processes. Groups such as Steeleye Span, for example, started to fuse verses with different refrains. Similar choices occurred due to aural forms of transmission: broader access to recordings expanded performance approaches beyond regional and historical boundaries, as tunes were not learnt through direct contact but instead from recordings. Many English musicians developed an eclectic performance approach that drew from various traditional and contemporary folk singers, while subsequently becoming models for the next generation. Indeed, a revival can continue previous repertoires in new versions adapted to modern contexts, evident in The Imagined Village's 'Tam Lyn Retold', which transfers the fairy-tale content of the original ballad into a migrant context. It could likewise include the reimagination of traditional themes. The band Mr. Fox, for instance, changed the ballad 'Reynardine' into a first-person narrative with a different ending. Finally, it might even expand the rediscovery of traditional instruments (such as the Latvian *kokles*) and the reconstruction of playing traditions through electrified variants and/or the integration of instruments and performance practices foreign to the reference tradition (for example, the *bouzouki* in Ireland or the integration of Irish fiddle techniques in Latvia). While this appears to be a natural process, heated debates signal that ideals of authenticity are at stake.

Owing to historical and contextual divides, revivals are never identical with the original reference traditions. As my introductory example illustrates, debates between the various revival strands have nevertheless been centred on violations of a prevailing notion of authenticity. Literally meaning 'original' or 'genuine', the term *authentic* denotes, among other things, the idea of 'conforming to an original' or 'true to one's own personality, spirit, or character'.[20] This might appear as a contradiction at first sight. However, as art historian Denis Dutton has outlined, 'authenticity' should not be approached as an essentialist concept, but rather as a relational term always defined by its opposite.[21] By asking under what conditions, by whom and for whom the concept of authenticity is debated and who profits from it, we can begin to understand its power and the purposes for which it is employed – for instance, to combat commercialism (or, in the case of the Latvian folk cultures, against homogenizing Soviet mass music ensembles).[22]

As Dutton argues, authenticity discourses mainly centre on two different, yet often intertwined perspectives.[23] One approach, described as *nominal authenticity* or authenticity of provenience, relates an object, in this case music, to a historic point of origin. This perception emphasizes a historical transmission line that is connected to local identity formations. Owing to its fluid and performative nature, nominal authenticity is much more difficult to determine in music than in art, which can relate this concept to an extant object (a Greek vase, for instance). Authenticity of provenience, however, becomes apparent in references to musical versions preserved in notated or printed collections (the Child Ballads being a good example). By putting themselves into a line with these texts or reference artists, folk revivalists establish a nominal idea of authenticity. A similar process can be seen with regard to performance practice. A central feature of the folk club scene was the ideal of unaccompanied singing, which seemed to resemble original ('undiluted') performance practices. This was likewise evident in the notated collections of first revivalists like Cecil Sharp, although traditional singers had occasionally accompanied themselves on instruments.[24] Nominal authenticity can also be found in internal debates on the 'correct' verse order traditional ballads, despite the central role of variation in living tradition.

The opposite position is defined by the idea of *expressive authenticity*, which perceives works of art as genuine expressions of an individual's or society's values and beliefs. A Romantic setting of an English folk song, for example, could hold expressive value for certain performers and audiences within the realm of classical music. Nominal concepts of authenticity, however, are often interwoven with notions of expressive authenticity. The folk club scene, for instance, understood unaccompanied singing from a political stance consciously set against both art and popular musics. This helps to explain why the reaction to electric folk was so extreme: it was perceived as an opposite, something representing commercialism and a greater distance from the audience. In contrast to the second folk revival with its intimate performance contexts in folk clubs, folk rock fusion approaches were thus considered a betrayal of its fundamental values. This corroborates Thomas Claviez's observation that authenticity always requires an external 'authentifier', a referential authority, who holds the power to decide what is accepted as authentic within a given context.[25] In the case of electric folk music, it was the core revivalists, as well as journalists with the most prominent voices, that came to be regarded as authorities.

Nostalgia and Utopia

In the case of folk music revivals, I want to suggest, these ideals of authenticity are strongly connected to nostalgia. Particularly within the context of an increasingly thick globalization in the late twentieth and twenty-first centuries, experiences of nostalgia seem to have been brought about by a perceived loss of identity and temporal displacement on multiple (individual, cultural, local, and national) levels. As Svetlana Boym has argued, nostalgia is in many ways a 'rebellion against the modern idea of time, the time of history and progress'.[26] The nostalgist (much like the folk revivalist), she continues, 'desires to obliterate history and turn it into private or collective mythology, to revisit time like space, refusing to surrender to the irreversibility of time that plagues the human condition'.[27] The motivation for a revival or reinterpretation of historical musical repertoires believed to be associated with the folk might therefore be explained by a shared loss of authentic reference points on both nominal and expressive levels.

Nostalgia is generally understood to be an 'excessively sentimental yearning for return to or of some past period or irrecoverable condition'.[28] We can find this kind of nostalgia, for example, in later adoptions of working songs that were initially tied to specific context and fell out of use due to contextual or functional changes of production and working practices.[29] This might include pre-industrial songs that were silenced through the industrial mechanization of work, as well as mining, industrial weaving songs, and sea shanties. The latter provide an especially succinct illustration of the central role of nostalgia in the folk revival process.

Connected to the different working tasks on sailing ships as well as entertainment, sea shanties started to disappear due to the altered working requirements on steam ships in the mid nineteenth century. As the German shanty revival illustrates, revival processes were partly stimulated by specific circumstances that provided time and space for nostalgia. The German movement was indebted to the *Knurrhahn* ('gurnard', which literally translates as 'growling rooster'), the sea pilot singing club that was founded when both the Baltic Sea and the Kaiser-Wilhelm Canal (now, Kiel Canal) froze over in the severe winter ice of 1928–29. With shipping at a standstill, sea pilots in Kiel-Holtenau were left unemployed and at a loss. This enforced inactivity inspired joint singing activities, resulting in the publication of the homonymous *Knurrhahn*. One of the major German sea shanty songbooks of the first half of the twentieth century, the *Knurrhahn* represented an early attempt to collect sea shanties for choir-related purposes, mostly in the tradition of the male singing clubs of the nineteenth century. Nostalgic sentiments are apparent in the language of the collection's preface that, largely oblivious to the hard work on these ships, reads as follows:

It was only natural that several pilots sat together over grog and pipe smoke and rummaged through the unforgettable experiences of their old sailing days. Fond memories were awakened; one seemed to feel the calm blowing of the Trade Winds and monsoons, saw the beautiful climes of the South Seas and other places familiar to every true seaman rising before one's eyes, heard the roar of the hurricane at Cape Horn with its terrible terrors.[30]

This preface points to the central aim of preservation for the sake of a 'poetry-poor afterworld', heralding the 'beauties of the vanished, romantic cruising days on our proud, sail-swept swans of the seas', and the hope of reviving these old songs so that they might 'flower eternally'.[31]

While such wording might be read as a form of unrealistic escapism, the preface contains traces of what Boym calls 'restorative nostalgia'.[32] Restorative nostalgia can be described as the attempt at a complete reconstruction of, in this case, monuments of the past, accentuating the idea of nominal authenticity. Characterized by a serious stance, restorative nostalgia dwells on ideas of a lost national past. Similar to what Eric Hobsbawm described as 'invented traditions', this form of nostalgia is characterized by a high degree of symbolic formalization.[33] In contrast, what Boyn characterizes as 'reflective nostalgia' is much more ironic and humorous. By playing with the 'patina of time' from a more self-reflective stance, this alternative form of nostalgia 'dwells on the ambivalences of human longing and belonging and does not shy away from the contradictions of modernity', aiming more intensely at individual and cultural memory.[34]

The first and second English folk revivals both fit the category of restorative nostalgia on many levels. These revivals were driven by an (often extremely serious) attempt at 'authentic' reconstruction, despite the unavoidable changes described earlier. In contrast, the electric folk approach might be described as much lighter, tending towards a form of reflective nostalgia, which, despite careful source studies, plays more ingeniously with its musical possibilities from a consciously modern perspective. This perspective still encompasses a basis in local traditions that are, however, expressed in modern ways of music-making (such as electric instruments or rock percussion). Indeed, some musicians who later embraced electric folk could not stomach the restorative tendencies of the earlier revival: Cecil Sharp's pedagogical impact had resulted in the presence of folk music in English schools, yet singers such as Maddy Prior could not relate to it as children, only discovering and adapting the songs later in folk clubs.[35] Nevertheless, relics of restorative nostalgia – with its search for alternative, imaginary spaces – are still apparent across folk revivalist scenes. On a visual level, this form of nostalgia was expressed through aestheticized elements of romance and fantasy, such as the utilization of Celtic designs and nature images on album covers or the adaptation of specific dress and hair styles, including medieval dresses for women and long hair styles (a prominent example being Jacqui McShee of Pentangle). This might appear to be mere escapism, yet it contains within it a vision of utopia.

Nostalgic longing in folk music revivals has often been seen as inseparable from more positive or even utopian ideas. As Boym puts it, 'nostalgia is not always about the past; it can be retrospective but also prospective'.[36] Generally speaking, a utopia can be defined as 'a place of ideal perfection especially in laws, government, and social conditions; an impractical scheme for social improvement; an imaginary and indefinitely remote place'.[37] As Ross Cole has argued,

> folk revivalism manifests a special kind of utopian thinking both in its commitment to more radically egalitarian forms of collective existence and in its envisioning of alternative places or futures for human flourishing. In a folkloric worldview, these possibilities involve the imaginative creation of different social spaces grounded in pastoral or premodern tropes, yet ones that are not simply nostalgic attempts at recreation or restoration, but rather aim at establishing new communities and ways of being ... impelled by a distinctive blend of hope and remembering.[38]

In essence, he shows, folk revivalism has often been driven by the political goal of fostering a more 'communal society' inspired by the past in which 'the conflicts of the present are resolved and a collective identity or community is finally re-established'.[39] Such visions are clearly evident in Johann Gottfried Herder's writings, which relate folk music to the rural as representing an ideal of the humanist-national condition.[40] As Herder first formulated in his correspondence about Ossian (1773) and further elaborated in *Stimmen der Völker in Liedern* (1778/79) he saw (rural) folk music as the 'living' (i.e. unadulterated, original) 'voice of the peoples'.[41] This ideal of simple, unembellished, and directly expressed emotionalism has to be read as an opposition to or even rebellion against the stylized – and almost, from Herder's perspective, 'dead' – baroque and subsequent rococo styles of that time. Herder's concept is also indirectly apparent in Cecil Sharp's seminal collection *One-Hundred English Folk Songs*, in which he writes that

> the essential characteristics of the folksong – its freshness, naturalness, and unconventionality – are the very qualities which are conspicuously absent from the popular song-music of the past ... A nation's music, for instance, must, at every stage of its development, be closely related to those spontaneous musical utterances which are the outcome of a purely natural instinct, and which proceed, it will always be found, from those of the community who are least affected by extraneous educational influences – that is, from the folk.[42]

According to Sharp, the evidence offered by folk song had ultimately 'restored the Englishman's confidence in the inherent ability of his nation to produce great music'.[43] Similar national futures, this time on the eve of the Second World War, were apparent in the foreword of the third *Knurrhahn* edition in which the intention of revival is made clear, 'that it contributes to awakening the joy of seafaring in wide circles of our people ... And I hope that contemporary sailing and the coming generation may also draw new courage and new strength from these songs for the benefit of the rising Germany'.[44] We can also understand local collecting activities in Latvia from this perspective. In this case, they occurred during the *Atmoda* – the so-called 'National Awakening' – as a utopian vision that aimed at national independence, gained in 1918.[45]

In contrast to these nationalistic ideals, the revival of historical songs of resistance and rebellion in West Germany following World War II became a form of political utopia set against the nationalism of earlier fascist movements.[46] The Nazi Era (1933–1945) marked a significant breaking point for both Germanies, as folk music was inevitably associated with nationalist standpoints. Dark utopian visions of blood-and-soil were implemented through such music at kindergarten age on a subconscious level. These repertoires on war-related or nationalist themes permeated into long-term memory and could not be separated from other more 'neutral' material and resulted in the post-war generation's either avoidant or extremely critical stance towards the concept of folk music, as it was intertwined with ideas of nationalism that were to be avoided at any cost.[47] The West German folk revival that started around 1964 – heavily influenced by the preceding American folk revival as well as the French chanson scene – was grounded in leftist critique and counter-reacted to this history by reviving political-historical repertoires as a statement against escapist mainstream culture and the silence of the parental generation. For revivalists, folk music represented not only a vision of freedom and internationalism (and, thus, resistance to preceding nationalism), but also of civil rights in the broadest sense, intertwined with the idealization of working class culture. Owing to the instrumentalization of folk music during the Nazi Era, a restorative approach became impossible. Instead, this movement was shaped by a self-distancing, reflective approach defined by adapting Anglo-American and British-Irish-Scottish instruments, arrangements, and performative styles from the late 1960s, exerting a strong impact on the perception of German folk music right up until the present day.[48]

Each of these revivals incorporated utopian visions drawing on rural, urban, or working-class ideals. Their nostalgia was not merely a displaced love affair with tunes and lyrics, but a political project motivated by the urgency to create counter identities and visions against the experience of modernity, globalization, and political environments that denied the freedom of individuality in the widest sense. As Cole points out, the utopia expressed through folk revivalism can be described as the counterpoint of an increasingly faster and more estranging modernity.[49] For example, Sharp was prompted above all by his antipathy towards the modern. As he remarks, 'with the passing of the last survivors of the peasant class, it would have been quite impossible to have recovered anything of real value, and the products of a great peasant art would have been irrevocably lost'.[50] For Sharp, the songs were not simply of aesthetic and scientific value; rather, he regarded his collections as a counterstatement against the dominance of the music hall and industrialization. The second English folk revival – where the breaking point was experienced as much stronger than in neighbouring Scotland or Ireland – was shaped in similar ways by the perception of the increasingly oppressive dominance of US popular culture. As Niall MacKinnon illustrates in the case of the British postwar folk club scene, nostalgia became a force of resistance to the modern by 'seeking to place past "low" cultures at its core, not seeking to elevate it to "high" culture as in the mode of many eighteenth- and nineteenth-century European composers'.[51] It is worth remembering, however, that such visions, espoused by core revivalists, are not necessarily shared by all. The contemporary folk revivalist scene, for example, has resulted in a significant loosening up of prevailing restorative nostalgic concepts towards a more reflective stance.

Revivals Today

I started out with the example of Fairport Convention's 1969 album *Liege & Lief*, as electric folk (or 'folk rock' as it came to be known) represents an extreme position on the revival spectrum. Neither fitting into the established folk club scene nor into the commercial ideals of the popular music industry, the band's idiosyncratic musical direction might simply be understood as an experiment. But it can also be seen as the product of a particular utopian vision grounded in (mostly rural) working-class musical reference traditions revolving around ideals of free human creativity as well as a timeless view of human emotion and experience. Whatever folk purists made of it at the time, it has since become a canonical album: as part of the BBC Radio 2 Folk Awards in 2006, the British public voted it the 'Most Influential Folk Album of All Time'.

Revivals generate a large and complex universe of meanings tied to what has been connoted as 'folk music' in different times and places around the globe. These meanings constantly change as they are adapted to new ideas, musical traditions, and socio-political contexts. Inevitably, folk music thereby involves change and transformation on multiple levels, and we need to accept change as a major inherent factor – not as a distraction or betrayal of original reference traditions. Whereas early folk revivals were stimulated by the overwhelming experience of industrial modernization in the West, globalization now appears as a similarly extreme and contradictory experience the world over, involving instant communication and information overload that yield opportunities and yet also lead to a loss of local grounding. This might well explain the continuing revival of old rural and urban working-class music cultures in the twenty-first century. These appear to provide space for more grounded counter-identities that re-echo a long history in which the folk have been positioned as the foil to modernity.

This calls for a more nuanced analysis of folk music revivalism in the modern world. On a primary level, analysis of the music and the central elements making up a revival culture provides us with an understanding of revivalism as a recurrent historical phenomenon with shared characteristics – the most notable being, to quote Livingston, an 'oppositional tendency' expressed as a 'rejection of mass culture (considered a hallmark of modernity)'.[52] On a second level, studying these revival processes and levels of change not only helps to understand the evolution of new folk music cultures, but also to avoid essentialist stances that have led to (mis)conceptions of folkloric authenticity. Livingston portrays this as follows:

Music revivals are a product of both specific historical circumstances as well as general intellectual and social trends. As these trends change over time, so do music revivals. I view music revivals as existing in a continuum; some revivalist attempts may never move beyond the planning stage, others are simply a phase which a musical movement passes through, still others endure for decades. The tension caused by static definitions of authenticity and historical fidelity may sow the seeds of the revival's breakdown; yet frequently the revival will have served as a cultural catalyst, stimulating new sounds, new textures, and new repertoires.[53]

A critical analysis also requires, on a third level, a much deeper contextualized study of the conscious or unconscious conceptual motivations behind these various revival activities.

Looking beneath the surface of repertoires that often include supernatural or imaginative themes affording a means of escapism, we need to situate folk revivalism as a form of nostalgia shaped by the experience of a troubled, overwhelming, and threatening present. At the same time, these traditions – whether revived or catalysed into new forms – can be explored as a form of utopianism. This is apparent in the nationalistic ideas of some English folk revivalists (such as Cecil Sharp) or in the German sea shanty revival, as well as in the more overtly radical intentions of the second revival generations, be they in England, Germany, or Latvia. In other cases, labouring repertoires such as mining songs can become an epitaph on disappearing cultures and human values that suggest directions for an alternative political future. These marginal repertoires contain a function beyond escapism and nostalgia, especially in the context of neoliberal globalization. It might even be the case that – as music revivals of pagan repertoires indicate – utopian elements become especially apparent when the original reference culture is remote in time or lesser known, as this situation provides more abundant space for projection of imaginative ideals. This can be observed with Celtic music as well as in the Baltics, where Old Prussian tribes that had disappeared in the tenth century became a central reference point.[54]

Ultimately, what is needed is to relativize the idea of folk music, moving away from the kinds of nominal authenticity that Dutton identifies – perspectives invested in authenticity of origin and transmission. If we accept, as Cole argues, that folk musics, as they appeared during the nineteenth century, are visions that were created through collecting and did not previously exist as coherent bodies, it does not make sense to be concerned with locating the most authentic versions or performance practices.[55] As the examples discussed in this chapter illustrate, folk music is highly flexible and versatile. Notions of authenticity need to be interpreted as indicators of strong emotions – those tied to personal or social values embedded in different ideas of 'folk music'. From this perspective, we need to approach authenticity debates as clashes and markers of contrasting perspectives in which claims to nominal and expressive authenticity are made and defended. Rather than perceiving the act of revival or electrification as a move away from pure to polluted, for example, we might speak of them as two contrasting sides of the same coin.

This is not to deny the existence of traditional music practices and cultures. On the contrary, it points towards the complexity of what traditional music and communities represent, be it as distinct or more diffuse repertoires that might change, disappear, or become the basis of further tradition lines and communities.[56] Tradition and revival, in essence, are not necessary opposites. Rather, revivals contribute to the continuation of musical genres over centuries, connecting past, present, and future in fluid and imaginative ways. How far might we therefore perceive revival not as the exception, but as an integral component of tradition? This calls for a different understanding of what folk music – but also of what tradition – means.

Notes

1. On this history, see Britta Sweers, *Electric Folk: The Changing Face of English Traditional Music*. New York: Oxford University Press, 2005.
2. See www.efdss.org/cecil-sharp-house/history-of-the-house#.
3. David Held, Anthony McGrew, David Goldblatt, and Jonathan Perraton. *Global Transformations: Politics, Economy and Culture*. Cambridge: Polity, 1999, 21–27.
4. This idea is explored in Mark Slobin, *Micromusics of the West*. Hanover: Wesleyan University Press, 1993.
5. See Svetlana Boym, *The Future of Nostalgia*. New York: Basic Books, 2001, xiv.
6. See, for example, Neil V. Rosenberg, *Transforming Tradition: Folk Music Revivals Examined*. Urbana: University of Illinois Press, 1993; Max Peter Baumann, 'Folk Music Revival: Concepts between Regression and Emancipation'. *The World of Music* 38/3 (1996): 71–86; Linda Fujie, *Folk Music Revival in Europe*. Special issue. World of Music 38/3 (1996); and Owe Ronström, 'Revivals Reconsidered'. *The World of Music* 38/3 (1996): 5–20.
7. Tamara Livingston, 'Music Revivals: Towards a General Theory'. *Ethnomusicology* 43/1 (1999): 66–85; Caroline Bithell and Juniper Hill, ed., *The Oxford Handbook of Music Revival*. New York: Oxford University Press, 2014.
8. Caroline Bithell and Juniper Hill, 'An Introduction to Music Revival as a Concept, Cultural Process, and Medium of Change', in *The Oxford Handbook of Music Revival*, ed. Bithell and Hill, 3–42, 3–4.

9. Bithell and Hill, 'An Introduction', 4.
10. Alan Jabbour, 'A Participant-Documentarian in the American Instrumental Folk Music Revival', in *The Oxford Handbook of Music Revival*, ed. Bithell and Hill, 116–132, 117–119.
11. Thomas Claviez, Kornelia Imesch, and Britta Sweers, 'Introduction' in *Critique of Authenticity*, ed. Thomas Claviez, Kornelia Imesch, and Britta Sweers. Wilmington, DE: Vernon Press, 2020, viii–xix.
12. Denis Dutton, 'Authenticity in Art' in *The Oxford Handbook of Authenticity*, ed. Jerrold Levinson, 258–274. New York: Oxford University Press, 2003; Thomas Claviez, 'A Critique of Authenticity and Recognition', in *Critique of Authenticity*, ed. Claviez, Imesch, and Sweers, 43–58.
13. Bertrand Harris Bronson, *The Traditional Tunes of the Child Ballads*, 4 vols. Princeton: Princeton University Press, 1959–1972; Britta Sweers, 'The Transforming Perception of German Folk Song: Some Case Studies' in *Orchestrer le passé / Singing the past*, ed. Christine Guillebaud, Sybille Emerit, and Julien Jugand, 151–174. Paris-Nanterre: Presses universitaires de Paris Nanterre 2024.
14. Roger Fiske, *Scotland in Music*. Cambridge: Cambridge University Press, 1983.
15. See, for example, Trish Winter and Simon Keegan-Phipps, *Performing Englishness: Identity and Politics in a Contemporary Folk Resurgence*. Manchester: Manchester University Press, 2013.
16. Britta Sweers, 'Towards an Application of Globalization Paradigms to Modern Folk Music Revivals', in *The Oxford Handbook of Music Revivals*, ed. Bithell and Hill, 466–486.
17. See the discussion in Bithell and Hill, 'An Introduction', 28–30, and Livingston, 'Music Revivals'.
18. Livingston, 'Music Revivals', 69.
19. See Slobin, *Micromusics of the West*.
20. www.merriam-webster.com/dictionary/authentic.
21. Dutton, 'Authenticity in Art'.
22. Claviez, Imesch, and Sweers, 'Introduction'.
23. Dutton, 'Authenticity in Art', 259–261; 266–268.
24. See Sweers, *Electric Folk*.
25. Claviez, 'A Critique of Authenticity'. See also Allan Moore, 'Authenticity as Authentication'. *Popular Music* 21/2 (2002): 209–223.
26. Boym, *The Future of Nostalgia*, xv.
27. Boym, *The Future of Nostalgia*, xv.
28. www.merriam-webster.com/dictionary/nostalgia.
29. Marek Korczynski, Michael Pickering, and Emma Robertson, *Rhythms of Labour: Music at Work in Britain*. Cambridge: Cambridge University Press, 2013.
30. 'da kam es ganz von selbst, dass eine Anzahl Lotsen sich bei Grog und Pfeifenqualm zusammensetzten und in den unvergesslichen Erlebnissen

alter Fahrenszeit umherstöberten. Schöne Erinnerungen wurden wach; man glaubte das ruhige Wehen des Passats und Monsuns zu spüren, sah die schönen Gefilde der Südsee und andere, jedem echten Seemann bekannte Orte vor den Augen aufsteigen, hörte das Brausen des Orkans bei Kap Horn mit seinen furchtbaren Schrecken' (Otto Wolters, 'Vorwort', in Richard Baltzer, ed., *Knurrhahn: Seemannslieder und Shanties*, 3rd ed. Kiel: A. C. Ehlers, 1936, n.p.).

31. Wolters, 'Vorwort', n.p.
32. Boym, *The Future of Nostalgia*, xvii.
33. Eric Hobsbawm, 'Introduction: Inventing Traditions', in *The Invention of Tradition*, ed. Eric Hobsbawm and Terence Ranger. Cambridge: Cambridge University Press, 1992, 1–14.
34. Boym, *The Future of Nostalgia*, xviii.
35. Sweers, *Electric Folk*, 211–212.
36. Boym, *The Future of Nostalgia*, xvi.
37. www.merriam-webster.com/dictionary/utopia.
38. Ross Cole, *The Folk: Music, Modernity, and the Political Imagination*. Oakland: University of California Press, 2021, 74–75.
39. Cole, *The Folk*, 75, 103.
40. Johann Gottfried Herder, *Stimmen der Völker in Liedern. Volkslieder. Zwei Teile 1778/79*. Heinz Rölleke, ed. Stuttgart: Reclam, 1975.
41. Johann Gottfried Herder, *Auszug aus einem Briefwechsel über Ossian und die Lieder alter Völker*. Hamburg: Bode, 1773.
42. Cecil J. Sharp, *One-Hundred English Folk-Songs*. Boston: Oliver Ditson Company, 1916, xiv.
43. Sharp, *One-Hundred English Folk Songs*, xiv.
44. '... dass sie dazu beiträgt, die Freude an der Seefahrt in weiten Kreisen unseres Volkes zu wecken [...] Und ich hoffe, dass die jetzt fahrende und die kommende Generation auch aus diesen Liedern neuen Mut und neue Kraft schöpfen möge zum Wohle des wieder aufsteigenden Deutschlands' (Kapt. B. Petersen, in Baltzer, ed., *Knurrhahn*, n.p.).
45. See Sweers, 'Towards an Application'.
46. Jürgen Frey and Kaarel Siniveer, *Eine Geschichte der Folkmusik*. Reinbek: Rowohlt, 1987; Sweers, 'Germany: History, Culture, and Geography of Music', in *The SAGE Encyclopedia of Music and Culture Vol. 3*, ed. Janet Sturman and Geoffrey J. Golson. Thousand Oaks, CA: Sage Publications, 2019, 995–1002.
47. See also Britta Sweers, 'The Power to Influence Minds: German Folk Music During the Nazi Era and After', in *Music, Power, and Politics*, ed. Annie J. Randall. New York: Routledge, 2005, 65–86.
48. Sweers, 'Germany'.
49. See Cole, *The Folk*.
50. Sharp, *One Hundred English Folk Songs*, xiii.

51. Niall MacKinnon, *The British Folk Scene: Musical Performance and Social Identity*. Buckingham: Open University Press, 1994, 66.
52. Livingston, 'Music Revivals', 81.
53. Livingston, 'Music Revivals', 81.
54. Sweers, 'Towards an Application'.
55. See Cole, *The Folk*, in particular 18–73.
56. On this topic, see Kay Kaufman Shelemay, 'Musical Communities: Rethinking the Collective in Music'. *Journal of the American Musicological Society* 64/2 (2011): 349–90.

14 | Music, Migration, and Belonging

HELEN PHELAN WITH HALA JABER, JOHN NUTEKPOR, AND EWA ŻAK-DYNDAŁ

I have spent most of my professional life working at the Irish World Academy of Music and Dance, located at the University of Limerick in Ireland. I joined the Irish World Academy in 1994, the year of its inception. Established by the musician, academic, and composer, Mícheál Ó Súilleabháin, its founding vision included the creation of an Academy where parity of esteem for all music and dance practices was built into the design and accreditation of every undergraduate and postgraduate programme, as well as its research agenda, community engagement strategies, and artist-in-residence schemes.[1] At the heart of this vision was the full and systemic integration of Irish Indigenous music and dance traditions into the Academy's offerings. This led to lengthy and sometimes contested discussions on how to label these offerings.

My first post in the Academy was as Academic Coordinator. A large part of this job involved generating the paperwork to move programmes through the university accreditation system. A decision was taken from this starting point to use the terms 'Irish traditional music' and 'Irish traditional dance' rather than 'folk' music and dance. My memory of the discussions around this resonate with Charles Keil's provocative paper, 'Who Needs "The Folk"?' Keil argued that the conceptualization of traditional music as 'folk music' was a nineteenth-century middle-class invention, and that 'there never were any "folk," except in the minds of the bourgeoisie'.[2]

Niall Keegan, a lecturer in Irish music at the Irish World Academy, notes that the term 'folk music' is more often used in Ireland in connection with the American and English folk revivals than with Irish music. He discusses the politicization of both 'folk' and 'traditional' in key Irish publications such as Breandán Breathnach's *Folk Music and Dances of Ireland* (1971) and Seán Ó Riada's *Our Musical Heritage* (1982), which sought to link Irish tradition with an ancient, 'high art' culture: 'Irish language aspects of Irish culture, thus, are not represented as "folk music" because of the implied definition of "folk" (peasant and illiterate) which conflicts with the idea that the music is generated by the denizens of an idealised Gaelic-Irish culture'.[3]

The Academy's decision to identify its programmes as 'Irish traditional music' and 'Irish traditional dance' was also connected to the importance of attending to questions of repertoire and style. This was evidenced in the naming of key programme modules, for example, as 'repertoire and style' or 'technique, repertoire and style' modules. While the focus was on identified bodies of repertoire (for example, dance tunes and songs from living practitioners and collections) as well as related traditions of technique and style, modules in 'materials and context' also recognized the changing sociopolitical and cultural frameworks within which this music existed. Far from understanding this as a static or decontextualized repertoire, the programmes continue to support a dynamic engagement with living traditions, embracing not only transmission but also innovation and composition.

According to Keil, the construct of folk music exists as a kind of foil, used to delineate 'culture' (otherwise known as 'high art') from everything else, helpfully corralled into 'countercultural', 'folk', or 'popular' cultural agendas. The Academy's insistence on parity of esteem for all cultural practices set out to contest these dialectics. An example is the Academy's biannual events brochure, produced for over thirty years, self-consciously titled *Comhaimseartha / Of Our Times*. *Comhaimseartha* is the Irish language word for 'contemporary', and producing an events brochure which included a substantial number of 'traditional' Irish music and dance events under this banner alongside a spectrum of contemporary, classical, and popular repertoires communicates a view of traditional music as co-existent with modernity, post-modernity, and contemporary practice.

As an American child of Irish migrants who returned 'home' to Ireland in the 1980s, the interface between musical practices and migrant communities has been core to my personal and professional identity. The origins of the Academy corresponded with the economic boom years known as the 'Celtic Tiger' in Ireland.[4] These years were characterized by an unprecedented change in Ireland's migration patterns. For the first time in its recent history, Ireland became a country of destination rather than departure. After over a century and a half of net emigration, Ireland reached its migration turning point in 1996, becoming the last member of the European Union to become a country of net immigration. This period of immigration was characterized by the widening of the immigrant demographic from beyond the Irish diaspora and Western Europe to include significant immigration from other parts of the world. My research interests in music and migration coalesced into an interrogation of the potential relationship between music and belonging for new migrants in Ireland.[5] Several of my doctoral students have taken this work further through focussed arts practice research with African (John Nutekpor), Middle Eastern (Hala Jaber), and Eastern European (Ewa Żak-Dyndał) communities in Ireland.

Although none of us have hitherto chosen to interrogate the musical practices we study through the lens of folk music, there is one perspective on such music that drew us to participate in this *Companion*. This perspective positions folk music as 'an artifact of the imagination'.[6] As Yuval Noah Harari reminds us, 'all large-scale human cooperation is ultimately based on our belief in imagined orders'.[7] Pieces of paper function as money because we collectively believe that they do. Nation-states, divinities, philosophies, and other non-tangible constructs for which we are prepared to live and die exist primarily in the realm of the imagination. This logic would suggest that whether or not folk music 'exists' is irrelevant. The fact that it has been *imagined* as a category or construct inevitably impacts our engagement with musical practices swept into this imagined realm. It would thus be foolish to dismiss folk music without trying to understand the effect of this collective, imagined category on communities of musical practice.

The Paradoxes of Folk Music

An important characteristic of this imagined world is the prevalence of paradox. Folk music is often presented as being strongly connected to place (via the use of place names in songs and tune titles) and time (via songs associated with specific historical events), but also includes repertoires whose time and place of origin are completely lost and may be of little concern to its performers. Folk music is frequently associated with rural ways of life and presented as simple, informal, and typically acoustic. Yet in today's world it is just as often connected with urban, commercialized recording and marketing practices. Folk music has been linked with traditions of social activism and social justice movements.[8] Yet outside the West it is also critiqued as an act of colonialism.[9] The term has been appropriated as a form of cultural nationalism, whereas today many young people encounter it as part of their post-nationalist, virtual, global sound world.

Migration creates its own set of paradoxes in its encounters with the imaginaries of folk music. Many migrant cultures seek to preserve an ideal of their 'home' culture, which bears little resemblance to the rich complexity of musical experiences they left behind. This idealized culture may become a new version of 'folk music', though only recognizable as such in the new location. This was certainly my own experience, growing up in the United States in an Irish-American community. I and my four sisters learned Irish dance tunes on our piano accordions from our Polish teacher, who had conducted piano accordion orchestras in his native Poland before emigrating to the United States. He also taught us to play four-part arrangements of Bach and Mozart on the accordion, as well as mazurkas and polkas. We had no idea until we moved to Ireland that the piano accordion was a twentieth-century newcomer to Irish music, with its melodeon and concertina cousins more embedded in the tradition from the previous century. No one in our Irish American community disputed the Irishness of our music. We sang songs we thought of as Irish in our parish-based Irish cultural club. We did not know that 'How Can You Buy Killarney?' and 'Did Your Mother Come from Ireland?' came to us via Bing Crosby recordings, or that 'Maggie Murphy's Home' and 'Has Anyone Here Seen Kelly?' were spawned in the fertile mixing ground of Irish-Jewish Tin Pan Alley culture.[10] Only when my family moved back to Ireland did we realize that these were not considered Irish songs in Ireland itself.

Whereas 'Indigenous' (traditional, vernacular, folk) musical practices are most often associated with national identity in the home country, migrant groups have tended to appropriate all kinds of musical repertoire (pop, rock, classical) to represent their ethnic or 'Indigenous' identity. A Polish pop song, for example, may be sung in Ireland primarily as an expression of Polishness, while such an association might be redundant or non-existent in Poland.[11]

The imagined construction of folk music, combined with its predilection for paradoxical meaning-making, creates a rich and complex terrain for studying musical practice. Add to this the enrichment or complexity of musical mobility, and the lens becomes even more kaleidoscopic. For these reasons, our exploration of folk music imaginaries among new migrant communities in Ireland is less an analysis of repertoires or styles (though these are important) and more a focus on what Mark Slobin refers to as the everyday strategic use of available resources.[12] This understanding of folk music sits comfortably with the diverse musical experiences of migrants. The following sections pursue this exploration through three inter-related theoretical frames in the study of music and migration: diasporic studies, migration studies, and social inclusion. The discussion is then anchored with reference to three arts practice research projects exploring the everyday musical practices of migrant and diasporic communities in Ireland.

Music and Diaspora Studies

The concept of diaspora was primarily a religious one until the twentieth century. Its earliest use was associated with the Greek translation of the Septuagint and referred to the dispersal of the Jewish people. This dispersal was described as punitive – a result of God's wrath.[13] Later usage saw the term migrate from religious to secular contexts, as well as from negative to positive associations. Contemporary uses commonly celebrate the heritage, language, ethnicity, and ancestry of groups who have migrated to live in other parts of the world. It also refers to their descendants, who may or may not have ever lived in the diaspora's places of origin.

Several scholars have noted the important role played by artistic practices in sense-making for diasporic communities.[14] These practices provide opportunities to express and structure changing identities. Music-making, for example, creates experiential spaces that allow for ambiguity and the reinterpretation of cultural identities. These identities can be tried out temporarily, allowing members of diasporic communities to inhabit and move through different cultural identities in different contexts. Just as diasporic identities change and adapt as they move through transnational spaces, so too do the artistic expressions that provide the medium for these adaptations. Diasporic realities, moreover, sometimes involve experiences of trauma. Such histories and stories can be revisited and remade through artistic practices.[15] The somatic memory carried in music and dance renders these particularly effective media for the transformation of trauma, remaking it at times into an expression of survival, resilience, and celebration. The performative nature of these forms of expression allows this remaking to be experienced not only by the artists but also by the audience and wider community.

There are some striking similarities in the experiences of diasporic communities and the imaginaries of folk music. Much diasporic culture develops through a fear of losing touch with a way of life, just as the impulse to collect folk music is often motivated by concern regarding its disappearance. In both cases, the act of preservation changes the very thing being preserved. The cultural capital of 'folk' music from a country of origin can change significantly in diasporic contexts. For example, second-generation members of diasporic communities may seek to distance themselves from the music of their parents' place of origin, viewing this as peripheral to their primary cultural identity. In some cases, it may even be seen as a source of embarrassment or shame. Conversely, the cultural capital of a practice may increase in its relocation to a new home.[16] Indeed, performing diasporic culture can be a lucrative business. This may involve the transformation of community-based 'folk' traditions that may have been performed by amateurs in countries of origin to an increased professionalization and the development of a career trajectory around these same practices in a diasporic context. Slobin's description of folk music – to which I return throughout this chapter – as the strategic use of available resources to engage in everyday musical practices is of particular importance for diasporic communities, for whom cultural practices are often a key strategy for carving out social space. Finally, nostalgia has a significant role to play in the cultural negotiations of diasporic communities as well as in the imaginaries of folk music. Diasporic communities define their relationship to a culture as much by their distance from it as by proximity. Nostalgia, memory, and experiences of belonging and unbelonging play a critical role in the character of much diasporic cultural practice.[17]

Music and Migration

Although there are significant overlaps between the experiences of migrant and diasporic communities, migrants are most often distinguished as having been born somewhere else and moved to a new location, whereas this is not necessarily the case for members of a diaspora. The International Organisation for Migration defines a migrant as 'a person who moves away from his or her place of usual residence, whether within a country or across an international border, temporarily or permanently, and for a variety of reasons'.[18] This includes people who have relocated for purposes of work, education, family, violence, adventure, or fear. While the case studies described in this chapter include examples of people coming to Ireland for such reasons, a significant number arrived as a refugee, that is, 'someone who, owing to a well-founded fear of persecution for several reasons, is outside the country of his nationality and is unable, or, owing to such fear, is unwilling to avail himself of the protection of that country or to return to it'.[19]

As with the secularization of the term 'diaspora', migration studies emerged in the early twentieth century with a focus on issues of global population mobility trends. Its emergence was linked to the problematization of migration and policy concerns regarding issues of integration and diversity.[20] This problematizing of migration casts contemporary migrants as 'bad' migrants, in contrast with 'good' migrants of the past who are portrayed as industrious and civilizing. Contemporary trends associating migration with crisis, conflict, terrorism, growing numbers of people on the move, and growing numbers of female migrants are all part of this problematizing narrative.[21] As Sam Miller writes, 'migration has, in fact, become a proxy for a whole range of other issues that impinge on our lives and our thinking: identity, ethnicity, religion, ideas of home, patriotism, nostalgia, integration, multiculturalism, safety, terrorism, racism'.[22]

The prevalence of paradoxical identities already identified in the imaginaries of folk music and diasporic communities continues in the narratives around migrants. For some people, this label is part of their self-identity; for others, it is imposed upon them, a category under which they are governed in their country of destination. Representations and policies regarding migrants reveal deep inconsistencies, as Martina Tazzioli writes: 'They are expected to assimilate and encouraged to remain distinctive, to defend their heritage and adopt a new one. They are sub-human and super-human, romanticized and castigated, admired and abhorred.'[23]

According to Martin Stokes, this crisis narrative influences the study of music and migration: 'The measured language of the social sciences and the humanities – contextualizing, explaining, interpreting – does not fit easily with the emotions many of us surely feel at the news that flashes across our screens.'[24] He notes the growth of more explicitly activist and interventionist approaches in ethnomusicology in response. Though not downplaying the real and drastic challenges faced by migrants (and non-migrants) as a result of wars, climate change, economic crises, and failed governance, he emphasizes the often inescapable pitfalls associated with this field of study, suggesting that 'the media's urge to locate the human story and create compassionate foci for action is, perversely and ironically, intimately connected to the ever-deepening construction in public debate of migrants as existential threats to citizenship and security'.[25]

In the interface between folk music imaginaries and human movement, the constructs of migration and diaspora are the dominant theoretical frames through which the impact of cultural encounter and displacement on musical experiences are explored. A third theoretical frame is the emergent interdisciplinary space of mobility studies. Mobility studies focuses not only on the movement of people, but also on the movement of other living beings, texts, objects, images, and ideas. Although less frequently applied to the study of music and migration, it serves as an important reminder that music moves not only through people, but also through the artefacts and ideas by which it is transmitted. Related to, but also distinct from this body of work is research focusing on music and refugees. This work has generated not only a different set of research questions and priorities, but also a growing interest in exploring creative, ethically driven methodologies for working *with*, rather than *on*, refugees. A dominant theme in this discourse concerns the role of music as a potential medium of social inclusion and belonging.

Music and Social Inclusion

Studies concerning music and social inclusion and the inclusion of refugees more specifically are on the rise. Much of this work presents case studies of projects, interventions, and musical activities designed by or for refugees, sometimes within the broader context of migrant and/or diasporic communities.[26] Refugees and asylum seekers have themselves reported that engaging with the arts supports the development of new social networks.[27] Although the rising number of such studies speaks to the contemporary relevance of research on music and social inclusion, Oscar Odena has noted that 'this increase in publications does not seem to provide a clearer understanding of how such impact may develop or of its value across settings'.[28] Publications in the area of arts and health have attempted to address this issue by exploring social inclusion as part of a broader focus on health and wellbeing. One study published in 2015, for instance, explored the impact of musical engagement with refugees and asylum seekers in Australia using Amy Schulz and Mary Northridge's health and wellbeing framework. Participant experiences generated a number of self-reported social determinants of health that were not part of this framework – including cultural expression, social identity, and music-making.[29]

Caroline Lenette nevertheless sounds a note of caution in this health-based approach to music and social inclusion. Biomedical studies are prolific in refugee research owing to the high proportion of trauma-related issues in post-conflict contexts. The important work being done on the role of music in such contexts should not overshadow its equally important place in the everyday fabric of the lives of refugees – not all of which is traumatic or linked to conflict. These wider documented outcomes concerning the role of music as a form of wellbeing include its contribution to, for example, 'cultural identity and associated practices, self-determination and agency, self-expression and representation, social connectedness and relationships, social inclusion and social justice, emotional stability and safety, cultural adjustment and integration, continuity of religious and spiritual practice, and engagement in social leisure activities'.[30]

With its emphasis on the social purposes of music, much of this research highlights the strategic use of resources in everyday musical practice, but offers less information on the musical practices themselves. Ethnomusicological publications continue to be the exception that proves the rule in this regard. Examples include the special issue on music and migration published by the *Journal of Ethnic and Migration Studies* in 2006 that incorporates a wide range of research on musical production in Sudanese refugee camps, *dabke* performance among Palestinian refugees in the Jordan Valley, the singing of migrant mine-workers in South Africa, the changing status of the *mizwid* in the context of rural to urban migration in Tunisia, and the music of Khalifa migrants in the United Kingdom and the New York Fuzhou community.[31] My own work has focused on the intersectionality between singing and ritual in the lives of refugees and new migrants in Ireland.[32] In this context, I have suggested five characteristics of singing that support its facilitation of experiences of belonging. These include resonance (relating the singing body to space); somatics (relating the singing conscious and unconscious body); performance (relating the singing, performing body with the receptive, social body); temporality (relating the singing body to time) and tacitness (relating the singing body to other singing and listening bodies). A common theme across these publications is the musical transformation that often characterizes migration. This transformation may encompass changing audiences, venues, instruments, stylistic adaptations, social roles, and musical values. Critically, music provides a medium through which migrants can tell their own stories: as John Baily and Michael Collyer put it, 'music offers a possible insight into migrants' own interpretations of their migrations and visions of their new societies'.[33]

New Migrant Communities in Ireland

Arts-based research approaches, including music-making, are growing in recognition and practice in refugee and migrant research. This is based on mounting evidence concerning the ability of music and singing to foster intercultural empathy, curiosity, and accelerated social bonding among diverse groups. Musical activities can redress power imbalances between migrants and host communities and provide important spaces for the expression of complex cultural identities.[34] Arts-based research methods are utilized by social scientists, educators, and a host of other researchers from diverse disciplinary backgrounds. Arts practice research, also variously known as practice as research (PaR), artistic research, and practice-based research, is another important methodological innovation, wherein artists harness their own creative practice as both a research method and as an intrinsic aspect of the research output.[35]

Arts practice research methods are increasingly utilized by community musicians seeking to integrate community participants into their research. This is the case for the three doctoral research projects discussed in what follows. The examples summarize one event from each research project, each exploring the contribution of music to imaginaries of belonging. Jaber's research focuses on community music interventions in the context of post-conflict migration, with particular reference to the Syrian community in Ireland.[36] Nutekpor utilizes arts practice approaches to explore the contribution of artistic pedagogy, curation, and performance to cultural dialogue, with particular reference to Ghanaian-Irish cultural encounters.[37] Żak-Dyndał's research explores ritual, music, and experiences of belonging, with a particular focus on the Polish diaspora in Ireland.[38] Before discussing these in more detail, it is important to articulate a theoretical understanding of belonging. Belonging is still a relatively new theoretical construct, yet questions of belonging are among the most important and pressing in the context of migration and its impact on identity.[39] As Christine Halse writes, we are living in

> an era marked by increasing transnational mobility and interconnectedness and the largest flow of refugees and migrants fleeing war, persecution and poverty in search of a safer, better life in recorded history. Around the globe, it is also an era of resurgent conservatism, nationalism and nativism, increasing physical, social and political attacks on racial, ethnic, cultural and religious minorities, and growing social and economic disparities within and between societies. Deeply entangled in these historical conditions are profound questions about what belonging – and not belonging – means, how it is enacted and experienced, and its effects on and implications for individuals, groups and societies. Some of these questions are ... what technologies, strategies, processes and social institutions are mobilised to enforce inclusion and exclusion?[40]

Music is one such technology, strategy, and process. As all four of us are musician-researcher-migrants, our positionality is key to our engagement with these imaginaries of belonging.

From Within a Woman's Heart (2019)

The first curated performance in Jaber's research identified emergent themes of loss, migrant isolation, performative politics, and the complex positionality of the community musician. Through the analysis of these themes and extended conversations and interviews with the participants, the idea of a social musical event emerged. The first performance organically transformed into a women's platform of self-expression. Investigating these elements led to an exploration aiming to establish social musical events dedicated to women, which then led Jaber to consider the concept of the social event as musical intervention. In the context of this research, intervention is understood as the identification and co-creation of musical experiences that support communities in the negotiation of belonging in new cultural contexts.

As a key goal of the project was to provide a space for women to meet other women, Jaber identified two Limerick based women's groups with whom she had previously worked to join the project: Our Lady of Lourdes Sing-Along and the Coffee Morning Ladies. Social singing and singing sessions in domestic or community spaces (the home, pub, or club) are popular social activities in Ireland.[41] Gathering to share news, tell stories, sing, and play games were also identified by participants from Arabic backgrounds as part of their cultural practice, noting that these frequently took place in women-only or men-only spaces. The co-designed women-only event combined socializing and musicking with a supervised children's corner. Irish and Arabic treats were shared and all activities were presented in English and Arabic. Contributions included Polish lullabies, Irish step-dancing, and a performance on the French horn by a Canadian musician. Our Lady of Lourdes Sing-Along group shared songs from America, South Africa, and Australia. Three traditional Arabic songs were performed by Jaber and a Syrian singer, recently arrived in Limerick as part of a refugee resettlement programme. The musical sharing ended with a suite of Palestinian wedding songs sung by a group of Palestinian women.

Post-event interviews, fieldnotes, reflexive journal writing, and other forms of expression such as poetry focused on the extent to which the event was identified as an experience of belonging, and if so, what elements contributed to this experience? One of the themes that emerged involved the importance of sharing one's own culture while experiencing the culture of 'the other' as a key aspect of sense-making in the dynamic and changing realities of both:

'... I felt that my voice, culture, and language are heard, I found a space for myself here.'

'... this event welcomes a lot of cultures and allows women from various cultures to participate and express themselves and their culture, which is especially important for a migrant.'

The safety of the space was also identified as critical to a sense of belonging:

'... I felt that the event was a safe environment to women of all backgrounds and beliefs to come together and enjoy the moment with music, singing, and dancing. All women were very relaxed and smiling away.'

'... I noticed people sometimes sitting or standing alone but they did not seem awkward or left out. It seemed ok to just be there, sometimes with others and sometimes alone.'

The vulnerability of performance as a way of sharing something very precious was also noted as a powerful aspect of the experience of belonging:

'... I felt that each of the women shared a little of her heart and a little of her life with us ... all struck me as coming from a desire to share.'

Linked to this was the invitation to take part:

'... as the acts went on, all the guests started being more participative and took part in each act by clapping, repeating the chorus etc.'

Strikingly, participants did not focus on the particularities of musical repertoire; instead, the invitation to include material from different cultural practices was highlighted as an important aspect of the sense of belonging generated by the event. Experiences of belonging, then, were not identified primarily through cultural *content* but through acts of cultural *sharing*. Sharing occurred along a continuum – moving from the performance or presentation of one's own cultural practice to singing along or perhaps learning songs from other participants.

The paradoxical nature of diasporic, migrant, and folk music discourses noted above resonates with the seemingly contradictory themes of safety and vulnerability identified in this work. Participants noted that the creation of a safe space supported their ability to be vulnerable in a new and unfamiliar environment. Safety, vulnerability, and belonging were performed through acts of sharing: songs provoked both tears and laughter, while singing supported synchronized clapping, stamping, swaying. In this way, music actively fostered inclusion.

Kutrikuku / Resilience (2020)

Whereas safety and vulnerability emerged as key ideas in Jaber's work, resilience was the core theme explored in Nutekpor's *Kutrikuku / Resilience*. This staged performance was co-designed with musicians and dancers from Ireland, Ghana, America, India, and Nigeria. Experiences of migration are frequently characterized by some degree of psychosocial suffering. These include the stress of displacement, the risks of the journey, and the often precarious and chaotic living conditions encountered in the arrival country.[42] Experiences in the arrival country may include uncertainty of legal status, challenges in accessing services, gaining employment, limited resources, and isolation. The loss of one's habitual social environment and cultural identity can also add to a sense of vulnerability. The ability of both migrants and host communities to address these challenges in a healthy and balanced way depends on high levels of resilience in both.[43] The potential role of intercultural practices in contributing to resilience-building was the focus of Nutekpor's work. Having to create and realize the performance during the height of the Covid-19 pandemic added another dimension of resilience to the original research design.

The multi-art performance commenced with film, photography, and voice recordings from Nutekpor's youth in Ghana, leading into the performance of 'Tutugborvi', a Ghanian lullaby. The second piece, 'Luŋa dialogue', combined a solo improvised piece on the talking drum with an Irish jig tune. 'Atsiagbekor dialogue' was based on an Anlo-Ewe traditional dance, featuring Nutekpor and an Irish student who learned the dance

Figure 14.1 John Nutekpor in *Kutrikuku / Resilience*, 2020. Photograph by Maurice Gunning.

from Nutekpor. 'Gahu dialogue' included an excerpt from the Anlo-Ewe traditional Kinka dance, introduced by poetry. The final piece, 'Afro-Irish dialogue' was choreographed by Nutekpor combining African and Irish-inspired dance movements. This piece used the framework of an Irish reel inflected with influences of Ghanaian highlife music.

Interviews with participants from this performance identified the shared experiences of music and dance as strengthening a sense of belonging and motivation:

'... *Kutrikuku* is not only a concept that I learnt from participating in John's performance; it is also a source of inspiration and motivation to keep creating, generating synergy with other artists, building bridges between cultures and enriching the exchanges we have with the people we encounter in life.'

'... The "resilience" section where I had the bell was exciting. I loved the energy and the spirit of it. For me it was like walking on a bridge with amazing friends not looking back. I was blown away by the intensity and passion of the music.'

'... The lullaby music was very soothing, and I had deeper concentration on my reflective thoughts on those precarious moments when everything seems not to work. The music gave me some new insights and how to overcome my doubts in these challenging moments.'

A key finding of this research is that cultural dialogue is characterized by both complexity (in cultural nuances, performative interpretation, and intercultural transmission) and adaptivity (utilizing creative processes, technological support, and dynamic performance spaces). Resilience is key to one's ability to negotiate such complexities and to calibrate constantly changing levels of adaptation in the context of migration. Belonging, in this sense, is understood as a performative stance – something enacted in complex sociocultural spaces. As in Nutekpor's *Kutrikuku*, this may take the form of nostalgic evocation or deliberate fusion. It embraces specialist cultural bearers as well as non-specialist enthusiasts from other cultures. Nutekpor's work exemplifies music's ability to transform challenge or trauma into a malleable performance of survival.

Droga / Where We Belong (2022)

Żak-Dyndał's performance focused on music and rituals associated with the lifecycle in Slavic and Irish culture, and how these are negotiated by the Polish diasporic community in Ireland. Sociocultural research on the Polish community in Ireland to date demonstrates a focus on economic and political issues, health and well-being, and religious ritual.[44] Although there are a small number of studies on music and ritual with migrant communities in Ireland, there is little evidence of rigorous investigation of this topic in the context of the Polish-Irish community.[45]

The performance consisted primarily of musicians and dancers from Poland living in Ireland, as well as musicians from Poland who travelled to Ireland for the performance. Devised as a theatrical project, it presented an exploration of identity and belonging through musical and ritual traditions drawing on Żak-Dyndał's own experiences, inspired not only by her Polish heritage, but also her training as a classical singer and engagement with Irish traditional song.

The performance commenced in the venue foyer with the audience invited to enjoy food, drink, smells, and sounds from a 'Polish village'. On entering the venue, they were visually immersed in a Polish rural scene through a filmed recording. Like Nutekpor's piece, the performance opened with a lullaby, 'Usnijże mi, uśnij'. The version performed was collected from the region surrounding Cieplice village. The song transitions into a scene of children playing, interrupted by a lament, accompanied by the hurdy-gurdy. The children evolve into young women / spinners in the next 'courtship scene'. 'Prząśniczka', written by Stanisław Moniuszko, was performed as an example of a domestic work song (spinning), followed by 'Oj chmielu, Chmielu', one of the oldest known Polish bridal songs sung with the 'white singing' technique – a traditional Slavic singing style characterized by bright, open sounds utilizing an open throat strongly associated with traditional ritual practices such as baptism, weddings, burials, and agricultural rituals.[46] This was followed by a second wedding song, 'Siadaj, nie gadaj' from central Poland, as well as the folk song, 'Lipka' with lyrics originating in the Wielkopolska area. Delibes' flower duet from the opera *Lakmé* was sung by Żak-Dyndał's and another performer, while 'An Caoineadh', a traditional Irish song of lamentation for a deceased child, was also performed as a duet, exploring encounters with Irish traditional song and classical music. This Irish lament was preceded by 'Żegnam Cię mój świecie wesoły', a sixteenth- to seventeenth-century Polish lamentation still sung in Polish funeral rituals. The performance ended with 'Modlitwa gdy dziadki idą spać' by Wacław z Szamotuł, a sixteenth-century contrapuntal song calling blessings and protection on children as they fall asleep at the end of the day and pray for a better tomorrow.

Żak-Dyndał followed the performance with an open audience discussion and post-performance interviews. One of her questions to participants concerned whether the experience evoked any thoughts concerning belonging or identity. A prevalent theme of the audience discussion concerned how different it was to perform 'belonging' in Ireland compared to Poland, noting the enhanced value 'traditional' repertoire had in the diasporic context:

' ... People are not like oh wow, they're singing this traditional Polish music [in Poland]. It's kind of like you hear it everywhere, actually. Because when you are abroad, when you're in a different country, you miss that culture. You miss to listen to this music, sing that music.'

'While in here, we miss Poland, and also, we actually start to see the emptiness, and we don't know what this emptiness is. It's inside us so, this is actually coming from our hearts, our souls. I think that it's more prominent in here because this is really who we are. We also just try to actually give you this energy that we feel.'

Even more so than Jaber and Nutekpor, Żak-Dyndał explicitly positions belonging as the central theme of this work. Music and singing are again identified as significant sites for negotiating ideas of being and commonality, complicated and enriched by the multivalency of identity typical of diasporic or migrant communities. While these three performances explore a range of themes related to fitting in (sharing, safety, vulnerability, resilience, identity), all harness music and singing methodologically in pursuit of this investigation. Likewise, they demonstrate the ways in which diverse cultures use musical resources to imagine and create experiences of belonging.

Imaginaries of Belonging

At the outset of this chapter I proposed, along with Harari, that successful, large-scale human cooperation is often based on imaginaries. Folk music is one such imaginary. Belonging is another. Using Slobin's framing of folk music as the strategic use of available resources in everyday musical practices, each of the research projects discussed here explore how migrant and diasporic communities strategically harness the musical resources available to them to conjure experiences of belonging. While the three examples present significant variations in style, structure, repertoire, intent, musical forces, ethnicities, and migrant realities, they also share a number of commonalities in how belonging is imagined, curated, and presented. All three draw the majority of their repertoire from 'home' cultures (i.e. Arabic, Ghanaian, and Polish sources), but none do so exclusively. Furthermore, the performance of repertoire from the home culture is not only performed by those from that culture, but also by non-native and non-specialist performers. This includes audience or community participation in simple refrains, clapping, or dancing. Although much of the repertoire shared from the county of origin might be described as 'traditional' and is referred to as 'folk' music in interviews and programme notes, it was presented side by side with more contemporary and popular pieces, which played a similar role in representing the home culture. All three performances incorporated instruments with strong associations with the home culture (e.g. the *ney, luɲa*, and hammered dulcimer) but also incorporated the piano / keyboard, guitar, violin, and other instruments associated with Western art music. Characteristics of traditional singing styles (e.g. open throat singing, thoracic breathing, hypernasality, ululation) were present in the performances, but so were examples of classical and popular vocal styles. In all cases, the majority of performers were migrants, while the wider community or audience also included people from the host country of Ireland.

The everyday lives of those involved – whether migrants or members of diasporic and/or host communities – fostered the need to create new imaginaries of belonging linked to the realities of migration. The 'imagined order' of these creations identified music as a primary strategic resource in its negotiation, presentation, and performance. A key insight from the three examples is that the primary meaning of folk music resides not in naming it, but in *playing* it. While scholars continue to debate and parse the semantic implications of 'traditional', 'folk', 'Indigenous', 'vernacular', 'world', 'art', and a whole host of other terms to describe the musics played by people, the performers engage in their own acts of musical shape-shifting, adapting the sounds and the words to fit the need and the context. This is thrown into particular relief in the context of migration, where 'folk' musics (or whatever else they are called) are alternatively fossilized, sentimentalized, stereotyped, commercialized, hybridized, ridiculed, or sanctified, depending on who is performing and why they are motivated to do so. Like all imaginaries, they thrive less on logic and more on the creative bridging of memory, observation, and opportunity.

Such imaginaries require new understandings not only of the concepts discussed in this chapter, but of culture itself. These new understandings must recognize that culture is deeply implicated in our formulations of belonging / not belonging. Migration presents one of the most significant challenges to any static or bounded conceptualization of culture, which is increasingly and more accurately understood as a complex web of interconnected networks and collaborations.[47] Both metaphorically and literally, music moves us and moves with us. At the cellular level, our ability to create an optimal balance or homeostasis involves constant, dynamic adaptation and environmental response. At a cultural level, music may provide us with the dynamic means to adapt and respond to our changing environment – seeking and constantly recreating a kind of cultural homeostasis characterized by imaginaries of belonging.

Notes

1. Mícheál Ó Súilleabháin and Helen Phelan, 'MEND-ing Music Education: The Evolution of the Irish World Academy' in *Music Education for the Twenty-First Century: Legacies, Conversations, Aspirations*, ed. John O'Flynn and Patricia Flynn, 31–50. Cork: Cork University Press, 2023.
2. Charles Keil, 'Who Needs "The Folk"?', *Journal of the Folklore Institute*, 15/3 (1978): 263–65, 263. This argument is developed more fully in Ross Cole, *The Folk: Music, Modernity, and the Political Imagination*. Oakland: University of California Press, 2021.
3. Niall Keegan, 'The Art of Juncture: Transformations of Irish Traditional Music'. PhD dissertation, University of Limerick (2012), 181.
4. Eamon Maher and Eugene O'Brien, ed., *From Prosperity to Austerity: A Socio-Cultural Critique of the Celtic Tiger and its Aftermath*. Manchester: Manchester University Press, 2015.
5. Helen Phelan, *Singing the Rite to Belong: Music, Ritual and the New Irish*. Oxford: Oxford University Press, 2017.
6. Cole, *The Folk*, 8.
7. Yuval Noah Harari, *Homo Deus: A Brief History of Tomorrow*. London: Vintage, 2017, 167.
8. William G. Roy, *Reds, Whites, and Blues: Social Movements, Folk Music, and Race in the United States*. Princeton: Princeton University Press, 2010.
9. James Barrett, 'World Music, Nation and Postcolonialism'. *Cultural Studies*, 10/2 (1996): 237–47.
10. See J. J. Lee and Marion R. Casey, ed., *Making the Irish American: History and Heritage of the Irish in the United States*. New York: NYU Press, 2007; James R. Barrett, *The Irish Way: Becoming American in the Multiethnic City*. London: Penguin, 2012.
11. Fintan Vallely, 'Playing, Paying and Preying: Cultural Clash and Paradox in the Traditional Music Commonage'. *Community Development Journal*, 49 (2014): 53–67.
12. Mark Slobin, *Folk Music: A Very Short Introduction*. Oxford: Oxford University Press, 2011, 3.
13. Stephane Dufoix, *Diasporas*. Berkeley: University of California Press, 2008.

14. Alpha Abebe, 'Performing Diaspora', in *Routledge Handbook of Diaspora Studies*, ed. Robin Cohen and Carolin Fischer, 55–62. London: Routledge, 2018.
15. See Ananya Jahanara Kabir, 'Affect, Body, Place: Trauma Theory in the World' in *The Future of Trauma Theory*, ed. Gert Buelens, Sam Durrant, and Robert Eaglestone, 63–75. New York: Routledge, 2013 and Ananya Jahanara Kabir, 'Oceans, Cities, Islands: Sites and Routes of Afro-diasporic Rhythm Cultures'. *Atlantic Studies*, 11/1 (2014): 106–24.
16. Dieu Hack-Polay, Mahfuzur Rahman, and Matthijs Bal, 'Beyond Cultural Instrumentality: Exploring the Concept of Total Diaspora Cultural Capital for Sustainability'. *Sustainability*, 15 /7 (2023): 6238.
17. Kathleen Newland and Carylanna Taylor, *Heritage Tourism and Nostalgia Trade: A Diaspora Niche in the Development Landscape*. Washington, DC: Migration Policy Institute, 2010.
18. www.iom.int/about-migration.
19. www.unhcr.org/what-refugee.
20. Peter Scholten, Asya Pisarevskaya, and Nathan Levy, 'An Introduction to Migration Studies: The Rise and Coming of Age of a Research Field' in *Introduction to Migration Studies: An Interactive Guide to the Literatures on Migration and Diversity*, ed. Peter Scholten. New York: Springer International Publishing, 2022, 3–24.
21. Marlou Schrover, 'Feminization and Problematization of Migration: Europe in the Nineteenth and Twentieth Centuries' in *Proletarian and Gendered Mass Migrations*, ed. Dirk Hoerder and Amarjit Kaur. Leiden: Brill, 2013, 103–31.
22. Sam Miller, *Migrants: The Story of Us All*. London: Abacus Books, 2023, 3.
23. Martina Tazzioli, *The Making of Migration: The Biopolitics of Mobility at Europe's Borders*. Thousand Oaks: Sage, 2019, 6.
24. Martin Stokes, 'Migration and Music'. *Music Research Annual*, 1 (2020): 1–24, 1.
25. Stokes, 'Migration and Music', 5.
26. Cohen and Fischer, ed., *Routledge Handbook of Diaspora Studies*.
27. Clelia Clini, Linda J. M. Thomson, and Helen J. Chatterjee, 'Assessing the Impact of Artistic and Cultural Activities on the Health and Well-Being of Forcibly Displaced People using Participatory Action Research'. *BMJ Open*, 9/2 (2019): e025465.
28. Oscar Odena, ed., *Music and Social Inclusion: International Research and Practice in Complex Settings*. London: Routledge, 2023, 1.
29. Naomi Sunderland, Lauren Istvandity, Ali Lakhani, Caroline Lenette, Brian Procopis, and P. Caballero, 'They [do more than] Interrupt Us from Sadness: Exploring the Impact of Participatory Music Making on Social Determinants of Health and Wellbeing for Refugees in Australia'. *Health, Culture and Society*, 8 /1 (2015): 1–19.
30. Caroline Lenette and Naomi Sunderland, '"Will there be music for us?": Mapping the Health and Well-Being Potential of Participatory Music Practice

with Asylum Seekers and Refugees across Contexts of Conflict and Refuge'. *Arts & Health*, 8/1 (2016): 32–49, 45.
31. John Baily and Michael Collyer, 'Introduction: Music and Migration'. *Journal of Ethnic and Migration Studies*, 32/2 (2006): 167–82.
32. Phelan, *Singing the Rite to Belong*.
33. Baily and Collyer, 'Introduction', 180.
34. Caroline Lenette, *Arts-Based Methods in Refugee Research*. New York: Springer, 2019.
35. Robin Nelson, *Practice as Research in the Arts (and Beyond): Principles, Processes, Contexts, Achievements*. New York: Palgrave Macmillan, 2022.
36. Hala Jaber, 'An Arts Practice Investigation of Community Music Interventions in The Context of Post-Conflict Migration, With Particular Reference to The Syrian Community in Ireland.' PhD dissertation, University of Limerick (2020).
37. John Nutekpor, 'An Arts Practice Exploration of Ghanaian-Irish Cultural Dialogue, through Music and Dance Pedagogy, Curation and Performance.' PhD dissertation, University of Limerick (2023).
38. Żak-Dyndał commenced her doctoral research, 'Performing Rites of Belonging', in 2020.
39. Eva Youkhana, 'A Conceptual Shift in Studies of Belonging'. *Social Inclusion*, 3/4 (2015): 10–24; Nira Yuval-Davis, *The Politics of Belonging: Intersectional Contestations*. London: Sage, 2011.
40. Christine Halse, *Interrogating Belonging for Young People in Schools*. New York: Palgrave Macmillan, 2018, 1.
41. Carolyn Louise Dike, 'A Singing Space: Re-contextualizing Tradition.' PhD dissertation, University of Limerick (2017).
42. Maria Ciaramella, Nadia Monacelli, and Livia Concetta Eugenia Cocimano, 'Promotion of Resilience in Migrants: A Systematic Review of Study and Psychosocial Intervention'. *Journal of Immigrant and Minority Health*, 24/5 (2022): 1328–44.
43. Chesmal Siriwardhana, Shirwa Sheik Ali, Bayard Roberts, and Robert Stewart, 'A Systematic Review of Resilience and Mental Health Outcomes of Conflict-Driven Adult Forced Migrants'. *Conflict and Health*, 8/1 (2014): 1–14.
44. See Torben Krings, Alicja Bobek, Elaine Moriarty, Justyna Salamońska, and James Wickham, 'Polish Migration to Ireland: "Free Movers" in the New European Mobility Space'. *Journal of Ethnic and Migration Studies*, 39/1 (2013): 87–103; Elizabeth J. O'Sullivan, Agnieszka O'Grady, Karolina Pawlak, and John M. Kearney, 'A Qualitative Exploration of the Attitudes and Experiences of Polish Breastfeeding Mothers in Ireland'. *Journal of Human Lactation*, 37/2 (2021): 370–79; Wojciech Sadlon, 'The Social Activity of Polish Migrants in the Republic of Ireland from the Perspective of Their Religiosity'. *Review of Religious Research*, 64/4 (2022): 907–32.

45. Phelan, *Singing the Rite to Belong*; Helen Phelan, 'The Untidy Playground: An Irish Congolese Case Study in Sonic Encounters with the Sacred Stranger'. *Religions*, 8/11 (2017): 249; Helen Phelan, 'Sonic Hospitality: Migration, Community and Music' in *Oxford Handbook of Music Education*, ed. Gary E. McPherson and Graham F. Welch. Oxford: Oxford University Press, 2018, 168–84; Helen Phelan, 'Religion, Music and the Site of Ritual: Baptismal Rites and the Irish Citizenship Referendum'. *International Journal of Community Music*, 2/1 (2009): 25–38; Neil Conner, 'Religion and the Social Integration of Migrants in Dublin, Ireland'. *Geographical Review*, 109/1 (2019): 27–46; Abel Ugba, *Shades of Belonging: African Pentecostals in Twenty-First Century Ireland*. Trenton, NJ: Africa World Press, 2009.
46. Anna Czekanowska, *Polish Folk Music: Slavonic Heritage-Polish Tradition: Contemporary Trends*. Cambridge: Cambridge University Press, 1990.
47. Perla Innocenti, *Migrating Heritage: Experiences of Cultural Networks and Cultural Dialogue in Europe*. London: Routledge, 2016.

15 | Artist Voice

Mythopoeic Singing or, The Mythopoeic Singer

ANGELINE MORRISON

> 'They that walked in darkness sang songs in the olden days – Sorrow Songs – for they were weary at heart.'[1]

W. E. B. Du Bois writes so emotively in 1903 of what he refers to as 'the sorrow songs', the body of folk song of the enslaved African populations in America and their descendants. His words speak to the power of song to transform – the sacred act of not simply singing, but of singing something into being. Disembodied, imaginal, or non-physical things can all be sung into being: an idea, a feeling, a narrative, a wisdom lesson, a philosophy, even an identity.

The process of bringing the human breath and its sonorous vibrations for the purposes of transformation can be thought of as a magical act. In the case of Du Bois' sorrow songs, one of the key things available for transformation is the inexpressible, unfathomable burden of suffering, grief, and loss carried by the populations of enslaved Africans and their descendants in America. Through shared song, these horrors would be transformed into moments of soaring beauty or deep, poetic sadness. The forms or 'bodies' of the songs themselves can be thought of as kin to the form of a ritual, or prayer, or incantation. This applies both to the spirituals made famous throughout Europe and the wider world by the epic touring of the Fisk Jubilee Singers in the late nineteenth century (who famously performed 'Steal Away to Jesus' and 'Go Down Moses' for Queen Victoria in 1873) and also to the secular songs of work, love, and comedy. Words are transfigured from textual form into living, vibrating being through the breath of humans engaged in song. The breath gives life.

The significance of a song's text is also thus enlivened – and where group singing is taking place, this significance is effortlessly shared. When a song has been sung many times over many centuries by many souls, when it has gathered a palimpsest of individual and group human feelings and experiences around it, the song can come to feel like a significant artefact in and of itself.

In terms of thinking about folk and traditional song, one of the most compelling aspects of Du Bois' essay is the feeling of 'recognition' he describes on hearing these songs: 'Ever since I was a child these songs have stirred me strangely. They came out of the South unknown to me, one by one, and yet at once I knew them as of me and of mine.'² It is common to hear people saying similar things about their relationship to the folk and traditional songs of Britain – that on first hearing they felt an immediate connection, a mysterious 'knowing', a familiarity.

I had the exact same experience myself. Growing up in a household rich with pretty much every genre of music except British trad, I recall the first time I ever heard such music with crystal clarity. A small child absorbed in my game, I was oblivious to the radio my parents were listening to. Oblivious, that is, until a most extraordinary sound vibrated across the room to me, and I was transfixed. It was an incredibly pure-sounding, unaccompanied human voice singing a melody that sounded at once exotic and strangely familiar, with archaic and peculiar language I only half recognized and the most intriguing musical cadences. Later, as a young adult, I discovered that this was Shirley Collins singing 'Our Captain Cried' on what must have been a programme about the history of the 1960s folk revival. But for me at the time it was a purely spiritual experience. I had never heard anything like this before – and yet I was captivated. Like Du Bois, I felt that I belonged to this music and it to me. Folk music often feels like it 'belongs' to those who sing and love it.

Figure 15.1 William Edward Burghardt Du Bois, 1919. Photograph by Cornelius Marion Battey. Library of Congress.

But is folk song really available and welcoming for everyone who loves it? The popular misconception that the Black presence in Britain only dates from 1948 and the docking of HMT Empire Windrush at the Port of Tilbury is happily now much less widely held, though it does persist. This misconception brings with it a feeling of discomfort, if not outright wrongness on occasion, around the notion of Black or other Global Majority people involving themselves with the traditional songs of Britain. Black and other Global Majority people, however, have a very long historic presence in these islands and it is inconceivable that these ancestors did not sing songs, play songs, create songs, and share songs. It is interesting that although in Britain we have evidence for a historic African presence dating back at least to Roman times, what we lack is evidence for a body of songs that these ancestors would have sung, shared and played. The British folk tradition doesn't seem to have an equivalent of the sorrow songs.

I have been thinking about the phrase 're-enchantment is resistance', and in particular about how this re-enchantment might be rendered into a more specific form of resistance – that of decolonization. The ingredients required for this include a willingness to engage in a kind of contemporary mythmaking. Myth here is not intended in the popular sense of 'something that is not true', but rather in the more ancient sense of 'something that has always been true'. We can mine the vaults of historic and traditional song and seek Black and brown-skinned characters in the narratives. We find them occasionally, often shrouded in negative stereotypes common during the songs' popularity or the period at which they were collected. However, what we find only rarely (and my research into this is ongoing), is a British traditional or folk song containing someone we can definitely read as a Global Majority character set in a positive or neutral role in the song's narrative. What I like to call mythopoeic singing can be a creative ally here.

Mythopoeic singing as it might be applied to the traditional songs of Britain would involve re-populating an imaginal historic landscape with figures we know to have been present in that landscape, but who may not be identifiable in the body of song that survives. These ancestors have quite literally been ghosted from the official narratives of history. They can be found in the footnotes or in the margins, or by happy accident when the researcher is looking for something else entirely. But we do now know, without doubt, that their historic presence on this land and in the life of these islands is real. This knowledge allows us to re-enchant our singing of the past with these historic figures who have always been present, yet whose absence is palpable.

Mythopoeic singing involves the use of the sonorous breath – directed through the instrument of the human body and the human imagination – to breathe vigour and life into these ghostly figures gathered in the lanes, in the fields, in the towns, and at the crossroads of our shared past. Mythopoeic singing involves repopulating this shared imaginal past with erased or ignored figures whom we know were really there, but who are very difficult for us to find at this point in history. In the cauldron of the human body, the mythopoeic singer brings the combined powers of imagination, sonorous breath, words, stories and community in an alchemical act of momentary healing and restoration.

The mythopoeic singer might also re-enchant ancient popular song by singing the commonly found descriptors of 'black' and 'brown' in the folk, traditional, and ancient vernacular songs of Britain as though they refer to the skin of a Global Majority character in the song. This subversive action steps quietly away from the generally accepted notion that these terms can only possibly refer to the hair colour of a European subject. This kind of mythopoeic singing can open up the sense of possibility in a song, if only for a moment.

In these ways, mythopoeic singing is an act of continuous re-enchantment that can also be an act of decoloniality.

Whether as a solitary pursuit or a group activity, singing has a power to it that can be hard to translate into words. Children often intuit that singing to themselves under their breath is a useful way of making themselves feel better. This is an intuition backed up by research. When we work with the breath, moving it rhythmically and harmoniously in and out of our bodies, it causes a re-regulation of the parasympathetic nervous system. When this is done in a group – for example, a choir singing in harmony, a group of friends singing together, people singing as they work, or a folk club singaround – the effects on personal and group wellbeing are profound.

The air that we breathe and that we intentionally move when we sing takes no account of our differences. This breath is inclusive in the truest sense: when we sing together, we are all breathing the same air and sharing the same words and melody (or harmonious deviations from the melody that create a shared polyphony). We become, for a moment, a single singing organism made of many diverse bodies.

So in thinking about the possibilities of re-enchantment for decolonization, perhaps we can begin by thinking about folk or traditional songs themselves as containers of bodies of knowledge, bodies of pain, experiential truths, wisdom lessons, ideas, narratives, and identities. If we think about the songs in this light, then the act of singing them together becomes an act of magical significance. By re-working old songs so that they reflect histories that lie outside of master narratives, we re-enchant our imaginal past from our position in the present. We are singing things into being, across time and across history, if only for the duration of a song.

Notes

1. W. E. Burghardt Du Bois, *The Souls of Black Folk: Essays and Sketches*. Chicago: A. C. McClurg & Co., 1903, 250.
2. Du Bois, *The Souls of Black Folk*, 250.

PART IV

Identities

16 | Reclaiming Black Folk Music

KATRINA THOMPSON MOORE

In 2011 the last group to win the Grammy Award for Best Traditional Folk Album was a string band by the name of the Carolina Chocolate Drops. Formed in 2006, this all-Black band rejuvenated traditional American sounds through a variety of instruments ranging from the jug, fiddle, bones, and washboard to the guitar and banjo, along with beautiful lyrical accompaniment. Beyond performing traditional 'old-time' music, the band brought together a number of genres, including rhythm and blues, country, blues, spoken word, and with African and Caribbean influences in their repertoire. As music critic Robert Loss noted, 'These different perspectives are partly what makes contemporary old-time music so interesting, and the Carolina Chocolate Drops so riveting'.[1] Regardless of the numerous accolades and awards the group had already received, the 2011 Grammy Award was still a major feat. Since the inception of the Grammys in 1958, accusations of racial bias have plagued its history.[2] Beyond the award's long history of neglecting Black artists and performers, folk music generally has been fraught with racism ever since its inception as a field of study and interest. Folk-music journalist Robin Denselow wrote that the group's winning of the Grammy 'provided a reminder that pre-war string band music was played not just by white country artists but also African American musicians'.[3] As this chapter shows, Black folk music has a long, complicated history, and the Carolina Chocolate Drops are just one part of a growing movement to recognize, rejuvenate, and amend the history of Black artists' contributions to American folk music.

Black folk musicians, scholars, and enthusiasts of America's traditional music have begun to grapple with the long history of stereotypes, racial bias, and the overall neglect of Black people's contribution to the genre and culture. Many Black musicians today seek to integrate the present-day events and experiences of Black people with long-forgotten sounds and experiences. US musician Jake Blount, for example, relates that 'when the Black Lives Matter movement started kicking into full force ... I remember going upstairs into the attic ... reading through these books of old spirituals and songs, kind of trying to figure out ... how they would have coped with this sort of violence'.[4] Similarly, British folk musician Angeline

Morrison was drawn to folk music – or rather the lack of Black folk music – by the rise of racial violence in the United States and the Black Lives Matter movement. 'When George Floyd was murdered, I really wanted to honour my Black ancestors', she said.[5] But retracing this history brought her down a very different path. In contrast to Black people in the United States, who grapple with navigating racism within the history of American folk music, in Britain, Morrison faced the complete silencing of Black people even though they have existed in the region for thousands of years. Morrison notes, 'The traditional songs of the United Kingdom are rich with storytelling and you can find songs with examples of almost any kind of situation or person you can think of ... While people of the African diaspora have been present in these islands since Roman times, their histories are little known – and these histories don't tend to appear in the folk songs of these islands'.[6] The lack of preserved Black folk music throughout Britain's long history speaks to neglect on the part of early folk scholars, who failed to recognize the importance of Black sounds and culture more broadly. The resulting disappearance of a culture reflects a racist past rather than the absence of generations of people who created a distinct soundworld. Therefore, while in America folk music is being rejuvenated and reclaimed, musicians like Angelina Morrison are 're-storying' or rather 'writing new songs about people and incidents in Black British history'.[7]

The Sound of Black America

For some today, the Carolina Chocolate Drops, Jake Blout, and Angeline Morrison may represent a new sound, or perhaps even a 'white' sound being presented through Black voices and experiences. However, as founding member of the Carolina Chocolate Drops Rhiannon Gibbens states, 'A whole swath of people either haven't heard this music in a long time or have never heard it or don't know the history of it'.[8] The journey of Blout and the Carolina Chocolate Drops in this genre and history began with the banjo. From the Black Banjo Reclamation Project, based in the San Francisco Bay Area, to the Black Banjo Gathering at Appalachian State University in North Carolina, the banjo and its full history is being reclaimed.[9] As Black banjo player Pete Ross states, 'Correcting the history of the banjo and making it clear that this instrument, so central to American cultural history that so many White people have their personal identities wrapped up in, is in fact African American, forces a shift in understanding the country's history as well as personal cultural identifications'.[10]

'The banjo is the quintessential American instrument and an object in our material culture that can tell us the story of the United States', writes Kristina R. Gaddy.[11] For many, the banjo is the foundational instrument in American folk music. This four- to six-stringed instrument may be uniquely American, but it descends directly from the African lute. This gourd instrument was introduced to North America by those captured and enslaved within the transatlantic slave trade. The Middle Passage carried not only Black bodies, but also a culture that was introduced to and became part of the foundation of what would eventually become American culture. The banjo, as well as other aspects of West African musical culture, were carried in captive Africans' memories, stories, and material objects. The frequent use of music for the purpose of 'dancing' by the captives within the Middle Passage is well-documented (Figure 16.1). The collection of native instruments in the slave trade contributed to cultural exchange between enslaver and captive. White slave traders were hence unwitting agents in the transmission and continuation of African culture in the New World. In 1796, one traveller observed 'a slave-ship, belonging to North America, and bound to Savanna in Georgia ... with a cargo of Negroes on board' who 'were made to exercise, and encouraged, by the music of their beloved

Figure 16.1 '(Traversée) Danse de Nègres'. Engraving from Amédée Gréhan, *La France Maritime*, 3rd Volume (Paris, 1837).

banjar'.[12] For over a century, the instrument referred to as banjo, banjar, bonja, and many other terms, can be seen in accounts throughout the developing slave societies in the North American colonies, and as the United States developed into a discrete nation.[13]

Among Black communities, the banjo was the most-used musical instrument until the 1830s, and for all intents and purposes it was a quintessentially Black instrument. It entered mainstream popular culture in North America, and later Europe, through blackface minstrel shows of the nineteenth century.[14] Set in the Northern regions of the United States, white, predominantly male actors donned blackface and tattered clothing and used exaggerated dialect in order to mock Black Americans. Within these racist performances the banjo became a primary instrument, appearing in both advertisements and staged performances. The popularity of the blackface minstrel transformed a Black folk instrument into an emblem of white American entertainment and popular culture.

The first nationally and indeed internationally recognized sound of Black America is the music of blackface minstrelsy.[15] 'Old Dan Tucker', 'Coal Black Rose', 'Jump Jim Crow', and 'Camptown Races' are just a few of the songs that were recognized as the first major and original sound of the United States. Although classified as Black music, minstrel songs in truth represented whiteness through the mockery and degradation of Black people. Blackened-face white men using exaggerated dialect to portray Black people (with the accompaniment of a banjo for authenticity) sang songs and performed skits to present an imagined construction of Blackness to assert their identity.[16] The popularity of blackface minstrel music spread quickly from the United States to Europe, introducing the banjo to a much wider audience. As Jeffrey Green argues, the music was so popular that 'men and women purchased banjos ... and played the songs at home in England'.[17] Likewise, Robert B. Winans and Elias J. Kaufman note that 'the American minstrel show carried the five-string banjo to England, in what was probably the first example of a genuinely American musical phenomenon influencing the English music scene'.[18] The introduction of this instrument profoundly influenced music traditions – and by the 1880s, English musicians, both amateurs and professionals, embraced a new, uniquely English, banjo that had a distinct style of play and a different number of strings. Paradoxically, the African lute and banjo of the mainly enslaved Black community thus became almost exclusively understood as a culturally white instrument, and it has remained that way to the present day. Beyond the instrument itself, the widespread popularity of the American folk sound of blackface minstrelsy greatly influenced broader perceptions of race in Britain.

Scholar Matthew D. Morrison has recently coined the phrase 'Blacksound' to represent the 'ways in which popular entertainment, culture, and identity have been shaped by the sonic and embodied legacy of blackface minstrelsy in and beyond the United States'.[19] Minstrel songs and their racial ideology formed the very foundation of popular musical culture in the United States and were placed within the category of apparently authentic Black sound. Following Emancipation, Black American musicians were expected to perform minstrel music, continuing the perpetuation of racist culture embedded within the folk sound of North America.[20] Black folk music has thus travelled, developed, and is often indebted to a racial construct originating with the blackface minstrel show. To properly interrogate the Black sound, then, its cultural and racialized origins must always be kept within view. In many ways, Black folk musicians and enthusiasts today are reclaiming the instrument from this racist, anti-Black history and returning it to its African and early American roots, all the while attempting to navigate the continual resonance of blackface sound and ideology.

The Sorrow Songs

The banjo is foundational to the American folk sound, but its legacy does not hold quite the same status in Britain, as evidenced by the manner in which musicians are reviving Black history in British folk culture. For Angeline Morrison, the murder of George Floyd and the rise of the Black Lives Matter movement, not the banjo, were the driving force behind her entrance into Black folk music and its past. In pursuit of this history, Morrison was reminded of a book she read as a youth, W. E. B. Du Bois' *The Souls of Black Folk* (1903). Morrison pondered several questions upon re-reading the book. 'Where are people of colour in British Folk songs?', she wondered. 'Why are there no equivalents of the African American folk songs, mainly spirituals, in our body of folk music?' 'Why is there no Black voice in British folk music?'[21] For Morrison, these questions and *The Souls of Black Folk* itself greatly influenced her music. She named her 2022 album *The Sorrow Songs: Folk Songs of Black British Experience*, referring to the chapter in the book titled 'Of the Sorrow Songs'.[22]

Hailed as a book that 'should be read and studied by every person, white and black' at the time of its publication, *The Souls of Black Folk* was the first work to truly capture the multiplicity of identities, experiences, and perspectives of Black Americans in the early twentieth century in a series of essay-chapters ranging from philosophy and history to politics.[23] Du Bois begins each chapter with either a short poem or song lyrics, illustrating that music is foundational within the daily life and culture of Black people. In 'Of the Sorrow Songs', the final chapter of the book, Du Bois expounds on the power of Black music. It begins with anonymous lyrics simply titled 'Negro Song':

> I walk through the churchyard
>   To lay this body down;
> I know moon-rise, I know star-rise;
> I walk in the moonlight, I walk in the starlight,
> I'll lie in the grave and stretch out my arms,
> I'll go to judgment in the evening of the day,
> And my soul and thy soul shall meet that day,
>   When I lay this body down.

These words articulate the 'message of the slave to the world', according to Du Bois: 'They that walked in darkness sang songs in the olden days – Sorrow Songs – for they were weary at heart'.[24] Coining the phrase 'sorrow songs' as the 'rhythmic cry of the slave', Du Bois takes spirituals, the religious folk songs of enslaved Black Americans, to be the true folk music of America.

Although 'Of the Sorrow Songs' is a short chapter and appears almost as an afterthought at the end of Du Bois' pathbreaking text, it can be seen as the starting point of a larger conversation about the importance of Black music. At the time of its publication many in the United States were intent on romanticizing the role of slavery in US history. Just five years after Du Bois' work appeared, journalist Ray Stannard Baker published *Following the Color Line: An Account of Negro Citizenship in the American Democracy*, in which he spoke to a 'Georgian woman' who remarked that Southern Black people 'don't sing as they used to'. She continues: 'you should have known the old darkeys of the plantation. Every year, it seems to me, they have been losing more and more of their carefree good humour ... I don't know them any more ... and I'm free to say I'm scared of them!'[25] This statement is illustrative of the culture that gained popularity in the United States in the 1890s and continued into the early twentieth century. A revisionist fiction known as the 'Lost Cause' influenced all areas of North American life from academia to entertainment, representing a culture of myths on the history of slavery and the causes and actors within the Civil War.[26] Altering the basis for the Civil War from a battle over the institution of slavery to a conflict over states' rights was one major myth of the Lost Cause. Moreover, Lost Cause culture also popularized the fallacy that Black people were happy, contented slaves – and the music of the enslaved was one example of their mirth.[27]

The idea of happy, singing slaves was not novel to the twentieth century, however. For over a century, the myth had been perpetuated and popularized especially within the blackface minstrel show.[28] The rise of 'coon' songs in the late nineteenth century further contributed to this musical culture already based on the debasement of Black people.[29] Initially, the term 'coon' represented the minstrel caricature Zip Coon and was derived from raccoon, eventually resulting in the emergence of a ubiquitous derogatory term for Black Americans during the Lost Cause era. By the 1890s coon songs were the perverse name of a genre of music that continued the racist styles of earlier minstrel music popularized by mainly Black artists. The white public in the United States and Britain often accepted minstrel songs (and later coon songs) as the true Black folk sound; Du Bois' work attempted to counter this narrative. Scholar Houston A. Baker, Jr. writes of removing the 'minstrel mask from his entire race' and reclaiming Black music from the mocking sounds of blackened face performers and coon music.[30] Sorrow songs and their proper recognition as Black folk music were a part of a campaign to break the stereotypes that had bound the Black musical world for generations. As Du Bois states, 'the debasements and imitations – the Negro "minstrel" songs ... [and] contemporary "coon" songs' at the time of *The Souls of Black Folk*'s publication represented the Black sound for many, and a 'novice may easily lose himself and never find the real Negro melodies'.[31]

Racialized Histories

Two decades after his pivotal work, Du Bois released another groundbreaking book, *The Gift of Black Folk: The Negroes in the Making of America*. In a chapter titled 'The American Folk Song' he begins with a simple, declarative statement describing the essay's remit: 'How black folk sang their sorrow songs in the land of their bondage and made this music the only American folk music'.[32] Beyond quoting a few sections from *The Souls of Black Folk*, Du Bois also incorporates references to media and scholarly discussion on the status of Black folk music. Although there were many disputes within the field at the time, Du Bois focused on the conflicting perspectives on Black folk music being classified as a distinctively American music. He quotes directly from one contemporary critic who states that 'The Negro's music isn't ours ... it is characteristic of the Negro, not the American race'.[33] Du Bois uses this statement as an example of a larger belief in the field. To this perspective, he responds that Black music was 'created in America under American influences and by people who are Americans in the same sense that any other element of our population is American'.[34] In this 1924 publication, he is entering into a broader conversation on the matter of how national identity and racial hierarchy are being constructed within the scholarship on folk music.

At the same time as Du Bois was campaigning for proper recognition of Black Americans' contribution to American culture, folk song collector Cecil J. Sharp was attempting to preserve and revive folk music in England. In 1916 Sharp remarked that 'music in England ... became divorced from the national tradition ... the collection and preservation of our folk music, whatever else it has done, has at least restored the Englishman's confidence in the inherent ability of his nation to produce great music'.[35] This 'romantic nationalism', as Jean R. Freedman puts it, can be seen in Sharp and several other folk music scholars in the United States and Europe, and reflects a sense of folk music as a form of 'racial inheritance'.[36] This perspective is clear in Sharp's fieldwork in the Appalachian region, in which he spends two years collecting the folk sound of white Americans who he believed were continuing an English cultural tradition – while intentionally avoiding contact with Black culture and inhabitants in the region. Sharp's focus on what he saw as English culture in Appalachia has contributed to a neglect of Black culture in that region until this day. Fred Hay, for example, argues that Sharp and many folk scholars that followed in his footsteps held 'romantic themes of cultural, moral, and racial purity' when approaching the 'isolated' Appalachia region in an attempt to preserve a 'previous, simpler, and more happy era'.[37] The racialized associations Sharp drew between authentic folklore and nationalist, Anglo-Saxon culture, however, were not unique.

Early on, scholars of folk culture recognized folk music developing in America from European countries, and mainly as an English cultural inheritance. As Samuel Forcucci writes in his *A Folk Song History of America* (1984), 'American folk music was strongly influenced by the music of the Anglo-Saxons, minimally by the American Indians, and interestingly, by the contributions of the Europeans nationals who emigrated to our shores during the nineteenth century'.[38] Although some recognition of different populations in early America such as Indigenous populations and the first generation of Africans are recognized, folk music is still predominantly viewed from a Eurocentric perspective. Furthermore, Black music in folk scholarship was often placed as either representative of a primitive sound that was a continuation of African music or an imitation of white traditions, and yet not accepted as a part of a nationalist identity. If Black music represented American music, then the hegemony of whiteness as synonymous with the United States was threatened. Folk music for many within the field was associated with white identity and national pride. As Ross Cole argues, 'not only did folk song research entrench and reflect this white frame, but in so doing it also framed those others under its gaze *as* other'.[39] This 'white racial frame' is embedded within the history of scholarship on Black and white folk music alike. Joe R. Feagin defines it as 'the dominant racial frame that has legitimated, rationalized, motivated, and shaped racial oppression and inequality'.[40] The tradition of defining folk music within scholarship is directly related to either supporting or opposing the white racial framework that is a part of the bedrock of folk music history.

For early scholars that did recognize Black music as legitimate within the broader category of folk music, such music was often recognized only as a mimicry of white, Westernized sound. The United States 'seem to have no native African compositions because the Negroes have become Westernized', to quote ethnomusicologist Bruno Nettl.[41] The 'sorrow songs' (or rather spirituals) that Du Bois writes about were predominantly recognized by early white folk scholars as adaptations of white hymns.[42] Ideas concerning the continuation of African cultural practices were under serious debate for many years, contributing to the belated acceptance of an authentic Black sound in the United States. Du Bois speaks concisely to this in 'Of the Sorrow Songs' when he states that 'The first is African music, the second Afro-American, while the third is a blending of Negro music with the music heard in the foster land'.[43] However, Du Bois adds a new – and in many ways transformative – statement in his assessment that 'the songs of white America have been distinctively influenced by the slave songs or have incorporated whole phrases of Negro melody'.[44] Although Du Bois does not go into detail when he makes this assessment, scholarship of the late-twentieth and twenty-first centuries has adopted this categorization in a manner that not only recognizes the continuity of African musical traits in Black and white sounds, but also that these 'traits and cultural practices not only survived but played a major role in the development and elaboration of African-American music'.[45]

Slave Music and Folklore

The origins of Black folk music can be traced back to West African traditions brought to North America by enslaved Africans during the transatlantic slave trade. Olaudah Equiano recalls in his personal memoirs, published in 1789, the experience of being a youth in West Africa (present-day Nigeria), captured and enslaved in the transatlantic slavery system, and eventually freed. Within this testimony, Equiano offers a simple yet powerful statement: 'We are almost a nation of dancers, musicians, and poets'.[46] Beyond the banjo and other instruments carried across the Middle Passage, musical traditions such as polyrhythms, call-and-response patterns, improvisation, and the use of various percussion instruments were transmitted and formed the foundation of a Black sound. Indeed, the Middle Passage was 'not a clean break between the past and present', but instead represented a 'spatial continuation' between Africa, Europe, and America.[47] Given the employment of music within the transatlantic trade, a distinctively Black sound began to emerge that was an amalgamation of the multiplicity of cultures represented on slave ships. One slaver mentioned that the hundreds of captives on board his vessel represented 'fourteen different tribes or nations'.[48] West Central Africans, Sierra Leone, the Bight of Benin, Senegal, Gambia, the Gold Coast, and the Bight of Biafra were the main regional sources of Africans brought to North America. Furthermore, instruments including drums and lutes collected from Africa and such instruments as bagpipes, harps, and fiddles from Europe have been recorded as a part of the Middle Passage experience. The first creolized sound that would continue to develop in North America and other regions throughout the West began during this Atlantic voyage. The music culture within this Middle Passage laid the foundation for what would become known as American folk culture.

The 1867 publication of *Slave Songs of the United States* is recognized by many scholars, to borrow Du Bois' description, as the 'first serious study of Negro American music'.[49] William Francis Allen, Charles Pickard Ware, and Lucy McKim Garrison compiled 136 song lyrics over several years and from a variety of sources: 88 songs originated from the isolated region known as the Sea Island regions (encompassing Georgia and South Carolina), while the others represented various other regions ranging from the Northeast Seaboard to the Gulf States. The first section of the book offers the background and details of this collection and states the reason for its publication: 'The musical capacity of the negro race has been recognized for so many years that it is hard to explain why no systematic effort has hitherto been made to collect and preserve their melodies'.[50] Although this was not in fact the first publication of 'slave songs' from the enslaved African community, it was the first widely recognized one and the most extensive study to date.

Slave Songs of the United States assisted in carving out the path of the professional discipline of American folklore studies. It represents a manifestation of the white frame that intended to illustrate newly freed Black people as 'serious and earnest'.[51] Throughout the text's introduction, terms such as 'barbaric' and 'civilised' are used to characterize the enslaved population and the effect of Emancipation respectively. They refer to the enslaved, for instance, as 'half barbarous people' in whom the 'chief part of the negro music is civilized in its character – partly composed under the influence of association with the whites'.[52] The white compilers over-emphasize the religious music of the enslaved population and how it was influenced by white Christianity and culture to evidence 'civilization'. At the same time, they intentionally undercut the importance of secular music, which they portray as 'devil's music', consistent with a then-acceptable (white) perception of Black people and culture. This resulted in what Jon Cruz has called 'a new *cultural-interpretive reservation*'.[53] 'Not only did the romantic perspective of the collectors prevent them from complete dedication to the transformation of the freedman's social status', as Sandra Jean Graham writes, 'but their limited recognition [also] confined black expressivity'.[54] First through the mockery of minstrelsy, then in the manner that spirituals were preserved and distributed, the Black sound was foreclosed by the white gaze – and through that gaze, Black voices and experiences were altered, ignored, or erased.

The mainly white public interest in Black spirituals moved from scholarly narrative to public performance with the rise of the Fisk Jubilee Singers in the late nineteenth century. '[T]he world listened only half credulously until the Fisk Jubilee Singers sang the slave songs,' writes Du Bois in 1903.[55] This singing ensemble began in 1871 as an initiative to raise money for Fisk University in Nashville, Tennessee – a school of higher learning that focused on educating the Black community. The all-Black ensemble sang the songs that were at one time only heard within the private world of the enslaved, but the sound was purposely choreographed and produced for white sensibilities. A white music teacher at Fisk, George Leonard White, meticulously arranged the music to balance white Christian traditions, the history and music from the Black tradition of the students, and the expectations of the Black sound held by the majority-white audiences and the group's benefactors. The Fisk Jubilee Singers (and the many singing troupes that followed them) presented spirituals to majority-white audiences across the United States and in Europe for the latter half of the nineteenth century and beyond. Their popularity contributed to their sound being recognized as an American, or at least Black American, sound to emerging folk scholars and enthusiasts precisely at the time when it was being developed as a formal academic discipline. However, the Black voices and culture of Black people were often veiled even within Fisk's and other Black ensemble performances.

The neglect of the Black voice, without the filter and influence of whites, does not mean that Black people have not produced material on their music culture, even before the 1867 publication of *Slave Songs of the United States*. Work songs were commonly mentioned in North America and throughout the West Indies as the sounds created by those enslaved. In the mid-eighteenth century, references to the enslaved singing unified songs during tasks such as rowing a boat, hoeing a field, or grinding sugar were documented as being accompanied by music. Leisure music was also well documented early in the North American colonies and was so commonly heard that areas such as South Carolina and New Orleans attempted to regulate the types of instruments allowed in weekly Sunday gatherings. Religious music was not as regularly documented in the early decades of slavery. These early references to work and recreation songs and other secular songs were nevertheless almost entirely ignored within the foundation of the formal focus on Black folk music. These early sounds that were transmitted orally and encompassed the experiences and cultures of those enslaved were undoubtedly a part of the foundation of Black American music.

The corpus of texts known as slave narratives published throughout the nineteenth century offered to the reading public first-hand accounts of the Black sound for those willing to listen. In 1824, George Tucker includes detailed descriptions of work songs, specifically relating to corn shucking, in his account of slavery, *The Valley of Shenandoah*. Former bondsman William Wells Brown mentions slave song lyrics and the role they played in the enslaved community in his *Narrative of William Wells Brown, A Fugitive Slave*, published in 1847, and Solomon Northup describes his experience as an enslaved fiddler in his 1853 work, *Twelve Years a Slave*. One of the most prolific orators and writers of the nineteenth century, Frederick Douglass, also offers great insight into the importance of the Black sound. He not only offers song lyrics within his autobiography but also addresses the complexity of the Black sound. He explains that these songs expressed the 'highest joy and the deepest sadness', and with an example of the simplest lyrics – 'I am going away to the Great House Farm! O, yea! O, yea! O!' – Douglass illustrates how the Black sound was often heard as 'unmeaning jargon, but which nevertheless, [was] full of meaning to themselves' (the enslaved).[56] Lydia Parrish, a white woman collector of

Black music likewise noted 'The secretiveness of the Negro is ... the fundamental reason for our ignorance of the race and its background'.[57] The true and complex meanings of the music of enslaved Black people – whether concerning recreation, work, religion, or any other activity – were always intentionally hidden from white ears, often out of necessity.

The Black voices of Brown, Douglass, and Northup, among others, testify to the fact that the Black sound, whether sacred or secular, existed even if sometimes silenced as the field of American folklore developed. The American Folk-Lore Society was formed in 1888, beginning with 104 signatories from Canada and the United States who committed to methods 'of a scientific character' in the study and preservation of folk culture. The first issue of the society's *Journal* recognized Black Americans, specifically in the South, as being important 'for the collection of the fast-vanishing remains of Folk-Lore in America'.[58] This acknowledgement of Black music in formal scholarship began with a white gaze, focusing on sources such as *Slave Songs* and minstrel songs while neglecting actual Black voices. However, the rise of Black singers that deliberately chose not to continue the minstrel or coon genres began to gain national and international recognition during the late nineteenth and early twentieth centuries and contributed to the changing of the scholarly narrative.

From Blues to Hip Hop

The turn of the twentieth century witnessed the rise of a staggering variety of Black sounds in the United States and beyond: jazz, gospel, ragtime, string bands, prison songs, and the blues. Surprisingly, by the turn of the century, Du Bois' 'sorrow songs' would be associated more with secular sounds such as blues and soul, while more jubilant 'songs of praise' would become associated with the new religious genre of gospel. Throughout the history of Africans in America, the sacred and secular have always existed together regardless of how many have tried to distinguish them; the religious and secular music of the twentieth century was no different. As David Evans and Richard M. Raichelson point out, 'many well-known blues performers have "gone to God"; and an equally large number of religious performers are attentive to the style, if not the ideology, of blues'.[59]

The genre of blues developed over time and has a multiplicity of subgenres that represent the continual progression of the Black sound, while also illustrating evolving ideas of folk music. The secular sound of the blues originated in the predominantly rural regions of the American South and was used to express Black inhabitants' joys, sorrows, and struggles. As Samuel A. Floyd, Jr. writes, the blues 'took its most significant features from the calls, cries, and hollers of field slaves and street vendors and from the spirituals of brush harbors and church house'.[60] The blues was the first major and distinctive sound created by African Americans after Emancipation. Blues material, as the name suggests, reflected themes of mistreatment, struggle, and perseverance. As the blues travelled and became commercialized through the development of the record company, there were debates if its sound should still be classified as folk music. In 1946, Huddie William Ledbetter, often referred to by his stage name Lead Belly, brought together traditional folk music and rural blues within an album titled *Negro Folk Songs*. He was first introduced to the scholarly field by John and Alan Lomax, two of the most influential American folklorists, during their time attempting to gather 'songs of the Negro labourer' within the segregated prison system across the Southern states.[61] Lead Belly would become synonymous with a revival of Black American folk traditions and assist with ushering in recognition of a secular sound that for many years remained hidden.

Intertwined with the blues, folk tales from Brer Rabbit to Anansi the Spider, are recognized as a vital aspect of Black culture.[62] Folk ballads are narratives that tell stories and create folk heroes, such as the popular John Henry folktale. Within the genre of blues, folk ballads began as part of oral traditions that were later composed formally, without losing their folk music attributes. The folk story and song known as 'Stagger Lee' (also found written as Stagolee, Stackolee, and other variations) illustrates the progression of oral tradition to music and eventually its commercialization and mass popularity. This, essentially, is the story of blues and many other Black folk sounds. The story goes that in 1895 William Lyons was shot by Lee Shelton after an argument at a bar in St. Louis, Missouri. Lee Sheldon, also known as 'Stag Lee', was reported in the local newspaper as a former 'Negro politician' and the proprietor of a brothel-style establishment.[63] With the public dispute and shooting, 'Stag Lee' received notoriety as a renegade and secured his place as a Black folk hero (or anti-hero). The first printed lyrics of the folk-blues song 'Stagger Lee' appeared as early as 1902 or 1903, and its widespread popularity was recognized by scholars such as John and Alan Lomax and various folklore societies in the early twentieth century. As Cecil Brown states, 'Stagolee is authentic African-American folklore ... Stagolee has taken musical shape as ballad, as blues, as jazz, as epic, as folk song, and as rap'.[64] In a little over a century, the story of Stagger Lee (with the name in its various iterations) has been the subject of over 400 songs that range dramatically in genres and are performed by renowned Black and white performers including Ma Rainey, Duke Ellington, Bob Dylan, Loyd Price, Nick Cave and the Bad Seeds, and the Grateful Deal among others.[65]

Popular Black music, as Kip Lornell argues, 'with its strong roots in traditional forms, the church, and in the streets, has witnessed the emergence and spread of rhythm and blues (R&B), Motown and soul, funk, and rap since the close of World War II'.[66] This statement encompasses a broad view of music and the evolution and influence of Black folk music. The racist foundation of the field – which debated the primitive-versus-civilized qualities of Black people and their ability to create an American sound – has progressed into conversations regarding the manifest diversity and widespread influences of Black sounds across the globe. The most popular Black music today may not seem to have any relationship with the banjo, African cultural continuances, or enslavement, but for those who understand the history and have a discerning ear, the connection is clear.

For example, rap music – a sound created within oral traditions and with strong regional associations much like the music of the enslaved and the blues – is not often thought about or categorized as folk music. And yet, as songwriter and rapper Shaughn Richardson declares, 'It's a culture born out of oppression ... I think hip hop is folk music because it represents a people, place and time where they are'.[67] Rap music is in many ways one more evolution of Black folk tradition in the oratorical skills from signifying, playing the dozens, call and response, and constructions of folk heroes, or anti-heroes. Much like folk music, rap can also be viewed as labour songs, protest music, and associated with many other groups through its narrative delivery style. Similar overlaps occur in the United Kingdom, where artists crossing folk, protest, and hip hop have been dubbed 'folk hoppers'. Charlotte Richardson Andrews describes this confluence centred on cities such as Bristol:

Since the crackle of dissent is rising out of urban spaces, it's hardly surprising that politically conscious, city-dwelling folksters are weaving their music with the strands of hip-hop. The two may seem odd bedfellows, having emerged out of different lands and eras, but the two have much in common. Both are oral traditions, rooted in community-driven narratives, and both are beloved for expressing the pleasures and struggles of everyday people.[68]

Comparably, the folk band Carolina Chocolate Drops intermixes foundational sounds from their ancestors, such as jugs and banjos, with the newer genre of rap by incorporating beatboxing – a vocal percussion technique using the mouth. As one country music reviewer wrote about the Carolina Chocolate Drops, 'Even though you think of beat boxing as a more modern art form, believe it or not, it does have some history in the roots, and fits firmly within the realm of the Chocolate Drops' throwback concept, especially since it is not a featured element in their music, but just another tool in their bag, no different than a banjo and the bones.'[69]

'I know little of music and can say nothing in technical phrase', wrote DuBois in 1903, 'but I know something of men, and knowing them, I know that these songs are the articulate message' of a people to the world.[70] These words from *The Souls of Black Folk* offer an almost prophetic message. Black music in the United States has a complicated history filled with racist ideas and constructs, but it offers a truly American sound. Whether pioneered by Shaughn Richardson or Angeline Morrison, the Black sound continues to evolve, as does its place within the world of folk and traditional music. The relationship between folk music studies and Black music can be summed up by white British rapper Dizraeli: 'The two scenes might not want a lot to do with each other, but they share huge common ground, and more people are coming to realize that. It's an exciting thing.'[71]

Notes

1. Robert Loss, 'Past Present Future: An Interview with the Carolina Chocolate Drops'. *PopMatters*, 27 February 2012. www.popmatters.com/154927-past-present-future-2495881822.html.
2. Sarah Esquivel, 'The Past, Present and Future of Racial Bias at the Grammys'. *Study Breaks*, 6 December 2020. https://studybreaks.com/culture/music/grammys-2021.
3. Robin Denselow, 'Carolina Chocolate Drops – Review'. *The Guardian*, 24 January 2012. www.theguardian.com/music/2012/jan/24/carolina-chocolate-drops-live-review.
4. Sophia Alvarez Boyd, 'Breaking Down the Legacy of Race in Traditional Music in America'. *National Public Radio*, 25 July 2020. www.npr.org/2020/07/25/895112760/breaking-down-the-legacy-of-race-in-traditional-music-in-america.
5. Garth Cartwright, 'Angeline Morrison: "I can count on one hand the times I've been in a folk club with other people of colour"'. *The Guardian*, 7 October 2022. www.theguardian.com/music/2022/oct/07/angeline-morrison-i-can-count-on-one-hand-the-times-ive-been-in-a-folk-club-with-other-people-of-colour.
6. Cartwright, 'Angeline Morrison'.
7. Cartwright, 'Angeline Morrison'.

8. 'Quick Hits: An Interview with the Carolina Chocolate Drops'. *PBS*, 18 June 2012. www.pbs.org/video/sound-tracks-quick-hits-interview-carolina-chocolate-drops/.
9. Jerome Weeks, 'African American Roots Music Fest Spotlights Banjos, Fiddles in Fort Worth'. *KERA News*, 16 March 2022. www.keranews.org/arts-culture/2022-03-16/african-american-roots-music-fest-comes-to-fort-worth.
10. Paul Ruta, 'A Quest to Return the Banjo to Its African Roots'. *Smithsonian Voices*, 16 February 2021. www.smithsonianmag.com/blogs/smithsonian-center-folklife-cultural-heritage/2021/02/16/quest-return-banjo-its-african-roots.
11. Kristina R. Gaddy, *Well of Souls: Uncovering the Banjo's Hidden History*. New York: W. W. Norton, 2022, 284.
12. George Pinckard, *Notes on the West Indies*, 2nd ed. London: Baldwin, Cradock and Joy, 1816, 97–103.
13. See Dena J. Epstein, *Sinful Tunes and Spirituals: Black Folk Music to the Civil War*. Urbana: University of Illinois Press, 1977.
14. See Robert B. Winans, 'The Folk, the Stage, and the Five-String Banjo in the Nineteenth Century'. *Journal of American Folklore* 89/354 (1976): 407–437.
15. See Dale Cockrell, 'Jim Crow, Demon of Disorder'. *American Music* 14/2 (1996): 161–184.
16. On this broader history, see E. Patrick Johnson, *Appropriating Blackness: Performance and the Politics of Authenticity*. Durham, NC: Duke University Press, 2003.
17. Jeffrey Green, 'Minstrel Shows in Britain'. In *The Oxford Companion to Black British History*, ed. David Dadydeen, John Gilmore, and Cecily Jones, 299–30. Oxford: Oxford University Press, 2007, 300.
18. Robert B. Winans and Elias Kaufman, 'Minstrel and Classic Banjo: American and English Connections'. *American Music* 12/1 (1994): 1–30, 1.
19. Matthew D. Morrison, 'Race, Blacksound, and the (Re)Making of Musicological Discourse', *Journal of the American Musicological Society* 72/3 (2019): 781–823, 782.
20. See Sam Dennison, *Scandalize My Name: Black Imagery in American Popular Music*. New York: Garland, 1982.
21. Cartwright, 'Angeline Morrison'.
22. David Pratt, 'Angeline Morrison – the Sorrow Songs: Folk Songs of Black British Experience'. *Folk Radio*, 26 September 2022. www.folkradio.co.uk/2022/09/angeline-morrison-the-sorrow-songs-album-review/.
23. See the Introduction by Henry Louis Gates, Jr. to W. E. B. Du Bois, *The Souls of Black Folk*, ed. B. H. Edwards. New York: Oxford University Press, 2008, vii.
24. Du Bois, *The Souls of Black Folk*, 177.
25. Ray Stannard Baker, *Following the Color Line: An Account of Negro Citizenship in the American Democracy*. New York: Doubleday, 1908, 28.
26. See Reiko Hillyer, 'Relics of Reconciliation: The Confederate Museum and Civil War Memory in the New South'. *The Public Historian* 33/4 (2011): 35–62.

27. See Gaines Foster, *Ghosts of the Confederacy: Defeat, the Lost Cause and the Emergence of the New South, 1865–1913*. New York: Oxford University Press, 1988.
28. See Katrina Dyonne Thompson, *Ring Shout, Wheel About: The Racial Politics of Music and Dance in North American Slavery*. Urbana: University of Illinois Press, 2014.
29. See James H. Dorman, 'Shaping the Popular Image of Post-Reconstruction American Blacks: The "Coon Song" Phenomenon of the Gilded Age'. *American Quarterly* 40/4 (1988): 450–471.
30. Houston A. Baker, Jr., *Modernism and the Harlem Renaissance*. Chicago: University of Chicago Press, 1987, 17. See also Scott Herring, 'Du Bois and the Minstrels'. *MELUS* 22/2 (1997): 3–17.
31. W. E. B. Du Bois, *The Gift of Black Folk: The Negroes in the Making of America*. Boston, MA: The Stratford Co., 1924, 182.
32. Du Bois, *The Gift of Black Folk*, 275.
33. Du Bois, *The Gift of Black Folk*, 280–281.
34. Du Bois, *The Gift of Black Folk*, 282.
35. Cecil J. Sharp, *One Hundred English Folk Songs*. Boston: Oliver Ditson Company, 1916, xvi.
36. Jean R. Freedman, *Peggy Seeger: A Life of Music, Love, and Politics*. Urbana: University of Illinois Press, 2020, 140.
37. Fred J. Hay, 'Black Musicians in Appalachia: An Introduction to Affrilachian Music'. *Black Music Research Journal* 23/1–2 (2003): 1–19, 5.
38. Samuel Forcucci, *A Folk Song History of America: America Through Its Songs*. Englewood Cliffs: Prentice-Hall, 1984, 23.
39. Ross Cole, *The Folk: Music, Modernity, and the Political Imagination*. Oakland: University of California Press, 2021, 105–106.
40. Joe R. Feagin, *The White Racial Frame: Centuries of Racial Framing and Counter-Framing*, 3rd ed. Abingdon: Taylor & Francis, 2020, 5.
41. Bruno Nettl, *An Introduction to Folk Music in the United States*. Detroit: Wayne State University Press, 1960, 54.
42. See George Pullen Jackson, *White and Negro Spirituals: Their Life Span and Kinship*. New York: J. J. Augustin, 1943.
43. Du Bois, *The Souls of Black Folk*, 181–182.
44. Du Bois, *The Souls of Black Folk*, 182.
45. Samuel A. Floyd, Jr., *The Power of Black Music: Interpretation of Its History from Africa to the United States*. New York: Oxford University Press, 1995, 5.
46. Olaudah Equiano, *The Interesting Life of Olaudah Equiano, or Gustavus Vassa, the African*. London: 1789, 45.
47. Maria Diedrich, Henry Louis Gates, Jr., and Carl Pedersen, 'The Middle Passage between History and Fiction: Introductory Remarks'. In *Black Imagination and the Middle Passage*, ed. Maria Diedrich, Henry Louis Gates, Jr., and Carl Pederson, 5–20. New York: Oxford University Press, 1999, 8.

48. See Thompson, *Ring Shout, Wheel About*, 42–68.
49. Du Bois, *The Gift of Black Folk*, 275.
50. William Francis Allen, Charles Pickard Ware, and Lucy McKim Garrison, *Slave Songs of the United States*. Boston: Applewood Books, 1867, i.
51. Allen, Ware, Garrison, *Slave Songs*, vi.
52. Allen, Ware, Garrison, *Slave Songs*, vi.
53. Jon Cruz, *Culture on the Margins: The Black Spiritual and the Rise of American Cultural Interpretation*. Princeton: Princeton University Press, 1999, 127.
54. Sandra Jean Graham, *Spirituals and the Birth of a Black Entertainment Industry*. Champaign: University of Illinois Press, 2018, 13.
55. Du Bois, *The Souls of Black Folk*, 276.
56. Frederick Douglass, *Narrative of the Life of Frederick Douglass, an American Slave*. Boston: Anti-Slavery Office, 1849, 31.
57. Lydia Parrish, *Slave Songs of the Georgia Sea Islands*, Athens, GA: University of Georgia Press, 1992, 20.
58. Frank Boas, T. Frederick Crane, and J. Owen Dorsey, 'Front Matter'. *Journal of American Folklore* 1/1 (1888): 1–96, 1–2.
59. David Evans and Richard M. Raichelson, 'Tennessee Blues and Gospel: From Jug Band to Jubilee'. In *American Musical Traditions, Vol. II: African American Music*, ed. Jeff Todd Titon and Bob Carlin. New York: Schirmer, 2002, 59–63.
60. Floyd, *The Power of Black Music*, 73–78.
61. John A. Lomax and Alan Lomax, *Negro Folk Songs as Sung by Lead Belly*. New York: The Macmillan Company, 1936, ix.
62. See, for instance, Courtney Terry, 'It Ain't Trickin' If You Got It: Pre-Colonial African Trickster Deity Traditions Manifest in New Millennium Rap Music'. *Phylon* 54/2 (2017): 58–79.
63. Richard E. Buehler, 'Stacker Lee: A Partial Investigation into the Historicity of a Negro Murder Ballad'. *Keystone Folklore Quarterly* 12 (1967): 187–191, 188.
64. Cecil Brown, *Stagolee Shot Billy*. Cambridge, MA: Harvard University Press, 2003, 4.
65. See Mike Hobart, 'Stagger Lee – From Bar-Room Brawl to Black Resistance'. *Financial Times*, 11 July 2018. https://ig.ft.com/life-of-a-song/stagger-lee.html.
66. Kip Lornell, *Exploring American Folk Music: Ethnic, Grassroots, and Regional Traditions in the United States*. Jackson: University Press of Mississippi, 2012, 288.
67. Sam Ray-Johnson, 'Hip Hop: The Folk Music of America'. *Funk Punk Lives*, 13 February 2021. www.funkpunklives.com/blog/hip-hop-the-folk-music-of-america.

68. Charlotte Richardson Andrews, 'Hip-Hop and Folk Meet in a New Wave of Protest Music'. *The Guardian*, 6 November 2012. www.theguardian.com/music/musicblog/2012/nov/06/hip-hop-folk-protest-music.
69. Trigger Coroneos, 'Carolina Chocolate Drops: True Diversity in "Leaving Eden"'. *Saving Country Music*, 9 March 2012. www.savingcountrymusic.com/carolina-chocolate-drops-true-diversity-in-leaving-eden/.
70. Du Bois, *The Souls of Black Folk*, 179.
71. Andrews, 'Hip-Hop and Folk Meet'.

17 | Women in the Margins

ELIZABETH BENNETT

In this chapter, I explore three female folk song collectors – and three women from whom they collected songs – to provide wider commentary on the contributions of women to the first English folk song revival and their marginalization. This work builds on my previous research into the role of women in folk music and feminist practices in the archive, and contributes to a growing resurgence of interest in women and folk music.[1] In recent years there has been a turn to recognize the contributions of female folk song collectors within the first folk song revival, as well as a renewed interest in the seminal contributions of women to the second folk song revival.[2] Additionally, a contemporary resurgence of curiosity about folk song has seen the role of women more widely discussed.[3] There has been vital work undertaken by Esperance Folk, The Bit Collective, and FairPlé on folk music and gender equality in the United Kingdom and Ireland.[4] Other important initiatives include Lucy and Lisa Ward's podcast 'Thank Folk for Feminism', Amy Hollinrake's 'Loathly Lady' project, and Lucy Wright's manifesta *Folk is a Feminist Issue*. Angeline Morrison's work has also been a crucial addition to this picture, with its focus on the experience of women of colour (particularly Black British women) in her 2022 albums *The Sorrow Songs* and *The Brown Girl and other Folk Songs*. George Sansome and Sophie Crawford's work on the 'Queer Folk' project, moreover, has begun an intersectional discussion of gender and sexuality.

Georgina Boyes argued in 1993 that 'as individuals and as a constituent part of the revival, women are at best marginalized, at worst trivialized or ignored'.[5] Consequently, we know comparatively little about the singing practices of women, as Steve Roud acknowledges: 'it is the "public" singing events which are documented the best, and it is in precisely this sphere that women's behaviour was most constrained by social and practical restrictions'.[6] In what follows, I contend that by paying closer attention to what is found *in the margins* of manuscripts and other archival material, it is possible to glean information on the singing practices of women. These notes in the margins often did not make it into the final edits of publication in books and journals, and yet they can offer us vital clues about women's experience. By exploring three examples of collecting in the first folk song revival – using collected archival material, census records, and letters to piece together these exchanges – I illuminate the women who operated in the margins of the folk music movement and have since been marginalized by its history. This research joins and speaks to wider work taking place globally on women in folk music.[7]

In a 1905 lecture, Lucy Broadwood explained the barriers faced by female collectors, noting that (unlike women) men can 'make merry with songsters in the alehouse house over pipes and parsnip wine, or hobnob with the black sheep of the neighbourhood'.[8] Male singers, moreover, were often reluctant to sing material that they deemed too rude for a woman:

> Perhaps my oldest singer was a fine old Surrey carter ... he sang many songs, but one day he stopped, saying 'I knows a wonderful deal more, but they are not very good ones, most of them being outway rude'. It is this 'rudeness' that makes it hard for a women to collect. The singer is far too kind to offend her ears, but is almost always unable to humm or whistle an air apart from its words.[9]

Analogously, male collectors faced barriers collecting from women, as Cecil Sharp noted in 1907:

> [women] never perform in public, and only very rarely when men are present. If you prevail upon a married woman to sing to you, you must call upon her when her man is away at work, that is, if he be a singer himself. She will never sing to you in his presence until you come to know both her and her husband very intimately.[10]

The domestic sphere is often mentioned as the most common arena for women's singing, accompanying everyday labour in and around the house. Sabine Baring-Gould, for instance, recounts an experience of collecting from a female singer in 1895 as follows:

> There is an old grandmother on Dartmoor from whom I have had songs. She sings ancient ballads, walking about and pursuing her usual avocations whilst singing. She cannot be induced to sit down and sing – then her memory fails, but she will sing whilst engaged in kneading bread, washing, driving the geese out of the room, feeding the pig: naturally, this makes it a matter of difficulty to note her melodies. One has to run after her, from the kitchen to the pigsty, or to the well-head and back, pencil and note-book in hand.[11]

A domestic setting may well have been only one of the spaces in which women sang, but it was where they were most commonly collected from. Ginette Dunn offers an illuminating perspective on the social constraints faced by women in her study of the vernacular musical practices of Blaxhall and Snape during the 1970s, for which she conducted extensive interviews with women who were born and raised between the two World Wars. She observed that

> Whereas the majority of the men in Snape and Blaxhall are pub centred in their singing, very few of the women have relied upon the pub as their place of performance. They have found their audiences variously in their children, in women's club meetings, and with the men at village concerts and socials, at harvest frolics, at charity concerts and old folks' meetings, at wedding parties, and also in the pubs ... Overall, the singing habits of the women have been far more varied than those of the men.[12]

This description underscores the importance of what Heike Roms has called 'archival practices of care', and that dedicated time with archival materials might begin to reveal more about women singers than we have previously known.[13] Furthermore, it confirms to me that rather than being fixed entities, archives are in fact a process to which we can contribute, 'constituted through continual practices of care'.[14] As a corrective to received accounts of folk song in England, the following series of encounters between women singers and song collectors demonstrates what we might be able to discover and indeed imagine about these neglected histories.

Lucy Broadwood and Lucy Grahame

Lucy Broadwood's life is one of the better documented of the women discussed here. Her diaries are held by Surrey History Centre and a biography of her was written in 2013 by Dorothy de Val. Arguably, however, the predominance of Cecil Sharp in the later stages of the first folk song revival worked to eclipse some of the vital contributions made by Lucy and other women. Consequently, this chapter joins with a wider movement to recognize Lucy's pioneering work.

Born in 1858, Lucy was the youngest of 12 Broadwood children.[15] The Broadwoods lived mainly in London until 1864, when her father inherited the family estate in Lyne, on the border of Surrey and Sussex. Lucy's family were middle-class landowners with a well-known piano manufacturing business, John Broadwood and Sons, and Lucy was able to live on a private income for her entire life. Music was important to her, with Lucy becoming an accomplished singer and pianist. After the death of her parents, she lived independently in her own flat in London. Carlisle Mansions was a large block of mansion flats in Victoria, and for many years she shared number 84 with her niece Barbara Craster, a housemaid, and a cook. Her financial independence meant that she was able to devote much of her life to a wide range of musical interests. She played a pivotal role in the first folk song revival, collecting both English and Scottish folk songs, and becoming a founding member of the Folk-Song Society.[16]

Her interest in folk songs was influenced by her uncle, Reverend John Broadwood (of private income) who lived in Sussex and later Lyne, and who produced a ground-breaking anthology entitled *Old English Songs* in 1843. During the 1880s Lucy collaborated with her cousin H. F. Birch Reynardson to bring her uncle's collection of songs to a wider audience. In 1889 they published *Sussex Songs*, with new accompaniments.[17] However, on publication the cover had Hubert's name, with Lucy's contribution only acknowledged in the preface.[18] In addition to the original sixteen songs, Lucy added nine new ones. As de Val notes, her methods included

> Soliciting songs from local people and her father. As her father had also had an interest in local song, there were family records of the tunes and texts, and the more obscure texts could also be checked against older printed sources, with which Lucy was becoming familiar... Lucy set the pattern for her later work by tracking down the origins of the tunes, checking the texts with printed sources and filling in any gaps or questionable lines with alternatives.[19]

Locations where her male contemporaries collected – such as local pubs, remote villages, and rural workplaces – were inaccessible to her as a woman. Given such obstacles, Lucy developed other means of collection, such as developing a wide written correspondence, though she would also actively seek singers herself and note their songs, as de Val mentions, 'often through the intervention of friends, who could provide introductions and mediate in some way'.[20]

Lucy Broadwood's class position afforded her a high degree of privilege. She could live independently, keep staff, remain unmarried, and draw from a private income to support her interests. As Joseph Williams affirms, her 'residence in London from 1893 onwards, combined with the private income afforded by her family's wealth, meant that she was able to wholeheartedly pursue her interest in folk music as well as participate actively in the music scene of the capital'.[21] Her family connections and social life in London, moreover, provided a wide and influential network. De Val states that she 'connected with a large number of people, many of whom were already famous, or would become so'.[22] However, considering aspects of identity through the lens of intersectionality allows for a more nuanced understanding of Broadwood's position to emerge. Intersectional analysis allows us to view 'categories of race, class, gender, sexuality, nation, ability, ethnicity, and age – among others – as interrelated and mutually shaping one another'.[23] In addition to the limitations of gender and class, illness, and disability are important factors in an intersectional understanding of historical figures. Lucy is known, for instance, to have suffered with depression and melancholy, which de Val states 'remained with her throughout her life, and she was often incapacitated by illness which kept her in bed for days, she often felt tired and ill and prone to what would now be called seasonal affective disorder'.[24] Lucy had contracted malaria and typhoid in 1887, with the after-effects of these illnesses continuing throughout her life and making her prone to fevers and chills; the more immediate effects of a treatment involving arsenic and iron meant that she lost nearly all her hair by her 29th birthday.[25] Using written correspondence as a collecting practice therefore enabled her to continue her work when she would not have been physically able to travel. Her significant contribution to the first folk song revival and key role in the Folk-Song Society, I suggest, were accomplished in spite of, and in response to, barriers of class, gender, and illness.

A woman by the name of Lucy Grahame sent Lucy Broadwood two letters in the spring of 1904. The first, sent on 23 April, contained four songs with words and music. On the top of the music manuscript for 'Lord Thomas and Fair Elinor', Lucy Grahame writes that 'these four songs were learnt orally from the daughters of a Kentish Squire; the last of whom died in 1865 at a very advanced age'.[26] She apologizes for the time it has taken her to send the songs, and discusses the difficulties of accurately noting down tunes she had heard in her childhood, her desire to help 'awaken an interest in the Folk Song Society' among her friends, and asking her niece to help copy out the words for 'Lord Thomas and Fair Annet', which Lucy Grahame had seen in an 1887 collection of old English ballads and believed shared many similarities with the version she knew as 'Lord Thomas and Fair Elinor'.[27] In the second letter, dated 16 May, Grahame thanks Broadwood for all she tells her about the 'old tunes' and agrees with her about the errors she may have made in transcribing the tunes. She also includes a fragment of the nursery rhyme 'There was an Old Women went up in a Basket', which Grahame describes as 'a song on the "gods and goddesses" which is not suitable for a lady to sing which I believe was composed by a Kentish Gentleman [probably] more than 100 years ago! – though I have seen a few verses of it in a Children's book'.[28] She includes only the first couple of lines, presumably owing to the rest of the version she knew not being suitable to relate to Broadwood. Returning to the similarities between the two Lord Thomas songs, Grahame also writes that 'in the course of a few weeks I may be spending a short time in London and if you think it likely that a personal interaction might be of any help ... I would be pleased to call and see you'.[29]

There is nothing in the existing archival material to suggest how, why, and when Lucy Broadwood and Lucy Grahame began corresponding or how they were put in contact with each other, and Lucy Grahame's biographical details are limited. However, it is possible through census, birth, marriage, and death records to flesh out some of the details of Lucy Grahame's life. She was born Lucy Rayden in 1833 in Deptford, Kent, to merchant W. H. Rayden and his wife, Sarah. In both the 1841 and 1861 census, she is living with her family in Greenwich, then part of Kent.[30] The next record I was able to find on Lucy was her wedding to William Grahame, a man of private means, in St. Leonards-on-Sea, Sussex, on 20 December 1877.[31] Thereafter, she lived with William and his children in a house in Richmond, where they employed four domestic servants.[32] William Grahame had been a successful merchant in Auckland, who later returner to London and held a position on the London board of the National Bank of New Zealand until 1893 and died aged 82 in 1894.[33] Following this, in the 1901 census, Lucy is listed as a 68-year-old widow living on private means at 3 Marwick Terrace, St. Leonards-on-Sea in Sussex.[34] She is head of the household, and living with her is her 66-year-old sister Marianna Rayden. At the time of sending the songs to Broadwood, Lucy Grahame was living at 3 Markwick Terrace and would have been 71 years of age. In the 1911 census, she is listed as a widowed 77-year-old woman living as a boarder at 57 Marina Street, St. Leonards on Sea, a private nursing home.[35] Lucy's death is listed in the probate as follows: 'Lucy Grahame of 3 Markwick Terrace, St. Leonards-on-Sea, widow dies 30th of April 1912 at 57 Marina Street St. Leonards on Sea. Probate 25 June to Marianne Rayden spinster and William Rayden esquire. Effects £7643 11s. 4d.'[36]

Though these facts are not extensive, they allow us to glean a little information about the singer and her life. They tell us that her father was a merchant, that she socialized with the daughters of a Squire, married a husband of private means and social standing, lived in houses that employed staff, and bequeathed a substantial sum upon her death. As C. J. Bearman has observed, 'there were substantial contributions from people of Lucy Broadwood's own social standing who remembered the singing of grandparents or nurses in childhood'.[37] Thus, both Lucy

Grahame and the sisters that she learnt the songs from were not part of the rural labouring classes more commonly associated with folk singing. This association between folk song and unlettered peasants was shaped in large part by the politically driven mythologizing of Cecil Sharp, whose nationalistic and indeed racist theories, became, as Ross Cole argues, 'despite severe criticism from a range of contemporaries ... the dominant way of understanding folk heritage across the world'.[38] An exploration of women in the margins of the folk music movement contributes to an understanding of the diversity of singers collected from and of collectors whose approach and discourse differed from Sharp's prevailing ideologies.

Anne Geddes Gilchrist and Agnes Ford

Anne Geddes Gilchrist was a prolific song collector in her home county of Lancashire and in Scotland, where her parents were from. She was a member of editorial boards for folk song societies for over forty years; gave public lectures; collected a considerable volume of songs, singing games, dances, and calendar customs; contributed a substantial number of annotations, articles, and reviews to learned journals, and received a Gold Badge from the English Folk Dance and Song Society as well as an OBE for services to folk music.[39] Despite these achievements, Anne remains a lesser-known figure, in large part, as Peter Snape argues, because she did not publish any books.[40] Nevertheless, as Lyn Wolz notes, 'Gilchrist's legacy to the folk music world is an important one, and her papers are waiting to be mined for further information'.[41]

Wolz notes that the majority of Anne's collecting was 'from family members or from people in the communities where she spent time' and that her 'connection was almost always through her acquaintance with someone the singers knew'.[42] Born in Manchester in 1863 to a 'large and artistic family', one of Anne's earliest musical memories was of her mother singing to the children.[43] Anne was musical from an early age and loved to listen to 'melodies of all kinds, not only her family's songs, but also church hymns, songs her nursemaids taught her, and singing games learned at her grandfather's house in Cheshire during Christmas visits'.[44] Both a singer and a pianist, she studied harmony and composition in Manchester and in '1886 was awarded a special Royal Academy of Music gold medal'.[45] Her father George Gilchrist is listed in the 1901 census as a retired bank manager, and the family employs domestic servants.[46] The Gilchrist family spent their holidays at Sunderland Point, a small coastal village near

Lancaster, and they became involved with the musical life of this community, arranging and performing in many concerts.[47] Anne later collected a number of folk songs from Sunderland Point and continued to visit her siblings who lived there for the rest of her life. She also collected songs in Southport, where she lived during the late 1800s and early 1900s, later settling in 1920 in the village of Stodday on the outskirts of Lancaster, which looks across the River Lune to Sunderland Point. During the first folk song revival, Anne was the only collector to focus on the North-West of England and contributed significantly to our knowledge of folk traditions in Lancashire.[48]

Anne's collecting in Sussex took place during her visits to her brother William Gilchrist, a presbyterian minister in Blackham, between 1905–07.[49] Anne mostly worked alone, writing out the words in longhand, although she sometimes used a sister or other helper to transcribe the lyrics while she noted down the tune.[50] There is only one letter on her collecting in Sussex, sent on 22 June 1906, in which Anne writes to Lucy Broadwood, 'I got altogether about two dozen songs from my few days with my brother at Blackham'.[51] Much like Lucy, Anne faced barriers in collecting on account of her gender and class, and whether certain songs were deemed suitable for her to hear as a woman. In her account of collecting from an old sailor in Southport, Anne recalled that he 'stopped halfway through a verse. Had he forgotten the rest? I asked. "It isn't that," he said solemnly "I'm trying to think of something that will do instead".'[52]

Agnes Ford of Withyham, Sussex, sang songs for Anne in 1906 and 1907. Anne also collected songs from Agnes' husband William and had already met and collected the song 'The Cottage in the Wood' from Agnes's daughter Ethel Ford in 1905. It is not clear how Anne knew to collect from Ethel. At the bottom of the manuscript she writes 'Ethel Ford from her father. Blackham, May 1905'.[53] She also notes under Ethel's version of 'The Farmer's Boy':

N.B. Do ask Ethel's father for 'The Old Grey Mare' (his crack song), her mother for 'Silvery' ('Silvery' was a riding on the King's highway – or something of the kind), a song about 'Barbery' (perhaps a version of Barbara Allen), and to ask Flora Coombes' mother for two songs 'The Mole Catcher' (the mole catcher returned home unexpectedly and caught a man in his traps 'the biggest mole that ever I did see' – a song apparently on the same theme as 'Hame came oor guidman at e'en'.) and 'The Banks of Sweet Dundee'.[54]

In the 1901 census, Agnes Ford is 42 and lives at Forge Cottage, Withyham, with her husband William Ford, a blacksmith aged 49, their 12-year-old son William and 8-year-old daughter Ethel.[55] This makes Ethel about 12 years old when Anne first collected from her in 1905, and Anne and William approximately 47 and 54 respectively in 1906. Agnes' birthplace is given as Cowden, just over the border from Withyham in Kent. Her father was a farmer who came from Brighton, Sussex, and her mother Jane Durrant came from Kent (no occupation given). Her husband William was born in nearby Chiddingstone, Kent. In the 1891 census, William, Agnes, and William are living in Southborough, Kent.[56] In the 1911 census, four years after Anne last visits in 1907, the Fords are still living in Withyham, Sussex, but at the new address of Blackham, Langton Green. They are still living there in the 1921 census; William is 71 and his occupation in shoeing and general smith; Agnes is 63 and her occupation is 'home duties'.[57] Agnes's death is recorded as 1924, making her approximately 65 when she died.[58]

Beyond these scant archival records, it is difficult to discover much about Agnes's life. However, the notes made by Anne Geddes Gilchrist afford a certain degree of insight into Agnes' singing practices. In her letter to Lucy Broadwood, Anne expresses hope that Lucy and the editorial board of the Folk-Song Society *Journal* will not be too disappointed by the songs, none of which show 'any signs of extreme antiquity' and which she fears are 'little more than texts on which to hang observations of various kinds!'[59] She reminds Lucy that 'it was you who encouraged me to write notes – and you can easily strike out what you consider superfluous or over-elaborate'.[60] At the bottom of 'Mother, Mother, Make My Bed' sung by Agnes in 1906, Anne notes 'Mrs Ford, learnt from her mother'; the same note is found in the margins of the manuscript for 'The Banks of the Sweet Dundee'.[61] Similar notes appear on other transcripts from other singers that Anne collected from in Sussex – by the side of the music for 'Green Bushes' a note reads 'Mrs Jenner, 70, from her mother Mrs Yeoman'.[62] Following Anne's note on 'The Farmer's Boy' to ask Flora Coomber's mother for two songs, she collected five songs from Elizabeth Coomber as well as three from Elizabeth and her husband William Coomber, a farm labourer (who also sang six for Anne himself). On the bottom of the manuscript for 'False Hearted Lover', Anne has marked 'Mrs Coomber from her sister'.[63] Next to the music for 'The Dark Eyed Sailor', Anne notes that this was sung by 'Mrs and the Misses Coombers'.[64]

Through close attention to Anne's notes insights can be gained into the transmission of songs between women, such as mother to daughter and sister to sister. The Coombers are living a few houses away from The Fords in the 1901 census, suggesting that Ethel Ford might have recommended

Elizabeth Coomber as a singer to Anne. On the manuscript of 'The Squire and the Milkmaid' collected from Miss Flora Coomber, Anne notes 'learnt from her mother. Her sister also sang it. Her mother had learnt it out of a song book'.[65] Anne's notes also show that women learnt songs from men, taught songs to men, and sang songs with men. Ethel Ford's version of 'The Cottage in the Wood', as well as 'The Farmer's Boy' carry the note 'learnt from her father the Blacksmith'.[66] On Mr Ford's song 'Sylvie', in turn, Anne has written the addendum, 'was learnt as a boy from the singer's "mother-in-law"' (i.e. step-mother).[67] The Fords and The Coombers represent the rural working classes commonly associated with folk song. However, Anne's collecting in Sussex also includes songs from Mrs Amabel Ludlow of Beech Green Park, who was married to Major Ludlow and had considerable private means. Anne collected three songs from Amabel, two of which have notes on where she learnt them from – 'Little Sir William' was learnt from a Miss Blythe and 'Lord Lovel' from her old family nurse.[68] One other song, 'Two Little Hares', is unattributed; however, it is written on paper headed with 'Beech Green, Withyham, Sussex', suggesting that it too was collected from Amabel, and indicating ways in which we might discover unattributed women's songs in the archive (where women's songs are sometimes catalogued under their husband's names).[69]

Dorothy Marshall and Bessie Knight

Dorothy Marshall was a folk song collector working in Sussex between 1912 and 1916 in partnership with the better known collector Clive Carey. Their material is housed in the Clive Carey collection at the Vaughan Williams Memorial Library at Cecil Sharp House in London. In the 1871 census Dorothy is four years old and living with her parents in Wiltshire, making her birth year approximately 1867. Her birthplace is given as France. Her father, Captain John George Don Marshall of the Gordon Highlanders, is a 45-year-old landowner, and her mother Catherine Marshall is 43. Also living at the property are her two-year-old brother Kenneth and three domestic servants.[70] I can find no entries for Dorothy in the 1881 and 1891 census (perhaps owing to Dorothy's father's job). In the 1901 census, Dorothy is 34 and living at Chithurst House in Sussex. She lives there with her parents, both of whom are now in their 70s, and three domestic servants (one of whom is Charles Moore, a 23-year-old coachman).[71] Following her father's death in 1906, in the 1911 census Dorothy is 44 and still living at Chithurst House with her mother; three domestic servants are recorded as living with them.⁷² Charles Moore is not recorded on the census, but Dorothy's correspondence to Carey confirms that he continued to work for them during this period. Dorothy died in 1916 and was buried in Chithurst on 27 April. At her time of death she was living in nearby Buriton, Petersfield.

Little is known about Dorothy's musical life before she began corresponding with Carey in 1911. However, George Frampton notes that Dorothy's father taught her three sea shanties he had learnt on an 'East India Company ship' in the 1850s, and that she knew some piano and had musical guests.⁷³ In her letters she discusses playing in the local Whistle and Fife band, many of whose members comprised the Chithurst Tipteeters (the Sussex term for Mummers, a festive troupe of actors), the revival of which Dorothy greatly encouraged. There is a black-and-white photograph of this ensemble taken in early January 1912, with seven tipteerers in full costume.⁷⁴ Two were Frank Dawtry and Frank Albery, singers from whom Dorothy and Carey also collected. Unlike Lucy Broadwood and Anne Geddes Gilchrist, no photograph remains of Dorothy Marshall, but through her letters and this photograph she documented some aspects of the people she collected from. In common with Broadwood, however, Dorothy faced an additional barrier to collecting on account of chronic illness, suffering badly from neuritis in both arms.

The Espérance Guild of Morris Dancers that Carey was working for at the time as a musical assistant contacted Dorothy in late 1910 to ask if she could assist Carey with his first collecting trip to Sussex. There is no evidence detailing how Dorothy was known to the Guild. However, even before Carey's arrival in Sussex on 27 February 1911, she had already collected nearly thirty songs from nearby villages.⁷⁵ Over the next two years, they collected together on Carey's visits, with Dorothy continuing to collect alone. Carey's final visits were in September and October 1912. Thereafter, there is no record of Carey visiting, although Dorothy remained in correspondence with him.⁷⁶ After her death in 1916, Carey visited her area of West Sussex in 1919 and collected from Mr Viney, the landlord of the George and Dragon, Houghton.⁷⁷

Her limited musicianship led to her recording singers on the phonograph – a novel method that preserved the singers' individual voices.⁷⁸ This introduced another vital contributor, her coachmen Charles Moore who sometimes drove her (and her phonograph) to singer's homes to collect songs. In addition to driving her, he would also occasionally undertake the collecting work himself when Dorothy was incapacitated. As she writes to Carey in July 1911, 'I did not get to Heyshott last night, but Moore [was] quite the collector, and his best find is "Lord Thomas and Fair Eleanor"'.[79] Her letters illuminate her understanding of, and respect for, the rural life and practices that these songs accompanied, and her participation in community activities such as the Trotton Whistle and Fife Band. In June 1911 Dorothy writes to Carey that the singers 'don't approve of singing on Sunday's and won't', and, moreover, to come down then would be pointless as 'there is a lot of Hay about and most of the men you want would very probably – almost certainly – be working till dark at it'.[80] She also attended and hosted practices for the band, writing in December 1911 to Carey that 'you would love the Tipteerers all stamping about in Mrs Brown's cottage & old Brown and Alberry reminding each other of all the songs they've ever heard – lots of them!', and in November 1911 that 'I have just had the whole of the "whistle pipe band" here, dancing and singing in my dining room – such a racket!'[81] She was also sensitive to the social nature of these songs and would organize communal singarounds for singers: 'I want to have a dance and a "singsong" while you're here and get the plough boys together'.[82] Dorothy used these singsongs to prompt singers struggling with their repertoires, including David Miles from Heyshott who knew 100 or more songs but forgot parts of them: 'Miles will collect the others and I will provide beer and Moore will take the phonograph, so we may do something and I will report if it is worth your while to come down then'.[83]

Dorothy collected from Bessie Knight with Clive Carey at some point during his visit between 1 and 3 January 1912, and then again on a solo visit later in 1912. In total Bessie sang ten songs for collection. On the manuscript for 'Caroline and her Brisk Sailor Bold', Dorothy notes that the song was collected from 'B. Knight, Minstead, Stedham, Keeper's daughter, songs learnt from her father'.[84] Her singing is also written about in an untitled newspaper clip, which forms part of the collection of papers donated to the Vaughan Williams Memorial Library by Dorothy's brother after her death. The newspaper clip describes a local performance of a Tipteerers play and a number of songs from local singers, and describes Bessie Night singing 'Fair Phoebe and her Dark Eyed Sailor', a song she had learnt from her father, as 'scor[ing] a great success'.[85] It also states that her father resides at 'Tyelands'. Although Bessie's area is noted as Minstead in Dorothy's notes, Tyelands is administratively in the neighbouring village Woolbeding in some records, and Bepton in others. In the 1911 census, Bessie (Elizabeth) is 26 and living at Tyelands with her parents John and Elizabeth Knight, and three elder sisters. Bessie is the youngest of seven, one boy and six girls. Her father's occupation is listed as gamekeeper, and although Bessie's occupation is not listed, her sisters' occupations include schoolteacher, ladies companion, and household work.[86] There appears to have been both a Tyelands House and a Tyelands Cottage, with the Knights living in the former. According to the 1921 census, Bessie is 36 and continues to live at Tyelands. Her parents are in their 70s, and three elder sisters also remain living at Tyelands. In the 1939 registry, with both parents dead, she still lives at Tyelands and her occupation is listed as a poultry farmer; three sisters also still live there.[87] Bessie's death is recorded on 25 May 1940; she is aged 55 years and resides at Tyelands.[88] It is difficult to ascertain census information on her, in part because she remained single, which has the effect of obscuring such women in the archive even further. However, what it is possible to observe is that of her six siblings, Bessie inherited a singing tradition and songs from her father, and that she sang as least once publicly to great success.

It is important to note that wherever possible Carey gave Dorothy full credit for her work. In a letter of October 1911, Dorothy teases him and makes it clear that she considered their work a joint endeavour, 'All right Mr Carey, I shall now go about saying that you have bagged all of our discoveries and are vaunting them as your own in the Sharpist way. Of course, they are yours as much as anybody's. I should never have got the music but for you' (her reference here being to Cecil Sharp).[89] But amateur collectors such as Dorothy consequently become obscured in and by the archive, placed under the headings of better-known figures. Even small details like her songs being catalogues under CC – Clive Carey – effectively hide her contribution, and it is incumbent upon historians to consider the ways in which, to quote Maryanne Dever, 'feminist thought and feminist practice [might] frame archives'.[90] Dorothy's work was further obscured through the loss of her phonograph cylinders, which are thought to have been discarded in the 1960s owing to damage. Had these survived they would have been a significant collection of recordings, and such a collection may have helped to link English folk music at the turn of the century with the names and voices of the singers themselves, rather than (as Boyes notes) with the names of collectors.[91] Dorothy Marshall's legacy to folk music is an important one, and her papers are waiting to be mined for further information on the singing practices of women.

Revisiting the Archive

By exploring the margins of archival material, it is possible to begin to see varied circumstances and rich biographical details that tell us something –

if not everything – about the women who were singing these songs. The three case studies show songs passing from mother to daughter, sisters to friends, fathers to daughters, mothers to sons, and recommendations of singers by other singers – suggesting not just a female familial tradition, but also one in which men participated. Moreover, to be known to each other, we see that these singers sang outside of family circles. Through census research, it is possible to know a little more of the circumstances of their lives. Such a focus also enables a more nuanced and intersectional approach to the women who collected these songs. All three collectors in this chapter were white, single, childless, musically educated, lived on a private income, and came from middle or upper-middle class backgrounds. To explore their gender, disability, and illness is not to negate their class advantage, but rather to add nuance to it. In some cases, their gender was a generative constraint – meaning that they drew on correspondence, their social circles, and the communities they lived in for their collection, rather than public houses or male-dominated work-places. Moreover, elucidating their physical and mental health allows us to see their collections in the context of their embodied experience and the challenges posed alongside their gender.

Lucy Broadwood's work involved songs being, as Cole writes, 'harmonized and arranged for voice and piano, uprooted from the field and conveyed as objects to the middle-class drawing room'.[92] But her collecting also demonstrates these songs being sung in their unaccompanied form by people from the middle classes. As we can see from Lucy Grahame's letters, moreover, correspondence as a form of collection often afforded access to the personal context of a song. Both Dorothy Marshall's participation in the local Whistle and Fife band and Anne Geddes Gilchrist's lifelong participation and organization of musical concerts in Sunderland are evidence of collecting practices embedded in their respective communities, suggesting that some collectors were at times concerned with the 'lived experience [and] the social world' of singers.[93]

Ultimately, an intersectional, feminist approach to the archive provides rich opportunities to discover more about female song collectors and the women from whom they collected. A project that explores women in the folk archives and their connections to each other is long overdue. By paying attention to the marginalization of women, other marginal subjects in the folk revival will in turn become more visible, such as the neglected folk traditions of northern regions exemplified by Lancashire in Anne's collection. There is considerably more to say about each collector I discuss here, and a vast amount of research still to be done on female singing traditions around the world, but this chapter demonstrates the insights that can be gained from exploring the margins of history and the importance of a feminist re-reading of the archive.

Notes

1. Elizabeth Bennett, *Performing Folk Songs: Affect, Landscape and Repertoire*. New York: Bloomsbury Academic, 2024.
2. See for example: Dorothy de Val, *In Search of Song: The Life and Times of Lucy Broadwood*. Farnham: Ashgate, 2011; Simona Pakenham, *Singing and Dancing Wherever She Goes: The Life of Maud Karpeles*. London: English Folk Dance and Song Society, 2011; Shirley Collins, *All in the Downs: Reflections on Life, Landscape and Song*. London: Strange Attractor Press, 2018; and Peggy Seeger, *First Time Ever: A Memoir*. London: Faber and Faber, 2017. Other initiatives include the Gilchrist Collective; Lucy Neal's 'Mary Neal Project', 'Access Folk', and the 2019 show 'She Moved through the Fair: The Legend of Margaret Barry' held at King's Place.
3. Notable examples include the mini-festival 'Trad. Reclaimed: Women in Folk Music' held at Kings Place in 2019, the 'Women and Traditional Folk Music' symposium at the University of Galway's Centre for Irish Studies in 2019, and a BBC Radio 4 Woman's Hour special on 'Women and Folk Music' broadcast in 2022.
4. See EFDSS, 'Movement for Positive Change Gathers Momentum'. 2021. www.efdss.org/about-us/what-we-do/news/10471-eds-esperance-momentum.
5. Georgina Boyes, *The Imagined Village: Culture, Ideology and the English Folk Revival*. Manchester: Manchester University Press, 1993, xii.
6. Steve Roud, *Folk Song in England*. London: Faber and Faber, 2017, 45.
7. See, for example, Anjali Capila, *Images of Women in the Folk Songs of Garhwal Himalayas*. New Delhi: Concept Publishing, 2002; Smita Tewari Jassal, *Unearthing Gender: Folk Songs of North India*. Durham, NC: Duke University Press, 2012; Carole Blackwell, *Tradition and Society in Turkmenistan: Gender, Oral Culture and Song*. Richmond: Curzon, 2001; and Brahma Prakash, *Cultural Labour: Conceptualising the 'Folk Performance' in India*. New Delhi: Oxford University Press, 2019.
8. Lucy Broadwood, 'On the Collecting of English Folksong'. *Proceedings of the Musical Association* (1905): 89–109, 95.
9. Broadwood, 'On the Collecting of English Folksong', 101.
10. Cecil Sharp, 'Folk-Song Collecting'. *The Musical Times* 48 (1907): 16–18, 18.
11. Sabine Baring-Gould, *A Garland of Country Songs*. London: Methuen, 1895, viii.

12. Ginette Dunn, *The Fellowship of Song: Popular Singing Traditions in East Suffolk*. London: Croom Helm, 1980, 112.
13. Heike Roms, 'Archiving Legacies: Who Cares for Performance Remains?' In *Performing Archives/Archives of Performance*, ed. Gunhild Borggreen and Rune Gade, 35–52. Copenhagen: Museum Tusculanum Press, 2013, 38.
14. Roms, 'Archiving Legacies', 48.
15. de Val, *In Search of Song*, 12.
16. de Val, *In Search of Song*, 4.
17. de Val, *In Search of Song*, 46.
18. de Val, *In Search of Song*, 47.
19. de Val, *In Search of Song*, 46.
20. de Val, *In Search of Song*, 150.
21. Joseph Williams, *England's Folk Revival and the Problem of Identity in Traditional Music*. London: Routledge, 2022, 160.
22. de Val, *In Search of Song*, 1.
23. Patricia Hill Collins and Sirma Bilge, *Intersectionality*. Cambridge: Polity Press, 2020, 1.
24. de Val, *In Search of Song*, 4.
25. de Val, *In Search of Song*, 44–45.
26. Lucy Grahame, 'Lord Thomas was a Bold Forester'. Vaughan Williams Memorial Library, 1904: LEB/5/182/1.
27. *Letter from Lucy Grahame to Lucy Broadwood, 23rd April 1904.* Vaughan Williams Memorial Library: LEB/5/184.
28. *Letter from Lucy Grahame to Lucy Broadwood, 16th May 1904.* Vaughan Williams Memorial Library: LEB/5/183.
29. *Letter from Lucy Grahame to Lucy Broadwood, 16th May 1904.*
30. Lucy Rayden, *1841 England Census*; Lucy Rayden, *1861 England Census*.
31. Lucy Rayden, *East Sussex, England, Church of England Marriages and Banns, 1754–1936*. East Sussex Records Office.
32. Lucy Grahame, *1881 England Census*; Lucy Grahame, *1891 England Census*.
33. William Grahame, Obituary. *New Zealand Herald*, 24 December 1900, 2 [supplement].
34. Lucy Grahame, *1901 England Census*.
35. Lucy Grahame, *1911 England Census*.
36. Lucy Grahame, *National Probate Calendar (Index of Wills and Administrations), 1858–1995*, 30 April 1912.
37. C. J. Bearman, 'The Lucy Broadwood Collection: An Interim Report'. *Folk Music Journal* 7/3 (1997): 357–365, 361.
38. Ross Cole, *The Folk: Music, Modernity, and the Political Imagination*. Oakland: University of California Press, 2021, 133.
39. See Lyn A. Wolz, 'The Anne Geddes Gilchrist Manuscript Collection', *Folk Music Journal* 8 (2005): 619–639 and Gilchrist Collective, 'Anne Geddes Gilchrist: the untold story of a vital figure in folk'. *Folk London Magazine*, 2022,

folklondon.co.uk/2022/12/anne-geddes-gilchrist-the-untold-story-of-a-vital-figure-in-folk.

40. Peter Snape, 'In Search of Folk Song: The Story of Anne Geddes Gilchrist', *Sunderland Point Blog*, 2023, www.sunderlandpoint.net/blog/2-5.
41. Wolz, 'The Anne Geddes Gilchrist Manuscript Collection', 628.
42. Wolz, 'The Anne Geddes Gilchrist Manuscript Collection', 619, 623.
43. Snape, 'In Search of Folk Song'.
44. Wolz, 'The Anne Geddes Gilchrist Manuscript Collection', 619.
45. Snape, 'In Search of Folk Song'.
46. Gilchrist, *1901 England Census*.
47. Snape, 'In Search of Folk Song'.
48. Snape, 'In Search of Folk Song'.
49. Wolz, 'The Anne Geddes Gilchrist Manuscript Collection', 623.
50. Wolz, 'The Anne Geddes Gilchrist Manuscript Collection', 623.
51. *Letter from Anne Geddes Gilchrist to Lucy Broadwood, 1906.* Surrey History Centre: 2185/LEB/1/236.
52. Anne Geddes Gilchrist, 'Let Us Remember' [reprinted]. *English Dance and Song* 54/3 (1992), 8–9.
53. Ethel Ford, 'The Cottage in the Wood' Vaughan Williams Memorial Library, 1905: AGG/8/16.
54. Ethel Ford, 'The Farmer's Boy' Vaughan Williams Memorial Library, 1905: AGG 3/6/6.
55. Agnes Ford, *1901 England Census*.
56. Agnes Ford, *1891 England Census*.
57. Agnes Ford, *1921 England Census*.
58. Agnes Ford, *England & Wales, Civil Registration Death Index. 1916–2007*. London: General Registry Office, 1924.
59. *Letter from Anne Geddes Gilchrist to Lucy Broadwood.*
60. *Letter from Anne Geddes Gilchrist to Lucy Broadwood.*
61. Agnes Ford, 'Mother, Mother' Vaughan Williams Memorial Library, 1906: AGG/8/48; Agnes Ford, 'The Banks of the Sweet Dundee' Vaughan Williams Memorial Library, 1906/7: AGG/3/6/2b.
62. Mrs. Jenner, 'Green Bushes'. Vaughan Williams Memorial Library, 1906/7: AGG/6/3/1A.
63. Elizabeth Coomber, 'Dark Eyed Sailor'. Vaughan Williams Memorial Library, 1905: AGG/8/22.
64. Coomber, 'Dark Eyed Sailor'.
65. Flora Coomber, 'The Squire and the Milkmaid'. Vaughan Williams Memorial Library, 1905: AGG/8/69.
66. Ford, 'The Cottage in the Wood', 'The Farmer's Boy'.
67. William Ford, 'Sylvie' Vaughan Williams Memorial Library, 1906: AGG/3/6/21.

68. Amabel Ludlow, 'Little Sir William' . Vaughan Williams Memorial Library, 1906/7: AGG/3/28a.; Amabel Ludlow, 'Lord Lovel'. Vaughan Williams Memorial Library, 1906/7: AGG/3/6/4d.
69. See Bennett, *Performing Folk Songs*, 157.
70. Dorothy Marshall, *1871 England Census*.
71. Dorothy Marshall, *1901 England Census*.
72. Dorothy Marshall, *1911 England Census*.
73. George Frampton, 'Clive Carey, Dorothy Marshall and the West Sussex Tradition'. *English Dance and Song* 48/3 (1986): 7–8, 7.
74. Frampton, 'Clive Carey', 8.
75. Frampton, 'Clive Carey', 7.
76. Frampton, 'Clive Carey', 8.
77. George Viney, 'The Cruel Father and Affectionate Lovers'. Vaughan Williams Memorial Library, 1919: CC/1/329.
78. Using such methods, however, proved contentious: see Cole, *The Folk*, 29–36.
79. *Postcard from Dorothy Marshall to Clive Carey, 22 Oct 1912*. Vaughan Williams Memorial Library, 1912: CC/2/183.
80. *Letter from Dorothy Marshall to Clive Carey, 20 Jan 1911*. Vaughan Williams Memorial Library, 1911: CC/2/131; *Letter from Dorothy Marshall to Clive Carey, 23 Jun 1911*. Vaughan Williams Memorial Library, 1911: CC/2/139
81. *Letter from Dorothy Marshall to Clive Carey, 8 Dec 1911*. Vaughan Williams Memorial Library, 1911: CC/2/161; *Letter from Dorothy Marshall to Clive Carey, 21 Nov 1911*. Vaughan Williams Memorial Library, 1911: CC/2/157.
82. *Letter from Dorothy Marshall to Clive Carey, Feb 1911*. Vaughan Williams Memorial Library, 1911: CC/2/132.
83. *Letter from Dorothy Marshall to Clive Carey, 18 Oct 1912*. Vaughan Williams Memorial Library, 1912: CC/2/182.
84. Bessie Knight, 'Caroline and Her Brisk Sailor Bold'. Vaughan Williams Memorial Library, 1912: CC/1/170.
85. Clive Carey, *Untitled Newspaper Cutting Fragment*. Vaughan Williams Memorial Library: CC/3/44.
86. Elizabeth Knight, *1911 England Census*.
87. Elizabeth Knight, *1939 England and Wales Register*.
88. Elizabeth Knight, *Civil Registration Death Index*.
89. *Letter from Dorothy Marshall to Clive Carey, 22 Oct 1911*. Vaughan Williams Memorial Library, 191: CC/2/154.
90. Maryanne Dever, *Archives and New Modes of Feminist Research*. London: Routledge, 2019, 1.
91. Boyes, *The Imagined Village*, 52.
92. Cole, *The Folk*, 55.
93. Cole, *The Folk*, 50.

18 | No Neutrals Here: Folk, Class, Labour

MARK STEVEN

For the militant oil workers of Southern California, folk songs were battle hymns. We hear this in Upton Sinclair's naturalist petrofiction, *Oil!*, a novel first published in 1927. Set during the early decades of the twentieth century, this intergenerational epic describes the expansion of the trade unions during the 1910s, when – under guidance from the Industrial Workers of the World – they began to combine into something greater and more powerful than the established craft or guild system, which had always been organized along separate industrial lines. The IWW's efforts were met with brutal animosity from the property owners and the conservative press as well as from many of the old-line labour leaders; members were criminalized, scapegoated, and subject to the full force of paramilitary suppression. In Sinclair's narrative, the resulting violence is compared to both colonial extermination and the slaughter of animals. So reflects the novel's hero, Bunny, the sole heir to an oil magnate who will eventually disavow his inheritance to embrace a life of socialism:

These 'wobblies' were now being hunted like wild beasts under the 'criminal syndicalism act' of California; every one who came into a labor camp or industrial plant was liable to be picked up by a constable or company 'bull', and the mere possession of a red card meant fourteen years in state's prison. Nevertheless, here they were in Paradise; half a dozen of them had a 'jungle' or camping place out in the hills, and they would lure workingmen out to their meetings, and you would see the glare of a camp-fire, and hear the faint echo of the songs they sang out of their 'little red song book'. To Bunny this was romantic and mysterious; while to Dad and Mr. Roscoe and the managers of Ross Consolidated, it was as if the 'jungle' had been located in the province of Bengal, and the sounds brought in by the night wind had been the screams of man-eating tigers![1]

So much of the IWW's alure – equipping the arduous and deadly task of organizing labour with requisite political charisma – emanates from their music. That is what Bunny and his father and all the workers hear echoing down from the hills and the canyons and into the populous oil fields: old folk songs, sung and shared between workers, the kind of thing intoned over an acoustic guitar or banjo or squeezebox, with the familiar words recorded for ease of transmission in a mass-published, brick-red booklet no larger than 6 by 5 inches.

Just as the songs supplied this movement with an aura of the 'romantic and mysterious', they were razor sharp in their political analysis, not only affirming the workers' collective or the union combination but also describing the social conditions under which labour is forced to subsist. We read about this elsewhere in Sinclair's novel. One of Bunny's love interests is Vee Tracy, an actress whose 'whole being was concentrated upon making it real and vivid', and who is said to have been perfecting her artistry only to 'buy more applause and attention, as a means of getting more thousands for more weeks.' This, for Bunny, is the aspirational and middle-class equivalent to the conditions experienced by the oil workers and narrated in their song. 'It was a vicious circle', he reflects, 'exactly like Dad's oil wells. The wobblies had a song about it in their jungles: "We go to work to get the cash to buy the food to get the strength to go to work to get the cash to buy the food to get the strength to go to work—" and so on, as long as your breath held out.'[2] Such is the fate of labour under capitalism, in which we work only to purchase what's needed to replenish our capacity to continue working, for as long as breath holds out, until the end. At the start of the twentieth century, in what was an historical phase of heightened class consciousness, with workers going into battle against the property owners and the employers with maximal vehemence, the purpose of folk music was to break the wheel and terminate that cycle.

Folk music, and especially in the United States, has frequently been grounded in the fertile soil of labour struggles. Developing an account of folk from Bob Dylan's insistence that music is less a science than a 'living art', Ross Cole suggests that, in folk, we encounter a spectral archive of forgotten voices, the words and sounds that will have belonged to the casualties of history. 'The instruments are acoustic and vernacular; the politics are radical, egalitarian, and opposed to the status quo; the subjects are rugged outlaws, wars, tragedies, hard manual labor, solidarity, loss, religion, and the untamed frontier.'[3] This kind of sonic hinterland is what we might hear still in the songs of legendary figures like Joe Hill, Harry McClintock, and T-Bone Slim, whose political commitments and proletarian lyricism would find their way into the little red book. It is also what shades into the work of more thoroughly mainstreamed musicians, ranging from Joan Baez through Bruce Springsteen. Published in the format of the little red book, however, the irreducible romance of folk is repackaged into an incendiary device to be used against the serried defenders of capitalist modernity. As the book's subtitle proclaims, these are songs 'to fan the flames of discontent', fuel for a conflagration yet to come.

Before any one song, the book's single-page preamble provides a succinct analysis of labour's situation within capitalism's class hierarchy and suggests a way to escape. 'The working class and the employing class have nothing in common', it begins. 'There can be no peace so long as hunger and want are found among millions of working people and the few, who make up the employing class, have all the good things of life.'[4] If this rhetoric is more akin to the political manifesto than the folk song, its messaging also finds form in two slogans, which together propose a mutually transformative relationship between labour, class, and the songs to follow: 'an injury to one is an injury to all' and 'abolish the wage system'. Folk, whose semantic origins would have this term relative to the people in general, may well be a means of solidifying collective identities between heterogenous working people, the one and the all. Here it enacts that movement with the ambition of ending a class system for which the wage is only ever a tool for extracting value out of those of us who possess nothing but our capacity to work.

Taking seriously the content of these slogans and combining them with the textual substance of folk song, the argument of this chapter is that, beginning with its forceful critique of exploitation under capitalism, folk offers a dialectical vision of the modern worker – that is to say, it sings of the worker as a figure in which two contradictory phenomena are experienced at once. The experience of labour, in this account, is to live under a curse but to also embody the promise of collective redemption, to know that, when labour acts strictly as a class, it might yet abolish all classes and with that bring about the conditions of its own emancipation. Counterpoised to its many descriptions of wage work – an exploitation enabled only by the reality of dispossession and the threat of immiseration – folk articulates an alternative and hopeful vision of the worker as a collective subject defined by expansive solidarity, class antagonism, and common property. To make this argument, the chapter listens to three well-known folk songs from within the context of their composition and with an ear to the indivisible politics of class and labour. As with all collective subjects, the subject of labour is riven with difference: race, gender, and indigeneity are but three variables that will introduce complications into the following songs. Moreover, if the story of the American Century is one of labour's degradation, a tale in which (to borrow political economist Harry Braverman's summary) 'the masters take over the entire process, repeatedly reshape and reorganize it to suit their own needs, and parcel it out as tasks to workers for whom the process as a whole is now lost', this chapter argues that folk is also a record of all that has been and continues to be lost as we labour under the mastery of capital.⁵ In other words, folk provides sounds and images and stories of what has been forced upon all working people and of what might otherwise be, but only if we make it so.

'Solidarity Forever'

What are we affirming when we sing 'Solidarity Forever', that century-old staple of all good picket lines? 'There is such a thing as human fellowship', reflected legendary trade unionist Eugene V. Debs, 'and solidarity means fellowship, fraternity, mutual sympathy, interest in each other's welfare, and in seeking to bring about solidarity in the ranks of workingmen', he adds, 'it must be apparent only the highest good is sought'.⁶ For political theorist Jodi Dean, solidarity is the 'mutual expectation of a responsible orientation to relationship', a process of defining and redefining group boundaries and commitments within a given situation. 'Simply put', she explains, 'solidarity can be modeled as an interaction involving at least three persons: I ask you to stand by me over and against a third.'⁷ Perhaps that is what we are singing together as we guard the gates to the place of work: join us, in our withdrawal of labour, against those who profit from our exploitation. But if the strike is what traditional Marxists have often described as a 'school of war', perhaps this folk song and its avowed solidarity might also be adjunct to labour militancy, the stuff of full-blooded armed conflict.

The song was first written by Ralph Chaplin, who describes it in specifically folk terms as something like a distillation of 'the Pacific Northwest in the afterglow of the rugged period of American pioneering'.⁸ Chaplin was also an organizer and artist who would later be known as the illustrator of the IWW's black cat logo, Sabo-Tabby, an immortal feline embodiment of industrial sabotage and the wildcat strike. While Chaplin attributes his radicalization to seeing, at age seven, a worker shot dead during the Pullman Strike in Chicago, Illinois, it would be a similarly violent context that informed 'Solidarity Forever'. During the infamous Paint Creek–Cabin Creek strike of 1912, a conflict that served as prelude to the more infamous battles of Matewan and Blair Mountain, Chaplin worked on the strike committee with the fabled Mother Jones. 'The strike was truly war', Jones would insist, 'with murders and assassinations, with dynamite and prisons. The mine owners brought in gunmen. The President of the Union urged the miners to arm to defend themselves, their wives and daughters. It was Hell!'⁹ Or, as Chaplin would later reflect, the version of himself that penned the song 'had been shaped by bitterly contested labour struggles, including a two-year strike against mine owners of Kanawha County, West Virginia', but it was not this event alone, or anything at all to do with its authorship, that made the song an anthem: 'it took the sustained militancy of the grass-roots Western Federation of Miners, in the face of equally ferocious opposition to put the hefty punch into "Solidarity Forever" that later on made it the theme song of the entirely latter-day labour movement'.¹⁰

Even without the lyrics, we hear in the music itself that collective solidarity 'over and against' a common enemy. Specifically, 'Solidarity Forever' is sung to the tune of the 'Battle Hymn of the Republic' and 'John Brown's Body', two anthems that together describe bloody conflict, in either the American Civil War or the armed insurrection of Harper's Ferry. It is the sound of war, then, but specifically war in the name of abolition – to such an extent that the song cannot help but let slip something like a racial unconscious, with a tacit sense that wage slavery might be relative to chattel slavery. This would make explicit the heritage of all folk culture in the United States. 'Here', writes W. E. B. Du Bois, 'we have brought our three gifts and mingled them with yours: a gift of story and song – soft, stirring melody in an ill-harmonized and unmelodious land; the gift of sweat and brawn to beat back the wilderness, conquer the soil, and lay the foundations of this vast economic empire two hundred years earlier than your weak hands could have done it; the third, a gift of the Spirit'.¹¹ So when, in the first verse, a union is conjured forth in militant rhetoric, perhaps we should listen for the boundaries of a community enacted in a country built on the lacerated backs of racialized slave labour:

> When the union's inspiration through the workers' blood shall run,
> There can be no power greater anywhere beneath the sun;
> Yet what force on earth is weaker than the feeble strength of one,
> But the union makes us strong.

There is something of a *détournement* in this, removing 'blood' and 'earth' from fascist ideology and reasserting them as the bodily stuff of labour, the sinews of all industry.

The imagery of sun and earth returns us to the land, but not as some exceptional georgic arcadia – it is, rather, the land on which labour takes place, through which the harrowtrough is ploughed and into which seeds are planted. It is, overwhelmingly, a land that has been shaped by the fieldwork of slaves. Similarly, the spectre of slavery reappears in subsequent verses, first in reference to the parasite of capital that would 'lash us into serfdom' and then, again, in describing the results of collective industry as 'ours, not to slave in, but to master and to own'. There are at least two ways of interpreting this. One would be to equate the song with the eighteenth-century tradition of invoking slavery as a metaphor, against which liberty must be defended, and thus likening its invocations to something like European liberalism. The other interpretation, which is the more compelling, would be to suggest that the song – whether its author was cognizant of this or not – seems to know that it describes a labour force that is descended from slavery at the levels of the individual worker as well as that of an entire social system. 'The power of the great slaveholders was broken', writes historian of slavery Robin Blackburn, 'but almost everywhere it was replaced by the rule of landowners, merchants and banks. Slavery would never return, but post-Emancipation societies remained racially stratified and oppressive.'[12] From within this historical and folkloric terrain, the atomized labourer, a solitary 'one', has their strength multiplied by the power of all living labour, to create a union that is strong precisely because it is a collective both multitudinous and diverse, an embodiment of solidarity between all working people, of all races.

The subsequent verses resound with spirited affirmations of such an expansive group identity, all delivered in the oppositional language of collective agency, 'us' and 'them', workers and owners, labour and capital. The grammar mixes the interrogative with the exhortative in a way that seems calculated to inspire and recruit. 'Is there aught we hold in common with the greedy parasite?' it asks. But the strength of capital, the parasite's influence over its host body, is nothing when compared to those who have been compelled to build its wonders. This, the unparalleled power of labour, is something to which only the workers can lay claim:

> It is we who ploughed the prairies; built the cities where they trade;
> Dug the mines and built the workshops, endless miles of railroad laid;
> Now we stand outcast and starving midst the wonders we have made.

The song thus conjures its vision of the folk, its imagined community, by appealing to the common experiences of ostracism and hunger, on the prairies and in the cities, down the mines and on the rails. But that immiseration only exists alongside, and in tension with, a sense of collective achievement – the things that 'we' have done, or have been compelled to do, and which without us would be nothing.

To account for this tension in overly schematic terms, the song describes two interlocking social relations – vertical class structure and horizontal class formation – both mediated by labour. Labour, in this song, is a force of class unity and simultaneously an index to the exploitation of one class by another: it is the mediating substance of solidarity with others but also an index to solidarity against another. That is what we hear in rhymes like this:

> All the world that's owned by idle drones is ours and ours alone.
> We have laid the wide foundations; built it skyward stone by stone.

And this:

> They have taken untold millions that they never toiled to earn,
> But without our brain and muscle not a single wheel can turn.

Animating the sociality of this song, defining not only its lyrics but also the community it seeks to establish and mobilize, is one of the most salient contradictions at the heart of capitalist modernity. This contradiction is what Marx once described as the 'dual-character' of labour. Once labour 'finds its expression in value', he writes, 'it no longer possesses the same characteristics as when it is the creator of use-values', therefore ceasing to be 'an eternal natural necessity which mediates the metabolism between man and nature, and therefore human life itself', devolving into a source of exchange value, from which profits can be made.[13] Or, put simply, when labour is employed within capitalist production, it is revaluated in terms of quantity, not quality, and its value is transferred from the workers to capitalists. That is the contradiction between the 'untold millions' in profits and the experience of brains and muscles and minds and bodies laying the foundations or turning the wheel.

By emphasizing the useful and well-nigh heroic achievements of labour, and by showing those achievements alienated from the workers, the song is a reminder of what labour has achieved but also what labour is losing to the predatory forms of capital every hour it works for a wage. This contradiction, revealed in the dual character of labour, crescendos into the final verse, which announces a climactic intensification of solidarities, an expanded horizon for the labouring subject. Here collective strength is beheld as a latent potential more potent than all the forces arrayed against the worker:

> In our hands is placed a power greater than their hoarded gold,
> Greater than the might of armies, multiplied a thousand-fold.
> We can bring to birth a new world from the ashes of the old
> For the union makes us strong.

Note the shift in grammatical mood, from the declarative to the conditional, from an affirmation of what collective labour is to a gesture at what it might achieve if unshackled. It is that third line which seeks a social order other than the one we have all been forced to inhabit. The organic metaphor is familiar in radical discourse, in which capitalism is often said to have birthed its revolutionary antithesis. But here, crucially, any birth of the new world comes at the expense of the old one; life released from exploitation is only possible once the forms and forces that enable exploitation have first been reduced to ash, in a fire blazed with solidarity as its fuel. It is in this final formulation that the song moves beyond the affirmation of labour and the condemnation of capital to make its reckoning with their absolute incompatibility.

'Which Side Are You On?'

Florence Reece is said to have written the words of 'Which Side Are You On?' in 1931 during a battle between union miners and the coal firms during Eastern Kentucky's Harlan County War or what is commonly described as Bloody Harlan. The song was written in response to an event that extirpated any residual illusions about the impartiality of the law in class conflict. Florence was the wife of Sam Reece, a union organizer for the coal workers. One night, Sherriff J. H. Blair and his thugs searched the Reece house, looking for Sam, terrorizing Florence and their seven children, then setting up camp outside to shoot Sam if he returned. The morning after, Reece tore a sheet from the calendar and on it wrote the words of a song, using the tune of 'Lay the Lily Low', an old come-all-ye ballad, here remodelled to enact a triplicate passage of solidarity from worker to union and from union to class. 'My songs always goes to the underdog', Reece would later reflect, 'to the worker. I'm one of them and I feel like I've got to be with them. There's no such thing as neutral. You have to be on one side or the other. Some people say, "I don't take sides—I'm neutral." There's no such thing. In your mind you're on one side or the other. In Harlan County there wasn't no neutral.'[14] Both the vernacular and the homiletic mode of address in this reflection animate the song itself, which articulates an almost contradictory poetics of organization to what we heard in 'Solidarity Forever'. If Chaplin's song projected a vision of labour simultaneously glorious and imperilled, but always taking place in the collective, Reece calls out the individual worker and urges them towards that collective. Whereas 'Solidarity Forever' has the feel of a marching song, to be sung together on the way to or from battle, 'Which Side Are You On?' has all the urgency of live conflict, with bombs and bullets flying overhead.

'Come all you good workers', it begins, 'good news to you I'll tell, of how the good old union has come in here to dwell'. While this first verse retains the feel of the hymnal, employing the language of the church to address its congregation, the chorus shifts register. The collective 'you' takes on the force of direct address: 'Which side are you on, boys? Which side are you on?' The 'you', in the form of a question that only becomes more insistent in its repetition, is what philosophers might describe as interpellation: it hails the subject, speaking directly to you as the worker, asking you to choose sides, and denying the very possibility of nonalignment. Indeed, the whole premise for this song is that labour is a political category that is already divided, that it can only ever serve one of two interests, and that there is absolutely no middle ground between them. Contributing to the force of how it articulates this premise are two layers of narrative woven throughout the verses. One is an appeal to the authenticity of experience, the lived experience of working in a very specific time and place; the other is a calculated deployment of the gendered language, a calling forth of the masculine.

Forming a personal countersign to the 'you' of the song's address, several of its formulations clarify a point of delivery, emphasizing that the singer or singers are, likewise, already part of labour's struggle. This is especially pronounced in the second verse:

> My daddy was a miner
> He's now in the air and sun
> He'll be with you fellow workers
> Until the battle's won

To work down the mines is, the song attests, intergenerational: that kind of experience is 'the air and sun', the very manner, of this embattled community. It would be too academic to put this in strictly sociological terms, whereby the exploitation dictated by class structure forges common interests between workers, but here that kind of thinking is precisely what underwrites the movement of solidarity. Note the shift in tense, from the past into the future. It is a shift from the individual to the fellowship, infused by the affective current of implied mortality through possible redemption. The working class, Walter Benjamin once noted, is defined by 'both its hatred and its spirit of sacrifice, for both are nourished by the image of enslaved ancestors rather than liberated grandchildren', and it is that energy which seems to underwrite this appeal to authenticity.[15] Fight, 'fellow workers', if you ever hope to redeem 'my daddy', who was one of you, and is with you now, in spirit if not in body.

Redoubling the force of interpellation is the song's appeal to masculinity. At a practical level, this is in part because the mineworkers in Harlan were almost exclusively male, or at least that was the official composition of the workforce. 'Although it is not widely known', writes ethnographic historian of the mines Marat Moore, 'women did mine coal in the first half of the twentieth century, whenever the need for their labour overwhelmed the tradition against it. These workers were largely undocumented; most laboured in small contract operations as an invisible component of a family work unit. Some disguised their sex for fear of detection. Very few were publicly acknowledged or accepted by coal operators as part of an established workforce.'[16] Although the mines would not have functioned without the unwaged reproductive and domestic labour of countless women, wage labour – and so the capacity to strike against the mining firms – was primarily undertaken by men. And yet, the strike was upheld by the miners' wives and sisters, their mothers and daughters, who fronted the picket lines, carried the community, and worked in the union. Notwithstanding the feminine authorship of the song, its abundance of masculine nouns contributes to the way it hails specifically those workers best positioned to withdraw their labour. While the chorus speaks affectionally to 'boys', the verse presents the idea of 'man' as something less given than which needs to be earned through action and integrity and which obtains in stark opposition to the epithet 'scab', as in this apostrophe:

> Oh, workers can you stand it?
> Oh, tell me how you can
> Will you be a lousy scab
> Or will you be a man?

The worker has a choice, and how they choose defines their entire being: either with us or against, you can either live as a man or endure as a scab, and these are your only two options.

There is something ontologically damning about the insult, 'scab', which had already been established by a popular text commonly ascribed to the author and journalist Jack London, 'Ode to a Scab', which describes its subject as the vilest thing to ever have crawled across the earth. 'A scab', it reads, 'is a two-legged animal with a corkscrew soul, a waterlogged brain, and a combination backbone made of jelly and glue. Where others have hearts, he carries a tumor of rotten principles. When a scab comes down the street, men turn their backs and angels weep in heaven, and the devil shuts the gates of hell to keep him out. No man has a right to scab as long as there is a pool of water deep enough to drown his body in, or a rope long enough to hang his carcass with.' Resonating with the song's vision of authentic community, and with its notion of man as a worker that stands with and who fights on behalf of that community, the scab, by contrast, 'sells his birthright, his country, his wife, his children, and his fellow men for an unfulfilled promise from his employer, trust, or corporation'.[17] If you don't choose to be a man, the song suggests, then you will only ever be a scab.

It is all of these tactics combined – the direct address, the refusal of neutrality, the appeal to authenticity, and the synonymy of masculinity with solidarity – that we encounter at once in the song's most celebrated verse:

> They say in Harlan County
> There are no neutrals there
> You'll either be a union man
> Or a thug for J. H. Claire

This verse localizes the fate of labour, grounding it in a very specific lifeworld, with its proper names and with its real heroes and villains – the union men and police thugs. The song thus grounds its politics in an authentic locale while simultaneously speaking in the cadence of myth ('they say … ') as though to suggest an exportable lesson for labour everywhere. And that is precisely how Reece would later describe the song's historical content. 'If you wasn't a gun thug', she explains, 'you was a union man'.[18] Which side are you on?

'This Land Is Your Land'

'THIS MACHINE KILLS FASCISTS', Woody Guthrie emblazoned in black paint across the body of his big acoustic guitar – 'and', he would rightly clarify, 'it means just what it says too'.[19] For Guthrie, music was a weapon and the guitar a tool for social transformation. When he arrived in New York City in 1940 to be embraced by the folk scene, it was this understanding that informed his writing, an insistence that any one song could tip the scale between fascism and freedom, between concentrated hierarchical power and the liberation of labour from exploitation and immiseration under capital. This was a time when the United States was moving into the second phase of the New Deal, which shifted emphasis from public works to fiscal stimulus, as though confirming the state's newly developed capacities as the accessory to capital. It was also a time when

Figure 18.1 Woody Guthrie, 1943. Photograph by Al Aumuller. Library of Congress.

Guthrie was thinking about music in terms of political contest. He wrote as much in 'Big Guns', a short essay published in 1942:

There's several ways of saying what's on your mind. And in states and counties where it ain't any too healthy to talk too loud, speak your mind, or even to vote like you want to, folks have found other ways of getting the word around. One of the mainest ways is by singing. Drop the word 'folk' and just call it real old honest to god American singing. No matter who makes it up, no matter who sings it and who don't, if it talks the lingo of the people, it's a cinch to catch on, and will be sung here and yonder for a long time after you've cashed in your chips. If the fight gets hot, the songs get hotter. If the going gets tough, the songs get tougher.[20]

This reads like a mission statement, or at least an affirmation of artistic principles, and it should guide how we sing and listen to what is arguably Guthrie's best-known tune, 'This Land is Your Land', which will be approached here as not only a utopian vision of earthly freedom, but simultaneously as a critical reckoning with the fortunes of labour during the mid-century.

Guthrie claims to have written the song as a rejoinder. In 1938, during the rise of Nazism in Germany, Irving Berlin's patriotic hymnal 'God Bless America' enjoyed a revival in popularity after being re-recorded and broadcast by the popular singer and 'First Lady of the Radio', Kate Smith. 'While the storm clouds gather far across the sea, let us swear allegiance to a land that's free', it begins, and it is to this very sentiment that Guthrie responds critically. Unlike Berlin and Smith's anthem – whose sense of freedom and whose calls for gratitude could only sound disingenuous at the tail end of the Great Depression and through the Dust Bowl years – Guthrie's song describes the material conditions that underwrite such freedom, and it frames those conditions as perilously embattled. What, this song asks, does it mean to take ownership of the land, of all land, as something worth sharing between all humans, and to do so at a time when property is primarily a means of dispossession and coercion?

The song opens with its chorus, which takes the form of a rhetorical chiasmus, in a line that repeats its titular noun four times: 'This land is your land, this land is my land.' If the pronouns here gesture towards collective ownership, suggesting that the land itself could be communal property, the specificity implied by 'this' is backfilled by the subsequent lines. 'From California to the New York Island, from the redwood forest to the Gulf Stream waters', from the southwest to the northeast, from the forests to the oceans: everything for everyone. A final line encloses the chorus, combining and condensing that first one, shifting from possessive to nominative pronouns, but also shifting tense from present to past: 'This land was made for you and me.' So much depends upon the verb and its tenses. This land, whose proper names and geological descriptors conjure forth as America, does not simply exist. Instead, it has, by some unnamed and pre-existing agency, been created, shaped, or moulded into that entity about which we now sing. America is, in other words, a product of labour. But it might no longer be labour's property.

One way to make sense of this song would be to emphasize the shift from God-blessed to God-given. Whereas Berlin and Smith would encourage gratitude for divine blessings, Guthrie seems more intent on rethinking what has been described in critical theory as the 'free gifts of nature', those organic materials that appear to humans as useful and enjoyable given that no labour seems to be involved in their making – hence the singing persona finds themselves ambling through 'a golden valley' and 'diamond deserts', geological formations whose descriptions index value. And yet, capital appropriates these free gifts of nature into accumulation, enclosing and privatizing and monetizing the organic lifeworld, and it does so by harnessing human labour. 'All life', writes Jason W. Moore, 'is actively, creatively, incessantly engaged in environment-making, such that, in the modern world, human ingenuity (such as it is) and human activity (such as it has been) must activate the work of particular natures in order to appropriate particular streams of unpaid work'. Indeed, the land explored by Guthrie's rambler is also replete with all the signs of that labour, from the 'ribbon of highway' to the 'wheat fields waving'. This land is, as Moore would suggest, 'a co-produced reality, bundling the life-activities of human and extra-human nature in the present, and accumulated over time'; if it is collective property, that is only because of the labour that went into its making.[21]

There is a further layer of tension to the relationship between land and property, and this is a tension that extends far beyond this or any other song, namely that any calls for justice or redistribution or collective betterment made from within the United States are also made on stolen land. 'That Anglo settler colonialism is inextricably linked to the emergence of a market in land', writes political theorist Robert Nichols in his comprehensive theory of dispossession, 'is most obviously true in the case of the United States'. Moreover, it was this process of colonial dispossession that converted the land, which had not been conceived of before as property, into something that could be privately owned. 'Specifically', Nichols clarifies, 'the dispossessive processes through which a system of land ownership was generated in the Anglo settler world was recursive in the sense that it used a form of widespread and systemic theft as a means to generate property, thereby producing that which it presupposes'.[22] Compounded by its invocation of American names, its personification of space and place with a quasi-divine 'voice', and its bequeathing land to a universalizing 'you and me', the song omits any references to the actual or historical collective ownership: namely, Indigenous land tenure, which ended in the dispossession that enabled both the privatization this song critiques and the kinds of labour it affirms. In this way, the song veers close to a treatise on eminent domain. 'Even if the song's intended message rejects the predations of capitalism and the ownership of land', writes Guthrie's biographer Gustavus Stadler, '"This Land Is Your Land" still neglects to mention the history that made the collectivist stroll it narrates possible for people of European descent, and that is a big problem, perhaps especially in the work of an artist committed to social justice'.[23] As with a history of racialized domination that inheres in the music of 'Solidarity Forever', or in gendered work obscured by the masculinity of 'Which Side Are You On?' here the representation of the worker and the affirmation of labour exist in relation to other, earlier modes of expulsion, domination, and wholesale eradication.

Where this song hones its sharpest edge is across two verses that are frequently omitted from performances, especially when the song is redeployed as something like a de-historicized song of accord, the kind of thing used to usher in newly elected politicians. The first of these verses describes enclosure as the antithesis to all the song affirms, with private property articulating as the founding lie of capitalist modernity:

> There was a big high wall there that tried to stop me;
> Sign was painted, it said private property;
> But on the back side it didn't say nothing;
> This land was made for you and me.

The other verse compounds this radicalism by reframing the song's egalitarian and collectivist ideals as the stuff of material aspiration, not simply given but for which we will need to fight:

> In the shadow of the steeple I saw my people,
> By the relief office I seen my people;
> As they stood there hungry, I stood there asking
> Is this land made for you and me?

It is here that the song's persona – an itinerant worker, perhaps, or even a wandering vagrant – experiences solidarity. The repeated 'my people' conjoins the rambling adventure of that first-person pronoun with that of the 'hungry' masses – those men, women, and children now seeking shelter and relief – and this newfound solidarity shifts the refrain from declaration to question. If anyone is denied the stuff of life, the gifts of nature or the fruits of labour, then the land and all it contains might not be for you and me after all, or at least not then, and certainly not yet.

Coda: A New England

Folk music is a living art and an art that has been used to raise the living standards of labour. It is also a way of linking struggles past to struggle present. If this is a form of historical truth, and one that lives on in the songs to which we have been listening, those of us who have sung their words will also know that truth from experience. Since migrating from the east coast of Australia to southwest England on the very last day of 2017, I have spent weeks out on picket lines as a member of the Universities and Colleges Union. Whereas this has all happened at a geographical and historical remove from the contexts discussed in this essay, folk music in general but especially the three songs discussed here have all featured prominently over several years of accumulated strike action. In February 2018, two months into working for the University of Exeter, a nationwide strike for university workers was called. One of my most enduring memories from picketing that winter was having my antipodean blood warmed by loud, raucous performances of 'Solidarity Forever'. Rhian Keyse sang gleefully and at maximal volume, Marc Owen Jones played guitar, and a band of comrades joined in chorus and supplied percussion on pots and pans. Rhian's singing is the reason why anytime I read the word 'solidarity' I now hear a Welsh accent. The dispute continued into 2019, and it is to then that this chapter owes its title. Emily Criss, an exchange student from the United States, turned up to a picket line in November that year with a big, homemade placard advertising a revision to the lyrics of 'Which Side Are You On?' 'There are no neutrals here', it read in giant blue letters, shifting the conflict from Harlan Kentucky to the West Country. And of course, Billy Bragg has played a few of our pickets and our rallies, which has only reconfirmed my love of his music, though I've still not heard a live version of his take on 'This Land is Your Land'. It was during a march between venues once that I thanked him for the performance, for his solidarity, and I apologized that so few of my colleagues seemed to know the words to The Internationale. 'I only work for one man', he told me, 'and his name is Woody Guthrie'.

Notes

1. Upton Sinclair, *Oil!* New York: Albert & Charles Boni, 1926–27, 336.
2. Sinclair, *Oil!*, 397–98.
3. Ross Cole, *The Folk: Music, Modernity, and the Political Imagination*. Oakland: University of California Press, 2021, 2.
4. *The Little Red Song Book: To Fan the Flames of Discontent, A Facsimile Reprint of the Popular Nineteenth Edition 1923*. Chicago: Charles H Kerr, 1989, front endpaper.
5. Harry Braverman, *Labor and Monopoly Capital: The Degradation of Work in the Twentieth Century*. Monthly Review Press, New York: 1974, 317.
6. Eugene V. Debs, 'The Solidarity of Labor?' *The Railway Times* 2/9 (1894), 1.
7. Jodi Dean, *Solidarity of Strangers: Feminism after Identity Politics*. Berkeley: University of California Press, 1996, 3.
8. Ralph Chaplin, 'Why I Wrote Solidarity Forever'. *American West* 5/1 (1968): 18–27.
9. Mary Harris Jones, *Autobiography of Mother Jones*. ed. Mary Field Parton. New York: Dover, 2004, 80.
10. Chaplin, 'Why I Wrote Solidarity Forever'.
11. W. E. B. Du Bois, *The Souls of Black Folk: Essays and Sketches*. Chicago: A. C. McClurg and Co., 1903, 262–63.

12. Robin Blackburn, *The American Crucible: Slavery, Emancipation and Human Rights*. London: Verso, 2011, 455.
13. Karl Marx, *Capital: A Critique of Political Economy*, Vol. 1. trans. Ben Fowkes. London: Penguin, 1992, 283.
14. Florence Reece in Guy and Candie Carawan, ed., *Voices from the Mountains: The People of Appalachia, their Faces, their Words, their Songs*. Athens, GA: University of Georgia Press, 1996, 119.
15. Walter Benjamin, *Selected Writings*, Volume 4: 1938–1940. ed. Howard Eiland and Michael W. Jennings. Cambridge, MA: Harvard University Press, 2003, 394.
16. Marat Moore, 'Hard Labor: Voices of Women from the Appalachian Coalfields'. *Yale Journal of Law & Feminism* 2/2 (1989): 199–238, 199.
17. This ode is also printed in some versions of the little red song book, and that is the version cited here. Jack London, 'What Is a Scab?' In *The Little Red Song Book: International Edition, 36th edition*, i. New York: Industrial Workers of the World, 1995.
18. Reece in Carawan, ed., *Voices from the Mountains*, 119.
19. Will Kaufman, *Woody Guthrie's Modern World Blues*. Norman: University of Oklahoma Press, 2017, 140.
20. Woody Guthrie, *Pastures of Plenty: A Self-Portrait*, ed. Dave Marsh and Harold Leventhal. New York: Harper Collins, 1990, 78.
21. Jason W. Moore, 'The Value of Everything? Work, Capital, and Historical Nature in the Capitalist World-Ecology'. *Review (Fernand Braudel Centre)* 37/3–4 (2014): 245–91, 262.
22. Robert Nichols, *Theft Is Property: Dispossession and Critical Theory*. Durham, NC: Duke University Press, 2020, 117.
23. Gustavus Stadler, 'This Land Is . . . Whose Land?: The History of Woody Guthrie's Song', *Al Jazeera* (26 Jan 2021). www.aljazeera.com/features/2021/1/26/this-land-is-whose-land-the-history-of-woody-guthries-song.

19 | Protest Song and the Popular Voice

OSKAR COX JENSEN

On 18 March 1985, The Smiths released the single 'Shakespeare's Sister', the lyrics of which included the memorable non-sequitur:

> I thought that if you had an acoustic guitar
> Then it meant that you were a protest singer
> Oh, I can smile about it now
> But at the time it was terrible

The previous month, The Smiths had released their second studio album *Meat Is Murder*, the title track of which became, anecdotally, one of the most effective protest songs on record, credited with turning many listeners to vegetarianism. The song's production is a world away from that of acoustic guitars, built instead around an electronic soundscape and remorseless samples that layer up to evoke an industrial abattoir and the lowing of slaughtered cattle. Had Morrissey, the group's lyricist, reversed the logic of his lyric (*I used to think that to be a protest singer you needed an acoustic guitar*), it might be interpreted as a rational realization, even an act of becoming: *I too am a protest singer, though I front an indie-rock band*. As it is, his typically gnomic meditation gestures to an unresolved tangle of contradictions at the heart of both protest and folk song.

This was the mid-1980s, something of a heyday for protest song in England in reaction to Margaret Thatcher's neoliberal government and the Falklands War. Eight months after 'Shakespeare's Sister' was released, the political musical movement Red Wedge was formed, led by Billy Bragg, a one-man incarnation of the mingling of folk, rock, and punk genres, and including 'folk' musicians such as Kirsty MacColl alongside pop/rock/indie groups such as The Style Council, Madness, Bananarama, Tom Robinson, and The Smiths themselves.[1] Evidently, in 1985, Morrissey was closely bound up in the making of political and protest pop music. But in 'Shakespeare's Sister', he alludes to an association of protest song with the acoustic guitar-toting singer-songwriters typified by, at the most canonical level, US artists of an earlier generation – Woody Guthrie, Bob Dylan, Joan Baez, Joni Mitchell – and, at a local level, the earnest buskers and party-poopers of every Western town and city, Morrissey's Manchester included.

Generically, stylistically, and ideologically, Morrissey implies more than the possession of an acoustic guitar: his lines invoke, even enshrine, the stereotype of the countercultural *folk singer*.

That they do this even as they hint at the wrongheadedness of the automatic association between folk and protest is also typical. Because, put simply, the elision of an idealized version of folk music and protest song is a historical fallacy. But it is a fallacy that has real historical heft and agency. Following Morrissey's assumed lead, we might place it most visibly in the 1960s, an era responsible for the archetype of the protest singer parodied in Neil Innes' mock 'Protest Song' of 1976 – a straight-up Dylan impression that targets tropes of over-sincerity, bohemia, musical monotony, a stylized vocal drawl, and lyrics combining the platitudinous with the incomprehensible.[2] From isolated examples such as this and, I would argue, our collective cultural memory, we can immediately derive the primary attributes of this supposed association of folk and political protest: authenticity, sincerity, a vernacular musical idiom, a valorization of traditional forms, and above all the political and cultural capital of an asserted *vox populi*. That ideal of folk song as inherently 'of the people' is perhaps the keynote of this association. In this light the Innes parody song proves deeply patronizing, even anti-democratic by portraying that popular voice as foolish and bathetic. Indeed, even more affirmative idealizations of simplicity and plain-speaking (both musically and lyrically) as an attribute of 'the folk' do something similar. But there is nonetheless a radical power, as much as a patrician scorn, implicit in that idea of a vernacular, straightforward, honest voice that speaks truth to power. This is self-evidently bound up in the myth-making of folk music that this book has delineated throughout.

We could leave things there, but that would be insufficient to explain the contradictory, even paradoxical nature of two practices that are in some ways inimical. In its purest form (which, though unreal, nonetheless exerts real agency), folk song is anonymous, either timeless or definitively old, an artless art form concerned with addressing fundamental truths of the human condition, consciously detached from urban technologies and mass media. Political protest and radicalism, by contrast, is necessarily of the moment, topical, tied to current affairs and media, seeking to make a deliberate, partisan intervention in public discourse and the political process. In this light, medium and message seem wholly incompatible. Yet from our vantage point of the early twenty-first century, folk song and protesting appear, reflexively, to be natural bedfellows.

In order to account for this paradox, as well as to demystify the relationship between these two ideas, we must treat the archetype of the 1960s folk-protest singer not as a starting point, but as the *outcome* of a much longer, richer, stranger historical process that stretches back centuries before the coining of the term 'protest song' in 1953 – indeed, centuries before the mid nineteenth-century conceptualization of both political protest and folk song, to at least the sixteenth century, when a recognizable mass musical culture of song production and consumption began in the wake of the Reformation and the spread of the printing press.[3] Working forwards from that point, we can get a better grasp on the connections between the people, protest, and song; the ideologies and practices that informed the prehistory of 'folk'; and the supremely self-conscious interventions of political ideologues that led up to that definitive moment of the 1960s.

First, a caveat: though both folk and protest song are demonstrably global phenomena and increasingly studied in that light, this is primarily a twentieth-century development.[4] In focusing on the longer history behind that phenomenon, I am necessarily concerned with the countries etymologically and conceptually responsible, primarily England and Germany, though a fuller study would do better at including not only North America but also much of the rest of Europe, especially – in the earlier nineteenth century – Scandinavia. I hope that, in sacrificing this breadth, I can compensate with a little more rigour concerning English political and musical history, and allow that history to be taken as in some ways exemplary of much more widespread currents.

Romney Marsh, 1583

This long history begins, not with a protest song, but almost the reverse – a vision of a harmonious social order depicted by the Elizabethan chronicler Raphael Holinshed. Romney Marsh in Kent, south-east England, 1583: a group of workers were building a dam. In half an hour, a flag would be raised that would allow them to put down their tools and rest.

But by the space of halfe an houre before the flag of libertie was hanged out, all the court drivers entered into a song, whereof although the dittie was barbarous, and the note rusticall, the matter of no moment, & all but a jest: yet is it not unworthie of some briefe note of remembrance; because the tune or rather the noise thereof was extraordinarie, and (being delivered with the continuall voice of such a multitude) was verie strange. In this and some other respect, I will set downe their dittie, the words whereof were these:

O Harrie hold up thy hat, t'is eleven a clocke,
and a little, little, little past:
My bow is broke, I would unyoke,
my foot is sore, I can worke no more.[5]

This workers' song was consensual, a 'jest'; if anything, it gave them the strength to continue working a little longer, rather than being a genuine cry of dissent. But the moment, and Holinshed's commentary upon it, is remarkable: he describes the song as a barbarous, rustical ditty and an extraordinary noise, noting the strangeness of its being voiced by such a multitude. Emanating from the page we hear for perhaps the first time in the annals of Anglophone history a collective, popular voice raised in a song itself rooted in custom, in a paternalistic tradition of contractual labour. For all that Holinshed's educated instincts are to dismiss it, he cannot help but add it to his chronicle – a history organized according to monarchs, concerned with great affairs, yet awed into including this raw, rude song of the people, articulating tiredness and hunger. From this point on, even elite history was written in awareness of this reality: that the mass of society might assert itself in song. In an anti-democratic age, with no conception of a public sphere in which ordinary voices might participate, this was indeed 'verie strange'.

Barely a century later, England had been through multiple revolutions. Not only Puritans and Royalists but Diggers and Levellers – genuinely popular, bottom-up movements – had written and performed songs of protest. As early as 1619, the song 'The Powte's Complainte', penned by the unknown Penny of Wisbech, had adopted the voice of a local fish to protest the draining of the East Anglian fens by the local aristocracy, combining an incipient eco-critical consciousness with a defence of customary popular rights.[6] Robert Coster's 'The Diggers' Christmas-Caroll' of 1650, though more demagogic than most songs of its era, was by no means exceptional in beginning with an appeal to 'You people which be wise' – an immediate dignifying of its unenfranchised, unpropertied, even unlettered listeners with good sense and a legitimate perspective on current affairs.[7] Eight years earlier, an anonymous anti-clerical ballad printed at London was even entitled 'Vox Populi. In Plaine English'.[8] Just across the sea, the Eighty Years' War for Dutch independence from Spain was fought to the accompaniment of 'Wilhelmus', a song written anonymously between 1568 and 1572 to a pre-existing French tune – a song from the perspective of a would-be monarch but envoiced by thousands of ordinary combatants and their families.[9] It is true that, even during periods of republican government, states across Western Europe, from England to the Netherlands to the cities and fiefdoms of the Holy Roman Empire, remained hostile to truly popular political expression, repressing – sometimes with extreme violence – the demands or manifestos of peasantry and labourers. But there was nonetheless a liminal political space in which custom and pragmatism allowed for bottom-up political engagement via cultures of petitioning and even ritualized demonstration. And song, though highly regulated in its print incarnation and subject to forces of state-sanctioned violence in performance, was one highly articulate medium for the rhetorical expression of popular protest and appeals to popular sentiment.[10]

This is not the same, of course, as a genuine tradition of bottom-up, labouring-class protest song. Barriers of education and access, as much as the political and legal situation, militated against any such flourishing: street balladry was a formalized music industry in which most writers had connections and reputation, as well as knowledge of the classics. In this early modern era, the tension between song and popular opinion was above all one of the influence song might have on that opinion, rather than song as a form of popular self-expression. The best-known theorizing of this relationship is in Andrew Fletcher's *An Account of a Conversation Concerning a Right Regulation of Governments for the Common Good of Mankind* (Edinburgh, 1704).[11] His key line, endlessly (mis)quoted out of context by commentators ever since, is: 'If a man were permitted to make all the ballads, he need not care who should make the laws of a nation'.[12] Whereas the utopian prospect entertained is a harmonious state that, by means of sung propaganda, effectively regulates the passions and opinions of its pliable subjects, the actual situation as described by Fletcher's treatise – and bemoaned by elite reformers for centuries – was one in which the people remained unruly, dissolute, and dangerous because they were susceptible to arguments propounded in subversive songs. Pre-modern authorities recognized the power of song as a tool for governing the crowd, mob, or rabble (and other pejoratives used in the absence of an idealizing notion of the 'folk' yet to emerge in English discourse). Repeatedly, and well into the nineteenth century, they sought to use it as a regulatory mechanism, to reform, instruct, and depoliticize. But they also feared song, as an instrument of dissent, immorality, democracy, or what we might now label populism. And they were right to do so.[13]

The Swinish Multitude

If 1583 marks our starting point and 1965 our destination (for reasons that will become clear later on), then 1789 is very much the central milestone. The reverberations of the French Revolution were crucial, not only in precipitating the events of the next generation that would weaponize Johann Gottfried Herder's pre-existing concepts of *Volk* and *Volkslieder*, but in raising both the stakes of and the enthusiasm for popular political expression in song enormously. Embraced, at least in England, as much by counter-revolutionaries as radicals, this was in the first instance a continuation of two centuries of practice. As a contributor to Reeves' Association – a reactionary network of volunteer groups set up in defence of the status quo – put it in a letter of 1792: '[A]ny thing written in voice & especially to an Old English tune ... made a more fixed Impression on the Minds of the Younger and Lower Class of People, than any written in Prose'.[14] This was a familiar argument, a paraphrasing of Fletcher's old axiom. Yet on both sides of the political debate, something genuinely new was going on.

The songwriters and pamphleteers of Reeves' Association itself were more radical than they supposed. Made up as they were of the lower-middling sort previously excluded from establishment conceptions of the nation and the public sphere, their public-spirited anti-democratic activities – such as songwriting – played a major part in democratizing the very space they sought to protect.[15] This was precisely what the Whig-turned-reactionary politician and thinker Edmund Burke sought to prevent in his *Reflections on the Revolution in France* of 1790, which used the infamous phrase 'the swinish multitude' to refer to what a later generation would call 'the folk' or 'the masses'.[16] Yet already it was too late: in this new age, the swinish multitude felt emboldened to reply. Embracing Burke's slur in journals such as *Pig's Meat* and songs such as 'The "Swinish Multitude's" Reply', a working-class voice joined with that of propertied and educated radicals.[17] In the wake of Robert Burns's rise to fame, a generation of self-consciously labouring-class poets and songwriters based their literary, musical, and political claims to attention upon that very identity as plebeian, vernacular, and untutored. Among many working-class songwriters of protest and political radicalism, the most eloquent came from the expanding industrial towns and cities of the midlands and the north: Joseph Mather of Sheffield, Samuel Bamford of Middleton, John Stafford of Manchester. Often, these songwriters couched their lyrics in local dialect. There had already been a pervasive sense that lower-class street-level *singers* could be said to embody a dangerous moral force because they in some sense spoke for, and were of, the mass of the people.[18] Now, this was allied to an ideology by which the songs' *writers*, too, leveraged moral capital from their lower-class credentials.[19] Mather, for instance, made much of his job as a file-hewer and Bamford styled himself 'The Weaver Boy'.

Increasingly, though the idea remained politically contentious, there was a growing cultural respectability, even a cachet, attached to the songs of self-described workers. Some of these remained in the primarily aesthetic realm of Romantic verse – the movement that valorized and indeed immortalized Burns, and saw William Wordsworth and Samuel Taylor Coleridge publish their own *Lyrical Ballads* in 1798: this phenomenon coalesced with the existing dignified and ultimately conservative antiquarianism of the likes of Thomas Percy's *Reliques of Ancient English Poetry* (1765). At its most artificial, this privileging of a supposedly 'authentic', suffering, bottom-up voice could be mobilized in aid of specific political causes such as abolitionism: any number of anti-slavery songs were penned by middle-class white writers ventriloquizing the voices of Black slaves, the best (and least offensive) of which is William Cowper's 'The Negro's Complaint', set to a tune – 'Admiral Hosier's Ghost' – by then seen as traditional.[20] At its most extreme, this assertion of a popular voice manifested in the incendiary songs of the Luddites in 1811–12: generally anonymous (because treasonous) protest songs in support of machine-breaking, often explicitly republican in nature.[21]

In all of this activity, we can glimpse ideological undercurrents that anticipate later connections between 'folk song' and 'protest song' – the assembling of political legitimacy and moral or cultural capital around subversive songs that were of and by 'the people', the workers, the swinish multitude. The word 'authenticity' in the relevant, modern sense of the term would not be available until 1938, but there *was* a strong sense of the 'fitness' of certain songs – that they were appropriate for their audience, not mere sermonizing or 'cant' (a word much more prevalent at the time), and the songs that were sung and endured were those most fit for this popular milieu, not those imposed from an external and socially removed political realm.[22]

There was also a strong association of *place* with credibility – and that place was rarely London. In Newcastle, John Bell – a lower-middling bookseller – published his *Rhymes of Northern Bards* in 1812 with Margaret Angus, owner of the city's long-established popular press. This collection of some 200 local songs begins with iconic, traditional Geordie lyrics such as 'The Keel Row'. But it soon segues into a series of topical, satirical, radical songs by members of Bell's own circle, often in Geordie dialect, protesting the war effort and the local authorities, and championing the city's miners and keelmen (those who ferried the coal downriver and onto the waiting ships). A glance at this volume's paratext is highly instructive. Bell's subtitle is *Being a Curious Collection of Old and New*

Songs and Poems, Peculiar to the Counties of Newcastle upon Tyne, Northumberland, and Durham. The frontispiece has an etching of the city's coat of arms. And its preface begins with Fletcher's maxim, misquoted, and goes on to frame its task as 'to rescue from the yawning jaws of oblivion the productions of the Bards of the Tyne; and by so doing, hand them down to future ages as Reliques of Provincial Poetry'. Ideologically, Bell was aligned with the radical antiquarian Joseph Ritson.[23] Yet his rhetoric borrowed consciously from Ritson's conservative enemy, Thomas Percy. And it was deployed in the service of a collection of vitriolic, irreverent, up-to-the-minute songs by his own friends, in order to package them as respectable 'reliques' or traditional songs – one might almost say folk songs.[24]

It is notable, even remarkable, that the German discourse of *Volkslieder* propagated by Herder in the later eighteenth century made no directly tangible, linguistic impression upon this primarily English and Scottish idealization of the radical labouring voice. That it formed part of the *Zeitgeist* (another word that would have to bide its time in English) of the era is undeniable, but though Herder read and even translated Burns' songs, the interest was not reciprocated, and the English term 'folk song' had to wait until the 1840s.[25] Even in German-speaking Europe, for all Herder's own support of the French Revolution, the connection between protest song and *Volkslieder* was tenuous and unstable. Whereas twentieth-century historians, looking back at this era, have favoured categories such as '*Volkslieder demokratischen Charakters*', the terms in use in the volatile period of 1815–1848 – during which calls for reform across the German territories grew into outright revolution – were more commonly '*Freiheitslied*' (song of freedom) or '*patriotisches Lied*' (patriotic song).[26] Such terms were much more reflective of the reality, in which a wide variety of protest songs were promulgated by a disparate set of activists, many of them students, writers, professionals – overwhelmingly not of the *Volk*, tied to the land, that was idealized in Herder's terminology. Far from possessing any markedly 'folk' characteristics, the radical songs that fuelled this revolutionary era were created, performed, and disseminated much as such songs had been across Europe for centuries: written primarily from above, their lyrics printed on cheap sheets distributed by street-sellers, and sung in urban spaces – streets and public houses – rather than in the rural and Romantic spaces of the folkloric imagination. Lyrics were topical, usually satirical and political, and tunes were taken from theatre or military march as much as from more venerable sources.[27] In 1848 Friedrich Hecker, a leading revolutionary hero and author of several of these songs, wrote a short treatise on 'the political song' in which he demonstrates his indebtedness, not to Herder and the *Volk*, but to the Enlightenment, the French Revolution, and the 'Marseillaise', writing of the functional potential of songs to instil revolutionary fervour *in* the people, rather than extolling songs as pure expressions *of* the people's inherent spirit.[28] Yes, the term *Volk* was used all over the publications Hecker and his comrades were involved with – but its more accurate translation in such contexts would be 'the people', not 'the folk'.[29]

Back in England – and, soon, America – the middle decades of the century might also be characterized as *the people, not the folk*. Successive waves of reformers and Chartists campaigned for popular rights and the extension of the franchise in movements that were genuinely working-class and democratic. Song was absolutely central to these movements. Although middle-class composers and writers were still involved in the cause – most notably the music-and-lyrics pairing of Eliza Flower and Harriet Martineau during the early 1830s – these writers often remained anonymous by design, deferring to a culture dominated by and celebratory of labouring-class production. Leading lights were Ebenezer Elliott, the 'Corn-Law Rhymer', and Thomas Cooper, one of many activists who wrote songs in prison.[30] But less celebrated, often anonymous songwriters added their voices – such as the 'Welsh Chartist woman' to whom Cooper himself attributed the prominent 1841 song 'The Lion of Freedom is Come From His Den'.[31] Many of these unknown writers contributed their effusions to partisan newspapers like the *Northern Star*, which played a central role in distributing the repertoire of Chartist songs that would be sung *en masse* at specific rallies and camp meetings.[32] This was the logical extension of the reactionary song campaign of the 1790s instigated by those enthusiastic writers-in to Reeves' Association: the participation of the masses in a democratic, radical song culture, extended across the British Isles by an increasingly efficient and accessible network of cheap, topical print. When its writers did not set their words to familiar melodies – from Burns' 'Scots Wha Hae' to 'God Save the Queen' – they increasingly favoured new musical settings, provided by obscure composers, the aim being to prove by harmonic and technical competency the credentials of the self-educated workers as putative participants in the running of the state. If they could sing new music in four-part harmonies, then surely they could be trusted with the vote.[33]

Though these movements were generally unsuccessful in achieving their stated political aims (at least in the short term), they entirely redefined British social and political culture, and their songs were highly instrumental in this: transparently demagogic; envoiced at times by hundreds of thousands at enormous meetings; eloquent, energetic, and concerned above all with confident self-definition. They sought to effect radical change and bring about a new age. They were hyper-literate. They were often explicitly internationalist, making common cause between workers of all nations. They were, in all respects, the antithesis of the idealization of 'folk song' that was coming into being at precisely this moment. It is, perhaps, too reductive an approach – based on too little evidence – to suggest that this democratic reality played a causal role in the reactionary creation of the folk song idea. But it is a chronological relation worth noting.

A Canon Emerges

By the end of the nineteenth century, things sounded rather different. While working-class political organs like the *Labour Hymn-Book* continued to promote the original productions of Chartists and post-Chartists across the Anglophone globe, the most prominent new voices in protest song were those of the Fabians and associated socialist thinkers: William Morris, Edward Carpenter, Edith Nesbit, James Leigh Joynes, and Henry Salt. These songs were collected and disseminated in highly aestheticized songbooks subsidized by the producers. Morris' *Chants for Socialists*, a pamphlet of seven songs, was sold for just a penny, not enough to cover the printing of its ornate 'The Socialist League' cover etching. Carpenter's *Chants of Labour*, the most ambitious collection, printed the notated music to its many songs. It also boasted a splendid pair of opening illustrations commissioned from Walter Crane featuring idealized labourers and families exulting in their Arts-and-Crafts immortalization – and looking very little like their real-world equivalents. Salt's *Songs of Freedom* did not run to musical notation or a spectacular frontispiece, but it nonetheless adopted the form and content of a luxury collection of poetry. Transparently removed from a workers' milieu in their material incarnation, these songs also tended to the patrician in their lyrics – the title of Joynes' 'What Ho! My Lads' is symptomatic of a general trend to paternalistic exhortation.[34] The tunes often remained familiar, singable, canonical – but these were not the songs of an autonomous working movement. Just as the founding members of the Folk-Song Society (inaugurated in 1898) were collecting, selecting, curating, sanitizing, and editing the songs they deemed representative of a folk tradition, so too a parallel cadre of elite leftist songwriters was making its own well-intentioned intervention in the

Figure 19.1 Drawings by Walter Crane from *Chants of Labour*, edited by Edward Carpenter (London, 1888).

songs of the people – just, in fact, as both reformers and radicals had done in the seventeenth and eighteenth centuries. The only difference being that there was a new ideology and indeed vocabulary of 'the folk' available to this generation. It is perhaps significant that Morris et al. eschewed its use in their own songs.[35]

Naturally, the radical political songs of the nineteenth century that are most often sung today within the folk tradition are not those of the Fabian

Figure 19.1 (cont.)

socialists. But neither are they the songs of the Chartists – and the same goes for the majority of widespread strike songs, union songs, and so on. Instead, the tendency has been to canonize those works that conform most closely to the folk ideal: either anonymous or expressive of a collective narrative voice (though Burns remains, as ever, an exception); undated; local and specific in geographical reference points, but more abstract when it comes to the politics at stake. A selection of such songs that still feature in many repertoires might include 'The Death of Parker', 'Here's the Tender Coming', 'General Ludd's Triumph', 'The Hand-Loom Weaver's Lament', 'My Old Hat', 'All Jolly Fellows That Follow The Plough', 'The Owslebury Lads', 'Poverty Knock', and above all, 'The Blackleg Miner'. A song such as 'Johnny I Hardly Knew Ye' – demonstrably, as Jonathan Lighter has shown in an excellent study, the product of US marching bands, the London music-hall stage, an Anglo-Irish composer, and a taste for off-colour satire – has been subjected to generations of myth-making to the extent that as recently as 2020, the children's author Michael Morpurgo could wax lyrical about this 'traditional folk song' on BBC Radio 4.[36] All these songs are and were important, and highly expressive of nineteenth-century struggles; they enrich our collective memory. But they occlude the equally if not more important repertoires of working-class movements that have disappeared from the sung record: repertoires that were self-published, self-confident, self-aware, and as such much less compatible with mid twentieth-century transatlantic folk revivalist ideology.

The most totemic of the canonical songs, 'The Blackleg Miner', secured its place in the later tradition when the folklorist and politically radical A. L. Lloyd included it in his 1952 collection *Come All Ye Bold Miners: Ballads & Songs of the Coalfields*. In the sleeve notes to their 1970 record featuring the song, Steeleye Span observed: 'It is strange that a song as powerful and as singable as this should be so rare, yet it has only once been collected', while in the 1978 edition of his collection, Lloyd himself noted that the 'song has become quite widespread since its appearance in the first edition of the present work'.[37] There is an obvious historical tension, even an irony here between the paucity of evidence for this song's contemporaneous nineteenth-century influence, and its ubiquity in the mid to late twentieth-century folk scene. When coupled with the (conscious?) neglect, in the latter period, of demonstrably widespread and influential nineteenth-century protest music sung by the masses across the Anglosphere, this disjuncture verges on the uncomfortable. We might sympathize with working-class songwriter (and subsequently academic) Mike Jones, who co-founded the literate pop protest group Latin Quarter in 1983 after attending one too many student folk/politics events. In 2022, Jones was interviewed by Our Subversive Voice, a research project into the history of English protest song featuring a number of such interviews. Twenty minutes in, he recalls the band's formation:

Latin Quarter comes out of Steve [Skaith] and I walking back from a fundraising event where we'd heard 'The Blackleg Miner' – I said 'If I have to hear the fucking

"Blackleg Miner" again, I'm going to fucking kill myself.' Punk had happened – why are we still listening to this? ... It was just so *worthy*. I said come on, let's try and write some songs that say the things that we believe but end up on *Top of the Pops*.[38]

In Germany, the political side of the folk revival played out rather differently, with scholars in the GDR after 1945, and then singers in the west in the 1960s, pointedly resurrecting the revolutionary democratic songs of the earlier nineteenth century, and especially of 1848.[39] As Dave Robb argues, the specific political stakes of the era led to a philosophy that was rather more receptive than that in the Anglophone world to the revival of self-conscious, engaged, and transparently partisan political songs of the past. Confronted with the Nazis' embrace of a *Völkisch* tradition, it is easy to see why writers like Steinitz and musicians like Peter Rohland were ready to favour the literate, urban, democratic songs of earlier activists over and above an anonymous blood-and-soil *Volk*.[40]

Authenticity Exposed

The German example returns us to a question that has been humming, drone-like, in the background of this chronology: that of authenticity. It is the centrality of authenticity as a constitutive value of both protest and folk song that brings us back to the 1960s moment, satirized in different ways by Morrissey and Innes, with which we began. There is no need for this chapter to retread the arguments of many others in this book, focusing on the intellectual, commercial, and ideological formations of folk music from the early modern period to the present. It is enough to be aware of just how important this idea of an authentic voice was in the construction of a set of values that informed understandings of 'folk' – and to combine that awareness with an appreciation of the much longer history of authenticity in music and politics.

For centuries, as we have seen, activists seeking to advance a political message via music had sought to exploit the authenticity, the moral credibility, that came from certain forms of musical presentation. Even in the seventeenth century – the era of 'Vox Populi. In Plaine English' – it mattered whether a publisher set political song texts in black-letter font (which 'the people' were used to reading) or white-letter (the roman fonts associated with a social elite).[41] In the 1780s–1800s, the conservative moral reform movement led by Hannah More that disseminated the Cheap

Repository Tracts made sure to efface their own top-down agency by using street singers as distributors, choosing familiar popular tunes, and printing their songs on cheap paper.[42] In the same, Burnsian era, the idea of the labouring voice began to accrue real cultural capital. And it was no different when, in the 1950s–1960s, Ewan MacColl sought to harness new conceptions of 'authentic' folk music in the service of the Communist Party of Great Britain. Although – in fact, precisely *because* – his songs and those of the wider Critics' Group were programmatic and artificial, it was essential that they conformed to the criteria of the folk revival movement; to the precedent set by Alan Lomax.[43] This is not to diminish the group's sincerity, simply to highlight the similarity of their methods to past movements. Writing of this period, Peggy Seeger – author of this book's next chapter – recalls her (superb) song 'I'm Gonna Be An Engineer': 'Ewan, who usually did the writing, said, "Look, I just haven't got time to write this. And anyway, you should write it ... [W]e've got to have that song and we've got to have it in a week"'.[44] In her recent memoir, she adds: 'I wrote it in two hours and took it upstairs to Ewan's cubicle in the cistern room. He was brisk. *The last verse is depressing, Peg. You need some hope.* Downstairs again, rewrote the verse.'[45] There is nothing here of 'authenticity', or of 'folk'. But in commissioning protest songs to a deadline, critiquing, and rewriting, MacColl and Seeger exactly replicated the techniques and partnerships of earlier eras: the protest songs produced in 1830s London by Harriet Martineau, Eliza Flower, and William Fox; by the circle of John Bell and John Marshall in Regency Newcastle; by the Wilson family – father and sons – of working-class songwriters in 1800s Manchester; by the network of 1790s radicals that included printer-writers like James Montgomery in Sheffield and Robert Thomson in London, and collaborators like William Roscoe in Liverpool and John Thelwall in the capital, all of them extended (and frequently imperilled) Critics Groups of sorts.[46] Similarly, when Bob Dylan borrowed and adapted the melody of 'No More Auction Block', a Black anti-slavery spiritual, for 'Blowin' in the Wind', he was doing exactly as political songwriters had done for centuries: whether we call it homage, contrafactum, or appropriation, it was an age-old technique of recruiting musically-derived authenticity in the service of a political position (albeit, in this case, one intentionally vague).[47]

However, what *was* novel in the 1960s – especially by 1965, the year of the legendary Newport Folk Festival when Dylan plugged in an electric guitar – was the *inverse* of this phenomenon. In folk rock, we can see the creation of a commercially lucrative new genre, swiftly assimilated into the music industry and packaged for mass consumption, that sought to borrow authenticity from its espousal of countercultural politics. That is, instead of a political movement turning to music for moral and cultural capital, we have a commercial music genre turning to politics for the same thing – a marketing tool to distinguish itself from what was construed as the vapid, apolitical, and thus purportedly superficial realm of 'pop'.[48] In the 1790s, Hannah More, Reeves' Association, and other reformist and reactionary forces had a political set of values to disseminate among the people, and self-consciously chose to do so by means of what they regarded as a shallow but beloved cultural form: cheap print, familiar melodies, the things that they knew appealed in particular to those of supposedly lesser intellect (the young, the poor, women). This phenomenon was perhaps the most cynical instance of a much wider and longer process. But in the origins of folk rock, there is perhaps an equivalent cynicism in the negative: in order to promote and capitalize upon a new iteration of a beloved cultural form and give it distinctive kudos, a nascent association with politics was exploited and writers of protest songs given a broader platform, not to spread the politics but to valorize and sell the product. As Kenneth Bindas and Craig Houston have put it: '[folk] rock, as a commodity, marketed these anti-Establishment themes in order to capture the consumer whose ideals it mirrored.'[49]

This is, of course, a proposition too vast, and an oversimplification too crashing, to explore fully here. And it is not to dismiss the canonical protest songs of the mid 1960s as insincere: it was the credibility of the artists that the whole thing was built upon. But it presents us, in the longer scheme of things, with a grand historical irony, the tables turned – folk music rooting its credibility in an association with political protest. This is why, returning to Neil Innes' 'Protest Song', we find the simple parody has bite. Innes' Dylan-esque singer has assembled all the superficial markers of folk rock – rootsy clothes, acoustic guitar, harmonica, nasal head-voice – but his lyrics are bathetically empty, making gestures towards a political integrity they do not in fact possess; the closest they come to a proposition in a tangle of metaphor being 'we're marching for freedom today, hey'. It is that borrowing of an assumed authenticity, exposed.

None of which is to call out the genre we recognize today as folk as especially inauthentic or artificial. Rather, it is to place the formation of that genre in a longer perspective, and demonstrate that the association of 'folk' with radical protest is merely one self-conscious move within a wider history of protest music and popular expression. Folk as a genre continues to produce important protest songs, but only because it is a living genre available to musicians with something to say, just as every other genre is, from grime to pop, reggae to punk, R&B to easy listening. To return to

England, many of the most significant protest songs born of its folk scene have been written by highly self-aware, reflective musicians, perfectly happy to marry a folk idiom with highly writerly and composerly rhetoric. Sydney Carter's 'The Crow on the Cradle' (1963) turns a series of nursery rhymes on their head in the shadow of the Bomb. Leon Rosselson's 'The World Turned Upside Down' (1975) takes its title, not from the seventeenth-century song of the same name, but from a book by Marxist historian Christopher Hill. Two winners of Best Folk Song at the BBC Radio 2 Folk Awards – Maggie Holland with 'A Place Called England' (2000) and Chris Wood with 'Hollow Point' (2011) – have created powerful protest from rich literary allusion and novelistic lyrical style respectively. Grace Petrie's 'I Wish The Guardian Believed That I Exist' (2016) takes issue with the argument that 'there's no such thing as a protest singer / We lost them when the mines all closed'. Pointing out that 'there's politics in everything we sing', Petrie argues that political protest can come in many musical and lyrical guises, reminding us of Jones's rejection of 'The Blackleg Miner'. It is Morrissey's realization all over again: the association of protest music with the acoustic guitar-wielding singer-songwriter is a function of a brief historical phenomenon. There continue to be urgent, incisive, excellent protest songs produced within the genre of folk music, not because folk is the sole natural, objective vehicle for the expression of such sentiments, but because it is a tradition that – like many others – can boast committed, politically engaged writers and audiences as a subset of its overall demographic, and – like many other musical traditions – it provides fertile conditions for those writers and audiences. But the full history of popular protest song is broader, longer, louder, and indeed queerer than folk alone – though that's another story.

Notes

1. For an analysis of the movement, see Simon Frith and John Street, 'Rock Against Red Wedge: From Music to Politics, from Politics to Music', in *Rockin' the Boat: Mass Music and Mass Movements*, ed. Reebee Garofalo. Boston, MA: South End Press, 1992, 67–80.
2. For detailed discussion, see John Street et al., *Our Subversive Voice: The History and Politics of English Protest Songs*. Montreal: McGill-Queen's University Press, 2025, chapter one.
3. For the dating, see www.oed.com/dictionary/protest-song_n, which cites John Greenway, *American Folksongs of Protest*. Philadelphia: University of Pennsylvania Press, 1953.

4. The outstanding example is Aileen Dillane et al., ed., *Songs of Social Protest: International Perspectives*. London: Rowman & Littlefield, 2018.
5. Raphael Holinshed, *Chronicles of England, Scotland and Ireland*. London: Reginald Wolfe, 2nd edn 1587, 1546. Accessible at https://english.nsms.ox.ac.uk/Holinshed/texts.php?text1=1587_9135#p17498.
6. Todd A. Borlik and Clare Egan, 'Angling for the "Powte": A Jacobean Environmental Protest Poem'. *English Literary Renaissance* 48 (2018): 256–89.
7. https://oursubversivevoice.com/song/11970/.
8. https://oursubversivevoice.com/song/11956/.
9. L. P. Grijp, 'Nationale hymnen. Het Wilhelmus en zijn buren'. *Volkskundig Bulletin* 24 (1998): 16–42.
10. For England, the leading authorities are Christopher Marsh and Angela McShane; see also www.100ballads.org/.
11. I discuss Fletcher's argument and its long afterlife in detail in Oskar Cox Jensen, *The Ballad-Singer in Georgian and Victorian London*. Cambridge: Cambridge University Press, 2021, 98–101.
12. Andrew Fletcher, *The Political Works of Andrew Fletcher, Esq*. London, 1737, 373–4.
13. For these periodic attempts at reform and anxieties around song in general, see further discussion in Cox Jensen, *The Ballad-Singer*, 81–121, and Cox Jensen, 'The Ballad and the Bible' in *Scripture and Song in Nineteenth-Century Britain*, ed. James Grande and Brian Murray, 29–47. London: Bloomsbury, 2023.
14. 'A friend to Church and State' to John Reeves' Association for the Preservation of Liberty and Property against Republicans and Levellers, 12 December 1792. British Library Add. MSS 16922, fol. 43.
15. Mark Philp, 'Vulgar Conservatism'. *English Historical Review* 110 (1995): 42–69, 52; and Oskar Cox Jensen, *Napoleon and British Song, 1797–1822*. Basingstoke: Palgrave Macmillan, 2015, 16–17.
16. Edmund Burke, *Reflections on the Revolution in France*. London, 1790, 117. There is a vast scholarship on the phrase and the reaction it prompted; a good starting place is Darren Howard, 'Necessary Fictions: The "Swinish Multitude" and the Rights of Man'. *Studies in Romanticism* 47 (2008): 161–78.
17. For the latter, see https://oursubversivevoice.com/song/12113/.
18. Cox Jensen, *Napoleon*, 27–30; Cox Jensen, *The Ballad-Singer*, 81–2.
19. Street et al., *Our Subversive Voice*, chapter two.
20. For a full discussion, see Julia Hamilton at https://oursubversivevoice.com/voice/the-same-old-poem-re-setting-william-cowpers-the-negros-complaint-to-music/.
21. https://oursubversivevoice.com/?s=ludd&x=0&y=0; Kevin Binfield, ed., *Writings of the Luddites*. Baltimore: Johns Hopkins University Press, 2004.
22. www.oed.com/dictionary/authenticity_n; for the fitness argument, see Cox Jensen, *Napoleon*, 21–2 and thereafter.

23. Stephanie L. Barczewski, 'Ritson, Joseph (1752–1803)'. *Oxford Dictionary of National Biography*. Oxford: Oxford University Press, 2004.
24. But see also Dave Harker, 'The Original Bob Cranky?' *Folk Music Journal* 5 (1985): 48–82, for a critical reading of Bell. For further context to this entire paragraph, see Dave Harker, *Fakesong: The Manufacture of British 'Folksong', 1700 to the Present Day*. Milton Keynes: Open University Press, 1985, 21–60.
25. Margery Palmer McCulloch, 'Volksdichter und Künstler: German Responses to Robert Burns'. *Studies in Scottish Literature* 33 (2004): 30–41, esp. 34. See Ross Cole, 'The Idea of Folk Music', in this volume.
26. Wolfgang Steinitz, *Deutsche Volkslieder demokratischen Charakters aus sechs Jahrhunderten*, 2 vols. Berlin: Akademie-Verlag, 1954, 1962. Eckhard John and David Robb, *Songs for a Revolution: The 1848 Protest Song Tradition in Germany*. Rochester, NY: Camden House, 2020, 13. But see Karina Kellermann, *Abschied vom "historischen Volkslied": Studien zu Funktion, Ästhetik und Publizität der Gattung historisch-politische Ereignisdichtung*. Tübingen: Niemeyer, 2000, for a counter-argument.
27. See John and Robb, *Songs for a Revolution* for the best study of these songs to date.
28. Friedrich Hecker, 'Das politische Lied', foreword to Karl Heinrich Schnauffer, *Neue Lieder für das Teutsche Volk*. Rheinfelden: F. Hollinger, 1848, analysed extensively in John and Robb, *Songs for a Revolution*, 1–11.
29. See John and Robb, *Songs for a Revolution*, esp. 10.
30. Oskar Cox Jensen, 'The Hymn as Protest Song in England and Its Empire, 1819–1919'. *Yale Journal of Music and Religion* 8 (2022): 104–24.
31. https://oursubversivevoice.com/song/12219/.
32. David Kennerley, 'Strikes and Singing Classes: Chartist Culture, "Rational Recreation" and the Politics of Music after 1842'. *English Historical Review* 135 (2020): 1165–94.
33. Kennerley, 'Strikes', and see also Cox Jensen, 'The Hymn', esp. 114–7.
34. https://oursubversivevoice.com/song/12278/.
35. For connections between Morris and folkloric thinking, see Ross Cole, *The Folk: Music, Modernity, and the Political Imagination*. Oakland: University of California Press, 2021, 74–103.
36. Jonathan Lighter, *'The Best Antiwar Song Ever Written'*. Northfield: Loomis House Press, 2012; Michael Morpurgo, 'Johnny I Hardly Knew Ye'. *Michael Morpurgo's Folk Journeys*, BBC Radio 4, 19 October 2020, www.bbc.co.uk/sounds/play/m000nll9.
See also https://oursubversivevoice.com/song/12269/.
37. Both citations are taken from the song's entry in the Mainly Norfolk database, at https://mainlynorfolk.info/louis.killen/songs/blacklegminers.html.
38. https://oursubversivevoice.com/interview/mike-jones/, from 21:15.
39. John and Robb, *Songs for a Revolution*, 303.
40. John and Robb, *Songs for a Revolution*, 311–15.

41. Angela McShane, 'Drink, Song and Politics in Early Modern England'. *Popular Music* 35 (2016): 166–90, 184–6.
42. Cox Jensen, 'The Ballad and the Bible'.
43. Street et al., *Our Subversive Voice*, chapter five.
44. In Lisa Garrison and Sarah Plant, 'Honing, Polishing, Casting Out: Peggy Seeger Talks about the Folk Process'. *Sing Out!* 28 (1980): 2–11.
45. Peggy Seeger, *First Time Ever: A Memoir*. London: Faber & Faber, 2017, 265–6.
46. Street et al., *Our Subversive Voice*, chapter six; Oskar Cox Jensen, '"Canny Newcassel": Marshall's Musical Metropolis of North Britain', in *Music in North-East England, 1500–1800*, ed. Stephanie Carter, Kirsten Gibson and Roz Southey, 282–302. Woodbridge: Boydell & Brewer, 2020; and Cox Jensen, *Napoleon*, 21, 32, 110–11 for the Wilsons.
47. There is an extensive literature on this. See, for example, Charles Hughes, 'Allowed to Be Free: Bob Dylan and the Civil Rights Movement', in *Highway 61 Revisited: Bob Dylan's Road from Minnesota to the World*, ed. Colleen J. Sheehy and Thomas Swiss. Minneapolis: University of Minnesota Press, 2009, 44–60; David Yaffe, *Bob Dylan: Like a Complete Unknown*. New Haven, CT: Yale University Press, 2011, 93–124.
48. For an early commentary on this, see Michael Orth, 'The Crack in the Consensus'. *New Mexico Quarterly* 36 (1966): 62–79.
49. Kenneth J. Bindas and Craig Houston, '"Takin' Care of Business": Rock Music, Vietnam and the Protest Myth', *The Historian* 52 (1989): 1–23, 4.

20 | Artist Voice

Multiple Identities

PEGGY SEEGER

As it's helpful to know who wrote what you are reading, here's me in a nutshell. I will be dealing not with folk *music* but with folk *song*, chiefly words and melody. I work only within UK and Anglo-American (UK/A-A) traditions. My parents were middle-class Yankees, Western classical music professionals who became folk music enablers in the 1930s and 1940s, drenching their children in field recordings collected by Alan and John Lomax et al. I have worked in the UK folk revival since 1959. I am not a folk singer *per se* but a singer of A-A folk songs that I have borrowed. I also write topical songs of all sorts. The web and my memoir *First Time Ever* will tell you more than you might need or want to know.

Of the multiple promised, I've chosen three basic entities: *community*, *singer*, and *song*. These are so interdependent that discourse upon one automatically involves the others. Communities are the social soil upon which human cultures germinate. They are global and local, virtual and real, very small and very large, connecting and spreading out like a genealogy gone mad. They breed and support singers who make, sing, and pass on the songs, which in turn act as group glue and create new communities.

Who Sings?

Queen Caroline Hughes, a Dorset Romani woman, was a *field singer* – a term used by collectors for their original sources. A custodian of more than a hundred British folksongs, she was 'the real source' (which I am not). Matriarch of her extended family of Travellers and probably illiterate, she lived in a traditional caravan and was always on the move with her people, a pariah social group harassed by the settled Gorgios. The songs were infinitely precious to them, a treasure trove to guard and pass down. Her whole community knew them but only Caroline sang them when required. When we questioned her about the old traditional ballads she said, 'Them's our relegends. Them's our history. Without them we're nothin'.

Like Caroline I am a song-carrier: she from one era to the next, myself from one social class to another, like post persons delivering a parcel. She shared within a stable community – I share with anyone. We have similar repertoires. We both have deep love and respect for the songs. Caroline kept the songs exactly as she learned them (which I often do not). She sang them to her community. I create new communities. The songs are deep within me. Without them I am much, much less.

Who Listens?

For the moment, let's stick with revival singers like me, who sing every time for a different company of individuals who will pass through stages of collective identity as the event progresses. We shepherd them into a herd using humour, contrasting songs, and many sorts of persuasion that we professional singers prefer to keep to ourselves. If the whole front row is sobbing over Willie's farewell from the grave to his weeping lover, 'If ever the dead may pray for the living, my love, I'll pray for thee,' you've done your job. Tears are a gift. Chatter as they exit? Who are they now? Silence? Maybe they're still upset by that angry man who stormed out after two feminist songs shouting that he 'didn't come to hear a concert of f***ing songs about women!' He shifted audience identity in fifteen seconds. The audience are not just listeners. They absorb with ears, eyes, heart, and brain, and can easily slip into boredom or urgent desire for change . . . any change. Be prepared for pulling hard on the reins and changing direction.

The community of that Kent folk club had multiple identities from the moment I met the organizer to the point where a US Army freedom-fighter rose in his seat and poured his beer over me. Organizer and audience fled. A pod of killer males trashed the whole room. One song was 'too many f***ing anti-Vietnam war songs' for them. They chased me down the M20 – I outran them, doing a ton in the Citroën. Identities clash.

. . . and the Songs?

Where's their identity in all this? Classical music has strict stylistic features and is hewn on staff lines and huge orchestral scores. You are told what to do and how and when to do it. There is formal training so we can produce the right voice and give forth what we think the composer intended. Misreading the dots on the lines can be life-threatening. It is rumoured that the poor bass player who missed his cue in *Sailing By* (for the Shipping Forecast) obsessed over it till the day he died. You interpret such music. You don't create it.

At one time, sheet music provided basic transcriptions of popular songs of the time whose 'style' was still relatively close to both folk and classical music. Now songs can be hewn (and accidentally lost) on a recording desk with a composer/engineer/producer/robot turning out zenith/nadir, heaven/hell creations. 'Change' being the market credo, a new song constantly replaces the old one after the latter's fictitious 'fifteen minutes'. Rather like the unemployed queues in the capitalist system, instability and insecurity are inbuilt. Quality, content, style are all at the beck and call of ever-moving media-driven supply and demand. Mind you, much stunning talent and emotional depth can go into it – but defining popular music and its many nomenclatures and performers feels like giving an identity to a whirlwind. I only attempt it in order to put traditional song-making and transmission into perspective.

Is Style Important?

UK/A-A folk songs were organic, made in a time when there were few outside musical influences entering the home community. What was the intent of the maker of a 1700s orally transmitted song and how do we honour it? In our traditions, these songs were most often sung unaccompanied in what is known as sing/speak or 'I sing it like I say it'. They were made primarily to tell a story. They were word-focused via narrative, dialogue, and simple poetic formats with no instrumental distractions. Finely trained voices seem more concerned with the melody than the words, displaying the voice via histrionics, swelling in volume, long drawn-out high melody notes, slowing down dramatically at the end, performances bordering on theatre – contrary to the understatement of the folk storytelling process.

'Brigg Fair', a Lincolnshire folk song, was recorded, notated, printed, and taken up by folk and classical performers, bringing it speedily from orality to literacy, from ur-folk to revival-folk to classical. Put four renditions, in this order, into your browser: Joseph Taylor, a field singer; then revival singers Shirley Collins and Ryan Boldt of The Deep Dark Woods; then Ian Bostridge, his voice focussed on its classical self, a full orchestral score. The unadorned fragment, recorded in 1905, spins through time and stylistic metamorphoses to the present where we who study folk music catch it like a frisbee and toss it into anthologies and critical studies. Its 360° 'identity' would include all the circumstances in which it was sung ... endless shapeshifting. How many angels or devils dance on the head of 'Brigg Fair'?

All this doesn't mean everyone has to sing 'Brigg Fair' like Joseph Taylor. The most important thing is the *story*, easily overshadowed if instruments and a 'beautiful' voice run the show. If a listener can't remember a single word of what I sang, have I honoured the intent of its maker?

The Songs . . . Again

Sitting in the chiropractor's office with that Halloween model of a skeleton, I flesh it out in my mind. Most UK/A-A songs are sturdy frameworks constructed chiefly of nouns and verbs. No adverbs (Stephen King would approve). Everyday adjectives: lovely, fair maid, ruby lips, cherry cheeks, raven-black hair and a spare narrative. In the cowboy westerns, the full orchestra hiding behind the tumbleweed tells us how to feel and respond, keeps us from contributing to the story. A traditional ballad well sung in sing-speak can be fed, clothed, and sheltered in seconds by the minds of listeners. I can reinhabit my childhood home, including the smell of chicken pie, when I sing 'Old Joe Clark'. I sang 'The Two Sisters' unaccompanied in a junior school then asked, 'What colour was the dress the younger sister was wearing?' It was red! No, it wasn't, it was blue, striped with long sleeves! No, it wasn't, she was wearing trousers! The kids were making their own stories out of it. In a school for children in trouble there was a quiet one in the third row biting her nails. I learned she was a victim of incest. She wrote a scorching poem shortly after, using the form and footage of 'The Two Sisters'.

Can You 'Write' a Folk Song?

No. A folk song 'becomes' if ongoing generations adapt it and, hopefully, forget who originally wrote it. Make a song like a folk song, in a folk idiom? Yes. Ewan MacColl wrote 'The Shoals of Herring' using the words of Norfolk fisherman Sam Larner and reworking an English folk song tune. It is now known in Ireland as 'The Shores of Erin' and few people know that Ewan wrote it. Larner himself declared, 'I known that song all my life'. Is it maybe on the way to becoming a folk song? These treasures have endured through chronological/social/geographical upheavals. Why not study how they do it?

What Now?

A notification flashed up on my phone: 'If you are looking for a community we can help you find one.' All they needed was my postcode. The communities that produced folk songs were united by work, isolation, proximity, social bonds, and their own music and stories. When such communities broke up – or were broken up by progress, growth, development, and the media intruding with its hydra-head – this song-making process dissolved and before long we became consumers not producers. Now there are few songs in England that we can sing together. We sing in church, at scouts, at football, but there is no unifying body of well-known songs to help us *feel* together when we *are* together.

Quite a while back, I trawled the folk clubs intensely. Occasionally they felt dusty and many songs were definitely un-PC, but at least they are a community of sorts. They're regular get-togethers with regulars attending, rather like Sunday dinners. Folk festivals ditto, where most anything comes and goes. Friends meet, strangers dance together, this or that old song is deconstructed, singer-songwriters strut their despair, ambition, love life, their instrumental skill or lack of it. The togetherness is addictive, but rarely do festivals give us something to take back home and do on our own. From the 1930s through the 1960s, big industry, unions, and tidal political movements used folk songs and folk formats to create singable songs. Sing together becomes belong together. Yes, belonging ... that's what folk-type music can do if we let it, right from singing in the womb to our mother's heartbeat to marching on a demo.

New Identities

We can do more than just guard a vanished art form. Folk songs make great templates. Their language is so close to our spoken language that we can go into schools and encourage children to make their own songs; bring isolated songwriters together; make songs about every possible local or global issue and sing them at community events; make choruses to groupsing and take home; encourage unaccompanied singing so that you don't have to have an instrument in order to sing. A chance for everyone to tell their own story in their own way – with others. Back to community, full circle.

All of us in this book, experienced in our fields and roughly on the same page(s), have gathered together, each with something of our own to offer on the same subject. Our joint terminology bound us together and many new identities will have sprung up during this process, including yours, dear reader. Take it and run.

Further Reading

Origins & History

Bendix, Regina. *In Search of Authenticity: The Formation of Folklore Studies*. Madison: University of Wisconsin Press, 1997.

Cox Jensen, Oskar. *The Ballad-Singer in Georgian and Victorian London*. Cambridge: Cambridge University Press, 2021.

Epstein, Dena J. *Sinful Tunes and Spirituals: Black Folk Music to the Civil War*. Urbana: University of Illinois Press, 1977.

Fox, Adam. *Oral and Literate Culture in England, 1500–1700*. Oxford: Oxford University Press, 2000.

Fumerton, Patricia and Anita Guerrini, ed. *Ballads and Broadsides in Britain, 1500–1800*. Farnham: Ashgate, 2010.

Gammon, Vic. *Desire, Drink, and Death in English Folk and Vernacular Song, 1600–1900*. Aldershot: Ashgate, 2008.

Gelbart, Matthew. *The Invention of 'Folk Music' and 'Art Music': Emerging Concepts from Ossian to Wagner*. Cambridge: Cambridge University Press, 2007.

Gregory, David. *Victorian Songhunters: The Recovery and Editing of English Vernacular Ballads and Folk Lyrics, 1820–1883*. Lanham: Scarecrow Press, 2006.

Harker, Dave. *Fakesong: The Manufacture of British 'Folksong', 1700 to the Present Day*. Milton Keynes: Open University Press, 1985.

Herder, Johann Gottfried and Philip V. Bohlman. *Song Loves the Masses: Herder on Music and Nationalism*. Oakland: University of California Press, 2017.

Marsh, Christopher. *Music and Society in Early Modern England*. Cambridge: Cambridge University Press, 2010.

McDowell, Paula. *The Invention of the Oral: Print Commerce and Fugitive Voices in Eighteenth-Century Britain*. Chicago: University of Chicago Press, 2017.

McLane, Maureen N. *Balladeering, Minstrelsy, and the Making of British Romantic Poetry*. Cambridge: Cambridge University Press, 2008.

Sedley, Stephen and Martin Carthy. *Who Killed Cock Robin? British Folk Songs of Crime and Punishment*. London: Reaktion Books, 2021.

Watt, Paul, Derek B. Scott, and Patrick Spedding, ed. *Cheap Print and Popular Song in the Nineteenth Century: A Cultural History of the Songster*. Cambridge: Cambridge University Press, 2017.

Politics & Identity

Appiah, Kwame Anthony. *Lines of Descent: W. E. B. Du Bois and the Emergence of Identity*. Cambridge, MA: Harvard University Press, 2014.

Cole, Ross. *The Folk: Music, Modernity, and the Political Imagination*. Oakland: University of California Press, 2021.

Filene, Benjamin. *Romancing the Folk: Public Memory and American Roots Music*. Chapel Hill: University of North Carolina Press, 2000.

Jassal, Smita Tewari. *Unearthing Gender: Folksongs of North India*. Durham, NC: Duke University Press, 2012.

Jordan, Daniel David. *Coros y Danzas: Folk Music and Spanish Nationalism in the Early Franco Regime (1939–1953)*. Oxford: Oxford University Press, 2023.

Maliangkay, Roald. *Broken Voices: Postcolonial Entanglements and the Preservation of Korea's Central Folksong Traditions*. Honolulu: University of Hawai'i Press, 2017.

Miller, Karl Hagstrom. *Segregating Sound: Inventing Folk and Pop Music in the Age of Jim Crow*. Durham, NC: Duke University Press, 2010.

Nicholls, David G. *Conjuring the Folk: Forms of Modernity in African America*. Ann Arbor: University of Michigan Press, 2000.

Roy, William G. *Reds, Whites, and Blues: Social Movements, Folk Music, and Race in the United States*. Princeton: Princeton University Press, 2010.

Shay, Anthony. *Folk Dance and the Creation of National Identities: Staging the Folk*. Basingstoke: Palgrave Macmillan, 2023.

Slominski, Tes. *Trad Nation: Gender, Sexuality, and Race in Irish Traditional Music*. Middletown: Wesleyan University Press, 2020.

Stone, Jonathan W. *Listening to the Lomax Archive: The Sonic Rhetorics of African American Folksong in the 1930s*. Ann Arbor: University of Michigan Press, 2021.

Street, John, Oskar Cox Jensen, Alan Finlayson, Angela McShane, and Matthew Worley, *Our Subversive Voice: The History and Politics of English Protest Songs*. Montreal: McGill-Queen's University Press, 2025.

Thompson, Katrina Dyonne. *Ring Shout, Wheel About: The Racial Politics of Music and Dance in North American Slavery*. Urbana: University of Illinois Press, 2014.

Winter, Trish and Simon Keegan-Phipps. *Performing Englishness: Identity and Politics in a Contemporary Folk Resurgence*. Manchester: Manchester University Press, 2013.

Folk Revivalism

Allen, Ray. *Gone to the Country: The New Lost City Ramblers and the Folk Music Revival*. Urbana: University of Illinois Press, 2010.

Bithell, Caroline and Juniper Hill, ed. *The Oxford Handbook of Music Revival*. Oxford: Oxford University Press, 2014.

Boyes, Georgina. *The Imagined Village: Culture, Ideology and the English Folk Revival*. Manchester: Manchester University Press, 1993.
Cantwell, Robert. *When We Were Good: The Folk Revival*. Cambridge, MA: Harvard University Press, 1996.
Cohen, Ronald D. *Rainbow Quest: The Folk Music Revival and American Society, 1940–1970*. Amherst: University of Massachusetts Press, 2002.
Dunaway, David K. and Molly Beer. *Singing Out: An Oral History of America's Folk Music Revivals*. New York: Oxford University Press, 2010.
Hair, Ross and Thomas Ruys Smith, ed. *Harry Smith's Anthology of American Folk Music: America Changed Through Music*. Abingdon: Routledge, 2017.
Laing, Dave, Karl Dallas, Robin Denselow, and Robert Shelton. *The Electric Muse: The Story of Folk Into Rock*. London: Methuen, 1975.
Lindsay, Bruce. *Two Bold Singermen and the English Folk Revival: The Lives, Song Traditions and Legacies of Sam Larner and Harry Cox*. Sheffield: Equinox Publishing, 2020.
Munro, Ailie. *The Democratic Muse: Folk Music Revival in Scotland*. Aberdeen: Scottish Cultural Press, 1996.
Olsen, Laura J. *Performing Russia: Folk Revival and Russian Identity*. London: RoutledgeCurzon, 2004.
Rosenberg, Neil V., ed. *Transforming Tradition: Folk Music Revivals Examined*. Urbana: University of Illinois Press, 1993.
Russell, Ian and David Atkinson, ed. *Folk Song: Tradition, Revival, and Re-creation*. Aberdeen: The Elphinstone Institute, University of Aberdeen, 2025.
Svec, Henry Adam. *American Folk Music as Tactical Media*. Amsterdam: Amsterdam University Press, 2017.
Sweers, Britta. *Electric Folk: The Changing Face of English Traditional Music*. Oxford: Oxford University Press, 2005.

Folklorists & Song Collectors

Adams, Byron and Daniel M. Grimley, ed. *Vaughan Williams and His World*. Chicago: University of Chicago Press, 2023.
Arthur, Dave. *Bert: The Life and Times of A. L. Lloyd*. London: Pluto Press, 2012.
Brown, Mary Ellen. *Child's Unfinished Masterpiece: The English and Scottish Popular Ballads*. Urbana: University of Illinois Press, 2011.
Cochran, Robert. *Louise Pound: Scholar, Athlete, Feminist Pioneer*. Lincoln: University of Nebraska Press, 2009.
Cooper, David. *Béla Bartók*. New Haven, CT: Yale University Press, 2015.
Dalos, Anna. *Zoltán Kodály's World of Music*. Oakland: University of California Press, 2020.
DiSavino, Elizabeth. *Katherine Jackson French: Kentucky's Forgotten Ballad Collector*. Lexington: University Press of Kentucky, 2021.

Karpeles, Maud. *Cecil Sharp: His Life and Work*. London: Faber & Faber, 2008.
Lomax, Alan. *Folk Song Style and Culture*. New Brunswick: Transaction Books, 1978.
Lomax, John A. *Adventures of a Ballad Hunter*. Austin: University of Texas Press, 2017.
Porterfield, Nolan. *Last Cavalier: The Life and Times of John A. Lomax, 1867–1948*. Urbana: University of Illinois Press, 1996.
Robinson, Suzanne and Kay Dreyfus, ed. *Grainger the Modernist*. Farnham: Ashgate, 2015.
Seeger, Ruth Crawford. *The Music of American Folk Song and Selected Other Writings on American Folk Music*, ed. Larry Polansky with Judith Tick. Rochester, NY: University of Rochester Press, 2001.
Szwed, John F. *The Man Who Recorded the World: A Biography of Alan Lomax*. London: Arrow, 2011.
de Val, Dorothy. *In Search of Song: The Life and Times of Lucy Broadwood*. Farnham: Ashgate, 2011.

Singers & Songwriters

Baez, Joan. *And a Voice to Sing With: A Memoir*. New York: Simon & Schuster, 2009.
Bernard, Sheila Curran. *Bring Judgment Day: Reclaiming Lead Belly's Truths from Jim Crow's Lies*. Cambridge: Cambridge University Press, 2024.
Collins, Shirley. *America Over the Water*. London: White Rabbit, 2022.
Copper, Bob. *A Song for Every Season: A Hundred Years of a Sussex Farming Family*. London: Heinemann, 1971.
Dylan, Bob. *Chronicles: Volume One*. London: Simon & Schuster, 2004.
Freedman, Jean R. *Peggy Seeger: A Life of Music, Love, and Politics*. Urbana: University of Illinois Press, 2020.
Guthrie, Woody. *Bound for Glory*. London: Penguin Books, 2004.
Hampton, Timothy. *Bob Dylan, How the Songs Work*. New York: Zone Books, 2019.
Harker, Ben. *Class Act: The Cultural and Political Life of Ewan MacColl*. London: Pluto Press, 2007.
MacColl, Ewan. *Journeyman: An Autobiography*. London: Sidgwick and Jackson, 1990.
Schumacher, Michael. *There But for Fortune: The Life of Phil Ochs*. Minneapolis: University of Minnesota Press, 2018.
Seeger, Peggy. *First Time Ever: A Memoir*. London: Faber & Faber, 2017.
Stadler, Gustavus. *Woody Guthrie: An Intimate Life*. Boston, MA: Beacon Press, 2020.
Winkler, Allan M. *'To Everything There Is a Season': Pete Seeger and the Power of Song*. New York: Oxford University Press, 2009.
Zack, Ian. *Odetta: A Life in Music and Protest*. Boston, MA: Beacon Press, 2020.

Global Traditions

Blackwell, Carole. *Tradition and Society in Turkmenistan: Gender, Oral Culture and Song*. Richmond: Curzon, 2001.
Bohlman, Philip V. *The Study of Folk Music in the Modern World*. Bloomington: Indiana University Press, 1988.
Čvoro, Uroš. *Turbo-Folk Music and Cultural Representations of National Identity in Former Yugoslavia*. Farnham: Ashgate, 2014.
Dubois, Laurent. *The Banjo: America's African Instrument*. Cambridge, MA: Harvard University Press, 2016.
Fiol, Stefan. *Recasting Folk in the Himalayas: Indian Music, Media, and Social Mobility*. Urbana: University of Illinois Press, 2017.
Inserra, Incoronata. *Global Tarantella: Reinventing Southern Italian Folk Music and Dances*. Urbana: University of Illinois Press, 2018.
Jones, Stephen. *In Search of the Folk Daoists of North China*. Farnham: Ashgate, 2010.
Lewin, Olive. *'Rock it Come Over': The Folk Music of Jamaica*. Kingston: University of the West Indies Press, 2000.
McKerrell, Simon and Gary West, ed. *Understanding Scotland Musically: Folk, Tradition, and Policy*. Abingdon: Routledge, 2018.
Motherway, Susan H. *The Globalization of Irish Traditional Song Performance*. Farnham: Ashgate, 2013.
Prakash, Brahma. *Cultural Labour: Conceptualizing the 'Folk Performance' in India*. New Delhi: Oxford University Press, 2019.
Ramnarine, Tina K. *Ilmatar's Inspirations: Nationalism, Globalization, and the Changing Soundscapes of Finnish Folk Music*. Chicago: University of Chicago Press, 2003.
Sherinian, Zoe C. *Tamil Folk Music as Dalit Liberation Theology*. Bloomington: Indiana University Press, 2014.
Slobin, Mark. *Subcultural Sounds: Micromusics of the West*. Hanover, NH: University Press of New England, 2000.
Strom, Yale. *The Book of Klezmer: The History, the Music, the Folklore*. Chicago: Chicago Review Press, 2002.

Index

'Bangston', 124
'Battle Hymn of the Republic', 22, 321
'Blowin' in the Wind', 62, 64, 348
'Brigg Fair', 356
'Bring Me Back My Blue-eyed Boy', 125
'Hey, Tutti Taiti', 195
'I'm Gonna Be An Engineer', 348
'John Brown's Body', 22, 26, 321
'Johnny I Hardly Knew Ye', 346
'Kong Christian stod ved højen mast', 17
'Mr. Tambourine Man', 67
'My Back Pages', 30
'Ndoenda Zvangu Kumandega', 135
'Nhemamusasa', 135
'O'Donnell's March', 200
'Our Captain Cried', 273
'Pretty Polly', 131
'Protest Song', 335, 349
'Reliya na bairi, jahajiya na bairi', 85
'Reynardine', 231, 238
'Roll Alabama', 186
'Rule, Britannia!', 200, 213
'Scarborough Fair', 66
'Scots Wha Hae', 195, 200, 342
'Skye Boat Song', 194
'Solidarity Forever', 320
'Stagger Lee', 292
'Tam Lin', 185, 231, 238
'The Blackleg Miner', 346
'The Shoals of Herring', 357
'The Two Sisters', 121, 357
'The Wellerman', 7
'This Land is Your Land', 328
'Tom Dooley', 58
'Tullochgorm', 110
'We Shall Overcome', 64
'Which Side Are You On?', 324
'Workin' on a Building', 134

abolitionism, 19, 23, 321, 340, 348
Act of Proscription, 153
Adorno, Theodor, 4–8

aesthetics, 4, 39, 73–74, 79, 82, 84, 88, 99, 101, 141, 143, 167, 169, 177, 193, 241, 340, 343
Africa, 21, 135, 146, 274, 281, 287
Agawu, Victor Kofi, 140, 142
Almanac Singers, 57
American Civil War, 22, 186, 284, 321
American Folklife Center, 47
American Folk-Lore Society, 38, 41, 291
Americana, 69
Anansi the Spider, 292
Anderson, Benedict, 29
Andersen, Hans Christian, 17
Anderson, Marian, 64
Anglo-Saxon, 16, 18, 41, 286
anthropology, 21, 27, 38, 47, 216
Appalachia, 27, 38, 41, 46, 56, 142, 147, 150, 210, 218, 286
Appalachian lap dulcimer, 150
appropriation, 75, 77, 173–75, 254, 329, 348
Arabic music, 155, 261
Archive of American Folk Song, 42, 44–45, 47, 152
archives, 154, 299, 313
Arkansas, 124–25, 134
artisans, 23
Arts and Crafts Movement, 343
arts-based research, 259
Aryan race, 25
Ashkenazi Jews, 145
Assman, Aleida, 154
Atlantic slave trade, 22, 146, 272, 281, 284, 288, 321, 340
Atmoda, 243
authenticity, 3, 35, 41, 60, 144, 154, 167, 172, 174, 231, 238, 246, 283, 325, 335, 340, 347
authorship, 23–24, 193–94, 201, 321, 326
Axon, William, 24

bagpipes, 101–2, 106, 153, 288
Baez, Joan, 58–60, 318, 334
Bahamas, 175

bahujan communities, 75
Baker, Houston A., Jr., 285
Bakka, Egil, 166
ballad, 2, 7, 15, 17, 20, 24, 26–27, 38, 41, 44, 113, 121, 185, 231, 239, 292, 300, 324, 338, 354, 357. *See also* broadsides, poetry, print culture
Bamford, Samuel, 339
Band, The, 69
banjo, 58, 124, 146–47, 280
Barbeau, Marius, 41
Baring-Gould, Sabine, 199–200, 300
Baroque music, 102, 109, 112, 242
Barry, Phillips, 28, 41, 120, 123
Bartók, Béla, 108, 214
basse danse, 110
Battle of Bannockburn, 195
Baudelaire, Charles, 6
BBC Proms, 212, 225
BBC Radio 2 Folk Awards, 245, 350
Beach, Amy, 204
Beat Generation, 60, 63, 69
beatboxing, 293
Beatles, The, 68
Beaton, Calum, 104
Bell, John, 340
belonging, 191, 200, 252, 260, 267, 358
Benjamin, Walter, 4, 325
Berlin, Irving, 328
Berlioz, Hector, 195
bhangra, 177
Bhojpuri, 85
bidesia, 85
Bihar, 75, 85
binary form, 106
birdsong, 100
Black Banjo Gathering, 280
Black Banjo Reclamation Project, 280
Black Lives Matter, 212, 279, 283
Black music, 23, 38, 42, 46, 65, 134, 147, 204, 223–24, 272, 279, 282, 286, 288, 291
Blackburn, Robin, 322
Blackburn, Stuart, 82
blackface minstrelsy, 147, 175, 282
Blake, James Vila, 24
Blaxhall, 300
Blount, Jake, 279
blues, 40, 44, 56, 65, 67, 69, 126, 279, 291
Board of Education, 200
Boas, Franz, 40
Bohemia, 196
Bohlman, Philip V., 216, 221
Boldt, Ryan, 356
Bonnie Prince Charlie, 194

Book of Kells, 112
Bordes, Charles, 198
Bosnia, 35, 93
Boss Morris, 170
Bostridge, Ian, 356
Botkin, B. A., 43, 45
Boyes, Georgina, 299
Boym, Svetlana, 232, 239
Bragg, Billy, 332, 334
Brahmins, 25
Brăiloiu, Constantin, 99, 108, 113, 115
breath, 272, 275
Breathnach, Breandán, 109
Bremer, Fredrika, 18
Brer Rabbit, 292
Bristol, 293
British Empire, 153, 173, 220. *See also* colonialism
broadcasting, 70, 126, 155, 193, 273, 328
broadsides, 27, 41, 123, 132
Broadwood, John, 302
Broadwood, Lucy, 27, 199, 234–35, 300–1, 306, 312
Broonzy, Big Bill, 66
Brown, Barnaby, 107
Brown, William Wells, 290
Brunel, Isambard Kingdom, 19
Bureau of American Ethnology, 41
Burke, Edmund, 100, 339
Burney, Charles, 104
Burns, Robert, 116, 195, 339
Byrds, The, 67

Cabaret Law, 149
California, 58, 317
call-and-response, 135, 288, 293
Cambridge Folk Festival, 236
Campbell, Angus, 102
Canada, 41
Canarese, 25
canon, 27, 64, 112, 153–54
Canteloube, Joseph, 198
cantometrics, 27
caoineadh, 100
capitalism, 2–4, 7, 19, 28, 30, 40, 70, 78, 85, 318–19, 322, 327, 356. *See also* class, mass culture, revolution
Carey, Clive, 308
Caribbean, 85, 146
Carolina Chocolate Drops, 279, 293
Carpenter, Edward, 343
Carter, Sydney, 350
Carter Family, 56, 126

Carthy, Martin, 66, 234
caste, 75, 79, 84, 88
Cecil Sharp House, 214–15, 231, 308
cèilidh, 103–4, 112, 150
Celtic folklore, 99
Celtic music, 21, 100–1, 195, 198, 200, 204
Celtic Tiger, 252
censorship, 156
Certeau, Michel de, 6, 25
Champfleury, Jules, 198
Chaplin, Ralph, 320
Chartism, 19, 342, 345
Child, Francis James, 27, 41, 231, 233
childhood, 19, 77, 93, 123, 303–5, 357. See also education, lullabies, nursery rhymes
China, 173
Chithurst Tipteeters, 309
choreography, 174
Christian Socialism, 201
Christianity, 167–68, 201, 289
Christmas carols, 66, 121, 198, 202, 337
Church of England, 199, 201
circle dancing, 170
Civil Rights movement, 7, 63, 65, 68
class, 24, 43, 302, 312, 318–19, 322, 324, 354. See also feudalism, middle class, nobility, revolution, working class
Cold War, 28, 45, 57, 63, 92, 167
Cole, Ross, 242, 312, 318
Coleridge, Samuel Taylor, 340
collecting, 23, 36, 50, 198, 201, 211, 219, 223, 234, 246, 286, 289, 299, 343
collective origin, 3, 108, 194
Collins, Shirley, 234, 273, 356
colonialism, 5, 25, 30, 37, 80, 82, 145, 150, 155, 193, 210, 253, 330. See also decolonization, indigenous culture, racism, white supremacy
Combs, Josiah, 151
communism, 19, 57, 91, 348
Communist Party of Great Britain, 348
Communist Party USA, 57
community, 3, 6–7, 36, 43, 55, 60, 68, 75–77, 121, 136, 152, 176, 191, 236, 242, 260, 306, 319, 321, 325, 327, 354, 357
comparative musicology, 38, 41
Concours des Musiques Pittoresques, 199
conservatoires, 103, 198, 204, 235, 251
contra dancing, 173
Cooley, Timothy, 50
Coomaraswamy, Ananda K., 5
coon songs, 285
Cooper, Thomas, 342
cosmopolitanism, 5, 201, 219

counterculture, 17, 69, 171, 335, 349
country music, 69, 212, 279
Covid-19, 7, 263
cowboy songs, 42, 57
craft, 143
Crane, Walter, 343
Critics' Group, 348
critique, 5, 30, 73–74, 84, 243, 246, 319, 329
Crosby, Bing, 254
cultural capital, 192, 255, 335, 340, 348–49
cultural conservation, 49
cultural memory, 144, 154, 175, 241, 255, 335
cultural sustainability, 49
curation, 186, 343
Cyprus, 221

dabkeh, 171
Dalits, 75
dance ethnology, 164
dance halls, 149
dark border morris, 169
Dartmoor, 300
Darwin, Charles, 3
Debs, Eugene V., 320
decolonization, 37, 51, 82, 210, 224, 274
Dean, Jodi, 320
Dearmer, Percy, 201
democracy, 19, 30, 36, 42, 73, 335, 337, 342
Denmark, 17, 20
Denny, Sandy, 234
Denselow, Robin, 279
Densmore, Frances, 40
Department of Ayacucho, 176
Des Knaben Wunderhorn, 17
desi, 77, 80
Dharwadekar, Aparna, 80
dialect, 18, 25, 185, 192, 339
diaspora, 79, 88, 147, 175, 252, 255
Diggers, 337
dissonance, 107
diversity, 214, 256
Dizraeli, 294
domestic sphere, 93, 300, 326
Donegan, Lonnie, 65
Dorson, Richard, 45
double-tonic, 106
Douglass, Frederick, 290
Dravidian people, 25
Du Bois, W. E. B., 27, 29, 272, 283, 285, 321
Dun, Finlay, 107
Dundes, Alan, 79
Dunn, Ginette, 300
Dutton, Denis, 238

Dvořák, Antonín, 193, 204, 214
Dylan, Bob, 17, 30, 45, 61, 66, 334, 348

early modern era, 2, 100, 338
East Anglia, 337
East India Company, 309
Eastern Bloc, 91, 164
ecology, 50, 76
ecomusicology, 50, 143
education, 5, 152, 191, 198–200, 217–18, 237, 242, 358. *See also* childhood
Eichner, Barbara, 196
ekonting, 146
Electric Telegraph Company, 19
Elliott, Ebenezer, 342
Emancipation, 204, 283, 289, 292, 322
embodiment, 82, 168, 172, 205, 259
Engel, Carl, 23
England, 18, 44, 170, 172, 194, 201, 211, 217, 233, 282, 299, 336, 341, 350
English Folk Dance and Song Society, 29, 213–14, 226, 231, 234, 305
English Folk Dance Society, 199, 201, 234
Enlightenment, 35, 56, 62, 110, 145, 342
environmentalism, 144, 169, 337
Equiano, Olaudah, 288
Espérance Guild of Morris Dancers, 309
essentialism, 174, 224
ethnicity, 49, 92, 121, 162, 166, 172, 174, 192, 196, 215, 255, 303
ethnochoreology, 164
ethnomusicology, 41, 45, 48, 232, 257
Evans, Nathan, 7
Evers, Medgar, 64
evolution, 1–3, 5, 27, 168
exoticism, 20, 196
exploitation, 210, 319, 323–24, 327. *See also* capitalism, working class

Fabianism, 3, 5, 343, 345
Fáil, Fianna, 150
Fairport Convention, 231, 244
fakelore, 45
Falkirk Tryst, 153
Falklands War, 334
Fanon, Frantz, 5
Fariña, Richard, 64
fascism, 5, 24, 26, 171, 203, 243, 327
Feagin, Joe R., 287
Federal Writers Project, 42
female warriors, 131
feminism, 299, 311, 355
feudalism, 19

fiddle, 141, 145, 288, 290
fieldwork, 37, 39, 48, 50
Findhorn Foundation, 170
Finland, 196
Finnegan, Ruth, 113
Fiol, Stefan, 77, 81
First Intifada, 155
Fisk Jubilee Singers, 7, 40, 272, 289
Fisk University, 289
flamenco, 203
Fletcher, Andrew, 338
Florida, 175
Flower, Eliza, 342
Floyd, Samuel A. Jr., 292
folk clubs, 234, 236, 239, 275, 355, 358
folk heroes, 22, 292
folklore, 15, 21, 29, 37, 45, 73, 164, 220, 289
folkloric imagination, 15, 19, 29, 232, 246, 274, 341
folk rock, 67, 231, 239, 241, 348
Folk-Song Society, 3, 199, 234, 302, 307, 343
Ford, Agnes, 306
formulaic patterns, 106, 108, 114, 122, 126, 136
Foster, Stephen, 67
fourth wall, 187
Fourtoul Project, 198
Fox, Adam, 2
France, 16, 196, 198, 203
Franco regime, 167, 203
Franklin, Benjamin, 10
Frazer, James, 169
Freiheitslied, 341
French Revolution, 194, 197, 199, 338, 341
French Third Republic, 202
Frith, Simon, 3
fRoots, 236

Gaddar, 85
Garfunkel, Art, 66
Gaza, 155
Geertz, Clifford, 48
Gelbart, Matthew, 192
Gencarella, Stephen, 73
gender, 28, 42, 84, 87, 93, 131, 168, 172, 174, 261, 299, 312, 326
genre, 2, 21, 80, 82–83, 147, 166, 172, 191, 212, 247, 279, 285, 291, 348–49
Germany, 16, 18, 30, 196, 220, 240, 243, 336, 341, 347
Ghana, 260, 263
Gilbert, Ronnie, 57
Gilchrist, Anne Geddes, 305, 307

globalization, 171, 232, 245. *See also* industrialization, modernity
Goldfaden, Avram, 93
Goldstein, Kenneth, 47
Gordon, Robert Winslow, 41
gospel, 291
Gover, Charles E., 24
Graham, Sandra Jean, 289
Grahame, Lucy, 303
Grammy Awards, 279
Gramsci, Antonio, 73, 86
gramyadharma, 78
Great Depression, 57, 149, 329
Great Famine in Ireland, 19
Great Fire of London, 122
Greece, 167
Greenwich Village, 17, 57, 60–62, 68
Gregorian chant, 24
Greig-Duncan Folk Song Collection, 113
Grimm, Jacob, 16, 108, 196
Grove, Lilly, 169
Grundtvig, Svend, 233
Guard, Dave, 58–59
Guthrie, Woody, 45, 57, 60–61, 63, 152, 327, 332, 334
Guyana, 221

Habermas, Jürgen, 55, 62
Hall, Stuart, 15, 27
halling, 173
Halse, Christine, 260
Hamilton, Andrew, 20
hammered dulcimer, 151
Hansen, Kathryn, 82
Harari, Yuval Noah, 253
Harishchandra, Bhartendu, 81
Harlan County War, 324
Harvard University, 35, 41, 57
Harwood, John Berwick, 20
Hawai'i, 59, 174
Hays, Lee, 57
Hayes, Red, 67
Hebrides, 102–3, 114
Hecker, Friedrich, 341
Henry, John, 292
Herder, Johann Gottfried, 15–16, 21, 30, 145, 192, 242, 339. *See also Volkslieder*
Herodotus, 37
Herzog, George A., 41
Higgins, Lizzie, 100
Highlander Folk School, 7
highlife, 264
hillbilly music, 40–41, 63

Hindu culture, 167
hip hop, 293
historiography, 3, 26, 193, 212, 223, 233, 274, 285
HMT Empire Windrush, 274
Hoberman, Mary Ann, 1
Hobsbawm, Eric, 29, 241
Hoerburger, Felix, 163
Holinshed, Raphael, 336
Holocaust, 91
Homer, 35
Hornbostel-Sachs system, 140
House Committee on Un-American Activities, 45
Houston, Cisco, 63
Howe, Julia Ward, 23
Howitt, Mary, 17, 20, 32
Hughes, Caroline, 354
humour, 184, 355
Hungary, 174
hurdy-gurdy, 142, 265
Hurston, Zora Neale, 27, 175
Hurt, Mississippi John, 65
Hutton, Ronald, 169
Huw, Robert ap, 107

identity, 17, 26, 49, 63, 65, 69, 82, 147, 149, 166–67, 172, 177, 191, 193, 197, 205, 217, 239, 254, 272, 282, 286, 302, 319, 322, 339, 355, 358
Iļǵi, 235
imagination, 7, 21, 76, 238, 253, 275, 282. *See also* folkloric imagination, nostalgia, utopia
Imagined Village, The, 238
improvisation, 60, 109, 135, 288
India, 5, 25, 73
Indiana University, 45
Indigenous culture, 23, 38, 73, 80, 107, 146, 156, 211, 217–18, 221–24, 251, 254
Industrial Workers of the World, 317
industrialization, 173, 240, 244. *See also* modernity
d'Indy, Vincent, 197–98
inheritance, 23, 102, 286
Innes, Neil, 335, 349
Intangible Cultural Heritage, 176
integration, 256
International Folk Music Council, 1, 28, 46, 163
interpellation, 325
Ireland, 99, 102, 145–47, 251, 261, 357
Irish music, 28, 147, 149, 204, 238, 251
Irish World Academy of Music and Dance, 251
Islamic law, 174

Israel, 57, 155, 167
Italy, 110, 196

Jackson, Mahalia, 64
Jacobite Rebellion, 194
Jackson, Bruce, 48
Jane Eyre, 19
jazz, 56, 60, 291
Jensen, Oskar Cox, 2
Joan of Arc, 195
John Broadwood and Sons, 301
Jola people, 146
Jones, Mike, 346
Joynes, James Leigh, 343
Judaism, 91

Kalyani, K., 85
Kanneh-Mason, Sheku, 213
Karpeles, Maud, 2, 46, 210, 234
Keil, Charles, 174, 251
Kent, 336
Kellerman, Fred, 57
Kennedy, John F., 63
Kentucky, 152, 324
Kerouac, Jack, 60
Kidson, Frank, 199
King Charles II, 125, 145
King, Martin Luther, Jr., 64
Kingsley, Charles, 202
Kingston Trio, The, 45, 58–59, 70
Kittredge, George Lyman, 41
klezmer, 7, 91, 95, 145, 197
Knight, Bessie, 310
Knurrhahn, 240
Korea, 221
Kurath, Gertrude, 164

Labour Hymn-Book, 343
lai, 16
lamentary music, 100
Lancashire, 305
land, 5, 26, 76, 82, 163, 170–72, 211, 321, 329–30, 341. *See also* nature, pastoral, peasant
Larner, Sam, 357
Latin Quarter, 346
Latvia, 231, 235, 243
Lead Belly, 57, 66, 130, 292
Lévi-Strauss, Claude, 26
Lincolnshire, 356
listening, 103, 185
Little Red Song Book, 317
Livingston, Tamara, 233, 245

Lloyd, A. L., 27–28, 234–35, 346
lok, 76, 80, 83
lokgeet, 76, 80
loksangeet, 76, 80
Longfellow, Henry Wadsworth, 21
Lomax, Alan, 27, 27, 42–43, 45–46, 133, 152, 235, 292, 348, 354
Lomax, John A., 27, 42, 292, 354
London, 122, 125, 199, 301
London, Jack, 326
Lord, Albert, 35, 103, 105, 108, 113–14
loss, 128, 260, 263, 272, 320. *See also* nostalgia
Lost Cause, 284
Lott, Eric, 147
Louisiana, 44
Lorimer, Robin, 106
love, 58, 62, 66, 85, 125, 128, 131–33, 184, 194, 355
LP record, 56, 59, 70
Luddites, 340
lullabies, 20, 100, 123, 263, 265

MacColl, Ewan, 27–28, 66, 234–35, 348, 357
MacColl, Kirsty, 334
MacDonald, Donald Allan, 102–3
MacDonald, Joseph, 105
Macedonia, 167
MacInnes, John, 103
MacIntyre, Duncan Bàn, 114
MacKinnon, Niall, 244
Macpherson, James, 100, 104, 194
Mahler, Gustav, 197
mandolin, 149
Manet, Édouard, 6
Manipuri dance, 83
Mannhardt, Wilhelm, 169
manual labour, 3, 15, 23, 28, 42, 82, 85, 99, 237, 290, 300, 317, 319, 321, 336, 343. *See also* mining, peasant, working class
Manuel, Peter, 80
March on Washington, 64, 67
Marcus, Greil, 30
Marshall, Dorothy, 308
Martineau, Harriet, 342
Marx, Karl, 19, 323
Marxism, 4–5, 28, 174, 320, 350
masculinity, 42, 173, 325
mass culture, 1, 4, 15, 30, 245, 339, 348. *See also* capitalism, popular culture
materiality, 143
Mather, Joseph, 339
mbira, 135
McGhee, Brownie, 59, 65

McShee, Jacqui, 241
Meir, Golda, 155
Memphis Slim, 59
Middle Ages, 16, 21, 95, 100, 107–8, 113, 135, 241
middle class, 17, 29, 56, 66, 73, 80, 191, 234, 237, 312, 340, 354
Middle East, 21, 155, 171, 261
Middle Passage, 281, 288
migration, 79, 85, 145, 150, 176, 238, 252, 256. *See also* refugees
Middleton, Richard, 3
Miller, Karl Hagstrom, 212
mining, 131, 201, 234, 320, 324, 326, 340, 346
misogyny, 85, 187
Missouri, 292
Mitchell, Joni, 334
Miyan, Rasul, 85
modality, 104, 192, 205
modernity, 4, 6, 15, 26, 30, 35, 55–56, 76, 156, 162, 191, 236, 244, 252, 318, 323, 331. *See also* globalization, industrialization, mass culture
Moiseyev, Igor, 174
Moldova, 93
Mollenhauer, Jeanette, 166
Moore, Jason W., 329
Moore, Marat, 326
Moore, Thomas, 195
More, Hannah, 347
morris dancing, 169
Morris, William, 5, 343
Morrison, Angeline, 280, 283, 299
Morrison, Matthew D., 283
Morrissey, 334, 350
Mount Saint Helens, 128
Mr. Fox, 238
music hall, 27, 219, 244, 346
music industry, 43, 62, 101, 115, 126, 212, 222, 244, 338, 348–49
mythopoeic singing, 274

Nahachewsky, Andriy, 165
Naithani, Sadhana, 220
Nakba, 155
Napoleon III, 198
narrative, 122, 127, 131, 185, 356
nation state, 55, 154, 167, 191, 196, 253
national airs, 23
National Endowment for the Arts, 46
National Endowment for the Humanities, 49
nationalism, 3, 5, 22–23, 26, 29, 75, 78, 154–55, 167, 170, 191, 205, 215, 243

Native American culture, 20, 24, 38, 40, 129, 204
nature, 20, 24, 26, 100, 143, 170, 329. *See also* land, pastoral
Naumann, Hans, 108
Nazi Germany, 146, 167, 243, 328, 347
neoliberalism, 88, 246, 334
Nesbit, Edith, 343
Nettl, Bruno, 46, 287
Newcastle, 340
Newcastle University, 237
New Deal, 42, 45, 327
New England, 39, 41–42
New York City, 24, 57, 61, 149, 152, 327
New Zealand, 7
Newport Folk Festival, 7, 29, 59, 67, 348
Nichols, Robert, 330
Nigeria, 288
nobility, 101, 110, 112, 115
Norfolk, 357
Northup, Solomon, 290
Norway, 173
nostalgia, 3–4, 19, 26, 39, 65, 77, 149, 156, 175, 211, 239, 256. *See also* imagination, loss
Nuova Compagnia di Canto Populare, 66
nursery rhymes, 1, 20, 68, 123, 303, 350

Ochs, Phil, 64
Odum, Howard W., 40
òrain luaidh, 109
oral-formulaic theory, 105, 114
orality, 2, 30, 35, 37, 43, 46, 101, 103–5, 108, 112, 115, 121, 125, 164, 237, 290, 292, 356
organology, 140
Orpheus and Eurydice, 100
Ossian, 16, 104, 194, 242
Ozark Mountains, 124

paganism, 21, 168, 171, 246
Paint Creek–Cabin Creek strike, 320
Palestine, 155, 171, 261
Palmer, John Williamson, 21
panegyric music, 101
Panhellenic Socialist Movement, 167
Paris, 198
Paris World's Fair, 199
Parrish, Lydia, 290
Parry, C. Hubert H., 3, 205, 217
Parry, Milman, 35, 103
Pasler, Jann, 196
pastoral, 24, 28, 202, 242. *See also* rural life
patriotisches Lied, 341

peasant, 5, 20, 35, 88, 164, 169, 174, 192, 244, 305. See also land, manual labour, working class
Pegg, Carole, 210
Pentangle, 241
Percy, Thomas, 16–17, 340–41
performance, 36, 47, 50, 73, 80, 184, 188, 219, 234, 237, 259, 356
persona, 60, 62–63, 329
Peru, 176
Peter, Paul, and Mary, 62
Petrie, Grace, 350
phonograph, 309–11
pibroch, 101, 105, 109, 194
poetry, 21, 35, 63, 103, 198, 343. See also ballad
Poland, 254, 260, 265
political radicalism, 19, 26, 45, 56–57, 67, 87, 317, 320, 324, 331, 335, 339, 341–42, 344, 349. See also Marxism, revolution, solidarity
popular culture, 2–4, 17, 24–25, 28, 30, 55, 242, 338. See also mass culture
Popular Front, 203
popular voice, 335, 337
populism, 211, 219, 338
post-revival, 235
practice-based research, 260
primitivism, 18, 26, 38, 100, 168, 175, 196, 205, 214, 216
print culture, 2, 23, 56, 112, 123, 131, 192, 233, 292, 302, 336, 338, 341–42, 348–49, 356
Prior, Maddy, 241
private property, 331
progressive rock, 231
protest song, 45, 62, 67, 334, 336, 348. See also topical song
Provence, 198
public folklore, 49
Public Hall Dance Act, 150
public sphere, 55, 61–62, 64–65, 68–70, 337, 339

Queen Elizabeth I, 146
Queen Victoria, 272
queerness, 133, 299

race, 24–26, 29, 193, 204, 210, 217, 219, 282, 286, 321
race records, 56
racism, 213, 218, 280, 282
Radio Jerusalem, 155
Radu, Nikolai, 94
ragtime, 69, 291
railways, 19
Rajasthan, 75, 88

Ramanujan, A. K., 77, 82
Red Wedge, 334
Reece, Florence, 324
reel, 110
re-enchantment, 274
Reeves' Association, 339, 342
Reformation, 336
refugees, 79, 155, 172, 256–58. See also migration
regional identity, 18, 30, 45, 57, 63, 77, 88, 166, 173, 192, 198, 203, 341
religion, 134, 142, 150, 168, 202, 289
representation, 6, 25, 37, 55, 147, 330
resilience, 262, 292
resistance, 4–5, 89, 153, 156, 175, 192–93, 243–44, 274
revivalism, 6, 27, 44–45, 101, 115, 149–50, 153, 156, 231, 236, 247, 346, 354
revolution, 5, 19, 41, 191, 198, 324, 337, 339, 341, 347. See also Marxism, political radicalism
Reynardson, H. F. Birch, 302
Richardson, Shaughn, 293
ring-shout, 134
Ritchie, Jean, 152–53
Ritson, Joseph, 341
Ritter, Frédéric Louis, 24
ritual, 81, 88, 121, 168, 265, 272
Robert the Bruce, 195
Roberts, Helen H., 39
Robertson, Jeannie, 236
rock, 3, 58, 67–69, 231, 235, 349
Rodgers, Jimmie, 56
Romani people, 21, 91, 354
Romania, 92, 115
Romanticism, 17, 30, 194, 340
Ross, Pete, 280
Rosselson, Leon, 350
Roud, Steve, 186, 299
rural life, 3, 23, 38, 56, 63, 76, 79, 88, 103, 152, 156, 162, 165, 167, 169, 172, 200, 203, 216, 237, 242, 253, 291, 302, 310. See also land, nature, pastoral, peasant
Russia, 20, 193. See also Soviet Union
Russian Empire, 196

sailing, 240
Saint-Saëns, Camille, 196
Salt, Henry, 343
Sandburg, Carl, 27
Sanskrit, 83
Sarkar-Munsi, Urmimala, 83
scab, 326

Scandinavia, 142
Scarborough, Dorothy, 40
science, 26, 36, 38, 45, 47, 218, 291
Scotland, 17, 44, 99, 121, 153, 194, 305, 341
scots snap, 110
Scott, Walter, 121
Scottish National Party, 195
Scottish Parliament, 116
sea shanties, 7, 240, 309
Seeger, Charles, 43
Seeger, Peggy, 234, 348
Seeger, Pete, 27, 45, 57, 59, 64, 152
Seeger, Ruth Crawford, 44
segregation, 212
sexuality, 133, 299
Shakespeare, William, 16, 21, 133
ShantyTok, 7
Sharp, Cecil J., 2, 5, 23, 27, 38, 108, 152, 169, 172, 186, 199–200, 210, 215, 217, 231, 234–35, 241–42, 286, 300–1, 305, 311
shastra, 83
Shay, Anthony, 165
Shelemay, Kay Kaufman, 6
Shenandoah Valley, 152
Sherinian, Zoe, 87
Sherman, William Tecumseh, 22
Sibelius, Jean, 193
Sibelius Academy, 237
signifying, 293
Simon, Paul, 66
Sinclair, Upton, 317
singer-songwriter, 68, 334, 350, 358
Singh, Namvar, 83
skiffle, 65
Skinner, James Scott, 110
slave narratives, 290
Slave Songs of the United States, 40, 288
Slobin, Mark, 254
Smetana, Bedřich, 193
Smith, Bessie, 129
Smith, Harry, 27
Smith, Kate, 328
Smith, Linda Tuhiwai, 223
Smiths, The, 334
Smithsonian Center for Folklife and Heritage, 47
Smothers Brothers, 70
Snape, 300
social Darwinism, 1, 27, 193, 218. *See also* evolution
social inclusion, 258
social justice, 224, 253, 258, 330
social media, 7, 175

socialism, 5, 28, 167, 317, 343
Society for Ethnomusicology, 46, 48
Society for International Folk Dance, 170
solidarity, 7, 63, 176, 203, 319–20, 322, 324–25, 327, 331–32. *See also* political radicalism, trade unions
Son House, 65
sonata form, 110
Sontag, Susan, 26
South Asia, 73
Southern United States, 46, 56, 126, 146, 212, 272, 284, 291
Soviet Union, 94, 164, 167, 174, 235
Spain, 131, 142, 167, 196, 203
Spencer, Herbert, 3, 218, 228
Spicer, Katy, 215
spirituals, 23, 40, 64, 126, 204, 272, 279, 283, 287, 289, 348
Springsteen, Bruce, 318
Stadler, Gustavus, 330
Stafford, John, 339
Stalinism, 92
Stanford, Charles Villiers, 200
Stanley Brothers, 59
Steeleye Span, 237, 346
Stivell, Alain, 66
Stokes, Martin, 257
Stowe, Harriet Beecher, 22, 26
strathspey, 110
street music, 219, 338–39, 341, 348
strikes, 67–68, 320, 326, 331, 345. *See also* manual labour, solidarity, trade unions, working class
string bands, 45, 279, 291
Súilleabháin, Mícheál Ó, 251
Surrey, 300
survivals, 169, 218
Sussex, 304, 306, 308
sustainability, 144
Svart, Itzik Cara, 92
Swarbrick, Dave, 234
Sweden, 18
sword dancing, 169
Syria, 171, 260

Tamil, 25, 83
Tamil Nadu, 78
Taruskin, Richard, 193
Taylor, Joseph, 356
television, 70
Telugu, 25, 88
Tennessee, 152
Terry, Sonny, 59, 65

Thakur, Bhikhari, 85
Thatcher, Margaret, 173, 334
The English Hymnal, 201
Thiesse, Anne-Marie, 191
Thoms, William, 15, 37
Thomson, George, 106
TikTok, 7
time, 16, 19, 27, 36, 60, 67, 104, 106, 120, 122, 136, 154, 194, 239, 241, 272, 276, 330, 356
Tin Pan Alley, 254
Toomer, Jean, 29
Topic Records, 7, 234, 236
topical song, 122, 335, 354. *See also* protest song
totalitarianism, 224
trade unions, 57, 317, 320, 324, 345, 358. *See also* strikes, solidarity, working class
tradition, 27, 29, 123, 150, 170, 231, 236, 245, 247, 252, 274
trans identity, 133
transmission, 28, 55, 125, 237
Travellers, 354
Treitler, Leo, 108, 113
Tucker, George, 290
Tylor, E. B., 3

Ukraine, 193
UKRI, 214
UNESCO, 176
United Kingdom, 38, 65, 199–200, 220, 274, 280, 283, 293, 342, 354
United Nations, 155
United States, 27, 35, 47, 55, 146, 149, 203, 254, 281, 287, 318, 329
Universities and Colleges Union, 331
University of Limerick, 251
Upadhyay, Krishnadev, 83
utopia, 242, 244, 328, 338. *See also* imagination, socialism
Uttar Pradesh, 75, 85
Uttarakhand, 75, 81

Val, Dorothy de, 301
Vance, J. D., 211
variation, 108
Vaughan Williams Memorial Library, 214, 231, 308, 310
Vichy regime, 203
Victorian era, 3, 15, 19, 168, 201, 210, 218
Vietnam war, 64, 67, 70, 355

Viking Age, 21
violin, 141
Virginia Minstrels, 147–50
Viscount Hersart de la Villemarqué, 198
Volk, 342, 347
Volksgeist, 163, 172
Volkslieder, 15–17, 21, 31, 34, 158, 339, 341, 352
Volksmusik, 23

Wales, 68, 99, 107, 198, 200, 342
Walker-Sweeney, Joel, 147
Washington Square Park, 61
waulking, 109, 114
Weavers, The, 57–58
Weckerlin, Jean-Baptiste, 198
Welch, Gillian, 69
wellbeing, 170, 258, 275, 303
Wellington, Sheena, 116
Wendell, Barrett, 42
West Bank, 155
West Virginia, 321
Western art music, 3, 21, 193, 213, 355
western frontier, 42
whaling, 7
White, George Leonard, 289
White, Richard Grant, 23
white singing, 265
white supremacy, 24, 26, 37, 41, 214. *See also* colonialism, racism, segregation
Wilco, 69
Wilgus, D. K., 41, 45, 123
Williams, Ralph Vaughan, 27, 199, 201, 234
Williams, Raymond, 76
Wiora, Walter, 164
women's groups, 261
Wordsworth, William, 340
work songs, 265, 290, 337
working class, 19, 24–26, 28, 30, 42, 45, 57, 147, 172, 201, 243, 308, 319, 325, 339. *See also* manual labour, peasant, trade unions
world music, 221, 235
World War II, 59, 164, 234, 243
Wosien, Bernhard, 170

Yiddish, 60, 92, 94
Yugoslavia, 35, 103

Zimbabwe, 135
zither, 150

For EU product safety concerns, contact us at Calle de José Abascal, 56–1°,
28003 Madrid, Spain or eugpsr@cambridge.org.

www.ingramcontent.com/pod-product-compliance
Ingram Content Group UK Ltd.
Pitfield, Milton Keynes, MK11 3LW, UK
UKHW050109230326
469255UK00020B/457